History of
SWEETWATER VALLEY, TENNESSEE

By
William B. Lenoir

Reprinted with a New Index, Introduction,
Table of Contents, Errata Sheet, and Maps

CLEARFIELD

Originally published
Richmond, Virginia
1916

Reprinted with a new Index, Introduction,
Table of Contents, Errata Sheet, and Maps
Regional Publishing Company
Baltimore, Maryland
1976

In Cooperation with
Monroe County Chapter
East Tennessee Historical Society

Copyright © 1976 Regional Publishing Company
Baltimore, Maryland
All Rights Reserved

Library of Congress Catalog Card Number 76-17472

Reprinted for Clearfield Company by
Genealogical Publishing Company
Baltimore, Maryland
1994, 2012

ISBN 978-0-8063-8007-0

Made in the United States of America

INTRODUCTION TO THE REPRINT EDITION

Some sixty years have come and gone since W. B. Lenoir's *History of Sweetwater Valley* was first published in 1916. Original copies of the book are quite scarce and are highly prized by their owners.

Consequently, in commemoration of our nation's Bicentennial Year, the Monroe County Chapter of the East Tennessee Historical Society (founded in 1972) is reprinting this *History* in cooperation with the Genealogical Publishing Company of Baltimore, Maryland.

We wish to express our appreciation to all who have assisted us in this endeavor, including, but not limited to, the following:

The Sweetwater Library and the Helen M. Cooke Memorial Library Association of Sweetwater for their interest and help.

Mr. W. F. Lenoir of Houston, Texas, and Mrs. Nathan Harris and Mrs. Kermit Ausmus of Sweetwater for the index included in the reprint.

Mrs. Charles L. Clark of Sweetwater for providing the "Table of Contents" page and the "Corrections and Addenda" page which apparently were prepared after the original printing.

The Bank of Madisonville, Tennessee, for their assistance in helping to finance this project.

The maps are provided by Society member Walter B. Lumsden, Jr., who made a tracing of the 1860 plat of Sweetwater which was found in 1959 when the old Love-Lowry dwelling at 310 South High Street in Sweetwater was razed to make way for the Wood-Presbyterian Nursing Home. The home sites shown on the Sweetwater "1852" Map were located according to the text from Mr. Lenoir's *History* and of personal knowledge of the area.

> *Publication Committee*
> Mr. Gene Worthington, Chairman
> Mr. James Burn
> Mrs. Kay E. Hatton
> Mr. M. Wesley Hatton
> Mr. Walter B. Lumsden, Jr.

MONROE COUNTY CHAPTER
East Tennessee Historical Society

The Monroe County Chapter of the East Tennessee Historical Society is the outgrowth of a county-wide meeting called by Monroe County Judge J. P. Kennedy on October 21, 1971, for the purpose of forming a county historical organization. At this meeting Gene Worthington was elected Temporary Chairman and Walter B. Lumsden, Jr., was elected Temporary Secretary. At the meeting of November 18, 1971, the group voted to organize as a Chapter of the East Tennessee Historical Society. At this meeting a Committee was appointed to write a Constitution and By-Laws, also a Nominations Committee was appointed. On March 16, 1972, the Constitution and By-Laws were adopted and officers for the year 1972-1973 were elected.

The Monroe County Chapter of the East Tennessee Historical Society meets on a regular monthly basis on the last Thursday of the month, usually at 7:30 P.M., in the Conference Room of the Fort Loudoun Electric Co-operative Building, Madisonville, Tennessee.

Following is a list of the Charter Members, and also lists of the Officers and Directors to date (1976).

ALPHABETICAL LIST OF CHARTER MEMBERS (1972)

Mrs. Greg Ashe
Mrs. S. B. Boyer
Mr. Ernest Browder
Miss Margaret Browder
Mr. James Burn
Mrs. S. S. Caldwell
Mrs. Antoinette Stickley Cate
Mr. & Mrs. Richard Cheatham
Dr. & Mrs. Tom Clark
Mrs. Joan Damico
Mr. & Mrs. Ed Dougherty
Mr. & Mrs. Fred Edgemon
Mr. Jerry Estes
Mrs. Wanda S. Franklin
Mayor & Mrs. Bob Harrill
Mr. & Mrs. M. Wesley Hatton
Mrs. E. R. Hensley
Mr. Dan Hicks
Judge & Mrs. Sue K. Hicks
Judge & Mrs. J. P. Kennedy
Mr. & Mrs. J. Lewis Kinnard
Mr. & Mrs. Bob Taylor Lee, Jr.
Mrs. Charles (Judy) Lee
Mrs. J. D. Lee
Mr. & Mrs. Walter B. Lumsden, Jr.
Dr. Houston Lowry
Mr. Ralph E. Moore
Mr. & Mrs. Joe Sherlin
Mrs. Greta Sliger
Mrs. Beth G. Spurling
Mrs. Joseph H. Stickley
Mr. & Mrs. Newell Thompson
Mr. Harold Witt
Mr. & Mrs. Clifford Wilson
Miss Emma Sue Williams
Mr. & Mrs. Gene Worthington

OFFICERS AND DIRECTORS 1972 - 1973
(Elected March 16, 1972)

President	Mr. Gene Worthington
Vice-President	Mr. Bob Taylor Lee, Jr.
Vice-President	Mr. Walter B. Lumsden, Jr.
Secretary	Mrs. Wanda S. Franklin
Treasurer	Mr. Clifford Wilson

Directors—Ex Officio
Mayor Charles Hall, Tellico Plains
Mayor Bob Harrill, Madisonville
Mayor Blanche Farnsworth, Vonore
Mayor Beverly Wood, Sweetwater

DIRECTORS

1972-1973	1972-1974	1972-1975
Dr. James H. Barnes	Mr. D. F. Heuer, III	Mr. J. Lewis Kinnard
Miss Margaret Browder	Mr. Dan Hicks	Mr. Joe Sherlin
Mr. Sanford Gray	Judge J. P. Kennedy	Mr. Harold Witt

OFFICERS AND DIRECTORS 1973 - 1974
(Elected June 28, 1973)

President	Mr. Bob Taylor Lee, Jr.
Vice-President	Mr. Walter B. Lumsden, Jr.
Vice-President	Mrs. Ann Stickley Cate
Secretary	Mrs. Kay Estes Hatton
Treasurer	Mr. Clifford Wilson
Immediate Past President	Mr. Gene Worthington

Directors—Ex Officio
Mayor Charles Hall, Tellico Plains
Mayor Bob Harrill, Madisonville
Mayor A. J. Kennedy, Vonore
Mayor George Cansler, Sweetwater

DIRECTORS

1972-1973	1972-1974	1972-1975
Dr. James H. Barnes	Dr. Thomas Clark	Mr. J. Lewis Kinnard
Mrs. Sarah Lee	Mr. Dan Hicks	Mr. Joe Sherlin
Mr. Sanford Gray	Judge J. P. Kennedy	Mr. Harold Witt

OFFICERS AND DIRECTORS 1974 - 1975
(Elected June 27, 1974)

President .... Mr. WALTER B. LUMSDEN, JR.
Vice-President .... Mrs. ANN S. CATE
Vice-President .... Dr. TOM CLARK
Secretary .... Mrs. BETH G. SPURLING
Treasurer .... Mr. ED C. DOUGHERTY
Immediate Past-President .... Mr. BOB TAYLOR LEE, JR.

Directors—Ex Officio
MAYOR CHARLES HALL, Tellico Plains
MAYOR BOB HARRILL, Madisonville
MAYOR A. J. KENNEDY, Vonore
MAYOR GEORGE CANSLER, Sweetwater

DIRECTORS

1972-1975	1974-1976	1974-1977
Mr. J. Lewis Kinnard	Mrs. H. G. Gangwer	Mrs. Kay E. Hatton
Mr. Joe Sherlin	Mr. Gene Worthington	Judge J. P. Kennedy
Mr. Harold Witt	Mrs. Wanda Franklin	Mr. Jim Burn

OFFICERS AND DIRECTORS 1975 - 1976
(Elected June 26, 1975)

President .... Mr. M. WESLEY HATTON
Vice-President .... Mr. NEWELL W. THOMPSON
Vice-President .... Mrs. ANTOINETTE S. CATE
Secretary .... Mrs. BETH G. SPURLING
Treasurer .... Mr. ED C. DOUGHERTY
Immediate Past President .... Mr. WALTER B. LUMSDEN, JR.

Directors—Ex Officio
MAYOR CHARLES HALL, Tellico Plains
MAYOR LEON HARVEY, Madisonville
MAYOR A. J. KENNEDY, Vonore
MAYOR GEORGE CANSLER, Sweetwater

DIRECTORS

1974-1976	1974-1977	1975-1978
Mrs. H. G. Gangwer	Mrs. Kay E. Hatton	Mrs. M. Wesley Hatton
Mr. Gene Worthington	Judge J. P. Kennedy	Mr. Harvey Price
Mrs. Wanda Franklin	Mr. Jim Burn	Mrs. Sarah Lee

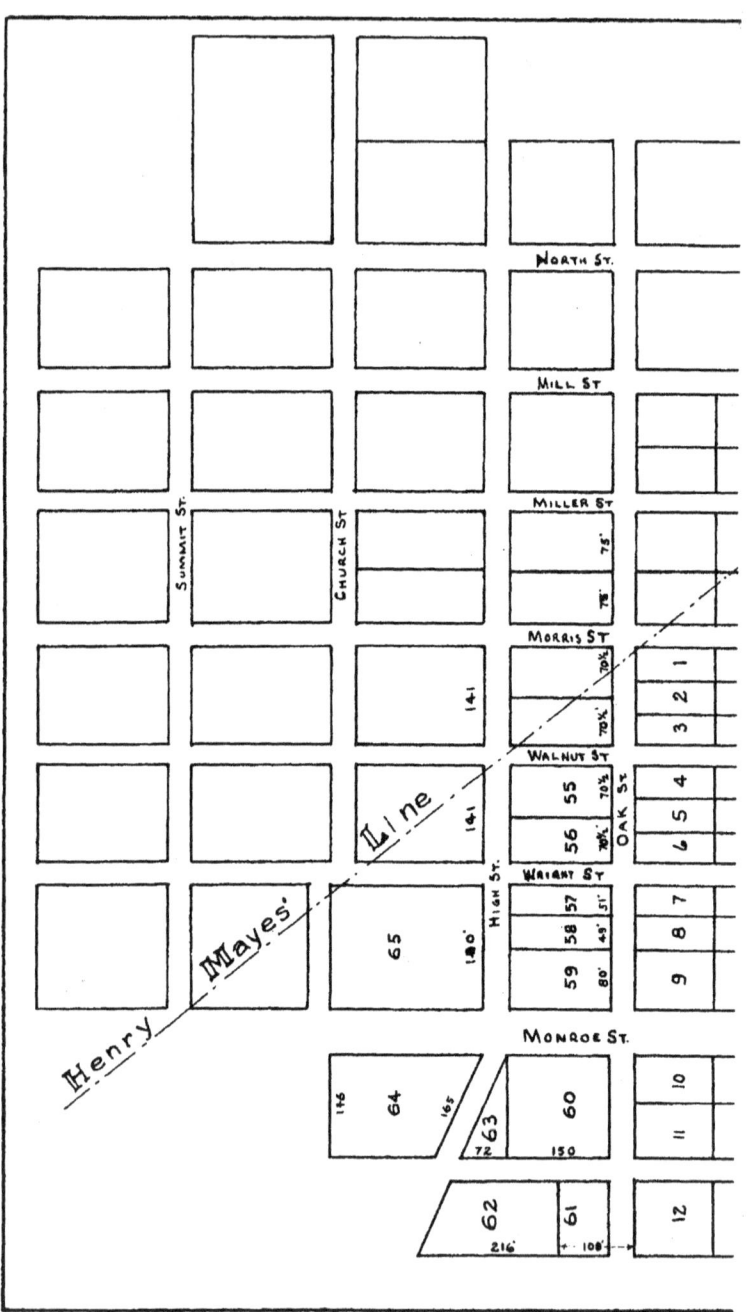

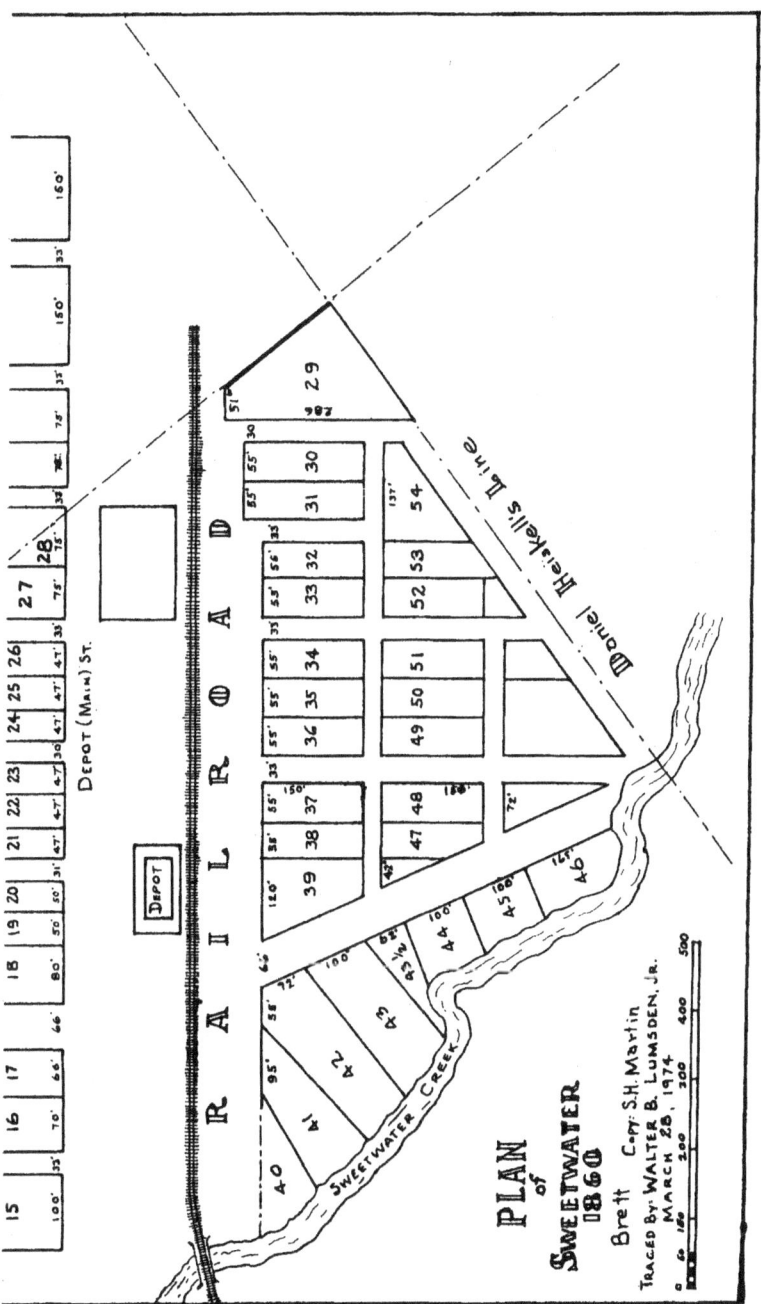

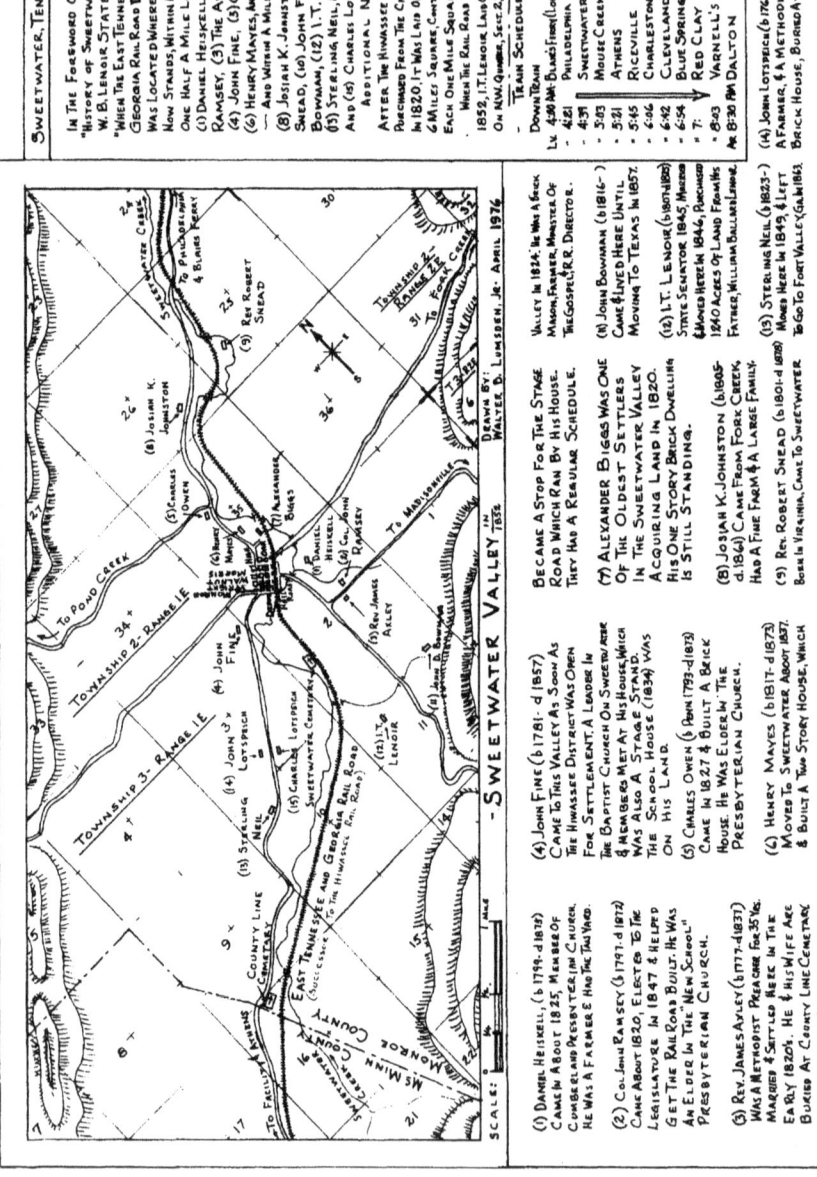

TABLE OF CONTENTS

Sweetwater Valley. Geology p. 14—Chemistry p. 16—Why ideal Place to live. 20—Earliest Inhabitants of—p. 21.

The Cherokees, p.26-Fort Loudon,p. 27-Treaty of 1777 p.29. Town of Refuge, p. 28—Indian Names of Mountains and Rivers, p. 29—"Soitee Woitee," p. 32

Chapter on Races. p. 37—Treaties with Cherokees, p. 37—Why necessary to remove Cherokees, p. 39—Encroachment of Whites, p. 43 Hiwassee Purchase, p. 44—Origin of Land Titles in Sweetwater Valley, p. 45.

Biographical—The Old Inhabitants and Decendants.
Order of Patronymics commencing with p. 51.

Axley, Brewder, Adkins Berry, Caldwell, Bellamy, Biggs, Bogart, Bowman, Brown, Calloway, Cleveland, Cannon, Childress, Cooper, Cozart, Smith, Cooke, Clark, Cunnyngham, (Cunnyngham-Pattons) (Cunnyngham-Pickels) Fine, Fry, Glaze, Goddard, Gregory, Heiskell, Janeway, Jones Johnston, Lenoir, (Waightstill Avery) Hogg, Lillard, Lotspeich, Mayes, Owen, Orr, Patton F. A., Rutherford, Row-Pennington, Ramsey Jno., Waren, Ramsey R. A., Rutherford, Rowan, Rowland, Reagan, Scruggs, Sheldon, Shell, Stillman, Snead, Young, Vaughn, Upton, Walker, Yearwood, Bradley, Carter, Montgomery, Coffin, Bachmar

CHURCHES, SCHOOLS, LODGES, RAILROADS, TOWNS.

H. M Cooke Memorial Library, p. 128—Cumberland Pres. Church, 163—Sweetwater, Founding of Town, p.199—Gift of Land to E. T. & Ga., R. R., p. 200—City Beautiful League, p. 204—Slaves in Sweetwater Valley, p. 215—Facts About E. T. & Ga. R. R.—First Train Schedule from Loudon to Dalton, 222—Railroad Elevations, p. 223—Plan of Sweetwater, p. 224—Baptist Church on Sweetwater, p. 355—First Baptist Church in Sweetwater, p. 369—M. E. Church, South, in Sweetwater, p 372—Presbyterian Church in Sweetwater, p. 372—History of Union Institute and Its Teachers, p. 377—Story of Stolen Horse, p. 391—A Civil War Episode, p. 402—The Town of Philadelphia, p. 404—The Battle of Philadelphia, p. 405—The Town of Loudon, p. 409.

Sweetwater Lodge, No. 292, F. & A. M., p. 380.
Newspapers of Town of Sweetwater, p. 386.
Members of General Assembly from Sweetwater Valley, p. 389.

CORRECTIONS and ADDENDA

Page 77 line 4, insert: He d. April, 1917..

Page 78, line 4 from bottom insert: O. K. Jr., was b Mch. 20, 1917.

Page 79, line 11 from bottom, insert: Susan Laird, d. May 8, 1917

Page 110, 11 from bottom insert: She died Mch. 10, 1917.

Page 111, after paragraph about (7), A. B. Cannon, insert:(8). Wm.Harry b. Feb. 13, 1877. Now (1917) U. S. Post Master at Gooding, Ida

Page 112, line 16, add: D. C. Young d. Sunday, July 1, 1917, at 11 p. m.

Page 116, after line 6. insert as heading:...John Smith.

Page 140, line 12, add She (E. P. T.) died Aug. 8 1911.

Page 170, line 3, from bottom add D. H. d. Nov. 23, 1917.

Page 176, line 5, eliminate"he d. in 1871" and add: She d. in 1908

Page 176, line 8, add· He d. June 16, 1913.

Page 176, for "Dyche" read Dyke.

Page 222, line 6, from bottom, for "4:59" read 4:39.

Page 308, line 14, read Joseph, for "James" Reagan.

Page 308, line 18, from bottom read 1810, instead of 1910.

Page 311, line 15, for "Hagwood" read Haygood.

Page 316, line 18, cut out "Five.   Arthur Bruce, fourth son of and read·   Two. Frank M. first son of R. F. and E. R. Scruggs.

Page 316, line 17, from bottom for "Margaret" read Annie Ssruggs

Page 325, line 22, read Frances M. b. May 26, 1883, at Sweetwater, and died at Knoxville, Sunday Jan. 13., at 8:30 a. m.

Page 338, line 13, add J. Forsyth Swords, d. at Dallas, July 9 1917

Page 347, line 14, for 1835, read 1853.

Page 414. line 20 from bottom, for "who" read whom.

Page 414, line 9 from bottom, for "laides" read ladies.

Page 282, line 13 trom bottom, add, She d. Feb. 8 Arequipa, Peru

Page 282, line 9 from bottom, read Margaret Caroline, b Feb. 26, 1896, in Mexico

Page 282, line 8 from bottom, read, Mary Elizabeth, b Jan. 6, 1898, in Mexico.

Dedication

To the natives of this valley and their descendants, wherever found; to the admirers of strength and loveliness of character, to the lovers of the beautiful in nature, to those who delight in fertility of soil and seek healthfulness of clime, this book is respectfully dedicated.

Preface

In this book can be found sermons and songs, humor and pathos, history and philosophy, geology and genealogy, and a great fund of information. If you do not find these, do not blame me. It is your deficiency, not mine.

Yours egotistically,

W. B. LENOIR.

EXPLANATORY NOTES

In setting forth the genealogical tables in this work to attain clearness and prevent puzzling the mind of the readers, I have used the following method:

One, Two, Three, etc., placed in front of names are children of at least one common parent.

1, 2, 3, etc., are children of One, Two, Three, etc.

(1), (2), (3), etc., are children of 1, 2, 3, etc.

a, b, c are children of (1), (2), (3), etc.

(a), (b), (c), etc., are children of a, of a, b, c, etc.

Abbreviations used are:
    b for born.
    m for married.
    d for died.

FOREWORD

My purpose as given in the *Sweetwater Telephone,* a weekly paper published at Sweetwater, Tenn., was set forth in what follows:

I contemplate writing a history of the early settlement of Sweetwater Valley, at least that part of it which includes the location of the town of Sweetwater and as much adjacent territory up and down the valley as far as I am able. My intention, also, is to take in as much of the country east of Sweetwater Ridge and west of Black Oak Ridge as was embraced formerly in the first civil district of Monroe County. This history, if it can be dignified by that name, will contain sketches of the people of this section of the long ago, whether they permanently remained here or removed to other parts of the country; and give genealogical table of the principal families; of the condition of the valley at the first settlement; then when the railroad was built, graded and finished. We will try to trace the gradual growth of the town, and tell of the people wherever coming from who helped to make it what it is. We, who live in this day, are much indebted to George Washington and the founders of this republic for many of the blessings we enjoy; but we who live here or have lived here, owe a far greater debt to those who dug and built, toiled and legislated for us in this our own valley. Those of the present generation who find improvements and resources ready made to hand often fail to think what is due to those who occupied and acted before us. This is to us an unearned and unpaid for increment. The people of this valley before the war did not incur bonded indebtedness for their descendants to pay. It is well that they did not then, for after the losses during the Civil War, their condition would have been indeed deplorable. Considering what they had to do aforetime they could have well been excused for bonding the county, but such was not the policy pursued.

When the Hiwassee, the district in which we live, was surveyed and sold in quarter sections, there were no Indians to fight and the country was not a lawless one, but roads were to be made, schoolhouses and churches to be built and at the same time the settlers had to prepare for themselves homes and get the land in a state fit for cultivation. Then the inhabitants of this valley not only raised what they ate and drank, except coffee, water and salt, but also made their own wearing apparel and produced the material for the garments and made their own wagons and farm implements. A blacksmith or a shoemaker was as valuable an asset in the community as a school teacher or a doctor. Thus neighbors were in a great measure dependent one upon the other; they swapped work and materials when money was not plentiful. This begot a feeling of common brotherhood and helpfulness, that nowadays is almost impossible to exist in our state of society.

When the East Tennessee and Georgia Railway depot (now the Southern) was located on the lot of land where the present depot now stands, within the radius of a half mile there lived Daniel Heiskell, John Ramsey, the Axleys, John Fine, Charles Owen, Henry Mayes and the Biggs, and within a mile or about that distance Josiah K. Johnson, Robert Snead, John Fryar, John Bowman, I. T. Lenoir, Sterling Neil, John and Charles Lotspeich. These were all farmers and got their mail at "Facility," postoffice at Reagan's, and Philadelphia. Some of those mentioned above had considerable families; all of them, however they might differ about religion and politics, were high-toned, honorable, public-spirited men—acted in concert and formed an almost ideal nucleus for a town. Some of those living farther away in the valley and across the ridges in the opposite valleys had almost, if not quite, as much to do with the upbuilding of the town as those mentioned.

The plan of these citizens in town-making was not to lay off a number of lots, exploit and advertise the place, get up an excursion, knock off to the highest bidder, for speculative purposes, but to get such people to come and live here as would become honorable and useful citizens and whom they could associate with on terms of perfect equality.

In getting up data for this work, I have spent much time at Madisonville examining the public records. The only office in which I found them at all satisfactory was that of register of deeds. Many of the records in the clerk and master's, the circuit court and the county court clerk's offices are missing or destroyed. The old court-house was burned in 1864, therefore the loss of the records is not due to inefficiency in past or present officers holding those places, but partly to the destruction of the court-house and partly to the fact that no vault or proper places had been prepared for their safekeeping. The vaults we now have in the new court-house at Madisonville are much too small and will soon be filled up.

Even the marriage records in the county court clerk's office are far from complete.

It is not until quite recently that it has been made obligatory by the State laws to keep a record of births, which has been the practice for a thousand years in England. Thus, the children of many prominent people could not prove by the public records their title to much valuable property were it to be disputed, unless by parole evidence. For these reasons the gathering of data for what I wish to do through sources open to the public, is a matter of much difficulty. I shall have to rely in a great measure on the assistance of those who personally know or have private sources of information about the subject and people of whom I wish to be informed.

It is not my purpose now, but may be later on, to bring records nearer to the present than 1867. From that time on to the present is much plainer sailing and can be done by any painstaking individual. Any facts not recorded in public offices or newspapers can easily be obtained from private individuals.

There were also very few even weekly newspapers published in this section in olden times and those did not deal much in personalities, or rather personals. Their columns were devoted mostly to news to be found on the first page of the newspapers published to-day and to the discussion of public men and measures. Now we can take the daily Knoxville and Chattanooga papers, with the assistance of the weekly papers published in places between, and compile the history of the community for any period desired.

History of Sweetwater Valley

ABOUT HISTORY—WHO SHOULD ATTEMPT TO WRITE IT.

One makes a statement. It is either true or false; or it may contain elements of both truth and error. Owing to the fallibility of human memory, the temptation to distort for interest or effect, the want of proper information, the lack of time for investigation, misstatements of one kind or another are nearly always found in a lengthy article.

If real persons are written about and what is published purports to be facts, we call it history or biography. If the people or narratives are imaginary we call it fiction. If animals other than men are told about, it is usually termed natural history. If inanimate things treated of, it is physics.

To be a satisfactory historian, one should have a discriminating, impartial mind, be a patient investigator, able to sift the false from the true, having good powers of observation, should not be swayed by malice or led to too much adulation by friendship or admiration.

In addition to this he should have such a command of language as to make his meaning clear, using concise sentences composed of simple words, able to be understood by people of average intelligence. No sentence should be ambiguous or susceptible of two meanings; but each should be written so that the sense cannot be changed by punctuation. If pains are taken by a good writer, this can be done.

Unfortunately the English language abounds in words of the same sound which when spelled differently have different meanings. This is why the phonetic system cannot be adopted for many years (if at all) in a history or scientific treatise. Also when a word is used in a restricted sense, explanation is sometimes necessary.

The word "water" in common language may mean any one of several things, fresh, salt, pure, impure, *et cetera.* To the chemist or druggist, water means a liquid formed from hydrogen and oxygen gases combined in certain proportions and expressed in chemical language, H_2O. It can exist in three forms, solid, liquid and gaseous. In the open air at sea level at a temperature of 32 degrees (Fahrenheit) and below, it is a solid (ice or snow), above 32 degrees and up to 212, it is a liquid (water), above 212 and up to an exceeding high temperature, it is a gas (steam). Pure water, when taken into the stomach, quenches thirst and is healthful, when taken into the lungs in sufficient quantities, destroys life. These facts are known to humanity in general, the knowledge of which is necessary to the preservation and comfort of the human race, therefore this is the most useful and highest form of knowledge. It has also the advantage of being able to be verified by the individual observer. The study of physics is more exact than that of history. Each individual drop of water under like circumstances acted, acts and will act the same manner yesterday, to-day and forever. Not so the individual people of even a limited section of country, although they may be of the same race and living under the same government and subject to the same human laws. When taken as a mass, however, we can formulate a general rule of conduct.

We assert as a fact that the East Tennessee mountaineer resists oppression and is quick to resent an insult; still this is not true of every individual, but only of the large majority. Any doubter can experiment and see what happens.

So much about how a history should be written. I have been asked more than once what good is there in delving into the past of this section and attempting to place the result before the public. The question is pertinent. Everyone should have a good reason for his actions. If what is written becomes a part of the record of the country in which he lives and is untrue, it helps to perpetuate error, which is undesirable. The Barbara Frietchie incident has been embalmed in story and song to such an extent that, though proved a hundred times to have no foundation in fact, is usually believed and accepted as history.

Even mere annals or the relation of dry facts have their uses. For instance, two persons, William Browder and Thornton C. Goddard, residing within a mile of each other, reached almost the century mark in age. Several things could and ought to be inferred therefrom; that the section they lived in was healthful; that there was much of clean living and thinking in the individuals themselves, to say nothing of clean eating and drinking; that their parents before them gifted them with good constitutions, sound minds in sound bodies. What does it profit a man if he gains a million dollars and fails to transmit to his children the mental and physical capacity to use and enjoy in a proper manner the wealth he leaves them?

We, as people, are anxious to get the pedigree of the donkey, and trace his ancestry back to the Andalusian mountains, to know that our horses have their origin in the desert of Arabia, our cows came from Jersey, that our breed of chickens came from the Isle of Minorca or from Cochin, China, our ducks from Pekin, our hogs from Berkshire, and our hound dogs from Virginia or Pennsylvania. This is all right and proper and no objection is registered. But there are some who seem to think their own people and the acts of long ago are of no importance. Such an one usually miscalls himself a self-made man. He acknowledges no indebtedness to the past. He is of himself, by himself and for himself. Such an one is not likely to make sacrifices for the community in which he lives; he will not rush into the breach to save his country; if he sheds his blood it will be by proxy.

I know there are those, because of inherited wealth and family prestige, who consider themselves better than others and think that they are exempt from toil and trouble and ought to be granted special privileges. This spirit is to be deplored wherever found. I am glad to say there has been and is little of this in our valley. The very opposite should be the case. If one's ancestors took a prominent place in school, society, church or State, it is his duty to maintain its traditions and not have it said the family died with his mother or father.

Sentiment plays and ought to play an important part in our lives. It is well that such pieces as mentioned below belong to the mental make-up of the average school-boy:

"Breathes there a man with soul so dead."—Scott.

"Oh, say, can you see in the dawn's early light?"—Key.

"This lovely land, this glorious liberty, these benign institutions, the dear purchase of our fathers."—Webster.

"An exile from home pleasure dazzles in vain."—Payne.

They have been said and sung to admiring audiences by every school-boy. He cons them over day by day. These, in connection with the deeds of the good and great taught in history, help to make him a patriot and self-respecting citizen. If sentiment is lacking in a man's composition, he may think himself rich with acquired wealth, but he is really poor. He misses the best things in life.

PREFATORY REFLECTIONS.

When a magazine writer perpetrates a particularly unreasonable story, clear beyond the realms of possibility, he remarks nonchalantly (to use a popular expression in vogue in our periodicals): "This illustrates how stranger is truth than fiction;" that is to say, more wonderful, marvelous and startling. Wonder is the child of ignorance and superstition. Also the things we see happen daily and hourly we take little notice of; they occasion no surprise. We stare at the aviator who rises in his spiral flight; we accept as commonplace the soaring of the bird, though the latter is far more wonderful. We are pleased to see the order of things reversed, the man to ascend triumphantly into the empyrean and the whirring bird to tumble at the shot of the expert. The commonplace does not attract us. We care not to see a man walk on his feet however gracefully he may carry himself, but we applaud when he stands on his head on the trapeze bar and kicks his heels in the air. We have heard so much of the serpent charming the ancient Eve in the garden of Paradise, "the cause of our woe and the loss of Eden," that we cheerfully spend a dime in the side show to see the modern Eve charm the serpent. We feel that evens things up. Then we part with fifty cents in the big show to observe how the fierce monarch of the forest cowers under the lash of the animal trainer. He may be as gentle as a kitten but he roars as if he could eat up a whole menagerie. He knows his business: no roar, no meat. If the public but knew the facts in the case, minus would be the blood-curdling thrills so dear to the feminine heart, and the "barker" at the entrance would be hunting another job.

The man was not far wrong who said:

"This world is but a fleeting show (traveling circus) For man's illusion given."

And while the clown in the ring is convulsing our country cousins his child may be dying in the dressing-room. The cop on the corner says, "Move on"; we can't stop.

But if I thought that it would be necessary to resort to the bizarre, to palm off fiction for truth, to give an undue value to small things or to belittle the great to make an interesting and instructive history of our valley and its people, I would be far from attempting to write it. Mistakes will necessarily be made, but they will not be intentional and every pains and means within my power will be taken to avoid them. Statements merely probable will be given as such.

What truth is, what life is, have never been satisfactorily answered by philosophers and chemists.

There are hundreds of definitions but they are all mostly juggling with words. It is folly for us to attempt it. For our own purposes, which we premise is purely arbitrary, we shall divide the kinds of truth as follows:

1. *Axiomatic.*—Such as "A straight line is the shortest distance between two points." Not susceptible of proof but acknowledged.

2. *Mathematical.*—"Certain properties of the right angle triangle." These you can prove by experiment.

3. *Moral.*—Philanthropy or love as a ruling power for the world is preferable to hatred. One is constructive, the other is destructive.

4. *Historical.*—Dependent upon the accuracy of the written and spoken testimony of observers and the works of man extant.

5. *Financial* (mathematical also)—If a section raises, gets and keeps within its borders more of wealth than it exports, then it will eventually become rich. The problem of political economy is to exchange the perishable that you cannot use for the more or less imperishable. Simple enough in stating but not easy in practice.

As to rules of evidence, about which hundreds of volumes have been written, time and space are the principal factors: that is to say, that no two bodies can occupy the same space at the same time, nor can anybody be in two separate places at the same time.

If John Smith committed an act, then the remainder of the world is absolved from that particular action.

If John Jones was in Sweetwater when a man was hit by a baseball bat in Philadelphia, then it naturally follows that John Jones was not the hitter.

Furthermore, for the doing of any act, whether termed good or bad, there must be present motive, opportunity and ability. This applies to other animals as well as men. These things are A-B-C's to the legal fraternity and to a great many others; however, a statement of the same stripped of legal verbiage may not be inapt.

These state some of the general plans of the history, the specifications will come later.

THE TESTIMONY OF THE ROCKS IN SWEETWATER VALLEY.

In speaking of a valley, writers usually mean the surface drained by some particular stream and its tributaries. Sweetwater Creek takes its rise partly from some large springs on the east side of Sweetwater Ridge, the waters from which run westward through a low gap in the ridge, joining with other streams in the valley, which have their sources near Reagan's. Below Philadelphia, two miles, the creek breaks through the Black Oak Ridge, and empties into the Tennessee River on the west side of the ridge.

Our use of the term, "Sweetwater Valley," includes the territory between Sweetwater and Black Oak

Ridges from the summit or divide of the waters running southwest to Mouse Creek and those running northeast, forming Sweetwater Creek, to where those ridges strike Tennessee River near Loudon. The divide is about midway between Reagan's Station and Niota. The valley proper is about eighteen miles long and a scant two miles in width. The stations and towns included in the valley are Reagan's, Sweetwater, Philadelphia and Loudon. The name "Summit" was given to the point on the old East Tennessee and Georgia Railroad as being the highest on that railway between Knoxville, Tenn., and Dalton, Ga.

"Day unto day uttereth speech and night unto night showeth knowledge." The firmament, the stars have not human language but to the reverent listener they sing together as at creation's dawn, flashing their vibrant message of light through the ether, repeating o'er and o'er the story of their birth to the uttermost confines of space.

There is not a rock, tree or flower that has not a tale of its own to tell. Observe them, read them! What they have to say far surpasses in interest the novel or the yellow journalism of the day; for their story is a true one. The testimony of the rocks, when rightly read, is unmistakable. There is no misprint, no typographical error. You can lie about a rock, but it never lies about itself. It tells you plainly of what it is composed and how it was formed, whether by fire, water or air, whether its origin was igneous (volcanic) or sedimentary or a combination of the two. The imprint of the shell upon the limestone informs you what animals lived in the deeps at that period. Break it, powder it even, like the shattered rose vase, it will speak to your senses still of what it once held.

The geology of the surface of Sweetwater Valley is not complex. The stratifications dip at no great angle from the horizontal. They have been subjected to but few folds or "faults." They are almost entirely sedimentary, formed by water, and are not extremely varied in their character. In common language (we try not to use chemical and geological terms unless absolutely necessary) it is a limestone region. The formation is neither very hard nor very soft. It is, however, hard enough to prevent the streams from wearing away deep channels, as is notably the case with some of the rivers in the State of Kentucky and in some instances in the middle basin of Tennessee, and yet not of sufficient hardness to prevent the gradual weathering of the strata. These thus become part of the soil, enriching it and furnishing food for plant life. For this reason also we have no sharp, conical peaks as in shale regions, but the hills present to the eye a beautifully rounded contour. Nor are the ridges of great altitude above the intervening valleys. Massive and majestic mountain chains, like the Unaka or Blue Ridge, are formed of more durable material, such as the granites, the shales and the sandstones, which are far more slowly deroded by the action of air and water.

Although many thousands of compounds are known to chemists and an almost infinite number possible, they reduce on analysis to a small group of substances which are called "elements," merely meaning by this term, the simplest form to which any compound can be reduced.

There are now (1913) known to chemists eighty elements. Sixteen of these have been discovered in the last forty years. Several of the late discoveries belong to the radium group, with which, however interesting they may be, we have nothing to do.

The elements differ widely in their abundance and in their distribution in nature. In speaking of the geological formation of Sweetwater Valley we have to deal with a few only of these elements. The metals found in the rocks in our valley with their chemical symbols in brackets are given below:

Aluminum (Al), Carbon (C), Calcium (Ca), Iron (Fe), Magnesium (Mg), Manganese (Mn), Phosphorus (P), Potassium (K), Silicon (Si), Sodium (Na) and Sulphur (S).

Gases: Oxygen (O), Nitrogen (N), Hydrogen (H) and Chlorine (Cl).

Aluminum—The most abundant of all metals. One of the constituents of our red clay and an essential constituent of all important rocks except sandstones and limestones. It occurs only in oxidized compounds.

Calcium—Next to aluminum the most abundant metal in Sweetwater Valley. Our limestone is a calcium carbonate. Our marble is a crystallized calcium carbonate.

Carbon—The characteristic element of organic matter; trees, plants, flesh, etc. Diamond is crystallized carbon; anthracite coal also nearly pure carbon.

Iron—Occurs as an oxide in the valley and ridges; also is found in small quantities as a sulphide. Brown iron ore on Black Oak Ridge north of Sweetwater; red fossiliferous ore (hematite) in many places in the valley. Much has been mined and shipped.

Manganese found in nodules; also in combination with the oxide of iron and gives to the latter its bluish cast. Valuable as an alloy in the making of steel.

Magnesium—Best known to our fathers and mothers as common epsom salts, which is magnesium sulphate. This salt is very soluble and is, therefore, found in many mineral waters. The carbonate forms part of magnesian limestone, which is fairly abundant in our valley. It is commonly called dolomite, which is sometimes tinted pink or brown, and is unlike the blue limestone. Limestone containing a large percentage of magnesium is not suitable for being burned into the lime of commerce.

Phosphorus—Important constituent of many plants and also in combination with oxygen and lime forms the greater part of the bones of animals. Found in the limestones in our valley in small quantities. However, there are no great beds of phosporites in our valley as in middle Tennessee. When cereals requiring a large amount of phosphorus are cultivated from year to year on the same land, the phosphorus should be supplied in some shape to the soil. Phosphorus oxidizes with a light. Notice faint light from rotting wood in damp weather.

We have said already that the prevailing metals in the rocks of the valley were Aluminum (Al), Calcium (Ca), Carbon (C), Iron (Fe), Magnesium (Mg), Manganese (Mn), Phosphorus (P), Potassium (K), Silicon (Si), Sodium (Na) and Sulphur (S).

We have discussed these in a brief manner above with the exception of the last four. We have yet to speak of the gaseous elements, Oxygen (O), Hydrogen (H) and Chlorine (Cl). These are not liquid at ordinary temperature, but all of the gases may be liquefied by intense cold and pressure.

Potassium—Found mostly in the igneous rocks, though in small quantities in the sedimentary rocks of our valley. It is a constituent of most terrestrial waters. It is found in the ash of woods, especially hickory ash, also a constituent of many plants.

Silicon—Next to oxygen the most abundant of all the elements on the earth, yet in our own valley it is far exceeded in quantity by calcium. It exists in all well, river and spring waters. It is readily taken up by plants and gives to the stem of not a few of them their strength and resisting power. Quartz is a silicon dioxide. It crystallizes hexagonally. Almost every one has seen these semi-transparent crystals, though not plentiful here. They are often colored by various substances. Quartz or sand when fused with sodium or potassium forms the glass of commerce. It is easily manufactured into various forms. The fact that it resists all acids, except hydrofluoric, a rare acid, makes it almost a necessity in our daily life. Quartz in some localities forms great boulders and cliffs; found in our valley only in small quantities.

Sodium—Is a constituent of all oceans and closed lakes, usually as a solution of common salt, chloride of sodium, invaluable to humanity as an antiseptic. It exists in small quantities in rain water and the air, decreasing rapidly in proportion as we recede from the oceans. Very little sodium in any form is found in Sweetwater Valley rocks.

Sulphur—Sulphides and sulphates are not common in our valley. Sulphuret of iron (pyrite) in small particles is found imbedded in our limestone. This is in color a bright yellow of cubical crystallization and is sometimes mistaken for gold, therefore occasionally called "fool's gold." This is plentiful in copper regions, being a portion of most copper ores. Sulphate of lime is the gypsum of commerce, very little of which is found here. It is soft and easily ground.

Barium—Little in our valley, though in valleys east and west of us it is abundant; there found in the form of a sulphate, barytes (Ba So 4). Large quantities have been shipped from the different railway shipping points in our valley. It is principally valuable in the manufacture of paints.

We have now discussed briefly the important mineral elements of our valley soil, we will say something of the gaseous elements. They are found surrounding the earth. Not knowing the composition of the atmosphere we would be ignorant of one of the principal sources of plant and animal life. Where there is no atmosphere there can be no life such as we know here. For this reason astronomers believe that the moon is perfectly sterile. Our atmosphere is not a chemical compound but a mechanical mixture.

The principal constituents are three gases given below:

	Chemical symbol.	Percentage by weight.	Percentage by volume
Oxygen	O	23.024	20.941
Nitrogen	N	75.539	78.122
Argon	Ar	1.437	.937
		100.000	100.000

The last, argon, is an inert gas not found in combination with any other element. The reason for giving it is that its one and a half per cent. weight is far greater than any other element in the air with the exception of O. and N. given in table; otherwise it need not be taken into account. The atmosphere, roughly speaking, is four-fifths nitrogen and one-fifth oxygen, mechanically mixed but chemically separate, ready to seize upon anything that either comes in contact with for which it has an affinity.

As oxygen is heavier than nitrogen it would naturally be supposed that in the higher altitudes the percentage of oxygen would be less, however, numerous chemical analyses have shown the contrary to be the case; that the air in mountainous regions is richer in oxygen than those nearer the sea level. In addition to the elements spoken of above the air contains in variable quantities the vapor of water, carbon dioxide, ammonia, sulphur, organic matter and other suspended solids and also innumerable animalculae or microbes. But it is these very constituents, or the absence of them, infinitely minor in weight and volume, that make a region desirable or possible to live in. A miasmatic exudation from a swamp might bring disease and death to numerous near-by people though neither in weight nor volume it composes one ten millionth of the atmosphere in that locality. Local conditions in a great measure determine the proportion of these minor constituents. Wherever animals breathe and fire burns oxygen is withdrawn from the air and locked up in compounds. Wherever plants and trees grow oxygen is given out and carbon absorbed. Near iron furnaces and manufactories where a vast amount of coal is consumed there is a greater proportion of carbon dioxide in the atmosphere; near copper refining furnaces more sulphur; near oceans and large bodies of water more aqueous vapor and chlorine. Volcanoes erupt many gases, some of them deadly, sometimes destroying plant and animal life near them. Oxygen is far the most abundant element in nature, constituting one-fifth of the atmosphere, nearly seven-eighths of the waters, from 45 to 53 per cent. of all important rocks, being almost one-half of terrestrial matter. The "corroding tooth of time" is nothing more nor less than oxygen combining with other elements. In fact, gold, silver and copper are about the only metals of importance found in the free State. That is one reason probably why they were used as coins or standards of value long before chemistry or even alchemy or processes of extracting metals from oxides and sulphurets were known.

WHERE HUMANITY COULD MORE HAPPILY LIVE.

Many writers have conceded that the ideal places for humanity to live, in especial the white race, would be in the United States, somewhere between 30 and 40 degrees north latitude; in a valley whose average elevation was not less than six hundred nor more than two thousand feet above the sea level; whose surrounding ridges abound in timber and ores; whose elevation above the valley is high enough to afford a convenient water supply but not so high as to make transportation over them difficult; with a rainfall of not less than fifty inches nor more than eighty during the year, distributed somewhat equally in the seasons; with enough incline in the valley to make good drainage, give the streams free course and also furnish water for power and other purposes; with an average temperature of from sixty to seventy degrees Fahrenheit, and where there are not too sudden and extreme variations between seasons as in some parts of the Northwest; a valley where the thermometer rarely rises above 90° Fahrenheit or falls below 10°; these advantages, experience proves, makes a healthful climate and a valley capable of supporting a numerous and prosperous people. There are more places in East Tennessee that answer these conditions than any other section of country with which I am acquainted. No one of them is more ideal, in my opinion, than Sweetwater Valley. Different elevations, temperatures, waters and soils may suit different individuals but we are speaking of what would suit the average white man. We recognize the fact that there is no great stream running through our valley, there are no coal beds, no immense bodies of ores, and for these reasons small likelihood of there being in the near future any great city in our borders; however, most of us are not crazy on the subject of increase in population. We fail to see why people cannot get as much out of life in a town of 20,000 inhabitants as one of 200,000. We are not obliged to have millionaires in our midst to be happy. Needless to say we have none. If congestion of wealth and population is necessary to our happiness it is still possible to live in New York or London and China. The Chinese claim that their country is not yet full of people. There is no doubt though that Sweetwater Valley is capable of supporting several times the population it now has and at the same time exporting a large amount of products. Congestion is not likely to occur for years to come. Yet at the same time there should be no fear but that we will not receive our proportion of people seeking new locations. Thousands of people, and ones who will make splendid citizens, too, are on the hunt for such places as our valley affords.

THE EARLIEST INHABITANTS OF OUR VALLEY.

It is generally agreed by archaeologists and the delvers into antiquities that what are termed the mound builders are the most ancient inhabitants. They are so called because of their custom of erecting mounds in which to bury their dead. In supposed populous communities some of these mounds were very large, being sometimes as much as fifty to seventy-five feet higher than the surrounding territory. There used to be various mounds in Sweetwater Valley, none of them as far as I know were very large. There used to be a mound in the field of Mrs. Love, a short distance north of the old Sweetwater Cemetery, and one in the field on the east side of the railroad, perhaps nearly a quarter of a mile from the one mentioned above. For a long time the soil upon them was very unproductive, and it could be easily seen exactly where they were located. Now they have been so plowed down, fertilized and cultivated that to ascertain their exact location is a matter of some difficulty. These mounds, so far as I know, were never dug into and the findings made a matter of record. They are, however, supposed to contain what was found in the mounds in this valley and in the valley of the little Tennessee River that have been examined and their contents preserved and classified. The United States government and various universities and historical societies have carried on a series of explorations for a number of years. The results of different ones differ in many points. However, there are other points in which most agree: That the American Indian did not erect these mounds. If any tribe did it, it was the Cherokees. If they did build mounds it was for defense and not for burial purposes. Their burial customs are different.

The skeletons and stone sepulchres show that the mound-builders were rather small people, and hardly so large as the American Indians who inhabited this section. They belonged to the stone age. There is no evidence of their having used any metallic weapons or instruments. They were sun worshippers, as shown by the position of the stone and slate sepulchres. In this they show their kinship to the Aztecs of Mexico. There are no remains here of temples, roads, aqueducts or prominent residences. It is doubtful if they ever used wood for building. There is no mark of sharp instruments in any of the oldest trees.

According to Thurston's Antiquities in some mounds, however, have been found bottles, spoons and cooking utensils of various characters, mostly earthenware. There are no inscriptions on these which have been deciphered, and it is presumed they had no written language.

Their arrowpoints are similar to those plowed up in the Roman Campagna, which far antedate any period of Roman history.

So far there is no agreement of exactly when they inhabited this country, when they were driven away or destroyed, what was their color, race or nation. From my reading I infer that they were rather a small, warlike people, as shown by the weapons; were more civilized than the American Indians, but not so much so as the Aztecs or the Arizona Cliff Dwellers; that they inhabited the bounds of the Hiwassee district in far greater numbers or for a longer period than did the Indian tribes; that the American Indians have no reliable account even by tradition of what sort of people they were.

When the mound builders disappeared, were destroyed or were assimilated is a matter of conjecture; probably more than five hundred years ago. For when Ponce de Leon landed in Florida in 1512 the Seminoles, a tribe of Indians, occupied that country and must have done so for many years. Later on in 1540 when De Soto, the discoverer of the Mississippi, started his wonderful invasion he found the Seminoles in Florida, and marching northwestward he encountered the Cherokees in what is now North Georgia. He wintered in Nacoochee Valley at the head of the Chattahooche River at the foot of Yonah, a peak of the Blue Ridge. Exactly what route he pursued from there to the Chickasaw Bluffs on the Mississippi River is uncertain. There are traditions of his passing through a part of western North Carolina. In Cherokee county in the Valley River Valley are the remains of old diggings and rude furnaces for the reduction of ores, known as the De Soto mines. This was certainly not done by the Cherokee Indians, who held possession of that section, as they neither had the energy nor the appliances for such work; nor was it done by the

English white settlers since their occupation. There is one of two things probable; either part of De Soto's invading army, tiring of the hardships of the campaign, deserted and did this mining, and afterwards were killed or amalgamated with the tribe and lost to history like the colony of Sir Walter Raleigh on Roanoke Island; or that the whole force of that commander crossed the Blue Ridge Mountains at the Yonah Gap at the head of the Hiwassee River in Towns county, Georgia, and thence marched down that river to the junction of the Hiwassee and Valley Rivers. Six miles above there is the site of the so-called "De Soto mines." There are not many streams in that section which have not produced gold in paying quantities, nearly all got by placer mining. De Soto's object was evidently to gain fame and riches by repeating the conquest of Pizarro in Peru and Cortez in Mexico.

How strange this lure and thirst for gold in all people and nations from the earliest "syllable of recorded time" down to the present! Most of the explorations, discoveries, inventions and the greater number of wars and crimes have been attributed to it. "The love of money," we are told, "is the root of all evil." If we can credit historians, man's main effort through the ages has been to get and keep gold, "hard to get and harder to hold." Nothing has ever induced him to part with it save the charms of woman—Anthony flinging the world away for the love of Cleopatra.

When Croesus, the Lydian tyrant, showed Solon, the Athenian, the greatest hoard of gold then in existence, taken, it is said, from the sands of the River Pactolus, and asked him, "Ought I not to be happy?" Solon replied: "I call no man happy while living." How true it was in Croesus' case: The barbarian afterward overcame him and made him swallow his own molten gold. "You always wanted gold, now take this." Or as Herodotus gives it he was captured by Cyrus and subjected to torture and the greatest indignities.

No great hoard of gold, no matter where placed or how carefully guarded, has ever been safe from the robber, the vandal and the pirate, and those who rob are often robbed in turn. What becomes of all the gold taken from the earth too is a mystery! Millions upon millions are buried in the depths of the ocean, as in the Titanic disaster. Great sums are in the teeth of people dead and living, but that has not been the case for long. Dentistry is comparatively a recent art. It must be that misers have hidden away innumerable treasures which have never been discovered. The greatest search for gold in history, undoubtedly on our own continent, taking into consideration the number engaged, was the ill-starred expedition of De Soto. 'Twas nothing to him to be the discoverer of the Father of Waters, naught cared he for the mighty forests of the East, the immense, fertile plains of the West; 'twas gold and gold only that he wanted. He and his followers preferred that their bones bleach in the unknown wilderness rather than to return to Hispania with their galleons unladen with "barbaric pearls and gold." The Jamestown colonists found "fool's gold," iron pyrites and took it to England. The Carolina colonists spent their first efforts in search for gold. These finally found something far more precious: "Liberty" and home. There was a rush to California for search for the precious metal. It so happens that the products now from that State in one year even, exclusive of gold, are worth more than all the gold ever taken out of it. Alaska's gold is but a drop in the bucket to the iron, coal, the copper and the furs of the animals in her border; but little was said of anything but gold until the other resources were about all gobbled up by a favored few.

In 1896 we had what some called the "silver craze." Wrong, all wrong. It was just the old time greed for gold. It was this struggle: The men who had silver wanted gold for it, and those who had gold were determined to keep what they had. Gold won, as it nearly always does one way or another. Every intelligent person acknowledges that, except as a medium of exchange, it is far less useful to humanity than iron, tin or copper and it is not near so indestructible as most people imagine. It is easily abraded on account of its softness. There are numerous natural solvents of gold, as shown by its wide distribution by deposition and the finding of it in a great variety of rocks and soils. Some suppose aqua regia the only solvent for gold. By no means true. Even so mild a solvent as ten per cent. solution of sodium carbonate is capable of dissolving it, though but slowly. But people love gold on earth below, whether wisely or foolishly seems to matter not; and it is the opinion of many writers and speakers that we will love it in heaven above. If not, why is so much stress laid on the golden streets and the golden crowns the elect are to receive, as if it were impossible to attain perfect bliss in the New Jerusalem without the sight of the yellow metal? Exactly what use the disembodied or re-embodied spirits would have for a crown (for whom would they govern there?), or why it should increase their happiness to walk on the streets of gold is not explained.

However, we return to the expedition of De Soto. If he came in his march to where Murphy, N. C., is now, two routes to Alabama and Mississippi, which territories he is known to have traversed, were feasible: one down the Hiwassee River and the Tennessee Valley to Alabama; the other to strike the little Tennessee by way of some of its tributaries, thence down it to Chilhowee Gap. From there on to Alabama, Mississippi and the Chickasaw Bluffs the march would not present very great topographical difficulties.

THE CHEROKEES.

From the time of De Soto to 1700 we have no history of the Cherokees. Ramsey's Annals, page 78, says: "Early French explorers aver that the Shawnees, a powerfully and unusually intelligent tribe of Indians (in 1700), occupied the country from the Tennessee River in west Tennessee to the Cumberland Mountains. They were driven out by the Cherokees or Creeks, possibly both, and went north and were incorporated with the Six Nations.

"When the pioneers settled in Southwest Virginia and the coterminous part of North Carolina, those sections had ceased to be, probably never had been, the settled residence of the modern aboriginal tribes. It was used as the common hunting ground of the Shawnees, Cherokees and other Southern Indians. East and north of the Tennessee to the Ohio there was not a single Indian hut. The Choctaws, Chickasaws and Cherokees, however, of the South, used to engage in war with the Miami confederacy of the North. In their excursions they no doubt had certain trails which they were accustomed to travel.''

The Uchees were a small tribe which once occupied the country near the mouth of the Hiwassee River. Their warriors were exterminated in a desperate battle with the Cherokees. This took place at "old fields" in Rhea county sometime between 1750-1775. The remainder of the tribe were incorporated with the Cherokees. "Chera" in their language means fire. Chera-tage, men possessed of divine fire—of great courage. They were formidable alike for their numbers and their passion for war. When asked to make peace with the Tuscaroras, their reply was: "We cannot live without war. If we make peace with the Tuscaroras we must find some other tribe to war with. It is our occupation."

According to Adair, in 1735 the Cherokees had sixty-four towns and could collect six thousand warriors. This included all the men not too old or too young to fight, which would probably be one-fourth of the population. In 1750 there were not so many, they having been decimated by wars with the Creeks.

(Ramsey, p. 89): "Little of the history of the Cherokees can be ascertained from their traditions. These extend little farther back than the early days of O-ka-na-sto-to, their chief, who visited George II. of England. He was practically their king. His seat of government was E-cho-ta (more properly E-tsawty) on the Tellico River, which afterwards became the property of John McGhee.

FORT LOUDON.

After the visit of Okanastoto, Hugh Waddell, as commissioner for North Carolina, negotiated a treaty with the Cherokees. In pursuance with that treaty, Governor Glenn erected a line of forts, the easternmost of which was Fort Loudon at the highest point of navigation on the south bank of Tennessee River, near the mouth of the Tellico, and on the east bank of this river.

This fort was erected, Ramsay says, in 1756; Haywood gives the date at 1757. The fort surrendered after a long siege on August 7, 1760, being besieged by the united forces of the Cherokee nation. The English were to be allowed to march to the white settlements unmolested. The marching consisted of men, women and children, amounting to about three hundred. They were treacherously assaulted and massacred about daylight on the morning of the 10th of August. They had marched about twenty miles up the Tellico River, which would bring them not far from the site of the terminus of the Athens and Tellico Railway, now a part of the Louisville and Nashville system. There were only three or four survivors. One of them escaped to the town of Chota.

THE TOWN OF REFUGE.

"Every Indian tribe," says Adair, "had a town or house of refuge, which is a sure asylum to protect a manslayer or an unfortunate captive if he can once enter it. Among the Cherokees Chota, about five miles above Fort Loudon, was their city of refuge. Thus passed Fort Loudon, the first place in the bounds of what is now Monroe county, that was inhabited by the whites. The story has been told by numerous writers. Romance and truth have become so entangled that it is a matter of extreme difficulty to separate them. What happened to those pioneers or early settlers forms one of the most interesting and pathetic stories in the annals of that time.

After the fall of Fort Loudon the next we hear (historically) of the Cherokees was in 1769. They invaded the country of the Chicasaws beyond (west of) the Cumberland Mountains. They had what was called a bloody conflict. Not much is known of the battle except that the Cherokees were defeated and retired to their own country. The Chickasaws were content with their victory and did not follow it up. "This defeat of the Cherokees," Ramsey remarks, "probably saved the Watauga settlement." Since the extinction of the garrison at Fort Loudon they had shown evidence of intention of attacking it.

A treaty was concluded at Fort (Patrick) Henry on the Holston (Hogehogee) River near Long Island, July

20, 1777, between the commissioners of the State of North Carolina and the Overhill Indians. By this treaty the Indians conveyed the upper Holston from the mountains and the Nolichucky River to the Virginia line. It is not necessary to go into details which, anyhow as to exact territory, are somewhat vague. I refer to it more than any other reason as showing who the signers were to the instrument.

Those on the part of North Carolina were Waightstill, Avery, William Sharp, Robert Lanier and Joseph Winston. The Indian signers were Oconostota, of Chota; Rayetawah (Old Tassel), of Toquoe; Savannech (Raven), of Chota; Quillanuwah, of Toquoe; Octossetch, of Hiwassee; Attusah (Northward Warrior), of Mouth of Tellico; Ooskuah or Abram, of Chilhowee; Rollowah, of Tellico River; Toostook, of Tellico; Amoyah (Pigeon), of Notchey Creek; Oostosseteh (Man Killer), of Hiwassee; Tellehaeveh (Chestnut), of Tellico; Que-lee-kah, of Hiwassee; Annakehujah, of Tuskeega; Suahtukah, of Citico; Atta-kulla-kulla (Little Carpenter), of Notchey Creek; Okoo Neekah (White Owl), of Notchey Creek; Kata Quilla (Pot Cloy), of Chilhowee; Tuskasah (Terrapin), of Chiles Toosch; Sunne Waugh (Big Island). The Indians made their marks. The witnesses were Jacob Womack, James Robins, John Reed, Isaac Bledsoe, Price Martin, John Kearns. Joseph Vann was interpreter.

INDIAN NAMES OF MOUNTAINS AND RIVERS.

Thus we see from the location or dwelling place of the principal men who signed this treaty that there were no Indian towns west of Notchey Creek. Ramsey aptly remarks the Indian proper names and the appellation of the creeks and rivers were euphonious. The names of the mountain ranges were smooth and musical, such as Alleghanee. Tenasee, Chilhowee, Unaka, Chattanooga, Dumplin, Sandy Mush, Calf Kilier, High Tower, Hangin' Dog, Beaver Dam, and even Sweetwater would grate harshly upon the ears of those who sang their war songs upon the banks of the Allejoy, Oustanallee, Etowah and Euphassee.

The Tennessee River was so named from the Little

Tennessee River. By Tennessee River is meant that river from the Unaka Mountains and probably eastward to the Tuckaseega and westward from its junction with the Holston clear to the mouth on the Ohio River. That is what the Tenasee River of the treaties means. The French called it Riviere des Cheraquis or Cosquinambeaux; the aborigines named it Kallamuchee. From Little Tennessee to French Broad, Agiqua (Racing River); Clinch, Pellissippi; Little River in Blount county, Canot; Hiwassee, Euphassee. Right here I think it proper to say that there is absolutely no foundation for the spelling or pronunciation Hi-a-was-see. The mistake must have arisen from confounding the word Hiwassee (more properly Euphassee) with the Hiawatha of Longfellow's poem. The district was spelled Hiwassee in the old surveys, the river the same, the college always too. Dr. J. H. Brunner, former president of Hiwassee College, agrees that this is the correct spelling. I would not feel called upon to mention this attempted change in spelling, and also of pronunciation, had it not received the sanction of so high an authority as an ex-president of the United States. I am glad to say, however, that his suggested changes in that line have not always met with eminent success; and I hope much that for the sake of preserving the real Cherokee names we have (I wish there were more), that this attempted change will also prove a failure. The Cumberland River was the Warioto, French name Chauvanon. We still have left the Indian names Lousatchie, Hatchee, Sequachee, Ocoee, Conasauga, Chestua, Tellico (Psallico), Watauga and others. Watauga (properly, Waughtaugah) signifies many islands, the river of islands. Haywood says in his History of Tennessee that the Holston, from its confluence with the Tennessee at what is now Lenoir City upward to the French Broad, was known as Watauga to the Cherokees. Until 1889 it was Big Tennessee from the junction of the Holston and Little Tennessee to its mouth. By an act of the General Assembly, approved April 6, 1889, it was enacted as follows: "That the Tennessee extend from its junction with the Ohio River at Paducah, Ky., past the Clinch and French Broad Rivers to the junction of the north fork of the Holston River with the Holston at Kingsport in Sullivan county, Tenn., all usages to the contrary notwithstanding."

It is greatly surprising that the Cherokee Indians, whose language was so musical, attempted so little in the way of song and had no musical instruments at all, unless the tom-tom and the rattle can be called so. Their chants and war songs were far from pleasing to the ear of the pioneer even though he did not happen to be tied to a stake during the ceremonial. Little of the Cherokee music so called has been preserved, and in an artistic sense is no loss. One hymn called "Lamentation," found in some of the old hymn books published in East Tennessee, is said to be an Indian air adapted to some English words.

Francis S. Mitchell, Athens, Ga., in *Confederate Veteran* of July, 1916:

The aborigines lived so near the heart of nature that they learned her secrets and were unconscious poets. Their language, abounding in vowels, was soft and musical. Every proper noun had a meaning that was significant and often wonderfully poetic, as Cohuttan (Frog Mountain), Tallulah (Terrible), Toccoa (Beautiful), Amicalolah (Tumbling Water), Hiwassee (Pretty Fawn), Okefinokee (Quivering Earth), and Chattahoochee (Rocky River), Nacoochee (Evening Star). Neither the Creeks nor the Cherokees had a written language, and their history is a matter of tradition. The Creek language bore a resemblance to classic Greek. Their legends—wild, romantic, often tragic—are still full of interest for their pale-faced successors.

Extract from M. V. Moore, in March *Harper,* 1889:

RIVERS OF TENNESSEE.

Tennessee! How were her rivers in the olden Indian tongue?
What syllabic rhythm had they ere the white man's changes rung?
Wascibia and Shewanee—thus the Cumberland was known,
With Obed, Caney, Obe, Sulphur, Harpeth, New and Stone.

Holston once was Hogeehogee; and from the mouth of
    French Broad down (which was then the Taquas-
    tah) Cootchla on to Chota-town,
This an Indian refuge city of an ancient, wide renown,
    where there empties into Tennesa, this the Little
    Tennessee;
Then began great Kalamuckee (Chalaqua in Cherokee),
Once Hiwasse was Euphasa, with its brawling Chestoee,
Estinaula, "where they rested," and Amoah or Ocoee.
Through Chilhowee comes the Little, once the red man's
    swift Canoee—
Where the wingless Pigeon flutters, once the Aguqua
    they knew,
Where Unaka sent his daughter Salacao is Tellico;
Where was once the Nalachuckee, simply Chucky now
    we know.
Thundering through the Alleghanies with the Doe is
    yet Watauga;
Out and in with Georgia pranking, straight to gulf goes
    Connesauga;
Out but never more returning, "stream of death" is
    Chicamauga.
By these waters fought the Shawnee, Uchee, Choctaw,
    Cherokee—
Dead and vanquished are these warriors, but the music
    of the rivers,
And the sweet syllabic rhythm of its names shall live
    forever.

The following article will illustrate how, sometimes, history which is not history is accepted as history. It is taken from the *Sweetwater Telephone*:

"SOITEE WOITEE."
By W. B. Lenoir.

"Which I rise to explain" that things do sometimes turn out peculiar. In a very readable article in the *Southern Field* as reproduced in the *Sweetwater Telephone* of February 12, 1913, occurs this paragraph:

"The name Sweetwater came about in an unusual way. The Cherokee Indians, who formerly occupied the section, called the creek and valley 'soitee woitee,' which means in the Cherokee language 'happy homes.' But when the early settlers came they heard the Indians pronouncing the name, and, getting the pronunciation only half correct, they referred to the section as Sweetwater, which is merely what 'soitee woitee' sounds to them.''

It may really not matter how a town or a valley may have gotten its name; and although the name Sweetwater is not uncommon for branches, creeks and towns yet people are usually curious to know why it is called so. They want some sort of an explanation; and if an explanation is not ready to hand one must be invented. Often the more unreasonable the explanation, the greater the credence given it. Repetition, too, gives it more and more a semblance to truth. Usually I would let such paragraphs as the above go uncontradicted, as no real harm could come of it. My main reason for writing this is that I feel myself partly responsible for having started the yarn. I am aware that fiction, fairy tales, fables and legends have their proper place in literature, and they often entertain and sometimes instruct. Santa Klaus and St. Valentine are patron saints and national institutions with us whether they ever had existence or not. Sometimes, too, a man writes an article, which is accepted as truth, when at the time of its writing nothing was further from his desire than to have it so accepted. This brings me to my confession, so to speak.

Something like a decade ago, the late Mr. D. L. Smith, the then proprietor of the *Sweetwater Telephone,* on one of its anniversaries, possibly the tenth, with commendable zeal got out a special edition or magazine exploiting Sweetwater and Sweetwater Valley. He requested me some time previous to its publication to write a paper on the legends of the Cherokee Indians. I told him I didn't know, couldn't find out any. If 'twas to indite a sonnet to beauty's brown mouth or rosebud eyes, I could sing my little song with more confidence. I then thought no more of the matter. I left town to visit a friend. Whilst on that visit I got another letter from Mr. Smith insisting that I send in my communication about legends of Sweetwater Valley Cherokees. Not wishing to disappoint Mr. Smith I consulted a friend who was versed in Indian lore and asked him what was to be done in the case. ''The Cherokees,'' said he, ''have few if any traditions or legends and never occupied Sweetwater Valley so far as is known" (see Ramsey's Annals, page 87), but that he would help me invent a legend. I agreed to this provided we evolved a legend that would not be taken at all as history. How would this do? he remarked. Have John Howard Payne on his trip from Virginia to Georgia travel through Sweetwater Valley, stop there and be entertained by a hospitable and highly intelligent chief and draw a fancy sketch of the beauty and fertility of the country as it appeared then; narrate that he was also so much taken with the happiness of the Indian home that it inspired him to write the words and music of the song of "Home, Sweet Home"; naming it "Swatee Watee," which in the Cherokee vernacular meant "happy home." As a matter of fact neither of us knew of such words in the Cherokee language, and if there were such words had not the remotest idea what they meant. There could be no equivalent in any Indian language to our word "home," with its hallowed associations and civilized embellishments. "What is Home Without a Mother?" when translated into the Indian's idea would be, "What is a (smoky) tepee without a squaw (maybe two or three squaws) to fetch and carry and dig and cook and bear warriors to scalp the enemy?" An Indian squaw was no better than a beast of burden, to be thrown aside when she became useless. As the article referred to was signed by myself, the responsibility for the statements rested on me. On the one hand I was guyed for attempting to "palm off any such silly stuff on an unsuspecting public," and on the other hand, which was worse, have the statements taken as true and come to me for confirmation. I was sometimes tempted to stick to what I said and let them believe the lie and go their way; but here I am confessing my sins like a little man, as I should do, and promising to refrain from doing the like again. But—John Howard Payne, O, John Howard Payne! I almost wish that Home, Sweet Home, had not evolved from your fertile brain. Ramsey says in his Annals that Sweetwater had no Indian name, and, if it did, it bore no resemblance to its present one.

A CHAPTER ON RACES.

There are recognized at least four races of men. Once geographically and more accurately than now they could have been named from the locations they occupied as the European, the Asiatic, the African, the American; or according to characteristics the Caucasian, the Mongolian, the negro, the Indian; in relation to color, the white man, the yellow, the black and the red. Adopting either the biblical or evolutionary origin of man, it is equally uncertain where the cradle of the human race was. It is generally given as the highlands of Asia. This is, however, more speculation than actual history. There are individuals and even nations that are difficult to be classed under any one of these heads and may resemble several of them. The most plausible explanation is that they are an admixture. In the early dawn of history, sacred and profane, the races were not so much inclined to amalgamate, but kept more distinct. Yet even the divine command could not keep the Hebrews apart from others. It is scarcely conceivable that the ten "lost" tribes of Israel were lost sight of except as being mingled with other nations of the globe. In the contest of races the strongest or, if you insist on the word, the "fittest" survives; mental and physical capacity and environment make men and nations. A Kentuckian might use the phrase "blood will tell."

In the scheme of humanity or nations only two of these races, the white and the yellow, need to be taken into consideration in the future as determining the destiny of the world. They already occupy or control much the greater part of it. The white men own by far the most territory, but have not a very large preponderance in number. Judging the future by the past it is more than probable at some time the whole habitable globe will be controlled by one race, and we think that will be the white man.

The black and the red men have been nomadic in their nature. They have not the same attachment to home and country as the white man. When an Anglo-Saxon gets hold of a piece of land he erects his castle, and there he stays until driven off by a more powerful foe or is dispossessed by legal process by the sheriff. The white man has the inventive power, he progresses. The yellow has only imitation, he is conservative. The white man has always held in slavery the black man, either by chains or commercially. The black man is no fighter. He doesn't know how to fight. The Indian lacks numbers, industry and persistence. It is impossible either to enslave him or impart to him successfully the civilization and habits of the white man. When once he loses against the white man the places that knew him once know him no more forever. In one hundred years from now the small boy will give his dime to see a pure blooded Indian in a side show. The "barker" will say: "Ladies and gentlemen and children, buy your tickets here and step right in and behold one of the few pure living descendants of the powerful red man, who once held undisputed sway over our mighty continent. He was finally overcome by superior arms and numbers and such was his pride of race that he preferred extinction to becoming the serf or underling of his hated conqueror. Don't neglect this wonderful opportunity; for it may be many, many moons before you have a chance to view his like again!"

The words of Pope have become so familiar that cartoonists sometimes name the Indian "Lo."

"Lo, the poor Indian! whose untutored mind
Sees God in the clouds, or hears Him in the wind,
His soul proud science never taught to stray
Far as the solar walk or milky way;
Yet simple nature to his hope has given
Behind the cloud-topp'd hill an humble heaven;
Some safer world in depths of woods embraced,
Some happier island in the watery waste,
Where slaves once more their native land behold,
No fiends torment, no Christians thirst for gold.
To be content's his natural desire,
He asks no angel's wing, no seraph's fire,
But thinks admitted to yon equal sky
His faithful dog shall bear him company."

"There is no good Indian but a dead one," said Kit Carson, and it used to be such a favorite phrase out

West as to become wearisome. Here you have the two views entirely opposite, the poet who knew the Indian from hearsay and the soldier and scout who thought he knew all about him from experience. However, Carson's experience was more with the Sioux, Comanche and Apache than with the Cherokee. The fact remains that an Indian is Indian, a negro a negro and the white man a white man, and the two hundred years they have lived under the same government have not changed them.

The Hon. John B. Brownlow in an issue of the *Knoxville Daily Journal* in speaking of how history is sometimes made, or how error or a lie may become an accepted fact among a people, says:

"A lie will beget permanent belief by constant iteration and reiteration. Constant dripping will wear a stone, and the muddier the water the faster the wear. We all believe a great many things which we know are not true. The thing most widely known about George Washington is that he cut down his father's cherry tree with 'his little hatchet,' and then expressed his inability to lie. No fact in the history of Washington has wider or deeper prevalence. We all know now that it is not true—but what is the use to 'argufy'? About the only thing that the best read people in the world know about William Tell is that he shot an apple off his little son's head. That never occurred—but why 'argufy' about it? * * * Lee did not surrender to Grant under an apple tree at Appomattox, but what is the use of taking issue with every old woman and school child in the land who says he did?"

It is just as popular an error that the Indians were cruelly treated when it was thought best to cause their removal across the Mississippi; but more of this hereafter.

TREATIES WITH THE CHEROKEES.

Cessions o the State of North Carolina and the U. S. Government.

In May, 1783, the General Assembly of North Carolina opened an office for the sale of western lands for the purpose of paying the arrears due officers and soldiers on that part of the continental line which was raised in North Carolina and for the purpose of extinguishing part of the national debt acquired in the progress of the Revolutionary War. Without previous consultation with the Indians they enlarged the boundaries as follows: "Beginning at the point on the line between Virginia and North Carolina due north from the mouth of Cloud's Creek; thence west to the Mississippi River; thence down said river to the line of 35 degrees of north latitude; thence east to the Appalachian Mountain chain; thence with the same to the ridge that divides the waters of the Nolichucky and French Broad Rivers; thence with that ridge to Brown's line (Acts of North Carolina, 1778); thence with Brown's line to the beginning."

This was going farther than the General Assembly had a right to do and was almost certain to involve the State and settlers in bloody and expensive wars with the Cherokees and other Indian tribes. However, before much of the territory mentioned had been taken up under this act, the Legislature saw the unwisdom of it, and for this and other reasons they ceded their claim to this and other territory to the United States with certain conditions attached. This was in the year 1784. Congress, however, refused to accept the cession, and the act was afterward repealed.

Then John Sevier and others claiming that the State of North Carolina had parted title to the land so ceded to the United States, organized the State of Franklin, and held a session of the Legislature in Greenville in 1785.

They elected United States senators, passed acts and attempted to exercise all the powers of a State. "Thus," says Ramsey, "in the beginning of 1786 was presented the spectacle of two empires exercised at one time over the same people and territory."

Then arose that wonderful series of events in which John Sevier was leader for the State of Franklin, and Jonathan Tipton was leader for the State of North Carolina, which came near involving the factions in the throes of civil war. The Congress of the United States, after much wrangling, however, did not recognize the senators and representatives from Franklin as belonging to a State and they were refused admission. For this, more than any other reason, the State of Franklin, by legislative enactment on March 1, 1788, ceased to exist.

From then until 1796, when Tennessee was admitted to the Union, the State of North Carolina exercised undisputed authority over her boundaries.

The history of those times, with Sevier and Tipton as central figures, forms chapters of more thrilling interest than the happenings of almost any State in the Union—far more so than bull moose hunting in Maine, witch burning in Massachusetts, or tales of mining in Dead Man's Gulch, and stage robbing in Wyoming and Nevada. It is a favorite theme with writers and historians; but however charming narrative could be made it is not within our province to write of them except the bare mention as leading up to other events in our immediate section.

WHY FROM WHITE MAN'S VIEWPOINT NECESSARY TO REMOVE THE CHEROKEE.

In 1735, Ramsey says, the Cherokees had sixty-four towns and six thousand warriors. These towns were scattered over North Georgia, Western North Carolina and a part of Eastern Tennessee. In 1750 there were not so many, having meanwhile been decimated by wars, the Overhill Towns with the Northern Indians and the Lower Towns with the Creeks.

In 1755 the authorities of South Carolina divided the whole Cherokee country into six hunting districts: Overhill Towns, Valley Towns, Joree Towns, Keowa Towns, Out Towns and Lower Towns; in all thirty-eight towns. They gave the Overhill Towns as Great Tellico, Chatugee, Tenasee, Chote, Toqua, Sittiquo and Tallassee.

Bertram's Travels (1773-1778) gives the Overhill Towns on the Tanassee or Cherokee River as Nuasha, Tallase, Chelowe, Sette, Chote, Jaco, Tahassee, Tamahle, Tuskeege, Sunne Waugh, Nilaqua. Now in the treaty of Waightstill Avery and others, commissioners on the part of North Carolina at Fort Henry on July 20, 1777, with the Overhill Indians (heretofore discussed) the towns given as the abiding place of the head men are: Chota, Toquo, Hiwassee, Mouth of Tellico, Chilhowee, Notchee Creek, Tuskeega, Citico, Chiles Tooch.

The term "Overhill" means the towns west of the Great Smokies and situated between the (Little) Tennessee and Hiwassee Rivers. The white men approaching the section mentioned from the east, the country then occupied by the whites, would naturally term the towns on the west of the Smoky or Unaka Mountain the Overhill Towns.

The word "town" as applicable to Indian settlements was not open to the objection given in the song of "Yankee Doodle":

"Yankee Doodle went to town; he wore his striped trousers,
He said he couldn't see the town for so many houses."

An Indian town was a collection of tepees usually located near a considerable water course; near the tepees were patches cleared from the cane brake, on which the squaws cultivated corn for bread and hominy. This with the game killed by the bucks furnished sufficient subsistence for those residing there. The tepees were made of skins of wild animals supported by poles. They were of conical shape and had an opening at the top for the escape of the smoke, and were of such light character as to be readily carried away by the squaws in case of emergency. The buck scorned anything so degrading as manual labor. Fighting and hunting were his only occupations. The head men of these towns were elective. Only those who had performed some exploit in war or the chase had any voice in the selection. From the statements of historians and from the signature of the head men of the Overhill Cherokees to the different treaties it is almost certain that in the bounds of what is now known as the Hiwassee purchase or district, embracing most of Monroe county and a part of Loudon and Roane counties, all of Meigs and McMinn and a part of Polk county, the Cherokees really occupied about one thousand square miles only of this territory, to-wit: Bounded on the north by the Little Tennessee River; on the west by the Notchey Creek knobs; on the south by the Hiwassee River; on the east by the Great Smoky Mountains. The Indian population within this boundary it is likely did not exceed five thousand in number. Thus counting five to a family would have given each family in the Overhills Towns a square mile if divided and not held in common. In the Calhoun treaty of March, 1819, Article 2 reads thus: "The United States agreed to pay, according to the treaty of July 8, 1817, for valuable improvements on land in the country ceded by the Cherokees and allow a reservation of six hundred and forty acres to the head of each family (not enrolled for removal to Arkansas) who elects to become a citizen of the United States."

In addition to this, a portion of Article 1 contains this proviso: "All the islands of the Chestatee and the Tennessee and Hiwassee Rivers (except Jolly Island at the mouth of the Hiwassee River) belong to the Cherokee Nation." This left the Cherokee Nation to keep or dispose of these islands as they saw fit. In relation to one of these islands in Little Tennessee River not far above the site of Old Fort Loudon the late Henry Bradley related to me this anecdote. Mr. Bradley was for years an employe of Colonel Charles M. McGhee, son of John McGhee, of whom the story is told. An Indian chief (name not remembered) owned or claimed an island in the river, the bank of which was owned by McGhee. McGhee had a very fine rifle of rare make which the Indian was anxious to buy, but McGhee was unwilling to part with. On one occasion the Indian visited McGhee and after hanging around for a while he remarked: "Big Chief had a dream. McGhee: "I hope it was a pleasant one; what did the Big Chief dream?" Big Chief dreamed White Chief give Indian his fine gun." "Oh, that's it, is it? Well, if Big Chief was told by the spirit in a dream that he is to have the 'fine gun' he must not be disappointed" (taking it down from the rack and handing it to him). The Indian left in great glee.

Not a great while afterward they met, and after the customary greeting, McGhee said: "How did you like your gun?" "Great gun, kill anything." McGhee, "White Chief had a dream, too." Indian, "Uh, huh! What?" McGhee, 'White man dream Indian chief made him a deed to the island over there." Indian, "Here, take gun back!" McGhee shook his head, "Can't do it; Indian dreamed it away from him, no good to him any more." After some minutes of gloomy reflection the

Indian replied: "Big Chief make you a deed to it, but Indian no dream against white man no more."

Thus in what is now Sweetwater Valley from 1817 back for four hundred years or more we have the spectacle of a section without inhabitants, with no roads and not a trail through it. It was even nameless, not forevermore, but for a long period.

With the exception of a mound here and there to show a once human occupation and their passing away, it was just as the geologic laws and time and weather left it. The Cherokees came not through it when they went to fight their Northern enemies, nor when they surprised and exterminated the Euchees at the mouth of Hiwassee River; the trail to the Chicasaws and Creeks was not near it. So far as humanity was concerned it was a deserted country without a history or a name; nameless also the streams and ridges. It was given over to the deer, panther, the wild cat, turkey, pheasant, the swan, the duck and other smaller birds and animals. When the white man took possession in 1820 he found it almost as nature made it—Adamless, Eveless and with no apple to tempt save the sour wild crab. On the ridges the chestnut, poplar, the red, black and white oak predominated, in the valley grew abundantly the sycamore, hickory, the gums, the elm, the willow and water oak. The creek flowed tranquilly through the valley on its clear winding way to the Tennessee River, spreading out into ponds and marshes, the home of the mallard, the coot and the crane. However desirable a country it might be to the white man it was not such as the Indian, that child of nature, loved. It had no great wide reaches to gladden the eye, no stream large enough to easily and safely carry his birch bark canoe. To him it was merely a preserve or breeding ground for game. When it got too plentiful here it went to the Tellico and Tennessee where the Indian lived.

So the Cherokees traded this country for land beyond the Mississippi "unsight, unseen" and "no rue back" as the horse swappers say. As it turned out it was a good trade for both. True it must be admitted that the white man had a slight advantage in knowing that the trade was going to be made and what the terms were to be. The Indian in his childlike simplicity left the details to "the party of second part," and Return J. Meigs, backed by the United States government, was principally the party of the second part, and he was no amateur when it came to a land deal. Be it known, however, that if you have any extra tears to shed over the sorrows of humanity, the Indian does not desire nor need them. Save your sobs for the heroes and heroines of the dime novel, or exploited heathens of the "rubber trust on the Congo, or the down-trodden Moros of Mindanao. Don't acknowledge there is much to weep over in home conditions; it is too trying on the nervous system. Leave it to the politicians to "point with pride" and "view with alarm": it's their principal stock in trade.

ENCROACHMENT OF WHITES ON CHEROKEE NEUTRAL GROUND.

As early as August, 1790, President Washington in a message to Congress brought up the subject of the encroachment of white settlers on Cherokee neutral ground. (See "Messages of Presidents," compiled by J. D. Richardson.)

It was alleged that there were five hundred families settled and were occupying places that they had no legal right to.

Negotiations moved more slowly in those days, and it was not till 1798 that a new treaty was made with the Cherokees and the southern line of occupation for white settlers was established, to-wit:

"Commencing at Wild Cat Rock near the Tellico Block House; thence down the northeast margin of the (Little) Tennessee River, not including islands, to a point one mile above the junction of that river with the Clinch; thence at a right angle (northwardly) to Hawkin's line leading to the Clinch River; thence with that line to the Clinch River; thence up Clinch to Emery; thence up Emery to Cumberland Mountain (Wallen's Ridge); thence northeast to Campbell's line."

In 1803 President Jefferson urged the removal of the Indian tribes beyond the Mississippi. Congress approved and in 1804 appropriated $15,000.00 for the purpose of negotiations, and commissioners were appointed to look into the matter.

By a treaty concluded October 27, 1805, and proclaimed

June 10, 1806, Return J. Meigs and Dan. Shields being commissioners for the United States, the Cherokees ceded:

(1) The section of land at southwest point, extending to Kingston and the respective ferries of the two rivers and the first island in the Tennessee River above the mouth of the Clinch. (2) The Cherokees consent to the free and unmolested use by the United States of a mail road from the Tellico to the Tombigbee River in the territory of Alabama. This road was made and was called the Federal road. That part through what was afterward the Hiwassee district began at Nile's Ferry, passed by Ho (Torbett's) by what is now Nonaburg and continuing, crossing the Hiwassee River not a great ways from the mouth of the Ocoee. (3) The consideration paid for these concessions was $1,609.00.

THE HIWASSEE PURCHASE.

Below we condense some of the material provisions of the Hiwassee Purchase or treaty with the Cherokees in 1819. To give in full would require too much space, and would not likely prove interesting to the general reader. Several of the articles as will be seen by the numbers given are not mentioned. Some of them are lengthy and relate minute particulars for the removal of the Indians in flat boats; what guns, ammunition, provisions, blankets, etc., are to be furnished them for their start in the new territory.

Treaty concluded February 27, 1819. Proclaimed March 10, 1819. Held at Washington, D. C., between John C. Calhoun, secretary of war, and the chief headsmen of the Cherokee Nation.

TERMS OF TREATY.

(Art. 1.) The Cherokee Nation cedes to the United States all of their lands lying north and east of the following line: Beginning on the Tennessee River at a point where Madison county in the territory of Alabama joins the same; thence along the channel of said river to the mouth of the Hiwassee; thence along the main channel of the last said river to the first hill that closes on this river about two miles above Hiwassee old town;

thence along the ridge that divides the Hiwassee and the Tellico Rivers to the Tennessee at Talassee; thence along the main channel to the junction of the Cowee and Nanteyalee (Nantog Yulee—Nantahala); thence with the ridge in the forks of the said river to the top of the Blue Ridge; thence along the Blue Ridge to the Unicoy Turnpike road; thence a straight line to the nearest main source of the Chestatee; thence along the main channel to the Chattahooche; and thence to the Creek boundary; it being understood that all the islands of the Chestatee and (those) in the Tennessee and Hiwassee Rivers (except Jolly Island at the mouth of the Hiwassee), which constitute a portion of the boundary, are the property of the Cherokee Nation.

United States right of way, according to the treaty of 1805, not affected; twelve miles square on the Tennessee River near the Alabama line to be sold by the United States and the proceeds to be invested, the interest to constitute a school fund for the benefit of the Cherokee Nation east of the Mississippi River.

(Art. 2.) The United States agrees to pay according to treaty, July 8, 1817, for valuable improvements on land within the country ceded by the Cherokees, and allow a reservation of six hundred and forty acres to the head of each family (not enrolled for removal to Arkansas) who elects to become a citizen of the United States.

(Art. 5.) Leases made under the treaty of 1817, of land in Cherokee country are void. All white people intruding upon lands reserved by the Cherokees shall be removed by the United States under the act of March 30, 1802.

(Art. 7.) The United States shall prevent intrusion on the ceded lands prior to January 1, 1820.

THE ORIGIN OF LAND TITLES IN SWEETWATER VALLEY.

It is a far cry from our time to that of Charles II. of England. We would naturally think that he would have had little to do with us here in Sweetwater Valley, yet the title to every acre of land in this section can be traced back to the grant given by that king to Edward, Earl of

Clarendon, and six other nobles on the 24th day of March, 1663. Those were merry times in Merry England, and Charles, the Merry Monarch, was the merriest of them all. The people had become tired of long faces, long parliaments and long prayers. During the Cromwellian period places of amusement and theatres were closed. No musical instruments were allowed in the churches, and even the exhibition of Raphael's Madonna would have been considered a species of idolatry. If a man smiled it was as if he mocked himself for being so festive. Such hymns as "I Would Not Live Alway" were, if not popular, most in vogue. Small wonder that when Oliver Cromwell passed from the stage of action and Charlie from over the water appeared upon the scene, the pendulum of human emotions swung far in the opposite direction, and the parquet, the boxes and galleries all applauded. The people were all weary of tears, tragedy and solemn asservations.

Charles, as principal actor, discounted in merriment the celebrated performances of

"Old King Cole, that merry old soul,
A merry old soul was he;
He called for his pipe and he called for his bowl,
And he called for his fiddlers three."

The populace in imitation of Charles, set out to have a rip-roaring, hilarious good time and proceeded to paint the town of London a vivid red. It was a Fourth of July and Christmas celebration all rolled into one.

'Twas in this era of good feeling that Charles, between drinks, which we are told were never very far apart, gave the grants spoken of to the overlords of Carolina, so named in honor of Carolus (Charles). This was likely accomplished in a space of time that the governors of the two Carolinas would occupy in discussing what beverage should next be consumed.

Oh, no! There was nothing small about Charlie. He was all obliging. To satisfy his courtiers and keep his head on his shoulders he would have given them the moon with equal good humor. This grant covered that part of North America included between the parallels of 31 and 36 degrees north latitude, and stretched from the

Atlantic to the Pacific Oceans. Just think of it, a domain three thousand miles long and three hundred miles wide, the finest land in the world and the inhabitants thereof! It embraced in its extent the greater part of the Southern States south of Virginia and Kentucky east of the Mississippi River, a part of Arkansas, Oklahoma, Texas, New Mexico, Arizona and California. In the game of giving Charles has Carnegie and Rockefeller bluffed to a standstill; their combined benefactions of half a billion dollars or so look like thirty cents beside his. But he minded not. If he owned the territory he wanted to shift the responsibility from his shoulders; for he possibly knew that there were savage beasts and still more savage men and the French and the Spanish, too, to fight. He was no fighter as his ancestors were. He preferred to feed his ducks in the ponds of Windsor Park, drink the effervescing wines of France and Italy and dance to the lascivious music of the lute. To use an advertising phrase, with him "ladies' society was a specialty." If he did not own the land, then the grim humor of the situation was like that of the father with no assets at all that left to his beloved son a million dollars—"to get."

The Earl of Rochester once said that Charles II.

"Never said a foolish thing,
And never did a wise one."

We are inclined to differ. This proved a wise act. However, if he had known that North Carolina and Tennessee would turn out prohibition States he might have balked. For his warmest friends and bitterest enemies would scarcely claim Charles as a "State-wider." I wish to remark here that we will get to Sweetwater Valley after a while. If we do not arrive on schedule time remember that there were no roads and very few trails in the old days I next will write about.

When I wrote the above about the origin of land titles in Sweetwater Valley I did not have access to a copy of the charter of Charles II. There is now before me a book entitled as follows:

LAWS
of the
STATE OF TENNESSEE,
including those of
NORTH CAROLINA,
NOW IN FORCE IN THIS STATE,
from the year
1715 TO THE YEAR 1820, INCLUSIVE.

BY EDWARD SCOTT,
one of the judges of the circuit courts of law and equity.

IN TWO VOLUMES.
Vol. I.

KNOXVILLE, TENN.
Printed by
HEISKELL & BROWN.

1821.

As to Charles' fondness for the bowl and amusements, his lack of attention to details, his carelessness as to what he signed or did not sign, provided it did not trench on his own personal privileges, his being guided by his favorites, male and female, the statements written are absolutely true and are not to be added to or subtracted from. That there was any carelessness in the preparation of the charter on the part of the grantees or in the protection of their own interests is not true. For the charter was a wonderfully comprehensive instrument. So far as I have been able to perceive, besides paying the small rent exacted, they were almost independent of the British crown. The overlords mentioned could make laws for the government of the colonists, pardon or punish as they saw fit. There was, however, a provision that the freemen should give their assent to those laws; but in the referendum who should call the elections and how the ballots should be counted was not stated. We insert some of the provisions of the charter which are not the exact words of the charter, unless the wording as given are marked as quotations. This charter is very long and occupies ten pages of this volume. The second charter granted by King Charles II. to the proprietors of North Carolina was dated March 24th in the fifteenth year of our reign (1665). The proprietors are Edward, Earl of Clarendon, High Chancellor of England; George, Duke of Albemarle, master of horse; William, Earl Craven, Counsellor John Lord Berkely, Counsellor Anthony Lord Ashly, Sir George Carteret, Knight and Baronet; Sir John Colleton, Sir William Berkely. King Charles grants to them all that territory called Carolina, "Situate lying and being in our dominions of America; extending from the end of the island called Luke Island, which lieth in the Southern Virginia Seas and within 36 degrees north latitude; and to the west as far as to the south seas and so respectively as far as the river Mathias, which borders upon the coast of Florida and within 31 degrees of northern latitude; and so west in a direct line as far as the south sea as aforesaid."

This territory, I take it to mean, was to extend from ocean to ocean. The land having been explored only a few hundred miles to the westward, the immense extent of the territory was not known. The instrument particularly cites that it conveyed all soils, lands, fields, woods, mountains, lakes, rivers, all whales and fish in the bays, the seas upon the coast, all veins, mines and quarries discovered or not discovered, all golds, silver, gems, precious stones, metals or any other thing found or to be found within the province, territory or islets in the limits aforesaid. They had power to grant religious liberty and had ample rights, jurisdiction, privileges, prerogatives, royalties, liberties, immunities of any kind whatsoever, and these privileges and rights were to extend to their heirs and assigns forever. The consideration for this grant was the fourth part of all golds and silver ore found within its boundaries, and the yearly rent of twenty marks. They had full power and authority to erect, constitute and make several counties, baronies and colonies, also to make and enact under their seals and to publish any laws and constitutions whatsoever either appertaining to the public state of the whole province or any particular county of or within the same or to the private utility of particular persons by and with the advice and assent of the free men of said province or territory or of the county for which said law or constitution shall be made; and the said grantees have power to remit, release, pardon and abolish whether before judgment or after all crimes and offenses whatsoever against that law.

They also had power to collect import duties, except that certain articles such as English tools, silks, raisins, almond oil and olives were to be admitted free of duty. They also had power to confer titles and honors except certains ones, such as dukedoms, earls and baronets, which were exclusively the right of the crown. They had power to designate ports of entry, stating where vessels should enter and trade under such regulations as were prescribed. They were given power also to convey absolutely by deed in fee simple any tract or privilege to the colonists which had been conveyed to them by King Charles except legislative and judicial functions. This charter had many other provisions conveying certain powers and privileges, making them, not the governors only, but the absolute owners of the vast domain. It is needless to state again that this territory included what is now the State of Tennessee, but this State would not form a tenth of this grant.

BIOGRAPHICAL SKETCHES.

REV. JAMES AXLEY.

There lie in County Line Cemetery, two and a half miles from Sweetwater near the Athens road, the remains of the Rev. James Axley and his wife, Cynthia Axley. On his tombstone is inscribed: "Rev. James Axley died February 23, 1837, aged sixty years. He was presiding elder in the Methodist Episcopal church for thirty years."

On that of his wife, "Cynthia, wife of Rev. James Axley, died September 31, 1882, aged eighty-two years."

Rev. R. N. Price, in Vol. II, Holston Methodism, gives a synopsis of his life.

That he was presiding elder for thirty years is clearly a mistake. He was, according to church records, preacher for only thirty-three years; circuit rider for seven, presiding elder for ten and located for sixteen years. By located is meant that he was not under the order of the bishop and though still licensed to preach, was entitled only to such pay as the churches that invited him in any locality chose to give him. Preaching or not was entirely voluntary.

Born in Cumberland county, Virginia; father and mother, James and Lemuanna Axley. They moved to Kentucky about 1799. The subject of this sketch was admitted to the Western Conference in 1804 and located in 1822. His charges were: 1804, Red River, in Cumberland district, a colleague of Miles Harper; 1805, Hockhocking, Ohio district; 1806, French Broad; 1807, Opelousas, Louisiana; 1808, Powell's Valley; 1809, Holston; 1810, Elk; 1811, presiding elder of Wabash district; 1812, he was appointed presiding elder of Holston district and remained in charge of it four years; he was two years in charge of the Green River district, and three years presiding elder of the French Broad district (1818-1821).

James Axley had two brothers and two sisters, his brothers were Pleasant and Robert. James and Pleasant were converted near Salem, Ky., where they lived in 1802. Pleasant was a local preacher for many years, but did not attain anything like the celebrity of his brother James.

There are wealth-made, school-made, God-made, and self-made men. George Washington, fortunately for our republic, was all of these. Heredity, environment, physical capacity, mental and moral attainments made him easily the foremost citizen of America. It is related that Axley had no school training and no advantages in his youth. His father was a strange man in his habits and manner of life. He was greatly devoted to hunting wild game and searching for minerals; he spent the greater part of his time this way and remained at home but little. The burden of the family support was upon the mother and older children. James Axley, the son, was also fond of hunting in his youth. He became powerful in frame, alert and observing of the habits of animals. It thus became much easier for him to learn men and the customs of polite society and correct the deficiencies of early life. From a hunter of wild animals he became a hunter of men.

As is often the case, especially with those who lack previous training the first efforts of Axley were considered very unpromising, so much so that he was refused a license to preach, and when one of his preacher friends advised him his efforts would meet with failure and it would be useless for him to try further, he is said to have replied that if he couldn't be a preacher with God's help he could make a first class exhorter. As R. N. Price says: "He was called of God to preach; he felt it, he knew it, and nothing ever deterred him from obeying the call." Demosthenes was told he could never make an orator, Jenny Lind that she would not be a success in opera, and the prophecies of Lincoln's career were even more adverse. These things show what a poor prophet the average man is when he attempts to predict what others may make of themselves.

Here is Dr. McAnally's estimate of Axley later in life: "I have listened to popular orators among our statesmen, to distinguished pleaders at the bar, to the preachers who were followed and heard by enraptured thousands, but the superior of James Axley in all that constitutes genuine oratory and true eloquence I have not heard."

"His height was near six feet, muscular frame, large bones, but little surplus flesh, chest broad and full features strongly marked, large mouth and nose, heavy, projecting, shaggy eyebrows, high and well turned forehead, dark gray eyes, remarkably keen, large head and hair worn short. His dress was plain and made of homespun material. In the pulpit he stood erect and nearly still, gesticulating but little, only turning from side to side that he might see his auditors. If the weather was warm it was common with him, after opening the service and singing and prayer, deliberately to take off his coat and hang it on the pulpit." Few men perhaps ever had a finer voice and never yet have I met with one who could control it better. So completely was it under his command that the manner in which something was said often affected the hearer more than the thing itself. He was a natural orator after the best models—those which nature forms."

James Axley came into the ministry at a propitious time for men of his type. He was a born fighter polemically. Those days required both moral and physical courage. Since 1775 there had been a long war with the British and many with the various tribes of Indians. Between the red and white men there was little other than animosity, it had been an eye for an eye, scalp for scalp, and life for life. The pioneers of that day had been compelled not only to keep rifles in their homes, but to take their arms with them to their fields, their meetings in the forest and to their rude log churches, for fear of an attack from their cunning and treacherous foes. They were liable at any moment to be called from the worship of the Prince of Peace to bloody combat. Bloodshed and retaliation were the order of the day. War and especially that kind of war where personal and race hatred is added to national conflict, has a most demoralizing effect on humanity. If the doctrine of returning good for evil, or turning the other cheek when one is smitten, had any place in the breast of the men of that day its application was among white men and did not apply to the red. They held that their own preservation and that of their wives and children required no mild measures but almost a policy of extermination. Treaties of peace availed little; the primeval instincts were much in evidence. Consequently religion and the churches languished. The people did not fully appreciate the educated ministry of the Presbyterians; there were too few of them to go round and there was more or less prejudice against written sermons. Few of the pioneers adhered to the church of England. They had declared and gained their civil independence and they wished entire religious independence. They wanted no written prayers and sacerdotal robes; life was entirely too serious for elaborate ceremonies.

Some authors in speaking of that period from 1780 to 1800 have attributed the wave of Atheism and Deism (Infidelity) that swept over the country to the French revolutionary ideas and the writings of Voltaire and to Thomas Paine's "Age of Reason." In western North Carolina, East Tennessee and eastern Kentucky we are inclined to think their influence was over estimated. The pioneers had not forgotten the parts the French had taken in the Indian wars and massacres and the prejudice had not been fully removed even by the fact that Lafayette played so important part in the war of the Revolution against the British. They had little time and less opportunity for extensive reading. I can not believe that the books of Voltaire and Paine had a large circulation in our mountain country. Besides the "Age of Reason" was written for scholastic minds like Adams and Jefferson (who though violent political enemies were at one in their notions of religion) and not for the mountaineer. In the beginning of the Nineteenth century the New England ideas of Unitarianism had not taken any firm hold in our mountain country. The decadence of religion might have been more apparent than real or the preaching later on could not have been attended with such remarkable results. Fire cannot burst into flame without the proper fuel to feed upon. The people of France were ripe for the Revolution when it came.

The early settlers of that period and section were not engaged in speculations about fine spun theories; they needed something virile and exciting to arouse them, such as sermons hot with hell fire and eternal punishment; "Except ye repent ye shall all likewise perish."

Then arose such men as Cartwright, Axley, Lorenzo

Dow, McKendree, Creed Fulton, Granade and Jesse Cunningham, and the celebrated revival of 1800, as it was called, commenced. It continued unabated for eight or ten years and with some vigor for ten or more years longer. The zealous, emotional, often uneducated preachers in the modern sense of the term, had their day. Their hearers would stand no sham or hypocrisy; they desired sincerity and earnestness; they cared not whether the preacher or exhorter, as the case might be, said sepul-chre or se-pul-chre, Geth-sem-a-ne or Geth-se-mane, so the thought was there. The intention of the listeners was to flee from the wrath to come.

During this revival came the days of the camp meetings. At their inception some accessible place was selected, preferably near some large flowing spring capable of furnishing plenty of water for men and beasts. If not already done a place was cleared and a stand was erected for the preachers. It was important that the location should be suitable one for stretching their tents. To hear the sermons the people stood up or sat on chairs and logs or sometimes climbed the trees near by. The inhabitants came from far and near bringing with them their tents and provisions. When the weather permitted many slept out in the open air. These meetings were usually held in the fall, the pleasantest season of the year. Hospitality was unbounded for the visitors from a distance and hundreds and sometimes thousands were fed in one day. Great preparations were made for the entertainment of all comers. These meetings were looked forward to for months beforehand. They annually, sometimes semi-annually, were a source of much religious and social enjoyment. Influences were brought to bear and friendships formed which lasted for a lifetime, and were profitable for the Here and Hereafter. The services sometimes continued night and day for weeks as long as the interest lasted or the preachers and exhorters could bear the mental and physical strain. When a place of meeting became popular and numerously attended, a shed was built for protection against the weather, and it was seated with slabs, the sawed or hewed sides turned up and the legs were driven into two holes bored angling, thus making a firm but not a very comfortable seat, as there were no backs to lean against.

Around the shed were built also camps for eating and sleeping in. The sleeping berths were arranged in tiers one above another so as to accommodate a greater number. The camp grounds best known in this section were the Methodist at Pond Spring, three miles west of Sweetwater, and the Cumberland Presbyterian, three and one-half miles north of Sweetwater.

Some very curious phenomena attended the early camp meetings. Different persons explained them differently. By some they were attributed wholly to supernatural causes, by others to material or natural causes, still others partly to both. Whatever may have been the true explanation the facts themselves were undeniable. These happenings extended over quite a wide territory; parts of Virginia, Kentucky, Tennessee, North Carolina and Georgia.

Dr. Price, "Holston Methodism," Vol. I, page 340-1-2 quotes a Presbyterian divine, Rev. James Gallaher, as saying: 'The awful solemnity which now arrested the public mind was accompanied with bodily affections as notable and singular as those of Saul on his way to Damascus. Stout, stubborn sinners, bold, brazen-fronted blasphemers were literally cut down by the 'sword of the Spirit,' under the preaching of the Gospel men would drop to the ground as suddenly as if they had been smitten by lightning. Among these were many men in the prime of life—strong business men, men whom no human being ever thought of charging with enthusiasm.

"Holston Methodism," Vol. II, has this from the pen of Lorenzo Dow: "I have seen Presbyterians, Quakers, Baptists, Church of England people and Independents exercised with the jerks, gentleman and lady, black and white, the aged and the young, rich and poor without exception, from which I infer as it can not be accounted for on national principles and carries such marks of involuntary motion, that it is no trifling matter.

"On the 20th (August, 1803), I passed a meeting house where I observed that the undergrowth had been cut down for a camp meeting and from fifty to one hundred saplings left breast high, which to me appeared so slovenish that I could not but ask my guide the cause, who observed that they were topped so high and left for people to jerk by. This so excited my attention that I went over the ground to view it and found that the people had laid hold of the stumps and jerked so violently that they had kicked up the earth as a horse stamping at flies."

Let us mount a motor car, speed along the streets of the populous city and approach the grand cathedral. As we draw near its twin towers rise into the sky line. The building planned by the mind of some Christopher Wren, though immense in its proportions, is intensely pleasing to the beholder even to the smallest detail. The architect makes the whole world tributary to him. The solid granite of the foundations is hewed from the Appalachian hills, the pure marble of the facade is from the quarries of Vermont, the heroic statues, the gargoyles and the figures which adorn the niches and cornices have been chiseled from stone transported from Italy. We enter the arched portals between the towers. We are struck by the grandeur and beauty of the interior, the lofty galleries are supported by columns of onyx and porphyry from Mexico; the dome is frescoed by great European artists; the stained windows are of glass manufactured from crystal quartz of the Rockies and colored with the blue of the sky, the gorgeous hues of the sunset, the purple from the hills of Arizona, the green of the mountain cedars, the variegated blooms of the garden flowers; the chancel is formed of costly woods from the isles of the sea; the magnificent organ is replendent with the gold of Alaska; the winds of heaven are made captive to the will of man, they breathe the soft notes of the flute, the plaintive strains of the viola, or give forth the hoarse roar of the tempest; the trained harmonies of the white robed choir float enchantingly down from the gallery through the incense laden atmosphere; the surpliced minister chants the lesson of the day in resonant tones; everything that wealth can purchase or cultivated taste suggest is there; every art of man has there some representative production; the least image in the niche and the great paintings in the dome all impress you; every sense is held and conquered by the surroundings; you swell with pride of race; you exclaim, "How wonderful, how complex is man; in movement how graceful; in conception how like an angel; in creative powers how like a god!"

Yet, how utterly false this all is; how prone we are

to be puffed up with our own self conceit and how easily we can deceive ourselves! We build a temple to the Almighty but shut out God's sunshine, and light a faint taper of our own upon the altars. We listen with delight to the paid singers and disregard the music of the spheres. We sit in our ten thousand dollar pew and hear the doctrines of the meek and lowly Jesus discoursed in words that cost us a dollar a minute. Under such circumstances how dare the speaker offend the pew holders?

After all, what have we mortals to take so much pride in? We know no more of the mystery of life, what it is, than when Adam delved and Eve span. We come not here of our own will and seldom go of our own will. A germ, a breath of gas, a drop of hydrocyanic acid and man becomes, as far as this world is concerned, less than a worm, merely a clod of dirt.

Scientists tell us that there are creatures so small that ten thousand of them can dance on the point of a needle and have plenty of room to spare. A man can destroy ten millions of them at a blow, but he can no more create the least one of them than he can make a world. Yet these animalculae bear no more infinitesimal relation to the earth than our planet does to the illimitable uniserve. Well might the psalmist say: "When we consider the (suns) the moon and stars, the work of Thy fingers, what is man that Thou art mindful of him, or the son of man that Thou visitest him?"

When Axley preached in his time it was often in the open. He was fanned by the invigorating breezes, shaded by magnificent forest trees, in hearing of the murmur of waters, in sight of the shining sun and the blue arch of heaven above. There were no works of man surrounding to hypnotize the senses and divorce the attention of the audience from the Father and Creator.

He (Axley), wanted no luxuries and therefore feared no withdrawal of salary. He hesitated not to attack what he considered the evils and vices of the day.

The preaching of those pioneers of the Methodist church in effect, though astonishing, is by no means without parallel. We are told that aforetime, "In those days came John the Baptist preaching in the wilderness." He was a man plain in raiment and food but multitudes flocked to him. He had a message to deliver. In the eleventh century a comparatively insignificant hermit priest came forth from his cave in the mountains and by the zeal and frenzy of his discourses stirred up all Christendom. He started a series of crusades which cost millions of lives and almost bankrupted every kingdom in Europe. His cry was, "Down with the Infidel. Rescue the tomb of the Saviour from dominion of the Mohammedans." Yet this was merely a sentiment and not inculcated by any tenet of the Christian faith. Axley's message, in conjunction with the salvation of sinners, was against Masonry, Slavery, Whisky, Tobacco and the Fashions. He had a discourse which he reserved for important occasions. Dr. Price calls it his sermon on the "abominations." The text he sometimes used was "Let us cleanse ourselves from all filthiness of the flesh and spirit, perfecting holiness in the fear of God." Yet he could on occasion denounce the evils as he considered them spoken of above, regardless of text.

It may appear strange to us now that a minister should attempt to start a crusade against Masonry or any benevolent organization. Brotherhoods are as thick now as leaves in Valhambrosa. (No matter where that is and however thick the leaves may be there.) A man who does not belong at this day to some society or brotherhood is as lonesome as Robinson Crusoe on the island before Friday came. One person can call another brother with perfect freedom. If he is not your brother in church or society or federation, he more than likely may belong or has belonged to your political party. In Axley's day, particularly in the latter part of his life, there was much prejudice against the Masonic order. A man named Morgan, who was or had been a member of the fraternity wrote a book purporting to expose the secrets of Free Masonry. Quite a while afterward he disappeared and if any one knew when or how, it was never made public. The Masons were charged with being responsible for his disappearance. The country was wrought up. Wm. Wirt, who had become famous as prosecuting attorney in the case of the United States against Aaron Burr for treason, was the nominee of the Anti-Masonic party at a convention held in Baltimore in 1831. Mr. Wirt was a finished orator and a very distinguished man. He is noted as the author of a life of Patrick Henry. If he had been really great he would not have allowed his name to be used in such a connection, for what could he have accomplished even if he had been elected? However he was ignominiously defeated. The opposition soon died away.

Not so with Axley. He quoted: "For every one that doeth evil hateth the light, neither cometh to the light lest his deeds should be reproved." With him secrecy was the synonym of darkness and publication of light. If there is any good in it why not give the world the benefit of it? Why hide your light under a bushel? Let everything be done in the open; do away with your secret signs and symbols; abolish your dark, mysterious meetings! He (Axley) did not know that there is no true Mason that is not an earnest seeker after Light. He was probably unaware that in the time of the Emperor Nero the Christians had a symbol by which one believing brother made himself known to another. A fish was drawn with a staff or switch upon dust or sand. If the explanation was known to the observer it was significant, otherwise it was meaningless. It is related that the Emperor never discovered the true explanation even by torture. His persecutions and that of others forced the Christians for purpose of worship and burial to build the catacombs beneath the city Rome. Even to this day they are considered among the wonders of the world.

He (Axley), had not the slightest conception that Masonry reaches back far beyond the dawn of written history. It was hoary with antiquity when the pyramids rose to their dizzy heights from the sands of ancient Egypt; before the sphynx smiled and Thebes flourished on the banks of the Nile, it was; Moses learned in all the arts of the Egyptians was a Mason; so Zerubabel, Solomon, Hiram of Tyre, the wise men, the Magi, who saw the Star in the East; Jesus was a priest after the order of Melchisedek, a degree of Masonry conferred upon Him by the Mahatmas of India; Richard I belonged to the order, Saladin, Washington, James K. Polk; thousands of worthies could be mentioned but without naming further one might say it was rather a respectable and ancient fraternity. The beauty and glory of Masonry is that it is world-wide. Any male of lawful age, with a belief in a supreme Being, and of good moral character and free born can be made a Mason; provided he obtains the unanimous consent of the members of the lodge to which he has been recommended for admission.

It differs radically from Christianity in this respect that it is not reformatory. A man ought to be above reproach before he is made a Mason. Most of the tenets of the Masonic fraternity can be known and read of the world. There is not near so much secrecy as is supposed. If one reads the Masonic Text Book of Tennessee carefully and thoughtfully he can know more of the principles of Masonry than some members of the order know. This can be bought through any reliable book store, if you are desirous of information.

Dr. Price relates: "Axley cherished an inveterate hatred to slavery, and often preached against it. While on the Opelousas circuit in 1807 in Louisiana his tirades against slavery brought on him not only the censure of the church but of the community, the most of whom were slaveholders. He took the extreme ground that no slaveholder could be saved in Heaven or was a proper person for admission into the church. His views presented from the pulpit made him so unpopular that he found it difficult to obtain food or shelter. But he continued inexorable till relieved of his charge by the presiding elder, who found him in rags and well-nigh famished from hunger."

On the subject of slavery he was in agreement with the early bishops of the Methodist Protestant Episcopal church. Then it had few apologists and no real defenders. The mountain people were not usually slave owners. John Allison in "Dropped Stitches in Tennesse History" says that the first abolition paper in the United States was started at Jonesboro, Tenn., by Elihu Embree. It required no particular exhibition of nerve to do so. Even long before this there had been various manumissions of slaves and at that time within the bounds of the Holston Conference if the majority were not abolitionists they doubted the moral right of one human being to hold another in enforced servitude. Yet in East Tennessee during Axley's day the people were not so highly wrought up over the question of slavery until after the secession of the Southern from their Northern brethren of the Methodist Protestant Episcopal church and the setting up of a separate church government in 1844. This happened some time after the death of Axley. Had he lived what action he would have taken is conjectural.

From that time on the Southern Methodists, if they did not contend for the absolute right of slavery according to the Bible, held that emancipation and making the negro citizens at home or emancipation and colonization abroad would be equally impracticable. The question was as bitterly fought in church as in politics and helped greatly to precipitate the Civil War.

In Axley's times the people were not so fully agreed as to the evils of alcoholic drinks. It was not commonly considered disreputable as now to make or sell whiskey or brandy. There was no internal revenue tax on the manufacture or sale of intoxicants. Fruits which would otherwise be a total loss could be made into brandy and thus be a matter of considerable profit. Twenty-five or thirty cents a gallon or even less was considered a fair price for what was called "good" whiskey or brandy. Most people kept it and it was not uncommon to pass the bottle around. They had it on hands presumably for sickness, as most of it was kept until it was of some age, what was drank then would now be termed a superior article. It is not a matter of surprise that indisposition requiring stimulants were not at all uncommon. A doctor who would not prescribe whiskey for ailments (with or without roots and herbs) was either a crank or did not understand the nature of symptoms; so they took it anyhow. Axley in private and public talked and preached against stilling, drinking and the traffic in drink in terms that raised a blister. I have heard the Rev. James Sewell, who was well acquainted with Axley, tell how one of his neighbors, who had become very angry with him for some remarks he had made in the pulpit about drinking, went to his house early one morning for the purpose of giving him a "genteel thrashing," unless he took back what he had said. After he had stated his business Axley quietly remarked that when he called at the gate he was about to have family prayers and as that was something he never put off or neglected, he would be very much pleased if he would join them, and afterwards if nothing else would do, he would try his best to accommodate him. He accepted the invitation. Axley prayed (not as the preacher Bob Taylor used to tell about when a bully threatened him, mentioning how many fights he had had and always been victorious) but it was equally effective. He offered up a fervent petition for the salvation of the young man and that he would see the error of his ways. When the prayer was over he thanked Axley, shook hands with him and went away without saying anything further of the whipping he was going to give him.

Axley was largely instrumental in changing public sentiment in regard to stilling and dram drinking in the Sweetwater community. He was especially severe on the women following the fashions, decking themselves out with jewelry, fine clothes, frills and furbelows. He read frequently the 3rd chapter of Isaiah commencing at the 16th verse. He denounced the wearers of "round tires" as he termed the hoop skirts worn at that time. The reasons he gave for this action I have not learned.

One of his illustrations (the sense not the language is given) was: Sometimes you farmers go out to the woods hunting for a good hickory tree to make a maul stick out of. After a while you spy one you think is well suited to your purpose. It is nice and trim and straight, the foliage is green and beautiful and it has every appearance of being sound, you therefore cut it down and when you come to examine it more carefully you find it is rotten at the heart; so many women are symmetrical and enticing but are useless in the family circle and unfit material for the church.

At other times he compared them with the blue jay that carries all he has on the back, but of no value except for the plumage and the top knot on the head.

Notwithstanding all this it appears that his admonitions were little heeded by the ladies. They considered it none of his business. No man is looked up to by them as the arbiter of fashion.

He failed not on occasion to express his opinion on the use of tobacco, snuffing, smoking and chewing; but chewing was his particular aversion. Judge H. L. White in Holston Methodism, Vol. II, is quoted to have said: "I confess that father Axley brought me to a sense of my evil deeds—at least a portion of them—more effectually than any preacher I ever heard." Going on he further quotes him in an exhortation as mentioning several things that he was not going to talk about and then remarked. "The thing I was going to talk about was chewing tobacco. Now I do hope than when any gentleman comes to church who can't keep from using tobacco during the hours of worship he will just take his hat and use it for a spit box. You all know we are Methodists. You all know that it is our custom to kneel when we pray. Now any gentleman can see in a moment how exceedingly inconvenient it must be for a well-dressed Methodist lady to be compelled to kneel down in a puddle of tobacco spittle. Judge White says further that during Axley's exhortation, "I was chewing and spitting my large quid with uncommon rapidity and looking at the preacher to catch every word and gesture. When at last he pounced upon tobacco, behold, there I had a great puddle of ambeer. I quietly slipped the quid out of my mouth and dashed it as far as I could under the seats, resolved never again to be found chewing tobacco in a Methodist church."

Axley preached much after "location" and much increased his former reputation. He was of such independent character as to be restive under the order of the bishop.

Although very much has been written of his quaint sayings and doings not much is now known of his early history and that of his family. It is proper here to give what one of the descendants says is the true history.

A grandson of Rev. Jas. Axley says that the history be told of himself as follows: "Axley, a Scotchman, and his wife and son named James, a boy of twelve years of age took passage in a sailing vessel to come to the United States in the year 1777. They had a rough and boisterous voyage. Before reaching their destination, Axley and his wife both took sick and died and their bodies were consigned to the sea. At the end of the voyage at some port of entry on the James River or Chesapeake Bay the boy, James, was bound out or sold to one Judge Stevens to help pay for passage. Thus he was born in Scotland, place not known, and not in Cumberland County, Va. Judge Stevens observing that he was a bright boy educated him with the intention of making him a lawyer and making him a partner with himself. As has been seen however circumstances and Axley's will determined otherwise. If there is any relationship between the Tennessee and Virginia Axleys it is not known what it is." Whatever may have been his early history, that he was uneducated is negatived by the report of his sermons and exhortations by the Hon. Hugh Lawson White and various others.

Something original and unique stirs the public pulse and brings out a crowd. He may have at times used slang and uncouth sayings for this purpose. Once he got the people together it is agreed on all hands that none knew better than he how to hold them.

Shakespeare has Hamlet say in his soliloquy: "To be or not to be that is the question," paraphrasing; to stay here or go yonder, or as Ty Cobb would put it, "remain on the base or try for a home run." This same Danish gentleman on reflection concluded "to bear the ills he had than fly to others he knew not of." He also advised Ophelia, his former sweetheart, against love and marriage. Trust not mankind. "We are arrant knaves all of us." I am myself a deep dyed villain and guilty of crimes unspeakable. "Get thee to a nunnery." Axley maybe knew what awful trouble this same Hamlet caused by his advice. Anyhow he faced a dilemma of "to be married or not to be married." Whether to take the advice of John Wesley and Francis Asbury, the founder and the bishop of the M. E. Church, and remain a bachelor or to marry and settle down. To marry and rear a family on $60 a year, the then maximum salary of a circuit rider, was entirely out of the question. Even could he reach the high office of a bishop the salary of Bishop Asbury in those times was $80 a year only. Besides that he endured innumerable hardships. He traveled great distances almost wholly on horseback and sometimes in inclement weather in the mountains he was compelled to spend the night in a hollow log and let his horse crop the wild grass for a living.

It is not at all surprising to us that Axley preferred marriage and a fine body of Sweetwater Valley land to a precarious support as a circuit rider even with a good chance of being elected a bishop. He was located by the Holston Conference in the year 1821. From the best information at hand at present he must have purchased the tracts from Matthew Nelson, Treasurer of East Tennessee and the then agent of the State and obtained the grants directly from the State. The tracts he owned were the northwest quarter of section 1, Township 3, Range 1, east, and the south half of the S. E. quarter of section 2, T. 3, R. 1 E. He built a house on the latter, near a large spring by the side of the Madisonville road one-half mile southeast from the Southern Railway depot in the town of Sweetwater. It is needless to state at that time the town and railroad were not in existence or scarcely thought of. He must have married and settled there in the early twenties soon after the Hiwassee purchase from the Cherokee Indians. The house he built is still standing though almost a century old. It is diagonally across the road from the J. C. Waren (old Ramsey) residence. It is one of the old landmarks of the valley. There is growing at this house an Isabella grape vine which still (1914) bears grapes and which was planted as a slip by Axley previous to his death in 1837; thus making it more than seventy-five years old. At the head of the spring not far from the house is a giant oak tree likely as much as one hundred and fifty years old. The two tracts of land mentioned were purchased in 1859 by Col. John Ramsey for the sum of $7,000.

He (Axley), married Cynthia Earnest one of a family of ten brothers and seventeen sisters. Oh: there were patriarchs and matriarchs in those days! The Earnests were Greene County people. Cynthia was a sister of Mary Ann Earnest who married John Lotspeich, Sr., one of the original white settlers of Sweetwater Valley. They resided in the brick near the Athens road one and a half miles southwest of Sweetwater. Cynthia was considerable younger than Mary Ann; the latter was born in 1789 and the former in 1800. The one died in 1878 and the other in 1882. They are both buried in County Line Cemetery.

Mr. and Mrs. Axley reared a large family. Numerous grandchildren and great grandchildren of theirs are now living.

In the marriage license book of Monroe County in

the County Court Clerk's office this record is found: License issued to Samuel Blair and Cynthia Axley. Ceremony performed July 30, 1844. James Sewell, Minister of the Gospel, M. E. Church. I am told the marriage did not turn out happily. They did not live together many years.

I make no apology for thus giving at some length the history of Rev. James Axley. He was not only one of the early settlers but a very remarkable man. He was by far the most prominent preacher of the M. E. Church residing in the valley. He was brave and outspoken and feared not to condemn what he thought wrong or commend the right and added to that an unblemished character. He would have been a man in any age and any country.

The children of the Rev. James Axley and Cynthia Axley were:

One. James, b. Sept. 8, 1825. d. ―――
Two. Samuel Douthard, b. 1827. d. 1903.
Three. Elijah, b. ――― d. ―――
Four. Marilla, b. ――― d. ―――
Five. Betsy, b. ――― d. ―――
Six. Jemima, b. ――― d. ―――
Seven. Matilda, b. ―――d. ―――

One. James Axley, married, first, Mary McKenzie Dec. 11, 1856.

Their children were:

1. James Thomas, b. Oct. 4, 1857. He is a railway conductor Ogden, Utah.

2. John McKenzie, b. Dec. 31, 1858. Broker in Kansas City, Mo.

James Axley married, second, Martha Ann Smith of McMinn Co., daughter John Pickens Smith of South Carolina, on August 7, 1860. She was born Aug. 12, 1832, and died Apr. ――, 1892. Their children were:

1. Mary Alice, b. May 23, 1861. She married George Reynolds of McMinn Co. They reside at Canyon City, Texas.

2. William Wesley, b. Sept. 23, 1862, at the old Axley place three miles west of Madisonville, Tenn. He mar-

ried Sarah F. Norris, of Lutherville, Ga., Dec. 19, 1895. She was the daughter of a Baptist minister. They lived first in Sweetwater for several years and then moved to Chattanooga, where they now reside. He is a traveling man. Their children are:
Robert Chapman (named Chapman from grandmother), born Feb. 14, 1897; Martha Francis, b. Aug. 31, 1898; and William Wesley, Sept. 20, 1901.

3. Charles Davis, b. Nov. 1, 1864. d. Oct. 5, 1885, at Troupe, Tex.

4. Samuel Wiley, b. Sept. 1, 1866. d. Mar. 10, 1911. Kansas City, Mo.

5. Ella, b. Dec. 4, 1868. Married Oscar Hunt, of Monroe County, Tenn., Sept. 6, 1894. They reside at Carson City, Texas.

6. Ida, b. June 6, 1870. Married S. P. Tolleson in 1900. He died in 1902 at Amarillo, Texas.

Two. Samuel Douthard Axley married Eliza Jane Dean Jan. 31, 1860. She was born in July, 1836, and is still living (1916). He went to California in 1849 and returned in 1857 or 1858 and located on Bat Creek, in Monroe County, where he lived on his farm until he died in 1903. Their oldest child died in infancy. Their other children were:

2. James, b. Sept. 14, 1862. Married Susan Eliza Johnson Mar. 3, 1886. She was born in May 1866. Was the daughter of Jacob Kimberland Johnson and Susan Swaggerty. He came to Philadelphia, Tenn., in 1886, and moved from there to the James Axley farm three miles west of Madisonville in 1898. He was elected Trustee of Monroe County in 1900 and re-elected twice. He is a member of the General Assembly of Tennessee, as representative of Monroe County, elected in 1914. He lives in Madisonville. The children of James and Susan Axley are:

(1) Walter Brunner, b. Jan. 17, 1887. Married Lois Kimbrough Nov. 1909. She was the daughter of Jos. Kimbrough. They have two children: Nannie Peck, b. Mar. 3, 1911, and James, b. Nov. 16, 1913.

(2) Jacob Johnson, b. Feb. 16, 1890. Post-office, Dairy, Oregon.

* * * * *

4. Fred, son of Sam. Douthard Axley, born Nov. 9, 1865. Died Nov. 17, 1914. He was a farmer on Fork Creek. He married Malissa Johnson, daughter of Frank J., and granddaughter of Louis Johnson. She was born Mar. 13, 1870. They were married Sept. 5, 1889. Their children are:

(1) Zelma, b. Aug., 1890. Married Horace King, of Sweetwater Oct. 27, 1911. They have one child, Lucille, b. Aug. 18, 1912.
(2) Beulah, b. Oct. 17, 1892.
(3) Hazel, b. Jan. 29, 1899.
(4) Flora, b. Apr. 6, 1901.
(5) Blanchard, b. Feb. 5, 1905.

3. Nevada, b. July 16, 1864. She married C. P. A. Woolridge on Oct. 7, 1891. He is a farmer and they live near Madisonville. Their children are:

(1) Birge Littleton, b. Sept. 8, 1892.
(2) Edna Bond, b. Feb. 12, 1894.
(3) Ralph, b. Feb. 11, 1896.
(4) Ivy Modena, b. June 16, 1898.

5. Arch Bacome, b. ———— Married Samantha Hull on July 16, 1896. Their children are: Antel Lee (about 18), Walter, James Douthard, Tennie May, Sarah, Blanche, Jay Hugh, Artie Lou, Gertrude Belle, and infant b. June, 1916.

6. Tennessee, b. 1872. Married Douthard Green, who is a farmer on Bat Creek, Monroe County. They have two children: Francis Irene, b. Feb., 1905, and Garland, b. 1907.

7. Philander, b. Apr. 22, 1873. Married Hattie Keller Nov. 14, 1900, who was born Nov. 5, 1880. Their children are: Delia Irene, b. Nov. 9, 1902; Vola Eulalie, b. Feb. 22, 1905; Nellie Maude, b. Mar. 9, 1907; Ruby Alta, b. Jan. 11, 1909; Georgia Lois, b. Feb. 8, 1911; Vastine Stickley, b. Jan. 27, 1913, and Raymond Philander. b. Apr. 2, 1915.

8. Tressie, b. 1875. Married J. Henry Brakebill, Mar. 23, 1897. Eight children, three of whom are dead. The living are: Robert, Alonzo, Stella, Willis and Clyde.

9. Artie Lou, ninth child of Samuel Douthard Axley, b. 1880. Married Austin Brakebill, Dec. 7, 1899. Four children: Mabel (sixteen), Mary Axley, John Douthard and Milburn (eleven).

* * * * *

Harriet Jeannette Axley, daughter of Elijah and Martha Jane Axley was born Aug. 10, 1870. She married Wm. Haun at Rome, Ga., on May 9, 1887. He is the son of Abraham Haun of Monroe County, a Baptist minister. He (Wm. H.), came to Sweetwater Dec. 17, 1912, and has been Marshal of the city for three years.

Their living children are:

1. Oscar C., b. Feb. 11, 1888.
2. Ella F., b. Oct. 26, 1890.
3. Davie Ann, b. March 7, 1893.
4. Ethel J., b. June 15, 1895.
5. Elijah C., b. March 27, 1900.
6. Cora Lee, b. Sept. 16, 1903.
7. Erskin R., b. Nov. 29, 1906.

Bessie, daughter E. Axley, married Chas. Rickett, Dec. 19, 1898.

Mack, son, E. Axley, married and lives at Chattanooga.

Charles, son, E. Axley, married Kittie Moser Dec. 14, 1899. One child, Eva, b. 1904.

Ernest, son, E. Axley, married Ellen Frost.

Four. Marilla, daughter of Rev. James Axley, married Jesse Fouche, Feb. 24, 1842. They had two children: Jesse and Matilda. Matilda married ——— Harold and they had two children: Margaret, who married Heneger, and Jesse, who is unmarried.

Five. Betsy, daughter Rev. James Axley, married Josiah McGuire, Mar. 4, 1850. They moved to Iowa, near Des Moines. One son, Carl McGuire, married Mary Wilmot. They are both physicians.

Six. Jemima, married Wm. A. Plemings, Feb. 20, 1860. They went to Weatherford, Texas, and then to Oklahoma.

Seven. Matilda, youngest child Rev. Jas. Axley, married Wm. Bryan, May 24, 1840. They went to Grainger County, Tenn.

Three. Elijah, third son of Rev. James Axley, married Martha Jane Forshee Dec. 23, 1858. Their children are: (1) Bascom, who married Angelina Kinser. They live on Dancing Branch, Monroe County, and have considerable family.

(2) Cynthia Ella, b. Feb. 24, 1864. Married George H. Foland, who was b. Jan. 19, 1862. Died in Sweetwater Apr. 15, 1909. Their children:

(1) Mollie b. Aug. 1, 1885. Married Ed. Colquitt, of Sweetwater. Four children: Willie, b. Dec. 21, 1907; Gracie, b. Aug. 3, 1909; George, b. May 6, 1911; Edgar, b. May 5, 1914.

(2) Gracie, second child George Foland, b. Jan. 31, 1887. Married Garfield Stephens, Oct. 4, 1909.

(3) Henry, b. Aug. 29, 1888. Died Nov. 21, 1913.

(4) Harvey, b. Sept. 26, 1890. Married Jella Queen, of Sweetwater, Sept., 1911. One child, Katherine, b. Sept. 25, 1913.

(5) Asbury, b. Jan. 9, 1893. Married Bessie Blanton May 31, 1908. One child: James Franklin, b. Apr. 22, 1915. Live in Sweetwater.

(6) Martha, b. Mar. 7, 1896. Married Fred Seymour Feb. 7, 1915.

(7) Hobert, b. Aug. 24, 1897. Married Gertrude Aiken June 27, 1915. She was born Jan. 2, 1898. Live in Chattanooga.

(8) Mary, b. May 22, 1899.
(9) Prudie, b. Feb. 5, 1901.
(10) Willard, b. July 22, 1903.
(11) Elijah Eugene, b. May 30, 1906. Died infant.

Elizabeth, daughter of Elijah Axley, married William Lambert Jan. 30, 1896, who is a guard at Brushy Mountain.

Mattie, daughter of Elijah Axley, married Lafayette Hudgens. They moved to Iowa where he was at one time a member of the Legislature.

WILLIAM BROWDER.

The following sketch was written for the Monroe Democrat and published in that paper of date July 9, 1890. The facts given were obtained from Mr. Browder himself shortly before his death. He died in Meigs County on Sunday, June 29, 1890. He had been living for a number of years at County Line in McMinn County but had gone on a visit to his son William in Meigs.

"Wm. Browder was born on February 10, 1792, in Chatham County, North Carolina, about twelve miles from Hillsboro and twenty-two miles from Raleigh. He was therefore at the time of his death 98 years, 4 months and 19 days old.

About the year 1800, two brothers, John and Darius Browder, moved from North Carolina to the Browder place between Lenoirs and Loudon. Darius Browder was the father of William, who was then about 8 years of age. At that time Knoxville was a mere village, having about seven or eight stores. The county around Lenoirs was a wilderness. Bear, deer, turkeys, wild-cats and game were plentiful.

Wm. Browder enlisted in the war of 1812. He served under Brigadier General White. This brigade camped for a long time at the famous Lookout Mountain awaiting orders and supplies. The war closed before the brigade saw much active service.

At the time of the encampment at Lookout, no white man lived there, as it was before the purchase of the land and the removal of the Cherokees to the Indian Nation. Jack Ross was then the Cherokee chief and resided in that section. Hence the site near the city, now Chattanooga, was first known as Ross' Landing.

Darius Browder, the father of William, died in 1812.

In 1814, William Browder was married to Elizabeth Lackey, of Roane County. He afterward moved to what is known as the Hugh Goddard place and in one winter cleared eleven acres of land. He subsequently moved to the Hagler farm on Paint Rock, where he resided until 1835. He then came to Pond Creek Valley, to the place now owned by his son, James M. Browder. He lived there until 1862, when he went to Georgia, returning to this section after the war was over. Since then he has lived principally with his son, David Browder, and since his (David's) decease, with his widow.

William Browder was a man vigorous in mind and body, of great industry and sterling integrity.

It would naturally follow that endowed with these qualities his life was eminently useful and successful. The history of his life would be the history of the section in which he lived.

When he came to Tennessee, John Sevier the first Governor of our state was still governor. The Cherokee Indians occupied our section and warred, roamed and hunted amid the virgin forests scarcely touched by the axe of the white man. He had seen the Indian go from their hunting grounds; the wheat and corn take the place of the forest; school-houses, churches, railroads and all the concomitants of civilization rise where erstwhile roamed the bear and deer.

He has seen a great number of his descendants grow to be good and useful men and occupy prominent positions in the country. He can count his descendants in various parts of the Union. There are few, if any of them who do not reflect credit upon the name. Many of his children and grandchildren have passed before him to the other shore. They will be there to welcome his coming at the Golden Gates.

He, more than most men, because of such a long and useful life, has seen the abundant harvests of his good works while still alive. Whatever was for good and for the upbuilding of society he has been foremost in, and has spent his time and money for its success.

One of his last works was the Browder Memorial Church, for the building of which he furnished the principal part of the money.

He was an ardent man and took an active part in business, in politics and church matters. In politics he was a democrat.

When President Cleveland visited Atlanta, Mr. Browder went down saying that he wished to shake hands with another Democratic President before he died.

When voting day came around, he was always to be found at the polls. He thought it as much a duty to vote as to go to church.

He was a zealous Methodist and contributed greatly

to the success of that society in this section of the country. He always went to preaching and there is hardly a man, woman or child in a circuit of ten miles who has not heard Brother Browder lead in prayer. He supported his church with time and means. He believed that each church should meet promptly its obligations, pecuniary as well as religious, and he labored to that end.

In all the relations of life, as farmer, neighbor, citizen, church member and as father of a numerous family, he has been everything that could be desired. Few men in any country have been loved, revered and respected as he was. He has indeed been a good and faithful servant and has gone to his reward."

Children of William and Elizabeth Browder: Maryline, oldest child, married James Stone. Their children were Malinda and Elizabeth. Malinda married Wm. Murray of Pond Creek Valley, in the fall of 1850. They moved to Missouri and reared a large farmily. Elizabeth was married to Estel Lowe in the fall of 1851. There were six of the Lowe children, 5 boys and 1 girl. James now living in Knoxville; David, dead; "Billy" lives in Texas; Samuel and Lee both dead; Josephine died at the age of 8 years.

Elizabeth Stone Lowe died in 1863 or 1864.

William, third child and second son of William and E. B., b. in 1822. He married Sarah Deatherage in 1848. She died at Harriman in 1911, aged 90 years. They lived in Sweetwater Valley many years, part of the time at County Line the D. A., now C. O. Browder place. They went from there to near Nashville. They came probably in the early 80's to Meigs County, where he died in 1906. They had no family.

Darius, son of William and E. B., was b. ─────. He moved to Bradley County, where he died in 1892.

John Jefferson (oldest son of W. and E. B.), b. Nov. 9, 1818; d. July 14, 1903.

James Madison (son of W. and E. B.), b. October 16, 1824; d. September 10, 1902.

Nancy Jane Crump (daughter of W. and E. B.), b. May 17, 1839; d. April 25, 1872.

(She married J. H. Pickel whom see.)

David A., youngest son of W. and E. B., b. March 2, 1835; d. April 6, 1883.

JOHN JEFFERSON BROWDER

Was born near Lenoir City, Tenn., on November 9, 1818. He was married to Elizabeth J. Lotspeich, December 12, 1844. (See Lotspeich.) She was born March 7, 1825. He was a farmer. They first resided in Pond Creek Valley and then afterwards moved to the Brickel place, a short time previous to the Civil War. He died there on July 14, 1903, and there his widow still resides. Their children were:

(One) Elizabeth A. Browder, b. October 10, 1845.
(Two) Mary F., b. August 24, 1847. Married Wm. Cleveland. (See his history.)
(Third) Amanda J., b. April 12, 1849. Married A. J. Dickey.
(Fourth) William L., b. November 29, 1850; d. July 7, 1878.
(Fifth) Sarah A., b. August 13, 1862; d. September 4, 1867.
(Sixth) John W., b. April 1, 1854; d. April 18, 1890.
(Seventh) Chas. D., b. January 27, 1856.
(Eighth) Nancy E., b. February 19, 1858; d. March 27, 1882.
(Ninth) Alice, b. March 11, 1866.
(Tenth) Samuel L., b. September 10, 1868.
(Eleventh) Charles D. married Nettie Adkins November 7, 1888. (See Adkins.) He is a farmer. Justice of the Peace. He resides near his mother. The family of C. D. and Nettie Browder are:
Mildred, b. August 14, 1889.
Ernest, b. December 9, 1890. He resides at Port Gibson, Miss.
Eli, b. May 27, 1894. Student at Emory and Henry College.
Margaret, b. August 29, 1897.

AMANDA J. BROWDER.

Amanda was the third child of Jno. Jefferson and Elizabeth L. Browder. She married Andrew J. Dickey, son of D. H. Dickey, of Pond Creek Valley, on April 16,

1872. He was born January 17, 1846. They resided in Pond Creek Valley until August, 1889, when they moved to the town of Sweetwater. Their children are five in number:

(1) Hugh Browder, b. March 6, 1873.
(2) Corry Rebecca, b. March 26. 1875.
(3) David Wesley, b. January 11, 1877.
(4 Lela, b. August 1, 1880.
(5) Cecil, b. December 24, 1885.

Corry Rebecca married John Brown, son of Hon. J. K. Brown, and Sarah E. Brown, October 29, 1895. He (Jno.) was born in Meigs County, Tenn., on November 24, 1869. His father came to Sweetwater in 1882. He is cashier of the Sweetwater Trust and Savings Bank. Their children are:

(1) Grace Rebecca Brown, b. October 8, 1896.
(2) Irene Elizabeth Brown, b. August 25, 1898.
(3) Leta Jane Brown, b. January 2, 1901.
(4) Gladys Brown, b. October 3, 1903.

D. W. Dickey was married to Mabel, daughter of W. L. and M. E. Clark on January 17, 1907. She was born January 18, 1875; died August 1, 1908. Of this marriage there was one child, Mabel C. Dickey, born August 1, 1908. He married (2) Miss Clarine Lee, daughter of Wm. Thomas, and Margaret Rhinehart Lee, of Waynesville, N. C., February 18, 1914. Mr. Dickey has been depot and express agent for the Southern R. R. Co., from 1902, up to the present time (1916).

Hugh Browder was married to Miss Buna Bowling of Coal Creek, Tenn., June 20, 1912. He is a grocer and produce merchant in Sweetwater.

Cecil married Major J. G. Engleman at Sweetwater on May 31, 1911. He was educated at Virginia Military Institute, graduating there in Elect. Eng. 1908. He was teacher of mathematics and modern language and assistant commandant at T. M. I. from 1908-1915. He was born in Lexington, Va., on August 26, 1886. His postoffice is now (1915), Lexington, Va.

Lela Dickey

Was the second daughter of Andrew J. and Amanda B. Dickey. She was married to Henry Lee Cecil, October 25, 1905. He was born in Pulaski, Va., on March 8th, 1865. He is secretary and treasurer of Taylor-Christian Hat Co., Bristol, Tenn. Their children are three in number:
1. Elizabeth Eloise, b. September 18, 1906.
2. Juanita Blanche, b. November 20, 1910.
3. Henry Lee, Jr., b. October 24, 1912.

Alice, the sixth daughter of J. J. and E. L. B., was married to Dr. Joseph Albert Hardin on April 16, 1900. He was born in Meigs County on December 10, 1866. He was the son of ———— and ———— Hardin. He received the degree of M. D. at Vanderbilt University in 1883. He was a partner of Dr. D. N. Browder from 1894 to 1899. Partner of Dr. ———— McClain from 1899 to 1905. He is now (1915) a practising physician in Sweetwater. He has had no partner since 1905.

James Madison Browder

Was born in Meigs County, October 16, 1824. He moved with his father to Roane County, then to the old Browder homestead and lived there in Pond Creek Valley. He bought this place in 1868 and lived there until 1893.

He married Letitia Laird Patterson of Meigs County, November 29, 1849. She was born June 20, 1829, and died at Sweetwater July 4, 1879, and was buried at Mt. Zion, Meigs County.

James M. Browder was a farmer. Served in the Confederate army as a conscripting officer and refugeed to Georgia in 1863. After remaining there one year he returned home to his family. He moved to Sweetwater, December 12, 1893. He was a member of the M. E. Church, South.

He died at Sweetwater, September 10, 1902, of pneumonia, and was buried at County Line Cemetery.

The children of his first wife were:
1. Mary, b. August 8, 1851; d. February 7, 1888.
2. David Newton, b. July 31, 1853; d. February 5, 1902.
3. Elizabeth, b. November 20, 1855.

4. Ellen, b. March 22, 1858.
5. James Patterson, b. November 4, 1860. Postoffice, Chattanooga, Tenn.
6. John Jefferson, b. October 15, 1863.
7. Horace Lackey, b. May 17, 1868.
8. Lucy Pickens, b. June 16, 1871; d. January 3, 1914.
9. Robert, b. July 27, 1874; d. April 16, 1908.
1. Mary Browder married J. L. Suddath of Harriman, Tenn., on October 25, 1887. Their children were:
(1) Jennie, b. August, 1880. Postoffice, Harriman, Tenn.
(2) Carrie, b. ———, 1882. Postoffice, Murfreesboro, Tenn.
(3) Frank, b. October 25, 1884. Emory & Henry, Va.
(4) George, b. September 5, 1887. ———, Texas.

* * * * *

2. David Newton studied medicine at the Electic College, Cincinnati, Ohio, and got his diploma in 1881. He married Emma Byrd, daughter of Thomas Byrd, of Roane County, on September 1, 1881, when he moved to Sweetwater.

He and Dr. J. A. Hardin were partners during the years 1894-1899. After acquiring a lucrative practice he attended lectures and took a course of hospital practice in New York City. He died February 5, 1902, and was interred in West View Cemetery.

Emma Byrd, his wife was born July 9, 1857, near Paint Rock Ferry, Roane County. She resides in Sweetwater. Their children are:

(1) Byrd, a daughter, born October 28, 1882. She was musically educated at the Conservatory in Boston. Her profession was music teacher. She married O. K. Jones on January 3, 1914. Their child : John M., Jr., b. Deeember 11, 1914.
(2) Thomas, b. October, 1885.

* * * * *

3. Elizabeth Browder married James N. Heiskell. (See Heiskells.)

* * * * *

4. Ellen married A. A. Green, formerly of Kingston, Tenn., now of Boyd, Texas, on October 30, 1879. He is a merchant.

* * * * *

3. James Patterson Browder was a druggist at Philadelphia, Tenn., from 1887 to 1892 when he moved to Harriman. He married Maude Critchell, October 2, 1895. He has been in the employment of the Standard Oil Co., since 1892. His present residence is Chattanooga, Tenn. His children are:
(1) Byron, b. Jan., 1899.
(2) and (3) James and Elise, twins.
(4) Dorothy, b. June 1, 1908.

* * * * *

6. John Jefferson Browder married Bettie Taylor, of Morristown, Tenn., on November 25, 1889. They moved to Washington in September, 1902, where he engaged in farming. Present postoffice is Oakdale. Their children are: Sydney, Anna, Laura, Van, Robert, Newton, John, Kyle, Elbert.

* * * * *

7. Horace Lackey Browder married Huldah Cleveland, daughter of Eli Cleveland on June 14, 1910. She was born in Sweetwater Valley, June 7, 1884. One child, Susan Laird, was born October 27, 1911. Horace L. B. is now postmaster at Sweetwater, since 1913.

* * * * *

8. Lucy Browder married W. K. Horton, a merchant in Sweetwater, on October 12, 1899. They moved to Waynesville, N. C., in April, 1909. Afterwards they moved to Harriman, Tenn. She died there. Their children are:
Helen, b. January 21, 1901.
W. K., b. May 17, 1903.
Lucy Browder, b. June 29, 1906.

* * * * *

James Madison Browder was married (second) to

Elizabeth Armstrong, daughter of ——— and Jane Armstrong of McMinn County, Tenn., on December 14, 1890. She was born September 16, 1858, and died at Sweetwater, April 17, 1909. Their children were:

(1) Samuel P., b. July 8, 1882; d. November 1, 1883.

(2) Clyde, b. ———, ———. Married May Rodgers, of Chattanooga, in 1907. They went to Nashville in 1909. Residence, 1403 Des Monbreun Street. Employee of the Standard Oil Co. Their children are:

Mary, b. July, 1908.

Robert, b. July, 1910.

(3) Zelma Lee, b. September 21, 1888. Married W. Roy Plott, now of Statesville, N. C., on April 22, 1914. They have one child, Elizabeth, b. March 13, 1915.

DAVID A. BROWDER.

David A., son of Wm. Browder, was born in Roane County, March 2, 1835. He moved to Pond Creek about 1840 or 1841. Married Rachel Dickey, October 12, 1858, the Rev. Mack Lillard, officiating. Rachel Dickey was born April 17, 1837. David A. Browder was a farmer. He was elected a member of the General Assembly of Tennessee, November, 1877, for McMinn County. He was a member of the M. E. Church, South. He moved to the Rowan (Brett) place, at County Line, in 1866, and died there April 6, 1883, and is buried at County Line Cemetery. He died of pneumonia. His children are:

(1) William D., b. July, 1859.

(2) Elizabeth, b. August, 1861.

(3) D. H., b. September 29, 1863. Commission merchant, New Orleans, La.

(4) Frank E., b. May 21, 1867. Manager milling company, Mankato, Minn.

(5) Chas. O., b. December, 1870.

(6) Hubert, b. October, 1878. Commission merchant, El Paso, Texas.

* * * * *

William D., married Adda Lou Peak, of Meigs County, October 5, 1887, who was born March 18, 1866. He is a farmer and live stock dealer. They both belong to

HISTORY OF SWEETWATER VALLEY 81

the Southern Methodist Church. Moved to Sweetwater in 1901. Their children are:
(1) Boy, d. in infancy.
(2) Hattie May, b. 1895.

* * * * *

(5) Chas. O., was married to Georgia Duncan, of Atlanta, Ga., June 16, 1906. She was born at Hayesville, N. C., August 1, 1869. Her father was J. W. Duncan, a physician. Her mother was Mary Curtis. Their children are:
David Duncan, b. May 29, 1907.
Chas. O., b. September 23, 1909.

ELI SANDERSON ADKINS

Was born in Massachusetts, January 6, 1824; d. February 20, 1889. His father was Henry Adkins, and his mother was Lucinda Grace Adkins, who was born November 6, 1792; d. Nov. 23, 1869, at Philadelphia, Tenn.

E. S. Adkins came to Talbot County, Ga., when a young man. He was twice married, first to Miss Harris, of Talbot County. They had three daughters: Mary Ann, b. July 19, 1849; m. E. W. Cozatt in 1866. They had three children: Minnie, b. 1878; Rose, b. 1880; Lee, b. 1888.

2. Louisa Jane, b. October 2, 1850; m. Joe M. Jones in 1869. He died in 1870, leaving one daughter, Josie.

Louisa married (second) M. C. Duncan in 1875. Their children were: William, b. 1875; Walter, b. 1877; Worth, b. 1879; Eli, b. 1881; Lenoir, b. 1883; Emma, b. 1886; Ethel, b. 1889.

E. S. Adkins married (second) Elizabeth Mildred Childs, of Talbot County, Ga. She was born March 12, 1841; d. March 7, 1874. They came to Philadelphia, Tenn., in November, 1865. Their children were:

1. Emma Sophia, b. August 31, 1857. Married E. C. Jones, September 15, 1873. (See Jones.)

2. Fannie Amelia, b. February 18, 1859, in Talbot County, Ga.; m. W. G. Lenoir. (See Lenoir.)

3. Nettie Gray, b. January 5. 1861; m. C. D. Browder in 1888. (See Browder.)

4. Eli Sanderson, b. April, 1863. Married. Wife died leaving one daughter who is married. E. S. A. is a merchant and ranchman and lives at Pony, Mont.

5. Annie Mildred, b. April 26, 1866; m. W. C. Cannon in 1890. (See Cannon.)

6. Henry, b. January 5, 1868; m. Kate Owen, of Sweetwater, Tenn., October, 1898. They have two daughters: Katherine, b. 1900, and Henry Taylor, b. 1902. They live at Pony, Mont.

7. Charles Childs, b. January 25, 1872; m. Grace Biglow in 1905. He died in 1911. They lived at Livingston, Mont. They had no children.

Franklin King Berry, Sr.

Was born near Williamsburg, Ky., March 25, 1809. He married Emily, daughter of Thomas Laughlin, of Philadelphia, Tenn. He died October 28, 1845. He was buried in the old cemetery at Philadelphia. His wife was born January 26, 1823, and died October, 1884. Mrs. Berry's second husband was W. R. Molleston, of Philadelphia, who died January 25, 1872, at age of 63 years. The children of F. K. and Emily Berry were:

One. F. K. Berry. He was born at Philadelphia, December 4, 1841. He was a practising physician and a farmer. He married Caroline Cleveland, daughter of Robert R. Cleveland on April 15, 1868. They had a handsome residence not far from the Cleveland Baptist Church on Sweetwater Creek, where they lived during nearly all their married life.

Mrs. Berry was b. February 2, 1843. She d. September 16, 1910. Buried in West View Cemetery at Sweetwater.

Children of Dr. F. K. and Mrs. Caroline Berry are:

1. Frank E. Berry; was b. January 28, 1869. He m. Julia, daughter of J. L. Willson, of Pond Creek Valley. He (Berry), is a farmer and lives at Marble Bluff in Loudon County on the Tennessee River, seven miles from Loudon, his postoffice.

2. Robert S. C. Berry, b. December 30, 1870; m. Bertie Healan, of Ringgold, Ga., December 9, 1897. He is a merchant and resides at Morristown. One child, Roberta, b. June 7, 1900.

3. Nina, b. October 14, 1873; d. July 27, 1897.
4. Emily Ethel, b. November 4, 1875; m. J. Frank McGuire, December 17, 1894. He is a farmer. They reside in Sweetwater.
The children of J. F. and E. E. McGuire are:
Charles Euclid, b. September 28, 1895; Dorothy Caroline, b. August 23, 1897; Frank Ralph, b. January 1, 1900; Hilda, b. January 7, 1903; Jean Nicholas, b. February 24, 1906; Halstead, b. October 11, 1909; Ethel B., b. September 16, 1912.
5. Luke Danton, b. July 26, 1879; m. Julia Stowers. Their address is Cushing, Okla.
Annie Eliza, b. September 21, 1881; m. Virgil T. Rausin, June 6, 1906. He is a merchant in Sweetwater. Children are:
V. T. Rausin, Jr., b. June 13, 1907; Kermit Wendell Rausin, b. April 1, 1910; Buford Quentin, b. March 25, 1916.

* * * * *

Two. Sidney, b. in Philadelphia, August 17, 1844. (See C. Y. Caldwell.)

CHARLES Y. CALDWELL.

Charles Y. Caldwell was born in Pike County, Georgia, February 17, 1847. He came to Sweetwater Valley with his mother in 1855, who came to Philadelphia, Tenn., in that year. He was married to Sidney Berry, of Philadelphia, on November 5, 1868. She was born in Philadelphia, August 17, 1844. He engaged in farming while located there. He moved to California in 1875 and moved back to Tennessee in 1876, where he farmed at the old home place until 1901, when he went to Wuakomis, Okla. Their children are:
Charles Sydney, b. December 20, 1872; m. Mary Kline, of Loudon, Tenn., May 6, 1896, going to Waukomis, Okla., where they now live.
Robert Marvin, b. June 7, 1878; m. Maude, daughter of J. L. Willson, January 18, 1911, going to Waukomis to make it their home.
Fred. Roy, b. April 7, 1883; m. Bertie D. Johnston, of Oklahoma City, August 6, 1913. They live at Wuakomis.

Martha Emily, b. in California, September 1, 1875; d. December 18, 1876.

Frank Berry, b. August 15, 1869; d. December, 1898.

Mary, b. January 15, 1871; d. December 18, 1876.

T. W. BELLAMY

Was born in Louisa County, Va., June 15, 1806. He came to Sweetwater Valley in 1853. He married Sarah Griffin, April 3, 1828. She was born June 4, 1809, and died December 27, 1887. T. W. B. died September 4, 1889. Their children were:

William, b. December 23, 1828; d. July 15, 1847.

Mary Ann, b. April 13, 1830; d. August 28, 1854.

John Daniel, b. September 20, 1831. Lives in Benton, Ill.

Newton Walker, b. June 28, 1833.

Thomas Conner, b. in Louisa County, Va., February 16, 1835.

He came to Sweetwater with his father in 1853. He was employed in the cooper shop of McClung, Dobbins & Clayton. He was married. His children were eleven in number: six boys and five girls. Four girls died single. Three of the sons are married. Andy, the oldest one, is the father of eleven children. He is employed by Moore & Co., barytes manufacturers.

Andrew Bellamy, son of T. W. B., was born October 15, 1838. In the Civil War he enlisted in Colonel Jno. A. Rowan's regiment, 67th, C. S. A., Company D., Captain Robert Rowan, Priscilla Frances, daughter of T. W. B., b. October 28, 1840; m. W. B. Sample, July 25, 1858. W. B. Sample was b. August, 1833; d. 1899. Elizabeth Melissa, b. April 4, 1843; m. Professor J. S. Cline; she died June 19, 1913. Henry Washington, b. December 26, 1848. He is a Baptist minister of Mendota, Va.

ALEXANDER BIGGS

Was one of the oldest settlers in Sweetwater Valley. He acquired land in 1820 soon after the Hiwassee District was open for settlement. On his tract adjoining Mayes and Heiskell near the large spring on the north side of the now town of Sweetwater, he built a one-story brick residence, which is still standing. This is one of the oldest brick houses in the valley. It was occupied continuously by the Biggs until the year ―― when the farm was purchased by G. M. McKnight. Information in regard to the Biggs family is now hard to obtain, as there are no living descendants in this section; one son went to California and his address is not known to the writer.

Alexander Biggs; date of birth, death and where came from, not known. Isabella Biggs (inscription on stone in Sweetwater Cemetery) was born January 7, 1789; died January 12, 1877. She was the wife of Alex. Biggs. Their children were:

Mary Ann, Nancy, Alexander Hamilton and J. M. Mary Ann and Hamilton never married. Nancy m. Rev. Thos. R. Bradshaw, April 2, 1861; no children. Mr. Bradshaw was a learned Presbyterian minister and was the second pastor of the New School Presbyterian Church at Sweetwater, Rev. Thos. Brown, of Philadelphia, Tenn., having been the first. (See history of Presbyterian Church.)

Solomon Bogart

Was the son of Abram and ―― Duncan Bogart, formerly of Washington County. They moved to Kingston, Tenn., and then to Athens, Tenn.

Solomon Bogart was born in Washington County on January 4, 1800. He died at his home (which was located where the Bogart High School building now stands), at Philadelphia, on June 9, 1878. His wife was Ann Moore. She was born December 21, 1821. She died November 24, 1860.

Solomon Bogart was a hotel keeper, teacher and land surveyor. He first kept hotel at Athens, Tenn., which he advertised as a strictly temperance hotel, meaning by that, that he allowed no one drinking or carrying whiskey with them to put up at his hotel. I have been told that he refused to keep General Winfield Scott because the general carried a bottle, and on stated occasions took his toddy.

Solomon Bogart came to Philadelphia, Tenn., from Athens, Tenn., in 1847. He was a leading member of the Presbyterian church, which was located in the cemetery across the creek from and west of the town of Philadelphia. He reared a large family, eight of whom reached years of maturity and became highly respected and influential citizens. These children were:

1. Franklin, b. May 23, 1827; d. May 8, 1887.
2. Margaret, b. July 12, 1829; d. August 5, 1879; m. J. W. Goddard. (See Goddard.)
3. Newton, b. October 14, 1831; d. May 26, 1889.
4. Columbus, b. ———, 1833; d. during the war at Danville, Ind. He was a soldier in the Civil War, serving on the staff of General Spears, U. S. A.
5. Susan, b. August 21, 1836; m. W. Cannon. (See Cannons.)
6. Elizabeth, b. February 8, 1839; d. July 6, 1898.
7. Barbara, b. September 19, 1840; d. July 22, 1866. (See S. Y. B. Williams.)
8. Martha, b. January 6, 1844. Resides at Philadelphia, with her sister, Mrs. W. Cannon.
9. Mary Cornelia, b. September 26, 1845; d. Nov. 21, 1864.

1. Dr. Franklin Bogart studied medicine and settled at Tellico Plains, Tenn. On January 21, 1857, he was married (first) to Elizabeth McEwen, daughter of George and Sarah Gaines. He came to Sweetwater soon after the town was started, purchased property and practised his profession until his death. His first wife died October 8, 1873. They are both buried in the old cemetery at Sweetwater. Their children were:

(1) Thomas Cannon, d. in 1860 at the age of 3 years.
(2) Walter G., b. April 13, 1858; m. Lorella Magill, October 15, 1884. He studied medicine at Nashville and graduated in the medical department of the University of Tennessee. He is also a post graduate of Belle View Medical College of New York. He practised his profession in Sweetwater until 1888. He then went to Chattanooga and was a partner of Dr. G. C. Magee. He was Professor of Diseases of Women and Obstetrics in the Medical College at Chattanooga for twenty-one years. He was founder of the Highlands Sanatarium in that city. Lorella Magill was daughter of Jas. Magill and Lizzie Lowry and granddaughter of James L. and sister of Harrison and Robt. Lowry.

The children of W. G. and Lorella Bogart are:
Elizabeth G., m. T. C. Olney in 1910. Franklin Magill, b. at Sweetwater in March, 1888.

(3) John Newton, b. June 2, 1862, third son of F. and E. Bogart; was a graduate of the University of Tennessee and took the course in literature at Johns Hopkins University. He afterwards took a similar course at the University of Oxford, England. He was a teacher of English in the schools of New* Orleans, La., at the time of his death.

(4) Anna, b. December 20, 1864; d. February 7, 1893.

(5) William Moore, fourth son of F. and E. Bogart, was born February 27, 1867. He married Keturah M. Thompson, November 10, 1892. She is the daughter of Franklin Blevins and Gurley Thompson, of Chattanooga. Their children are Franklin Blevins, b. May 15, 1894; Martha Josephine, b. June 7, 1898, and Emma Mary, b. January 7, 1901.

W. M. B. is a practising physician at Chattanooga.

(6) Frank Augustus, b. in 1868; d. at 3 years of age.

Dr. Franklin Bogart married (second) Martha Ellen Cannon, daughter of Robert and Ann Galbraith Cannon, on October 28, 1879. She resides at Sweetwater.

3. Newton, second son of Solomon and Ann Bogart, when a young man was employed by William Lenoir and Brothers at Lenoir's, Tenn., in the early fifties, and remained with them until 1870, when he was employed by the E. T. V. & G. R. R. as master of trains, and, afterwards as superintendent. He was a director and stockholder of the East Tennessee National Bank of Knoxville, Tenn., and died possessed of a considerable fortune, a part of which he left to Loudon and Monroe counties, the interest on the amounts given to be applied yearly to the public school fund.

JOHN D. BOWMAN.

The Bowman family, as the name implies, came from England.

John D. Bowman was born in Blount County, Tenn., March 4, 1816. He was married to Susan Jackson, who was born March 5, 1820. She was the oldest child of Josiah and Mary Jackson, of Blount County. They came to Sweetwater Valley and settled near the big spring one and one-half miles south of Sweetwater, on the tract now owned by Kilpatrick. They lived there until October 1, 1857, when they moved to Texas, where he purchased land in Collins County, dying at Plano, February 27, 1852. Collins County was very sparsely settled at the time he moved there as one of the pioneers—his descendants are now prominent among a prosperous and numerous people.

The children of John D. and Susan Bowman were:
1. Mary, b. February 2, 1839; d. February 25, 1875.
2. Julia, b. February 1, 1840; d. September 5, 1868.
3. Jackson, b. November 6, 1841.
4. George, b. April 19, 1844.
5. Nancy.
6. James, and Callie, all three of whom died when children, at the Bowman place near Sweetwater, of scarlet fever in the epidemic of that disease, in the summer of 1856. They were buried in the old Jackson burying ground, in Blount County, on the Little Tennessee River.
8. Fannie, b. in 1852, m. James Florence, of Plano, Texas; had no children.

1. Mary married Wm. Lovelace. Their children were Laura, John, William, James, Ella and George.
2. Julia married Joseph Russell, of Plana, Texas, and had one child, John.
3. Jackson married Dora Dye, of Plano, whose daughter, Flora, married Edgar Wall, of Tampa, Fla., whose children were: Jack, Minnie, May and James B.
4. George W., who married Eliza McFarland, February 3, 1875, who died January 29, 1890. They had one son, J. Richard Bowman, who was born April 17, 1876. He was a lawyer a Plano, Texas, and died July 17, 1914. He was married to Edna Dilley, of Palestine, Texas, on February 1, 1911. Their children were:
Edna, b. January 22, 1879. Died October 20, 1885.
Russell, b. July 17, 1888; d. September 11, 1910.

The father of these children, J. Richard Bowman endowed a school in honor of his mother, Eliza, at Cienfuegos, Cuba.

George W. Bowman married (second) Mrs. Honaker, of Tampa, Fla.

Henry Bowman married ------. Had three children.

Rev. Thomas Brown

Was born in Rockbridge County, Virginia, December 27, 1800, and was the son of James Brown, who came to Blount County, Tenn., in 1803 or 1804. When a young man Thomas Brown went first to Bradley County, Tenn., locating at a town called Columbiana, which place does not now exist. There he followed his trade as blacksmith until he went to Kingston, Tenn. He then entered school to prepare himself for the ministry. On April 10, 1834, he married Jane N. Patton, who was the daughter of David and Elizabeth Patton, of Kingston, at which place Jane Patton was born on November 19, 1817.

Thomas Brown was ordained a minister of the Presbyterian church, September 22, 1827. He took charge of the Presbyterian churches at Kingston and Philadelphia in November, 1828, and remained with them until 1866, when, on account of ill health, he gave up the work. He preached at Sweetwater Presbyterian Church, as first pastor, in 1859-60. He died at his home near Philadelphia, April 21, 1872, and his wife died there on January 28, 1897. They are both buried at the Philadelphia cemetery.

The Rev. Thomas Brown took both the theological and literary courses at Maryville College, Maryville, Tenn.

The children of Thomas and Elizabeth Brown were:
1. Ignatius Cyprian, b. March 10, 1835; d. March 21, 1900.
2. Mary, b. March 30, 1836; d. September 29, 1837.
3. Rowena, b. July 2, 1838; d. December 9, 1908. (See T. J. Moore.)
4. William Leonidas, b. January 9, 1840.
5. Nancy, b. 1843.
6. David J., b. March 26, 1844.
7. Mary E., b. January 19, 1846; d. August 2, 1888.
8. Susannah, b. January 13, 1847; d. April 23, 1849.
9. H. Virginia.
10. Laura A.

1. Ignatius Cyprian Brown married Ruth Hamlet, of Indiana. He died at Columbus Junction, Ind. They had four children:

(1) Jennie, m. Hall. Live at Columbus Junction, Ind.
(2) W. T., is a druggist at that place.
(3) Harry L., unmarried. A pharmacist at Denver, Col.
(4) Hadley, unmarried. A physician at Okatee, Okla.

4. William Leonidas, second son of Thomas and Jane Patton Brown, was born at Kingston, Tenn., and came with his father to Monroe County in 1847. He was married to Sydney G. Hood, daughter of Parker and Amanda Torbett Hood, on February 9, 1875. She was born August 17, 1847, and died October 18, 1894.

Hon. W. L. Brown is a farmer and lives on his farm, and in the house built by his father in 1848, one mile south of Philadelphia, on the Fork Creek road. He was a member of the Forty-seventh General Assembly of Tennessee, upper house, 1891-92. He was elected justice of the peace for the Fourth District of Monroe County in 1875, and has served continuously until this time, 1916. The children of W. L. and Sydney H. Brown:

1. Clara Maude, d.
2. Cecil, m. Buena V. West. He is teacher in high school at Sweetwater, Tenn.
3. Thomas G., m. Nettie Walker in August, 1907, in Jefferson County. He is superintendent of city schools at Calumnet, Mich.
4. John P., b. 1883; m. Hazel Jones, Morristown, Tenn. He is a civil engineer.
5. Huldah.
6. Jane Sydney.
7. Lois Amanda, b. January 31, 1893; d. September 24, 1901.

Major John Calloway.

The history given below was mostly obtained from Mrs. Sarah Willson, widow of James Willson, deceased, of Niota, Tenn.

Major John Calloway came from the upper Yadkin valley, Wilkes County, N. C., where Eli and Presley Cleveland and William B. Lenoir came from. They were all descendants of King's Mountain heroes. From the purchases of land made by them in this country it is almost certain that they were in fairly comfortable circumstances when they moved from North Carolina to Tennessee.

John Calloway moved to Knox County and settled on Beaver Creek. He was sheriff of that county at one time.

When the Hiwassee District was surveyed and opened to purchase in 1820, the Clevelands and the Calloways bought numerous tracts. John Calloway was the purchaser of the northeast quarter of section 18, township 1, range 2, east. Date of sale was November 29, 1820.

Eli Cleveland and John Calloway, together, purchased entry number 365, 160 acres, the southwest quarter section 17, township 1, range 2, east. Eli Cleveland bought the southwest quarter of section 18, township 1, range 2, east. The records of the Baptist church, then constituted on Fork Creek in 1820, afterwards the Baptist church on Sweetwater Creek, near the old Eli Cleveland place, show that he was connected with that church in 1821. As to John Calloway, the church books of that church show that he joined the church by letter, in May, 1827. It is probable that he did not move to the valley until about that time. He built the first brick house that was built in the valley, if not in the county. Mrs. Willson thinks that it antedated the old Meigs residence, which stood west of the old Reagan residence, at Reagan Station. The brick house built by Calloway stood at or near the site of the Berry residence, near the Cleveland Baptist Church, two miles southwest of Philadelphia.

John Calloway was prominent in church affairs. His name was often mentioned with Snead, Fine and Cleveland, as a delegate to Baptist associations and conventions. The members of the Calloway family have records in the Baptist church in Sweetwater as follows:

John Calloway, received by letter the fourth Saturday in May, 1827.

Sarah Calloway, received by experience fourth Saturday in January, 1830.

Joseph Calloway, received by experience fourth Saturday in July, 1832.

Joseph, liberated for exhortation fourth Saturday in April, 1833.

Joseph, ordained a minister fourth Saturday in November, 1838.

Joseph, granted letter of dismission fourth Saturday in January, 1839.

Nancy Calloway (Webb), received by experience and baptism July, 1832.

Judy Ann Calloway, received by experience and baptism July, 1839.

James Calloway, received by experience and baptism fourth Saturday in July, 1839.

E. Malinda Calloway, received by experience and baptism fourth Saturday in July, 1839.

Hugh L. W. Calloway, received by experience and baptism fourth Saturday in August, 1842.

Judy Ann Calloway (Moffatt), dismissed by letter, fourth Saturday in August, 1842.

On the fourth Saturday in February, 1844, there were granted letters of dismission to Louisa Hatchett and also to John Calloway and family, viz: Sarah (his wife), Nancy Webb, Hugh L. W., Polly (Mary) McReynolds, Malinda Walker and James H. Calloway, also to colored persons (his slaves), Abraham, Pinckney, Patsy and Chloe.

John Calloway sold out to Eli Cleveland and moved to Harrisonville, Cass County, Mo., in 1842, so Mrs. Willson says. The family got their letters of dismission from the church, as above recited, in 1844, but as not infrequently happens, they sent back after them.

Thomas H. Calloway, whose father was a brother of John C., used to live with his uncle until he, John C., went to Missouri. Thos. C. became a very wealthy man and was afterwards president of the East Tennessee and Georgia Railroad.

John Calloway married Sarah Hardin, of South Carolina. Their children were:

One. Marshall, died on Sweetwater Creek.

Two. William Saunders.

Three. Hugh L. W.

Four. Joseph, d. near Springfield, Mo., in 1869.

Five. James, d. in Cass County, Mo.

Six. Nancy, lived and died in 1872, in Cass County, Mo. Married Webb.

Seven. Judy Ann, d. in Cass County, Mo.; m. Moffatt.

Eight. Mary, d. in Harrisonville, Mo., August 8, 1854; m. McReynolds.

Nine. Rebacca, d. in Harrisonville, Mo., in 1872; m. Reagan.
Ten. Malinda, d. in Lee's Summit, Mo., in 1873; m. Walker.

One. Marshall Calloway was a physician. He married Grace Meigs, a sister of Return J. Meigs. He died at the Calloway place, as above stated. They had two children: Farrar, who married Julia Castella, and Marshall, who married Caroline Kirby. They lived in Bradley County.

Two. William Saunders Calloway married Sarah Hurst, daughter of Elijah, and sister of John and Russell Hurst, of McMinn County. He was clerk of the county court of Monroe County 1832-36. He moved to McMinn County, near Riceville, Tenn., and resided there until his death. He was buried in the family cemetery on his farm. They were the parents of eleven children:

1. Marshall; 2. John; 3. William; 4. Thomas; 5. Elvira; 6. Sarah; 7. Malinda; 8. Emma; 9. Laura; 10. Cornelia; 11. Addie. Emma and Laura were twins.

1. Marshall was killed in the Civil War; m. Sarah Mayo, leaving no children.
2. John, moved to and died at Mountain Home, Idaho; m. Laura Durham, Sparta, Ga.
3. William, m. Ida, daughter of Rev. N. Goforth. Moved to Mountain Home, Idaho.
4. Thomas, d. unmarried.
5. Elvira, m. Geo. Hill (October 16, 1871, R. Snead, M. G.), who was reared at the Schultz place, near Niota. His mother was Elizabeth Lane, daughter of Isaac Lane. They went to an Indian reservation in Idaho.
6. Sallie, m. Dr. Frank Durham, of Sparta, Ga. She died at old Governor McComb's summer residence, near Milledgeville, Ga. She left two sons: Calloway and Dr. Frank Durham, both of Sparta, Ga.
7. Malinda, m. Thomas Epperson, who lives near Riceville, Tenn. Their children are: Calloway, m. ———; Charles, m. ———; Sallie, m. Wiseman, of Los Angeles, Cal.
8. Emma, m. Dennis R. Isbell, who lived near Mt. Harmony, on December 28, 1871. J. B. Kimbrough, M. G.

Their children were: John, m. Josephine Walker in Utah, and Earnest, who is a bachelor and lives at the old home in Monroe County.

9. Laura, m. Henry H. Matlock on November 14, 1870. J. B. Kimbrough, M. G. He is a farmer and lives nine miles west of Athens, Tenn. Their children are Mary, m. Henry Tittsworth, of Knoxville, Tenn., who is a conductor in the employ of the Southern Railway; they have four children: two sons and two daughters. The second child of H. H. and Laura Matlock, Sarah, m. John Thornburgh, a lawyer of Knoxville, Tenn. They have two children, a son and daughter.

10. Cornelia Calloway married W. P. Willson near Mt. Harmony. He died at Athens, Tenn., and was buried at the cemetery at Sweetwater, Tenn. They had four sons, two of whom, Frank and Robert are dead. Their son, William, married Katie Brown, of Murfreesboro, Tenn. She died. He lives at the old Doc Lane place between Niota and Reagans. Elbert, son of Cornelia and W. P. Willson, married Lucy Smith, of Oak Grove, Knox County. They live at Athens, Tenn.

11. Addie, youngest child of William Saunders and Sarah Hurst Calloway, married Robert Cooke, son of Dr. Cooke, of Madisonville, Tenn. They live in Los Angeles, Cal. They have two children: Henry, who married a daughter of Lawrence Henderson, three miles east of Madisonville, Tenn. They live in Los Angeles, Cal. Ella, second child of Robert Cooke, married ——— Rumsturm in Idaho.

Three. Joseph Calloway married Mary Willson, of Meigs County (no relative, as I understand, of the James Willson, who married Sarah McReynolds). The church history of Jos. Calloway has already been given. His children were: Mary, who married a Cunningham, and James who married Minerva, a sister of the late Hon. S. J. Martin. There were two other children but I have not been able to get their names or history.

Four. Hugh Lawson White Calloway married Caroline, daughter of Sam'l McReynolds, brother of David McReynolds, grandfather of Mrs. James Willson. They moved to Saline County, Mo., in the settling of that state. There were three children, two daughters and one son:

Sarah married in California; Potter Calloway, the son, lives in California.

Five. Nancy. Married George Webb some time previous to July, 1832, as she joined the Baptist church on Sweetwater, at that time, as Nancy Webb. Geo. Webb built the Second Presbyterian Church in Knoxville, at the corner of Prince Street and Clinch Avenue. He was buried in the churchyard there, but his remains were removed, with others, when that property was sold, and the new church built at the corner of Church Avenue and Locust Street. Mrs. Webb died in 1872, her husband many years previous. They had three children:

1. John. Never married.
2. Asenath, m. Thos. Hodge. No children.
3. Sarah, m. Dr. Logan McReynolds, son of Joseph McReynolds, Saline County, Mo., another brother of David McReynolds.

Six. Judy Ann Calloway, m. Thos. D. Moffatt, October 18, 1838, R. Snead, M. G. He was a merchant in Philadelphia, until about 1842, when he moved to Cass County, Mo. T. D. and J. A. Moffatt were the parents of three children: Sarah, m. James Woolridge, a lawyer at Harrisonville, Mo. They left a son and daughter who both died without heirs.

Seven. Mary Calloway, m. Coleman McReynolds, a young physician of Meigs County, Tenn. They moved to Harrisonville, Mo., in 1842. He died in 1852 and she August 8, 1855. They were the parents of five children:

1. Sarah, b. February 24, 1838.
2. John C., b. 1840; d. 1865.
3. David M., b. February 2, 1845.
4. Hugh, b. July 2, 1848; d. September 21, 1893.
5. Minta, b. July 2, 1848; d. March, 1871. Hugh and Minta twins.

1. Sarah, came back to Tennessee, to the Sweetwater Valley home of elder Robert Snead, on a visit to her aunt, Samantha McReynolds, who had married Mr. Snead September 17, 1852. Mrs. Snead was the daughter of Tely Jane and David McReynolds, of Selma, Ala. On the 12th of April, 1857, Sarah McR., was married to James Willson, of Mouse Creek (Niota), Tenn., and at once moved to that place. He was born in Sevier County, the son of James and Sarah Willson. He was a

successful business man and farmer. He died at his residence, near Niota, August 2, 1869. Their children were:
1. Hugh, b. June 30, 1858.
2. Robert S., b. May 6, 1860; d. October 10, 1907.
3. Ellie, b. May 17, 1862; d. June 17, 1887.
4. Mintie, b. July 5, 1864; d. July 23, 1887.
5. Sallie, b. May 10, 1866; d. August, 1869.
6. James C., b. July 7, 1869; d. September 17, 1887.

1. Hugh Willson married Carrie, daughter of Augustus P. and Dorcas Henderson Gaines, of Fork Creek Valley, on January 26, 1893. She was born October 2, 1862. (A. P. Gaines and Dorcas Henderson were married July 19, 1856.) Hugh Willson is a farmer and owns the place formerly owned by Russell Hurst, 1 and 1-4 miles southwest of Niota. He was president of the East Tennessee Farmers Convention in 1915. The children of Hugh and Carrie W. are: James Gaines, Dorcas Henderson, Mintie McReynolds and Sadie Gaines.

2. Robert Snead Willson married Lillian Boyd, of Sweetwater, November 18, 1891. She died September, 1907. He was a farmer and lived 1-4 mile from Niota. Their children were: Sarah Louise, Mary Lillian, Ellie, Mintie, Sallie and James C.

2. John C., son of Coleman McReynolds, was a soldier in the Confederate army, in Captain Forrest company of Colonel Bradford's regiment of Tennessee volunteers. He died at Abingdon, Va., in March, 1867.

3. David M. McReynolds married Laura Rice, of Athens, Tenn. He studied theology at Princeton, N. J., and was afterwards ordained a minister at Mt. Harmony, Monroe County. He was pastor of the First Baptist Church in Sweetwater in 1883-1889. He then moved to Chattanooga, and was pastor of the Central Baptist Church. He was then called to the Boise, Idaho, Baptist church where he was pastor for several years. They had no children.

4. Hugh McReynolds married Martha Rice, daughter of Wm. Rice, and sister of Laura, David McReynold's wife. He studied medicine and obtained his diploma at Jefferson Medical College, Philadelphia, Pa. He began the practice of medicine at Mouse Creek, but afterwards

moved to Chattanooga, where both he and his wife died. They had no children.

Nine. Rebecca, fourth daughter of John and Sarah Calloway, was married to Jesse Ragon. They moved to Cass County, Mo., and they both died there, he in 1873, and she in 1871. They had four children: Mary, Malinda, Nannie and Hugh.

Ten. Malinda, fifth daughter of Jno. and S. H. Calloway, married Jno. F. Walker of Fork Creek. She joined the Baptist church at Sweetwater, on the fourth Saturday in July, 1839, as E. Malinda Calloway, showing that she was not then married. She was granted a letter of dismission as Malinda Walker on the fourth Saturday in February, 1844. They moved to Cass County, Mo., where she died, leaving three children.

THE CLEVELAND FAMILY.

The Cleveland family have to their credit many illustrious names both in England and the United States. The most celebrated of these on this side of the water was Grover Cleveland, thrice a candidate for and twice elected president of the United States.

James Butler Cleveland, of Oneonta, N. Y., published a book in three parts in 1881 about the Cleveland family. We have had access to Part I and from this we glean the following information: From the year 1200 A. D. up to the present the family have spelled the name in a variety of ways, sometimes the same individual in the family spelling his name at different times in his life in more than one way. It is found spelled "Cliffland, Clyveland, Cliveland, Clieveland, Cleaveland and Cleveland; the last way was the one adopted by the members of the family who came to this state. There used also to be a "de" before the name but that was dropped when they emigrated to this country as being undemocratic. Sir Guy de Cleveland was knighted at the siege of Boulogne in ——— by King ——— and was therefore entitled to place "de" before the name and to have a coat of arms, a crest and a motto. (For description of crest and coat of arms see J. B. C.'s book about the Clevelands.) They seem to have had rather more than their share of mottoes, claiming two as belonging to them: "Pro deo et patrio," translated, "for God and country" showing them to be both a religious and a patriotic family; and another motto "semel et semper," "once and always," meaning, "once a (friend) always a (friend)" or the opposite. Both mottoes, I think, have been somewhat characteristic of the family.

For given names the Clevelands used Bible names of abstract qualities such as Faith, Hope, Perseverance, Justice, Mercy—answer to Prayer, Abigail, Sarah, Ephraim, Abraham, Benjamin, Jacob, and by no means were Joseph and his Gypsy wife, Asenath, forgotten. However I have not found in my reading about them that any of them were named either Judas or Esau; these they avoided.

The Butler Cleveland book deals mostly with that part of the Cleveland family descended from Moses Cleveland, who came to the colonies (Massachusetts) in 1635. His numerous descendants are dispersed over various states of our union. They have had many towns and counties named for them; probably had much to do with naming them themselves. The most noted of these for commercial prosperity, its Euclid Avenue and location and the most notorious as having been the home of Mark Hanna, Rockefeller and Tom Johnson is Cleveland, Ohio, on the Lakes. It is the largest city in the world named for a citizen of the United States.

The father of Benjamin and Robert Cleveland (the latter part of their lives citizens of Wilkes County, N. C.), settled probably early in 1700 in Orange County, Va. There on Bull Run Creek Robert was born. In 1736 he married Aley Mathis of Kentucky. This is a very common name among the Clevelands and their descendants. Robt. C. was twice married and was the father of 15 or 16 children. Jeremiah, one of the sons, was the grandfather of the Marietta, Ga., Clevelands.

Wheeler in History of North Carolina (page 462), has this to say of Benjamin Cleveland: "Colonel Benjamin Cleaveland, the hero of King's Mountain, and after whom Cleaveland County is called, lived and died in Wilkes County." (Cleaveland County was formed in 1841 out of Rutherford and Lincoln counties.) "He was a brave and meritorious officer. A serious impediment in his speech prevented his entering political life."

(However he was senator to the General Assembly from Wilkes County, N. C., in 1779.) "In 1875 he was appointed an ensign in the 2nd Regiment of troops and served at King's Mountain and at the Battle of Guilford Courthouse. He was also the hero of a hundred fights with the tories. He was the surveyor of Wilkes and lived at the place where Little Hickerson now (1850) resides. Some incidents of his life, dangers and daring conduct are recorded under Watauga County, their scene of action."

Captain Robt. Cleaveland was little less distinguished than his brother Benjamin. He was with his brother Benjamin in the majority of the campaigns mentioned.

Presley and Eli Cleveland were sons of Robert. In giving a sketch of Eli C. we can not do better than to quote an obituary of him written by Elder Robert Snead.

In that, though Mr. Snead did not mention it, he made a deed of gift in perpetuity to the parcel of land on which the Baptist church on Sweetwater is situated, and the gift of a cemetery lot for a public burial, or more correctly speaking, a neighborhood burial place. But for our present purpose it does not matter, for in giving a history of the Baptist on Sweetwater a copy of the deed and will as far as it pertained to those lots, are given in this book.

ELDER ELI CLEVELAND.

An obituary written by Elder Robert Snead.

Eli Cleveland was born in Wilkes County, N. C., on October 1, 1781. He was united in marriage with Polly Ragon the 28th of December, 1803. He was baptized the third Sabbath in December, 1813, and united with Baptist church in Ashe County, N. C., having obtained a hope in Christ a short time previous. Soon afterward he commenced exhorting and preaching to sinners "to flee the wrath to come."

He moved with family to Knox County, Tenn., in 1817. He was ordained to the full work of the ministry in 1818 by request of Beaver Ridge (now Brick Chapel) Church. He moved to Sweetwater Valley in 1821. He united with the church here (on Sweetwater) the fourth Saturday in January, 1822. He was chosen moderator soon after;

which office he was eminently qualified to fill and which he retained until his death. This being a newly settled country he preached much and was instrumental in building up and establishing a number of churches.

For many years he has been, at times, the subject of severe afflictions which kept him from traveling much; but he never neglected to meet with his own church and fill his place in the house of God, when his health permitted. We, who were present the last time he met with us, will long remember the earnest, warm and faithful exhortation he gave. Having lived to a good old age he died on the 23rd of November, 1859, of disease of the heart. He retained his mind to the last and died trusting in Jesus only. His motto was "Born a sinner, but saved by Grace." (Note. This is the epitaph on his tombstone.) The writer of this was with him the evening before and the morning of his death. He spoke of being fully conscious that the time of his departure was at hand. In his last conversation he said: "I shall not long be here; I have given up; I have no desire to stay here at all; this world is nothing to me. I am perfectly resigned to go at any time it is the will of God to take me. I have great reason to be thankful for His goodness towards me. My trust is altogether in Jesus, because I could not trust in anything on earth or in myself. I want you to pray for me that I may go easy, for God answers the prayers of His people.

About thirty minutes after speaking thus he fell asleep in Jesus without a groan or a struggle.

Presley Cleveland was born in Wilkes County, N. C., September 14, 1779. He died in Sweetwater Valley, May 31, 1861. He was married to Elizabeth Johnson. She was born February 17, 1792, and died November 20, 1854. These two brothers and their wives are buried in the (Cleveland) Baptist Cemetery. For history of Eli Cleveland see obituary by Elder Robt. Snead.

Eli Cleveland purchased the following tracts of land in the Hiwassee District from Matthew Nelson, treasurer of East Tennessee: northwest quarter, section 19, township 2, range 3, west, on December 2, 1820; entry number 1323, northwest quarter, section 20, township 1, range 2, east, on June 10, 1825; grant 684, September 7, 1827; entry 5145, southeast quarter, section 13, township 1, range 2, east; entry 5146, southwest quarter, section 18, township 1, range 2, east; granted 3212, dated February 13, 1838. He bought from John Calloway entry 320, southeast quarter traction, township 2, range 3, west.

The children of Eli and Polly Cleveland were:

One. Robert R. He was born September 15, 1808; d. April, 1868. He married Sydney G., daughter of Matthew Nelson, of Philadelphia, January 20, 1835. She was born July 15, 1811, and d. October 3, 1884. He was a wealthy farmer and merchant of Philadelphia, Tenn. They had one daughter, Clemintina, who married Dr. Franklin King Berry. (See Berry.)

Two. Matilda. She married John Chesnutt, son of Henry Chesnutt. They moved to Ooltewah, Tenn. Had no children.

Three. Caroline. She married Joseph Walker, of Fork Creek Valley on March 1, 1838. They had no children. (See Walker.)

Four. Jesse. Married Miss Spriggs, of Bradley County, Tenn., and lived on Candy's Creek.

Five. Eli Matthew, b. 1827; m. Emeline, daughter of Jno. Pennington, September 28, 1843. d. 1871. They had eight children, six girls and two boys. They moved to Hamilton County, near Ooltewah, Tenn., where he died three or four years after the Civil War; aged about 58 years.

Six. Aley Mathis, b. May 7, 1813; d. May 30, 1855; m. J. D. Jones, whom see.

Seven. Clarissa, b. September 6, 1815. Baptized March, 1833; d. March 11, 1880. She m. Jesse F. Jones (brother of J. D. Jones), whom see.

Eight. David H., b. November 5, 1824; d. August 10, 1900. He joined the Baptist church in August, 1842. He married first, his cousin, Elizabeth A. Johnson, daughter of Louis Johnson, July 11, 1844. R. Snead, M. G. She was b. January 5, 1827; d. December 31, 1882. She was a member of the Baptist church. They lived on his father's, Eli Cleveland's, place which Mr. Cleveland owned at the time of his death.

The children of this marriage were:
1. Jesse F., b. July 11, 1845; d. October 27, 1846.
2. Mary Katherine, b. January 4, 1847.

3. Eli, b. December 11, 1848.
4. Sydney, A.
5. Louis J., b. February 17, 1853; d. October 4, 1853.
6. Callie, b. August 17, 1854.
7. Robert Mathis, b. November 9, 1856.
8. Joseph Jones, b. November 20, 1858.
9. Eliza, May 5, 1861; d. October 1, 1862.
10. Aley, b. December 11, 1863.
11. Viola Jessamine, b. December 15, 1865.
12. Benjamin, b. December 4, 1867.

D. H. Cleveland m. Malinda Sherman (second), and their children were:

13. (1) John Sherman.
14. (2) Malinda Neil.
15. (3) Davy Grace.

2. Mary K., married Seth McKinney, son of David P. Walker, January 3, 1862. He then lived at Boiling Springs in Fork Creek Valley. In 188-- they moved to Sweetwater. Went to Sherman, Texas, in 1887. Mrs. Walker died there in April, 1906. In a communication March 14, 1916, Miss Faun Yearwood, of Knoxville, gives me as follows about the S. M. and Mary K. Walker family.

They were the parents of twelve children:
1. Jennie Anne.
2. Alice Elizabeth.
3. David Franklin (died in infancy).
4. Eliza Caroline.
5. Joseph (died in infancy).
6. Zeb McKinney.
7. Lena Ula.
8. Katherine.
9. Robert.
10. Helen (died in infancy).
11. Emmett.
12. Eugene (died in infancy).

1. Jennie A. Walker married Richard Jarnagin Yearwood, January 10, 1883. Now living in Knoxville, Tenn.

Have three children:
1. Maude, married John Staub Fouche, April 6, 1904, and have one son, John S., Jr. Live in Chattanooga, Tenn.
2. Faun, Knoxville, Tenn.
3. Richard Horace, U. S. N.
2. Alice Elizabeth Walker married John B. Montgomery, September 5, 1883. Now living in Knoxville, Tenn. Have one child:
1. Helen Louise, married Walter B. McLean, May 25, 1904, and have one daughter, Louise. Live in Knoxville, Tenn.
3. David Franklin, died in infancy.
4. Eliza Caroline.
5. Joseph, died in infancy.
6. Zeb McKinney Walker, married and lives in Sherman, Texas.
7. Lena Ula Walker married John Henry Hurst, at Bonham, Texas, February 24, 1888. Now live at Longview, Texas.
Have five children:
1. Henry Eugene Hurst, unmarried, employed by Ford Motor Co., Dallas, Texas.
2. John Russell, Longview Texas.
3. Edith Isabella, married Collie Carr Moye, January 1, 1912, and have one daughter, Edith Earline. Live in Longview, Texas.
4. Lewis, Beaumont, Texas.
5. Julian Harrison, Longview, Texas.
8. Katherine Walker, married George Blair. Now live in Sherman, Texas.
Have two children:
1. Jeff.
2. Raymond.
9. Robert Walker, married and lives in Sherman, Texas.
10. Helen Walker, died in infancy.
11. Emmett Walker, died in Philippine Islands, U. S. A., 26 years.
12. Eugene Walker, died in infancy.

3. Eli, son of D. H. Cleveland, m. Susan Martin, dau. Polly Griffitts Martin on November 22, 1881. He is a farmer owning a large tract of land about half way be-

tween Sweetwater and Philadelphia. He lives in the town of Sweetwater, where he is interested in the hardware business. The children of Eli and Susan Martin Cleveland are:

(1) Annie, b. September 4, 1882; m. Edgar Heiskell, whom see.

(2) Hulah, b. June 7, 1884; m. Horace Browder, whom see.

(3) Elizabeth, b. April 18, 1886; m. Myrtland Rollins. He is assistant city attorney of the city of St. Louis, Mo.

(4) David Martin, b. October 13, 1888. He is in the hardware business at Sweetwater.

(5) Martha Waren, b. 1890; m. Frank Dykeman Ruth. He is a manufacturer of wood veneer at Buchanan, Va.

(6) Eunice Eli.

(8) Susan Marguerite.

4. Sydney A., fourth child of D. H. Cleveland, m. Benj. F. Hudson. son of Richard Hudson. He is a farmer living in Fork Creek valley. Their children are: Eli, David, Jessie, d.; Cleo. m.; Pearl, m. Kimbrough, Ruby, m.; Garnett m.; Vanoy, m. Jessie Simpson.

5. Callie, m. James A., son of W. E. Johnson and grandson of Louis Johnson, on March 4, 1875. He was born January 31, 1849; d. February 26, 1899. He was a farmer in Pond Creek valley and afterwards moved to Sweetwater. After his death his wife and family moved to Oaksdale, Wash., March 21, 1910. Their children are:

(1) Sydney, b. September 3, 1876.

(2) David Cleveland, b. September 30, 1878.

(3) Eliza A., b. June 13, 1880; d. May 13, 1908.

(4) Maud, b. September 13, 1883; d. July 12, 1912.

(5) William E., b. June 18, 1886; d. December 13, 1886.

(6) Elizabeth, b. May 11, 1890.

(7) James A., b. March 3, 1892.

(8) Robert M., b. November 13, 1894; d. June 19, 1895.

7. Robert Mathis, was born November 9, 1856. Came to the town of Sweetwater, first as a clerk and then in the mercantile business for himself. He married Maggie Carmichael, of McMinn County, on December 7, 1884. He was an alderman of Sweetwater for many years and was mayor of the town in 1890. He was a justice of the

peace of the first civil district of Monroe for sixteen years. He moved to Chattanooga in 1902, where he engaged in the retail grocery business until his death. His widow resides at 110 Findlay Street, Chattanooga. Their children were:

Frances, b. December 8, 1886; m. J. Rollins, newspaper man, June 11, 1908.

Sammie, b. January 5, 1889.

Alena, b. January, 1891; m. O. L. Holt, a manufacturer, Chattanooga, August 17, 1911.

Robert Mathis, b. November 13, 1900.

8. Joseph Jones, b. November 20, 1858; m. Sallie, daughter of Hon. W. H. Turley, of McMinn County, June 28, 1882. They lived in McMinn County, where his first wife died. He went to Hamilton, Texas, in September, 1886. There he married (second) Irene Perry on April 23, 1887. He is a school teacher. Their children are:

(1) Geo. G., b. April 17, 1888; m. Fay Reid, Henrietta, Texas, April 13, 1913. Farmer.

(2) Joe J., Jr., b. June 9, 1890. Assistant cashier Hamilton National Bank, Hamilton, Texas.

(3) Charles C., b. August 18, 1894. Student Baylor Medical College, Dallas, Texas.

10. Aley, m. William Jones, son of Joshua Jones, of South Carolina, May 27, 1881. Their children are: (1) Alex., m.; (2) Rhea; (3) Ophelia; (4) Sydney; (5) Frank; (6) Ole; (7) Pearl; (8) ———

11. Viola Jessamine, m. R. L. Carter July 1, 1886. He was born January, 1859. Children:

(1) Matt, m. Nannie Martin, of Chattanooga, April 27, 1914. He is a bank employee there.

(2) Bess.

(3) Clifford, in the produce business with his father at Sweetwater.

(4) Bland L., m. Alan B. DeArmond October, 1915. Reside at Athens, Tenn.

(5) Robert L., Jr.

(6) Gladys.

(7) Fred.

12. Benjamin, the twelfth child of D. H. and Elizabeth Johnson Cleveland, was born December 4, 1867. He went to Spokane, Wash., where he married.

David H. Cleveland married (second) Malinda Neil, daughter of John Sherman, of Niota, Tenn. She was at that time the widow of Bart Forrest. Their children:

(13) John Sherman, b. October 28, 1885; d. September 26, 1891.

(14) Malinda Neil, b. February 4, 1888; m. J. Gid. Johnson November 10, 1910. He is a farmer and is also engaged in the jewelry business at Sweetwater. They have one child, J. Gid, Jr., b. May 17, 1913.

(15) Davy Grace, b. August 29, 1890; m. G. W. Fallin, of Fort Worth, Texas, on December 23, 1913.

Presley Cleveland

Was born in Wilkes County, N. C., September 16, 1779; he was the son of Captain Robert Cleveland and the brother of Eli Cleveland. He died in Sweetwater Valley May 31, 1861. His wife was Elizabeth, the sister of Louis Johnson. She was born February 17, 1792, and died November 30, 1854. They were both members of the Baptist church on Sweetwater and were buried in the cemetery near that place.

Presley Cleveland was a farmer and acquired lands as follows: 370 acres from the State, the northeast and northwest quarters of section 24, township 1, range 1, east, and 50 bought of Jno. Pennington, south side of southeast quarter sec. 13, township 1, range 1, east.

The children of Presley and Elizabeth Cleveland were:

One. Robert, d. August, 1854.

Two. Aley, b. October 14, 1816; d. November 3, 1824.

Three. William, b. October 11, 1820; d. August 22, 1835.

Four. Eliza Ann, d. 1911.

Five. Larkin, b. 1825.

Six. Caroline, b. November 25, 1827; d. November 10, 1896.

Seven. Harvey H., b. March 18, 1830; d. September 25, 1854.

One. Robert, m. Elizabeth Snead, daughter of Robert Snead, on June 4, 1840. They moved to Bradley County, Tenn., where he died and was buried. His widow came back to Sweetwater Valley and lived for some years across the creek from the Robert Snead residence. She

Children of Wm. and Mary Cleveland

Corrections, p. 107

(1) Addie V. b. Mch. 6, 1868; m. Mark L. Hardin, Aug 16, 1892, d. Jan'y. 10, 1895.
(2) Charles d. infant. (3) Ora, (4) Julia.
(5) Edgar, b. June 3, 1876; m. Julia Ballard, dau. W. L. B., Nov. 16, 1911. Two children, Wm. B. b. Dec. 26, 1913 and Marg. Frances, b. Nov. 21, 1915. E. C. is farmer in Sweetwater Valley.
(6) William, b. Aug. 25, 1879; m. Myrtle Laycock, Oct.5, 1904. d. Oct. 10, 1909.
(7) Henry b. Mch. 8, 1882; m. Jennie Burk, of Sherman, Tex., Dec. 30, 1907. Farmer in Sweetwater Valley.
(8) Ellis, b. Nov. 5, 1886. Moved to Olustee, Okla. m. in Mch. 1918

died July 27, 1875, and was buried at the old Sweetwater cemetery. She was a member of the Baptist church. The children of Robert and Elizabeth Cleveland were:
1. William, b. April 9, 1843. He served in the Confederate army during the Civil War; was a member of the Methodist Church, South. He was a progressive farmer and lived on the Athens road one and one-half miles south of Sweetwater. He died February 10, 1902, and was buried in old Sweetwater cemetery. He married Mary F., daughter of J. J. Browder, on June 24, 1867. Their children were:

(1) Addie V., b. March 6, 1868; m. Mark L. Harden, August 16, 1892; d. January 10, 1895.

(2) William, b. August 25, 1879; m. Myrtle Laycock October 5, 1904; d. October 10, 1909.

(3) Henry, b. March 8, 1882; m. Jennie Burk, of Sherman, Tex., December 30, 1907. He is a farmer in Sweetwater Valley.

(4) Ellis, b. November 5, 1886. Moved to Olustee, Okla., where he now (1916) lives.

(5) Ora.

(6) Julia.

2. Presley, second son of Robert and Elizabeth Snead Cleveland, was born in Bradley County, Tenn., January 28, 1845. He married Belle Bryant in McMinn County July 4, 1867. She was the daughter of Ellis and the sister of Louis Bryant. They moved to Gentry County, Mo., in 1877. He is a farmer. His address is Albany, Mo. He and his wife are members of the Baptist church. Their children were:

(1) James H., b. in McMinn County, April 24, 1868.

(2) William, b. November 11, 1871; d. February 6, 1901.

(3) Mary E., b. October 15, 1874, in Monroe County, Tenn.

(4) Allison B., b. February 16, 1868.

(5) Annie, b. November 1, 1880.

(6) Allie V., b. August 24, 1882.

Four of these children live in Gentry County, Mo. (3) Mary E. lives in Clarkston, Wash.

3. Mary E. aunt of above Mary E., sister of Wm. and Presley Cleveland married Horace F., son of Francis A. Patton, whom see.

4. Robert, third son of R. and E. Cleveland was b. in 1852. He m. Georgetta Martin nee Wallace and lives at Blue Spring, Tenn.

Four. Eliza Ann m. William E. Johnson. He was a farmer and resided on Pond Creek just above old Osborne (Dyche) farm. They were the parents of four children.

Five. Larkin Cleveland, b. in 1825; m. Minerva Parker. They reared a large family. Seven of them went west. Of their history little is known. Nannie m. John Rausin and lives in Oregon. Alfred married and lives in Missouri; Cordie and Eliza are married; names of husbands and residences not known.

Six. Caroline, third daughter of Presley and Elizabeth Johnson Cleveland. married Samuel Jesse Martin October 24, 1859. He was the son of S. J. and Polly Ragon Martin. His father and mother both died when he and his younger brother, Charles B. were quite young. They were taken and reared by their kinsman, Elder Eli Cleveland. When about 15 years of age Jesse went to Hamilton County, Tenn.. and lived four or five years with John Chesnutt, husband of Matilda Cleveland. He there learned the carpenter's trade and returned to Eli Cleveland's. He was the first layman to be moderator of the Baptist church on Sweetwater, and also the first layman to be moderator of the Sweetwater Baptist Association. He was a popular man with the people and was elected joint representative of Loudon and Monroe counties to the Thirty-eighth General Assembly of Tennessee, over H. A. Chambers, Democrat, in November, 1872. His children were:

(1) Sallie, b. July 15, 1861; d. May 27, 1879; m. Pryor, son of Humphrey Schultz, of Niota, Tenn., February 16, 1886. They had two children.

(2) Carrie Belle, m. Geo. Cline, son of Geo. Cline, works with Knoxville Traction Co.

(3) Samuel, b. October 22, 1862; m. Amanda Patton, of Cumberland County, Tenn., January 21, 1892. She was the daughter of John Patton who lives nine miles northeast of Crossville, Tenn. Samuel M. is a farmer and civil engineer. Their children are: Jesse, Charles, Luther, Scott, Lucille, Beatrice, Zirkle, ————, McClain and Winona.

Charles B. Martin, younger brother of Samuel J. was educated for the ministry, mostly by Elder Eli Cleveland, assisted partially by the Baptist church on Sweetwater Creek. When he was about 21 years old, in about 1856, he went to Van Buren County, Mo.

Seven. Harvey H., fourth son of Presley and Elizabeth Johnson Cleveland, married Mary Ann, daughter of John and Alpha Pennington, in March,1854. He died about six months afterwards, September 25, probably of cholera.

THE CANNONS.

John Cannon was born in Caswell County, N. C., on March 18, 1744, and died in Grassy Valley, Knox County, Tenn., in October, 1906. He was the son of William Cannon who first lived in Cumberland County, Virginia, and then moved to Caswell County, N. C. The wife of John Cannon was Ann Whitlow, who was born in North Carolina on November 18, 1747. She died in Knox County, Tenn., on July 1, 1830. John Cannon moved from North Carolina to Sevier County, Tenn., some time before 1795, when he came to Knox County, Tenn. He had three sons, William, John and Robert, and one daughter, Cynthia. Cynthia married M. C. Rogers. She died at Huntsville, Texas, November 24, 1855. Robert Cannon was born September 30, 1781, in Sevier County. He died at his residence in Roane (now Loudon) county, between Loudon and Philadelphia, on August 21, 1854. Ann Galbraith, wife of Robert Cannon, was born July 15, 1792, in Knox County. She died April 29, 1859. They are said to have eloped, when they married in 1812, and located in Roane County (now Loudon), on what is known as the old Matlock farm near Lenoir City, Tenn. Their children were:

1. Evaline, b. August 5, 1813; d. of yellow fever Huntsville, Texas, about 1854.
2. John G., b. 1815; d. December 21, 1827.
3. Louisa, b. April 16, 1819; d. at Philadelphia, Tenn., September 13, 1894.
4. Elizabeth Martin, b. June 11, 1822; d. in Indiana. (See Moore.)
5. William, b. November 10, 1824; d. Feb. 2, 1897.
6. Charles, b. ———, 1826; d. June 26, 1888.

7. Sydney Ann, b. April 19, 1830; d. July 21, 1854. (See J. W. Clark.)

8. Martha Ellen, b. April 25, 1833. (See Solomon Bogart.)

Of the above Cannon children the first three, Evaline, John and Louisa were born at the Matlock place, near Lenoir City, and the others were born at the Cannon place near Philadelphia, Tenn.

1. Evaline Cannon married Henderson Yoakum, the historian of Texas and a lawyer of Huntsville, Texas, in 1832. Their children were:

(1) Elizabeth, b. at Murfreesboro, Tenn., in 1832; m. ———— Campbell, a lawyer at Huntsville, Texas. She died at Los Angeles, Cal., leaving one son, who resides at Los Angeles.

(2) Martha, d. in infancy.

(3) Mary, married ————

(4) Annie, d. April, 1871, at Springfield, Texas. Unmarried.

(5) Robert, lives at San Marcos, Texas.

(6) Houston, b. 1858; married; d. San Marcos, Tex., about 1912.

(7) Henderson, d. in youth.

3. Louisa, third child of Robert and Ann Cannon, married (first) Laurence, son of Mathew Nelson, in 1834. After his death she married (second) James Chesnut. He was born April 5, 1808. He died of cholera July 31, 1854. She married (third) Joseph D. Jones, on December 6, 1861. (See J. D. Jones.)

5. William, fifth child of Robert and Ann Cannon, married Susan Bogart, daughter of Solomon and Ann Moore Bogart, on February 28, 1856. She was born at Athens, Tenn., October 21, 1836. Their children were:

(1) Robert Newton, b. December 28, 1856; d. at Philadelphia, Tenn., March 28, 1898. He was a grain broker and land owner at Paullina, Iowa, for a number of years before his death.

(2) Frank, b. October 27, 1859; d. March 28, 1894.

(3) Charles Columbus, b. January 28, 1862; m. Grace Jennings at Paullina, Iowa, on ———— 18—. Their children were: William, b. ———— d. ————; Susan, b. ————190 ; Margaret Bogart, b. October 4, 1902; Mary Matilda, b. May 15, 1908, and d.—

(4) Willie, b. January 10, 1865; d. October 8, 1867.
(5) Annie Yoakum, b. May 21, 1868. (See W. F. Lenoir.)
(6) Mary Louisa, b. June 18, 1871. She married Joseph M. Logan, son of the late Judge S. T. Logan, of Knoxville, Tenn., on July 22, 1897. Their children are: Maria Louise, born at the old Cannon place, Meadowbrook, near Philadelphia, on October 6, 1898, and Josephine, born at Knoxville, Tenn., March 9, 1908.
(7) Arthur Bogart Cannon married Julia Clark Thomas at Nashville, Tenn., on December 29, 1908. Their children were: Elizabeth, b. October 25, 1909; Sarah, b. August 12, 1912; d. ------ 191 ; and Arthur Bogart, b. February 3, 1916.

6. Charles, second son of Robert and Ann Galbraith Cannon was born at the old Cannon place near Philadelphia. He was married (first) to Lodusky Caroline, daughter of J. D. and Aley Cleveland Jones, on February 11, 1852. They moved from Philadelphia to the Fine place near Sweetwater, in 1859. Their children were:

(1) Mary Alice, b. January 20, 1854. She married Joseph H. Bean, of Knoxville, on November 26, 1890. He was born in Monroe County, September 15, 1853. He learned the printers trade in Knoxville; he was editor and proprietor of the Monroe Democrat, a weekly published in Sweetwater, from January, 1876 to January, 1890; he was manager and proprietor of the Knoxville Tribune, a daily paper published in Knoxville, from 1890 to 1892. He is now a member of the firm of Bean, Warters and Company, printers, bookbinders and stationers, at 706 Gay Street, Knoxville Tenn. The children of J. H. and Alice Bean are: Helen Lodusky, b. May 21, 1892; m. Geo. Rogers, teacher, of Charleston, S. C.; they reside at Charleston, S. C.; Alice, b. November 24, 1893.

(2) William C., son of Charles Caroline Cannon, was born February 4, 1860. He married Annie Mildred, daughter of Eli S. Adkins, on ------, 1890. She was born April 26, 1866. They have one daughter, Louise, born July, 189 . William C. Cannon lives at Philadelphia in the old home of his grandfather, J. D. Jones.

Charles Cannon married (second) Helen Graham, of

Pond Creek Valley, on December 17, 1868. Their children were:

(1) Martha Bland, who married David Carter Young on December 14, 1897. He was born August 18, 1865, the son of the Rev. Jas. N. and Sarah Carter Young. He attended school at Roane and Sweetwater colleges and studied law while teaching school. He was a law partner of his brother, Colonel Sam Epps Young, at Sweetwater, from 1888 to 1911. He is at present practising law at Sweetwater. He is also a farmer, real estate owner and dairyman. He is a member and elder of the Presbyterian church and has been Sunday-school superintendent. Their children are: David Graham, b. August 27, 1900; Helen Graham, b. May 6, 1904; Bland Elizabeth, b. December 10, 1906, and Sarah Louise, b. July 22, 1910.

(2) Sue Graham, second daughter of Chas. and Helen Cannon, married S. J. Pickel. (See Pickel.)

(3) Louise Caroline, third daughter of Chas. and Helen Cannon, married Everett Grace, son of the Rev. W. C. Grace, former pastor of the Baptist church at Sweetwater. He was born September 9, 1873. He is a broker at Birmingham, Ala.

(4) Ann Elizabeth, fourth daughter of Chas. and Helen Cannon, married Jno. F. Hargrove, of Fork Creek valley. He is a merchant at Robbins, Tenn.

(5) Ida Clark, youngest daughter of Chas. and Helen Cannon, married A. J. Binzel, trainmaster of the L. & N. Railroad at Knoxville, Tenn. Their children are Catherine and Alvin John.

DAVID BURTON CHILDRESS

Was born in Sullivan County, Tenn., April 14, 1831, the son of Finley Childress. His mother was Betsey Perry, a direct descendant of Commodore O. H. Perry. David Burton Childress came to Athens, Tenn., in 1857, where he clerked there for A. McKeldin. He married Miss Mary Jones on December 20, 1860. She was an older sister of Mrs. James M. Heiskell. She was born in Wilmington, N. C., May 11, 1841. They came to Sweetwater in 1865. He engaged in the general mercantile business with W. B. McKeldin as partner, for a year or two, when the partnership was dissolved, Mr. McKeldin returning to his former home at Athens. Mr. Childress remained in business until a short time before his death which occurred November 21, 1887. Some of the clerks for D. B. Childress were Hugh M. McKeldin, Sam Scott, R. E. Magill, Millard Hudson and J. H. Dickey, all successful business men afterward. For history of R. E. Magill see "Magill Family Record," page 103, by Robert Magill, Publisher, Richmond, Va. History of J. H. Dickey see Goddard, this book.

He was interred in the old Sweetwater cemetery. He first lived in the house now owned by S. H. Sharp. On April 5, 1873, he bought 15 1-2 acres, now the property of Mrs. J. R. Love, on the Athens road, and built and moved there. He was both mayor and an alderman of Sweetwater a number of times. The children of Mary and D. B. Childress were:

1. Samuella, b. June 14, 1862. She married James I. Carter on December 27, 1881. He was born January 11, 1858, the son of John G. Carter, of Charleston, Tenn. He was in business with J. H. Patton for several years, then a merchant in Sweetwater in partnership with his brother, John Carter, until about 1884, when he went to Chicago, where he was a member of the Board of Trade. He is now a capitalist in Chattanooga, with a city residence on Bluff View and a summer residence near the incline on Lookout Mountain.

The children of J. I. and Samuella Carter are:

(1) John Garnett, b. February 9, 1883. He m. Frieda Utermoehlen, a musical composer.

(2) Mary Lynn, b. April 7, 1885.

(3) Paul Burton, b. February 10, 1888. He is in business with his father.

(4) Lucille, b. August 30, 1891; m. James Glasscock, now with Proctor & Gamble, at Cleveland, O.

(5) Doris Inman, b. March 3, 1900.

2. Laura Edna, second daughter of D. B. and Mary Childress, b. January 18, 1868. She was married October 12, 1887 to L. P. Thatcher, wholesale grocer, of Chattanooga. He died in 1906. Their children were:

(1) Burton Craighead, b. 1888.
(2) Samuel Eugene.
(3) Hugh Lynn.

(4) Elizabeth.
(5) Louis P.
(7) and (8) Wendell and Laurette, twins.
(9) Kenneth.
(10) Douglas, about 10 years old. These are all living; the sixth child, Justis is dead.

3. Hugh Lynn, b. January 28, 1870; d. February 4, 1898. He was an expert telegrapher and fine business man. When he was 27 years of age he was superintendent of the southern division of the Postal Telegraph Company, the youngest in the service.

4. Berta, b. September 23, 1872. She m. David Rankin, of Chattanooga, June 23, 1896. She d. October 2, 1897.

5. Nellie Elizabeth, b. August 12, 1875; m. I. N. Steely, a lawyer of Williamsburg, Ky., on May 21, 1908. Children, three: (1) Hugh Childress; (2) Joe Francis; (3) Garnett Carter.

6. James Finley (John), b. May 22, 1878; m. Lyda Boykin at Chattanooga, on June 17, 1903. One child, Margaret Evelyn. He is a druggist in Sweetwater.

7. Annie Ellen, youngest child of D. B. and Mary Childress, b. April 2, 1884, m. to Samuel E. Johnson, at Sweetwater on December 27, 1905. Four children: (1) Nellie Elizabeth; (2) Samuel G.; (3) Lynn Cannon and Mary Childress.

JAMES COOPER.

Lived on Mrs. Mira A. Reagan's place, one-half mile south of I. T. Lenoir's residence, for probably as much as twenty years, from about 1840 to some time in the early sixties. My information as to the family is somewhat meager. What is given about them merely is as I remember it. James Cooper, I think, was twice married. Name of first wife unknown to me. The children of the first wife that I remember were: Washington, Patsy, Jane, David and James. He married, second, Miss West. Their children were: Cannon, Wesley, Levi, Nick and Joseph and two daughters, ——— and ———, Washington joined the Confederate army, I think Rowan's company, and was killed, soon after the commencement of the war, in the Cumberland mountains. Patsy married Matthew McGuire on December 21, 1858. Levi married Ellen Hayes December 31, 1878. Washington, the oldest child of the first marriage was born about 1838-9. Cannon, the oldest child of the second marriage was probably born about 1850. Joseph Cooper is a conductor on the street railway at Knoxville.

ABRAM WHITENACK COZART

Was born near Harrodsburg, Ky., on February 11, 1822, and died at Columbus, Ga., on February 20, 1889. He was buried at Philadelphia, Tenn., with other members of his family. He was first married to Julia A. Caldwell in Monroe County, Ga., in about 1847. Their children were:
1. Joseph H., b. about 1848 in Macon, Ga. He married February 13, 1870, Addie, daughter of George Montgomery Cuson, near Philadelphia. He died near Waukomis, Okla., leaving several children, who reside there.
2. Mattie, who married (first) the Rev. Joseph McGhee. They had one son, Joseph L. McGhee, Ph. D. (Johns Hopkins University), who is now professor of chemistry in the Southwestern University at Georgetown, Texas. She m. (second) B. E. Tallent.
3. Jacob Abner, m. Belle Snavely of Virginia. They live at Bridgeport, Sask., Canada.
4. David, died near Philadelphia, in early manhood. He was a medical student. The children of A. W. and Julia A. Cozart were, I think, all born in Georgia.

Julie A. Cozart died August 16, 1854, near Philadelphia, Tenn., to which place A. W. Cozart had moved a short time previous. After her death he married her sister, Martha G. Caldwell, who was born September 28, 1827. She died in Georgia January 2, 1899, and was buried at Philadelphia. Their children, who were born at the old home one mile east of Philadelphia, were:

(1) Samuel, who married Mary Wilson. Died at Colorado Springs, Col.
(2) Hugh Walker, unmarried and lives at Pocatello, Idaho.
(3) Hattie, m. Joseph Gates, Manatee, Fla.
(4) John, m. Addie Caldwell, of Knoxville. Resides at Knoxville, Tenn.

(5) Linneaus, died at Atlanta, Ga., in early manhood. Buried in Philadelphia.

(6) Abram Whitenack, b. June 14, 1870; m. Susan, daughter of Judge Brown, of Columbus, Ga. He lives at Columbus, Ga., where he practices law, and has served as judge of one of the courts.

History says there was once a man whose name was Andrew Smith and he took as a wife Miss Ellen Seater. He settled or temporarily resided in Orkney Isles; for there on the Mainland, the largest of the group, a son of his and hers first saw the light of day or possibly more correctly the fogs of the north sea. This son was born on the 20th of May, 1797, at Kirkwall. They searched diligently for a name for him and finally settled on John; not Ian, but just plain John without any frills to it. And why not John? There were John the Baptist, and John Knox, the Presbyterian, John the beloved disciple, and King John of Magna Charta fame and a host of other distinguished Johns. Anyhow if there was anything wrong with his being saddled with the name of John Smith and being born in the Orkneys John was not to blame for it; he couldn't help it. He was not obliged to stay there however, and when he grew to manhood he moved about as far away from there as he could.

The Orkneys are among the bleakest lands in the habitable parts of the globe. A frith separates them from the northernmost point of Scotia or the "land's end" or the "ultima thule" of the Romans; not a great ways north of them are the Shetland Isles, and like these islands they raise barley, ponies and rough and hardy breed of cattle. In the Orkneys there are nine months of winter and three months of rather cool weather; though in those three months of so-called summer the sun shines most of the time. The hills and cliffs around Kirkwall are about the same elevation above sea level as the depot at Sweetwater. Hoy, west of Mainland Isle, is a horneblende, Gnessoid islet rising sheer out of the sea to a height of more than 1,500 feet. On this uninhabitable, intractable rock the intense cold produces no impression and the storm king and the mad waves of the north sea beat in vain. In summer from the towering cliffs of these islets the sunsets and the starry nights are beyond compare. Formerly before the European war no wealthy Britisher's life was complete without a yatching trip to the north of Scotland.

Are there flowers there? We would think so; because the great Creator in some way has rendered beautiful and attractive the most barren and inaccessible parts of the earth, the coldest and hottest. The edelweis blooms amid Alpine snows; the acacia waves her yellow hair in Arabian sands, the cactus sheds its perfume in the rainless tracts of Arizona; gems sparkle in the fathomless depths of ocean.

This contention with the forces of nature on such shores as the Orkneys has given to the Scotch thus renders life in most climes easy. What chance would an Otaheite islander or a tropically reared man have against a descendant of the McGregors or a Scottish highlander with equal conditions. For the Scot it would be like taking candy from a baby.

What time John Smith came to Scotland proper we are not informed. He undoubtedly must have received his ministerial education there.

At the age of 29 he was married to Mary Bland, of Dumfries, on April 4, 1826. She was born July, 1808. She was the daughter of Robert Bland and Mary McGregor. Soon after marriage he was sent as a missionary to China: to what particular part is now not known. From the dates of his childrens' birth and where born he could not possibly have remained very long in China. We give the history as furnished us by Mrs. Bland Clark:

Robert Andrew Tomlinson, born at Malacca January 17, 1827. Helen Margaret, born at Malacca September 22, 1828. Mary Ann Aldersey, born off the coast of the isle of St. Helena, December 10, 1829. James Henry, born at Montreal, Canada, November 30, 1831. Bland Elizabeth (Mrs. Clark) born at Kingston, Canada, February 6, 1834. These were the children of the first wife.

He married (second) Elizabeth Bland, a sister of his first wife (Mary Bland), in Canada on August 9, 1835. She was born at Dumfries, Scotland, October 30, 1800. Her children were:

Wm. Henry. b. at Brockville, Canada, July 9, 1837; d. in infancy.

Jane Isabel, b. at Brockville, on September 30, 1838. Angeline Henrietta, b. at Union Village, N. Y., February 16, 1840. Wm. Henry (2), born at Troy, September 28, 1843. Caroline Emily Hutchinson (afterward Mrs. Buell), b. at Troy, N. Y., September 23, 1845.

There were some peculiar circumstances connected with this Smith family. That having a family he should traverse the oceans to Malacca and then to China, returning to Malacca and back again to England or Scotland and thence to the British dominions in North America soon after. He made the voyage to British Isles from Malacca in 1829, as evidenced by the birth of one of his children off the coast of St. Helena. That also shows that he did not go direct from Asia to Canada, for in that case he would not have gone from the Cape of Good Hope by St. Helena, made historic as the prison of the great Napoleon. This was at a time when the canal on the isthmus of Suez had scarcely been conceived. It was some voyage then in a slow sailing vessel especially when buffeted by contrary winds. I assume also that John reared on the brink of a tempestuous ocean did not dread the waves and was never sick at sea or he would not have spent so much of his time on ships. Yet with the best accommodations then obtainable it was hard on the youthful mother of three children, she being twenty-one and a half years old and the eldest child less than three.

He married two daughters of Robert Bland and Mary McGregor. One he married when she was 18 years of age and the other (the second wife) when she was 35 years old. His first wife was also eight years the younger of the two. Each was the mother of five children. He was born in the land of the diminutive shetland pony, two of his children in the region of the mighty elephant; one on the high seas, one in Montreal and one in Kingston, Canada. These were the children of the first wife. The five children of the second wife were born as follows: Two were born at Brockville, Canada, one at Union Village, N. Y., and two at Troy, N. Y. To three of the children were given the name of Henry: one James Henry and two William Henry, the first William Henry dying in infancy. We infer from this that either John or his wives were very partial to the name of Henry but did not care to perpetuate the name of John; he had had enough of it. Mrs. Clark says too that though the grandchildren and great grandchildren are very numerous that not one of them living bears the surname of Smith.

Also when once his children left the place of their nativity, which they usually did early in life, none returned to reside, like Roderick Dhu, on their native heath and very rarely set foot on it. His descendants are dispersed from Canada to Brazil and not a Smith among them to perpetuate the name. There are however a few Smiths left in New York City, so the directory says.

Mrs. Helen Margaret Cooke.

I take this from the Chattanooga Times of December 5, 1915.

"Kirkwall is a little place with about 4,000 inhabitants in the island county of Orkney. Its location may be fixed in the minds of the reader by the statement of the fact that it is between 20 and 30 miles north of the famous 'John O. Groats', the most northern point of Scotland. Because of its commodious harbor, in which can be held hundreds of vessels, and on account of the fact the harbor space is not occupied, it is used by the British as the most available place for the internment of detained United States ships. This has given it a prominence it might not otherwise have obtained."

"It is of interest to note that Kirkwall and its surroundings furnish one of the most interesting places in the world for sightseeing. History and tradition combine to trace the civilization and architecture back to the times of Scandinavian supremacy. The castle, palace and cathedral are buildings of remarkable interest and the scenery of the surrounding country is described as beautiful."

The springs and creek which supply the waters that flow through our town and by a thousand devious channels for thousands of miles find their way to the Gulf of Mexico. And are they lost there? By no means. Warmed by the suns of Yucatan they become part of the Gulf Stream, the mightiest water course on our globe—mightier even than the Bosphorus that empties from the Black Sea into the Mediterranian and the former affording ten times the volume of the Mississippi. This, the Gulf Stream, sweeps northeasterly in its irresistible flow and tempers the climate of many lands. It renders habitable the Orkneys and blesses wherever it goes. Thus one part of the world gets its food, its climate, its civilization and often even its religion from another part. "Am I (not) my brother's Keeper?"

"And east is east and west is west and never the twain shall meet, Till earth and sky stand presently at God's great judgment seat." A very pretty jingle, Mr. Kipling, but is it true? No, though we should endeavor to isolate ourselves on an uncharted isle of the Pacific, soon or late some ship would come our way and insist on knowing what we were there for.

Mr. Smith was educated at Oxford, England; was a teacher and preacher and was possessed of a magnificent library.

Mrs. Cook was born in Malacca and "Little Ellen," as her mother called her, sojourned some months in Singapore, Asia, traversed two oceans, lived in Montreal, Kingston, Brockville, and Bath in Canada, Troy and Union Village in New York, Selma, Ala., Athens, Cleveland and Sweetwater, Tenn., and Fort Valley, Ga., and also in Florida. There she spent her last days.

With these advantages of parentage and education and being associated with the best people in many sections and being a bright and attractive woman one can well conceive what her influence in life must have been.

She came south to Selma, Ala., about 1850. She m. there Professor H. G. Cooke, a teacher of music on the violin and piano. They came to Athens, Tenn., probably in 1853. She taught there a private school till the fall of 1856. She taught also at Cleveland, Tenn., in 1857. At Athens Mrs. Julia R. Love, Mrs. D. B. Childress and Mrs. S. J. A. Frazier were among the number of her pupils.

In 1858 she came to Sweetwater and became the principal of the girls' school in the Union Institute, now the Baptist Seminary. She taught in this building until the schools were closed on account of the occupation of this section by the Federal troops.

She was intensely southern in feelings. She always was very partial to the southern people and the climate of the south and the majority of her friends were in this section of the country. During the war she hesitated not to express her opinions and even her husband, a former Massachusetts man, was also a southern sympathizer. She entertained General John H. Morgan on one of his raids through this country. For this or more probably because she was under accusation of giving information to the "rebels" through a secret, then termed an "underground mail system," she was sent through the lines, by whose order I am not informed. She finally reached Fort Valley, Ga., where the family of Sterling Neil "refugeed" when the Federal troops occupied this valley. Stella Neil, now Mrs. J. C. Slappy, had been a pupil of hers at Sweetwater.

Before the Civil War she contracted for lot No. 127, bounded by High, Morris, Church and Walnut streets, adjoining the Union Institute lot 126 and built a residence thereon. The street between the two lots has since been closed by the town authorities.

Some time after the war she returned to her home in Sweetwater. She had a small building erected on her own lot and taught a private school there. These buildings now have both been removed or torn down.

She also taught a school in the lower floor of the Masonic Hall then occupying the site of the Methodist Episcopal Church, South.

She moved to Bridgeport, Florida, ———— ————. She died there on May 13, 1896.

Mrs. Cooke in her teaching strenuously insisted on thoroughness, industry and obedience to rules. Being such an indefatigable worker herself she could not tolerate a lazy pupil. Yet she was patience personified when the scholar was dull but really trying to learn. She was a strict disciplinarian and though firm she was always kind and managed to gain not only the respect but love of her pupils. I have heard many of them, most of whom are now passed away, express a devout thankfulness that they were taught by Mrs. Cooke.

She turned out many who were afterward teachers, both in the academical and musical departments. Few indeed were there of her pupils who were not well grounded in the "three R's" and numerous ones were shining lights in the higher branches. She taught nearly everything but domestic science; this her girls were expected to learn at home so far as they could.

She was a member of the Presbyterian church and owing to her disposition never neglected church or Sunday-school duties.

William did you mean it? "Mean what," said the shade of the immortal Shakspear? "what you said about the evil that men do lives after them, the good is oft interred with their bones."

* * * * *

"Get thee to a sanitarium, you mast fed East Tennesseean, you, I'm not answering fool question today; but this I will say, a part of it I meant and a part I didn't. Take your choice. Good-bye."

"William, sorry I disturbed you, take a rest and a coca cola for your nerves."

Now there may be those who may have minds sceptically inclined. They may refuse to believe that I called his spirit up at all from the—the vastly deep—as the Sweetwater telephone thitherward is not in working order—and if I did call, there was no answer or if there was an answer it was not Shakspear but his stenographer that answered. Again the language attributed to him is not Shakspearian and he had no knowledge that East Tennesseeans fed on acorns like the Druids of old.

But you can have it your own way; take it or leave it; I'm agreeable. I am about to give you the contents of a paper showing that the good Mrs. Cooke did live after her and that her soul is "marching on" but not in the John Brown direction, which is bad for John B.

The paper to which I refer was compiled and written by Miss Miranda E. Yearwood for the H. M. Cooke Memorial Library some time this year (1915). It is very highly interesting and instructive and almost a complete history of the library movement in the town of Sweetwater and surrounding country. That the town sorely needed a library goes without saying. Read her article, ye moneyed men and women, and loosen up your purse strings! And do not wait till you are worth a million to do it, but help endow the library so that it will not have a hand to mouth existence year after year.

Right here permit me to say, whether pertinent or not, if any one, after reading Miss Yearwood's paper, is bold enough to assert that the women of the first civil district of Monroe County have not sufficient intelligence and principle to transact business and cast the ballot, I would like for him to come forth and exhibit himself.

True the ladies usually get what they want as it is, but not always when they want it. I have several times been told by some of them how I must vote or suffer the penalty, and I have no legal boss either.

Some oppose female suffrage because they fear that the ballot will corrupt the women without elevating the franchise. A point not well taken. Is the sunbeam corrupted when it shines on a heap of garbage?

The paper of Miss Yearwood follows:

HELEN M. COOKE MEMORIAL LIBRARY.

On February 11, 1905, twenty-three persons from the town and surrounding country met in the Sweetwater Seminary building, then used by the "Tennessee Military Institute," to discuss plans to establish a public library in the town of Sweetwater.

Mrs. J. Harrison Lowry was chairman of the meeting. She stated the purpose of the meeting and stressed the special need for a library in the town. Miss Bess Love told of the start made, stating that when the Misses Coffin were preparing to leave Sweetwater they had given her mother, Mrs. Julia Reagan Love, thirty-five books. Mrs. Love offered these books with others she would donate toward a public library. Many others offered from three to six books and numerous magazines. For the present Colonel O. C. Hulvey offered a room in the school building, rent free, for a home for the library.

On voting the name was made the "Sweetwater Public Library Association," books to be obtained from membership fees, gifts, and by money earned by public entertainments, teas, etc.

The membership (fee) was placed at $1.00 per year, thus making a membership within the reach of all. Without charge any one can use the reference books or read in the library when open to the public.

Colonel O. C. Hulvey was made president, Mrs. J. H. Lowry, vice-president, and Miss Bess Love, secretary-treasurer. A committee was named to draft By-laws and a Constitution, one to solicit memberships, one to select books. The books were to be judiciously proportioned as to subjects in history, biography, fiction, nature, travel, essays, etc.

The officers of February, 1905, served until September, 1907. Then on February 7, 1907, S. T. Jones was elected president, Mrs. J. R. Love, vice-president, Miss Nancy Jones, recording secretary, Mrs. J. R. Bradley, corresponding secretary, and Clarence E. Young, treasurer.

Early in 1908 the room heretofore donated by Colonel O. C. Hulvey was needed for school purposes and the books and furnishings were removed to a small building in the yard of S. T. Jones, which we used rent free.

On March 21, 1908, Mrs. Bland E. Clark offered as a gift the small building and the ground on which it stood, opposite the Southern Methodist Church, for a home for the library, provided the name be changed from the Sweetwater Library Association," to the "Helen M. Cooke Memorial Library," in memory of Mrs. Clark's sister, Mrs. Helen Margaret Cooke, one of the pioneer educators in this community. Mrs. Ida Clark Hutcheson offered $100.00 to the building fund provided Mrs. Clark's offer was accepted. It was with great pleasure that the association made the change in name by a unanimous vote.

Several parties made an effort to secure a charter but each time failed in some essential. C. E. Young, treasurer, took the matter in hand and secured a charter for the "Helen M. Cooke Memorial Library" in September, 1910. It was signed by S. T. Jones, C. M. Young, Mrs. L. E. Heiskell and Misses Bess Love and Miranda E. Yearwood.

A building committee was appointed composed of Mrs. Bland E. Clark, C. E. Young, Mrs. S. T. Jones, and Misses Bess Love, Nancy Jones and Miranda E. Yearwood. The building given by Mrs. Clark was originally a small barn which had been converted into a dwelling. The committee could not dispose of this building to advantage, so concluded to remodel and add to it; which was done. When completed it was convenient and commodious. A circular was issued signed by pupils of Mrs. Cook now residing in this community and mailed to all her former pupils whose addresses we could learn, telling of the proposed memorial to her name and asking for donations toward the building fund. Among the replies received enclosing check, was one from Mr. Will Price (of Chicago), sending $25.00 and promising that when the building was completed he would donate a piano of his firm (Price and Peeple, Chicago) make. This he did. $200.00 was subscribed by citizens not pupils of Mrs. Cooke and the balance to complete the building was made by various entertainments. The building was completed April, 1911, at a cost of $1,036.70 and all paid.

The assembly room is finished in mission style, beamed ceiling, hardwood floor, built-in window seats, stone chimney, tinted walls, green stained woodwork and bookcases; large library table and piano to correspond. Electric light fixtures, rugs and window shades also to correspond. Clarence E. Young denated a mission clock and Mrs. Clark a Morris chair for this room.

Adjoining the main room is the kitchen, furnished; sink with water connections, table and dumb waiter to the second floor. In the pantry adjoining the kitchen there are numerous utensils and odd dishes in addition to three dozen small plates, three dozen large plates, three dozen cups and saucers, three dozen sauce dishes with green band and the "Helen M. Cooke Library" in green. These dishes were donated by Mr. and Mrs. Robert N. Penland. Across the end and down back side of the building is a wide porch lighted by electric lights. The stairs (enclosed) ascend from the side porch and enter the main room on the second floor (also hardwood) and which has built-in seats and shelves. Adjoining this main room is a storeroom and serving room with dumb waiter coming from the kitchen. The main room on the second floor is rented by the United Daughters Confederacy chapter as an assembly room.

The entire building with its contents is rented (when desired) for private or public entertainments at a reasonable rate and is an ideal place for holding receptions, etc. There are folding tables and folding chairs. The library owns about 1,800 books and subscribes for fourteen magazines; ten magazines are donated.

The library is open to the public three hours every Saturday afternoon. Different ones serve as librarian, donating their services.

At the fair in 1914 in connection with the "City Beautiful League" the members of the library served lunch and realized for the treasury $100.00. We have no income excepting membership fees and are compelled to resort to lunches, entertainments, etc., to replenish our bookshelves.

We make an order for new books four times a year and have added new bookcases, rugs and curtains that were badly needed.

When the plans of the building were submitted there was not enough ground for the building contemplated, so Mrs. Clark donated more ground to extend to yard fence of Mrs. Hutcheson and to extend to the wire fence of her (Mrs. Clark's) garden.

1915 officers are Mrs. S. T. Jones, president, Mrs. J. R. Love, vice-president, Clarence E. Young, secretary-treasurer, and Miss Nancy E. Jones, librarian.

CHILDREN OF MRS. H. M. COOKE.

Henry B. Cooke was born at Athens, Tenn., May 8, 1854. He married Fannie S. Meir, of Boulder, Col. She was born in Mitchell, Ind., November 27, 1861. He and she both are members of the Baptist church. After learning his trade, that of brick-mason and plasterer, at Sweetwater under Captain W. L. Clark he went to Boulder, Col.. then to Ash Grove, Mo., then to Coffeeville, Kan., thence to Cedaredge, Col. At the last named place he died on January 15, 1912. Their children are: Harry D. Cooke, Red Cliff, Col.; C. M. Cooke, Cedaredge, Col.; Nellie M. Cooke, Cedaredge, Col., and Mrs. Susan McCormick, Red Cliff, Col.

CHARLES MAYNARD COOKE

Was born at Athens, Tenn., July 1, 1856. He got his education from his mother and the public schools of Sweetwater. He studied law and went to Fort Smith, Ark., in 1882. There he married Sarah B. Luce, daughter of Rear Admiral John Bleecker Luce on June 2, 1884. He has been city atttorney and mayor of Fort Smith and was assistant United States district attorney for the Western District of Arkansas in Mr. Cleveland's first administration. Since 1908 he has been a Christian Scientist. He moved to Harrison, Ark., in 1912.

The children of C. M. Cooke and wife are:

1. John Bleecker, b. May 17, 1885. In United States Navy at Mare Island.
2. Charles Maynard, b. December 19, 1886. In United States Navy at Brooklyn Navy Yard. Lieutenant in command of Submarine E-2.
3. Helen m., b. November 8, 1888; m. Johnson, Fort Smith, Ark.
4. Cornelia P., b. July 21, 1890. Now at Pennsylvania Hospital, Philadelphia.
5. William Forester, b. July 8, 1892. 4229 South Benton Boulevard, Kansas City, Mo.
6. Stephen Bland, b. August 23, 1898. Attending school in Philadelphia, preparatory to entering Annapolis Naval Academy to which he has an appointment.

NELLIE COOKE (McLIN)

Was born at Sweetwater May 1, 1859. She married Chas. E. McLin on January 3, 1882. He was born in Blount County, September 3, 1858. Mother and father were George A. and Jane McConnell McLin. C. E. McLin is secretary and treasurer of Anchor Duck Mills at Rome, Ga. Children: Clifton, b. June 23, 1885; d. August 7, 1901. Helen, b. January 6, 1895.

JAMES W. CLARK

Was born in Washington County, Va., December 23, 1825. He came to Monroe County, Tenn., probably early in the forties. He helped to build some of the residences in and around Madisonville. He had received a common school education and was not afraid of work. He and laziness did not have a speaking acquaintance.

He first married Sydney Ann, daughter of Robt. Cannon, who owned a large farm on the stage road one and a half miles northeast of Philadelphia, on November 20, 1847. They had been married scarcely seven years when death came suddenly. The summer and fall of 1854 there was a great scourge of cholera in this section of the country. It was very prevalent and very fatal in Sweetwater Valley. The people were panic-stricken and I am told that half or more that took it died.

Mrs. Clark died of this disease July 29, 1854. She was born September 19, 1830. Robt. Cannon, father of Mrs. Clark, died also on the same date as his daughter. Previous to that time there had been no deaths in the family for a great number of years.

The Loudon Free Press, a newspaper then in the town of Loudon, published the fact that in August, 1853, E. P. Clark, and J. W. Clark, and R. T. Wilson afterward a New York millionaire, were each commencing the erection of a new residence in that town. Mr. J. W. Clark never occupied his.

Mrs. S. A. Clark left an infant daughter, Ida, who was born January 20, 1853; she married C. H. Hutcheson on December 30, 1887; she died at her residence in Sweetwater, January 28, 1915.

Mrs. Hutcheson was a faithful member of the M. E. Church, South, and one of the church's strongest supporters. She devoted a great deal of her time in later years to the church and its various organizations—the Sunday-school, missionary societies, etc. She also took great interest in the schools of the town and in the H. M. C. Library Association.

Mr. J. W. Clark married a second time, this time to Miss Bland Elizabeth Smith at Weston Mills, Cattaraugus County, New York, at the residence of her brother-in-law, H. P. Weston. She was born in Kingston, Canada, February 6, 1834. In 1855 she came south with Robt. McEwen, a merchant then of Athens, Tenn., who had gone to New York to purchase his stock of goods. The trip then was a toilsome one, and a young lady needed an escort. Miss Bland, came to Athens on a visit to her sister, Mrs. Helen M. Cooke, who was principal at a school for females at that place.

When Mrs. Cooke came to Sweetwater in 1857 Miss Bland came with her and here she met Mr. Clark and as stated they were afterward married.

Mr. Clark was a contractor and builder. He and his brother, W. L. Clark, built many houses in Sweetwater, both business and residence.

He was a zealous member of the Methodist Episcopal Church, South. He superintended the construction of the new church here and he was the largest contributor in money possibly with one exception, the Hon. Jno. K. Brown. He (Clark) spared no time or means to make the church and the parsonage adjoining such as would be an honor and a credit to the denomination and the town. The church stands on the site of the old Masonic lodge, afterwards Victoria College, under charge of the Athens District Conference. He was a considerable stockholder in the bank of Sweetwater. The Sweetwater Flour Mill and the Sweetwater Woolen Mills. He was one of the town's most honored and respected citizens.

From the time Sweetwater was incorporated he was either mayor or an alderman, so long as he would consent to accept the position. He died at his residence in Sweetwater on October 13, 1897, and was interred in West View Cemetery.

Mrs. B. E. Clark survived her husband almost nineteen years. She died at her residence in Sweetwater on Sunday, July 23, 1916, at 4:20 p. m. One of her last acts a short while before death was to donate $1,000.00 to build a Sunday-school annex to the Methodist Church, South.

CAPTAIN W. LEONIDAS CLARK

Was born near Abingdon in Washington County, Va., October 19, 1829. Mr. J. W. Clark was an older brother.

He took the gold fever and went to California in 1857. He went by the Panama route I think. The tribulations were not so great as in 1850 when General Vaughn went by that route, but it was still far from being a Sunday-school picnic excursion. I do not know exactly in what part of California he sought his fortune, but I have heard him speak of being with J. F. Owen and others. They were successful enough in their search for gold to get money enough to get back on, which was by no means always the case. Mr. Clark returned to this valley in 1860, as I am informed, as did also Mr. Owen. He

(Clark), after his return to Sweetwater commenced the study of medicine under Dr. M. C. Parker to learn how to cure people and ameliorate the ills of humanity; however, before being fully equipped for "curing" he was called on in 1861 to go and help kill the hated "invaders of our sacred southern soil." He joined Co. —— of —— Regiment, Tennessee Vol. Cav., C. S. A. (I have not his army record at hand but it is in the archives of Jno. A. Rowan Camp at Sweetwater.) He came out of the war a captain. He did not resume the study of medicine but was a mason, plasterer and contractor and builder. He wrought at these with the same energy and determination with which he had fought the "yankees" and with much more satisfactory results. He soon acquired a competence.

On November 12, 1870, he married Mrs. Mary E., widow of Mr. J. J. Sheldon (of whom a sketch has been given in these columns), and thereby hangs a tale if not a romance.

He was both an operative and a speculative mason. He was W. M. many times of Sweetwater Lodge No. 292, F. & A. M. The Grand Lodge formerly held its sessions in Nashville in November instead of January. Captain Clark and Mrs. Sheldon planned to get married just previous to the session of the Grand Lodge but kept their intentions secret. They went to Nashville on their bridal tour. The captain was considerable of a practical joker and therefore sometimes became the victim of one himself. However he was always good humored about it and would "acknowledge the corn" which would mean in later phrase "'the treats are on me." Some of his Masonic brethren in Sweetwater thought he should have given some inkling of his intentions so that they could have given him a good send-off. As that pleasure was not afforded them they sent a dispatch to the chief of police at Nashville somewhat as follows: "Arrest W. L. Clark, of Sweetwater, who has absconded with another man's wife." Word was sent. The arrest was made according to schedule. But when the brethren tried to explain to the chief that it was all a practical joke he refused to listen and said it was no joke with him, that he was simply doing his official duty. The matter was becoming serious and it took the Grand

Lodge and the remnant of the Southern Confederacy to get his quick release. As the Captain laughingly said when he got back home: "I Scotts, boys, you like to have got me in the jug, sure enough." Which goes to show that practical jokers sometimes go farther than they intend with their jokes and you can't always tell whom the joke is on. The senders of the telegram might have gotten into trouble.

In 1878, Captain Clark bought 20 acres off of the Lenoir farm southwest of the town. He built a residence on the hill on the Athens road where he resided at the time of his death. He died April 20, 1889. He was a member of the Methodist Episcopal Church, South.

He possesed a good library and read much. He conversed intelligently and interestingly on a variety of subjects. He had a contempt for shams and superficial knowledge. He said it was far better not to know anything at all than to "know" it wrong; for then you would not have to unlearn what you thought you knew. Entire ignorance was better than action on wrong assumptions, which subjected you to loss and ridicule.

The children of W. L. and M. E. Clark were:
1. Charles L., b. October 11, 1873.
2. Mabel E., b. January 18, 1875.
3. Frances J., b. October 14, 1879.

1. Charles L. m. Annie Rhea, daughter of Jno. R. Gaines, of Sweetwater on January 12, 1905. She was b. September 4, 1880. Their children are: James W., b. March 31, 1906, and John Craig, b. November 3, 1910. Charles Clark resides at the W. L. Clark residence in Sweetwater. He was educated in Sweetwater and is secretary and treasurer of The American Textile Company.

2. Mabel E., m. Wesley Dickey, January 17, 1907. (For his history see Browder family.) She died August 1, 1908. There was one child, Mabel, b. August 1, 1908.

3. Frances J., m. Robt. C. Copenhaver, of Abingdon, Va., May 10, 1906. He is a manufacturer of iron and lives at Abingdon. She died there Nov. 16, 1908. She was buried in West View Cemetery at Sweetwater. They had two children: Robert C., b. June 10, 1907, and Frances Clark, b. October 28, 1908.

THE CUNNYNGHAMS.

The above is the way the family have commonly spelled the name in this country. The English use "i" instead of "y." I am inclined to think, however, without a thorough investigation, that the Scotch orthography was "Conyngham," meaning the home of the Conyngs. The Scotch word "hame" means home. From the song "Comin' thro' the Rye" we quote:

"What's his name or where's his hame
  I dinna care to tell."

James Cunnyngham was Scotch-Irish. He was an Episcopalian. He lived in Ulster, North Ireland. He married Arabella Good. They emigrated to this country in 1769. They came through Philadelphia, Pa., and settled in the Shenandoah Valley of Virginia. He died there sixteen or seventeens years later. (Holston Methodism, Vol. 2.)

Their children were six in number: James, William (Henry), Arabella, Charlotte, Magdalen, and the name of the other not known.

Shortly after the death of her husband, Mrs. Arabella Cunnyngham moved with her family and some others to Tennessee, to what was known afterwards as "Taylor's Bend" of the French Broad River. The year is given as 1786. James and William were born in Ireland, the others in Shenandoah Valley. James was killed by the Cherokee Indians. Charlotte married George Turnley of Botetourt County, Va. Arabella married John Winton and they were the ancestor and ancestress of the Roane County Wintons.

William was born in Ireland July 3, 1765 He died in Sevier County, February 11, 1845. He married a Miss Lewis, a daughter of Amos Lewis. He was converted under the preaching of the Rev. Thos. Wilkerson and became a minister of the M. E. Church. Their children were Jesse, John, Wiley, Wilkerson, Polly, Betsey, Jane and Charlotte.

Jesse was born in Jefferson County on the French Broad River ten miles above Knoxville, October 25, 1789. His M. E. Church history is as follows: He was converted in 1805; admitted to Holston Conference in 1811; was Presiding Elder in 1816; located in 1826; readmitted in 1849 and superannuated. He died in 1857. He was married to Mary Etter on December 16, 1819. She was born in Fincastle, Va. She was quite a noted woman. (See Holston Methodism.) She died at the residence of her son-in-law, Robert Craven, on May 28, 1868. Mr. Craven lived near Chattanooga on the side of Lookout Mountain. They both were buried in the cemetery near Athens, Tenn.

Jesse Cunnyngham's home from probably about 1826 till the time of his death was in Monroe County not far from the head of Eastanallee Creek. This was afterward known as the Edwards, now the W. F. Orr place. He was a noted revivalist. I heard a darkey talking about his preaching once. He was telling some other negroes: "He shore is a skeery preacher. I don't like to listen to him; he makes me dream of the devil and the bad place."

Jesse Cunnyngham was one of the four commissioners appointed by the county court in 1835 to lay off Monroe County into districts; the other commissioners being William Bayless, John Callaway, Senior and Thomas L. Toomy. They divided the county into seventeen districts; the number was afterward increased to twenty.

Dr. Price in speaking of Jesse Cunnyngham and his wife says: "They reared a large family of children, brought them up in the fear of God, and they became ornaments to society and an honor to their parents. The Rev. W. G. E. Cunnyngham, one of his sons, came to eminence. He was for a number of years missionary to China and for a long time afterward was the Sunday-school secretary and an editor of the Methodist Episcopal Church, South."

JAMES R. CUNNYNGHAM,

son of Jesse Cunnyngham, was born January 28, 1828. He married Caroline S. Weathers, June 18, 1857. He died at his home on Eastanalla, October 3, 1898. Caroline S. Cunnyngham died at her home on Eastanalla December 16, 1901. Children of J. R. and Caroline Cunnyngham:

(1) Virginia M., b. March 9, 1858. She married Thos. Hunnycutt January 11, 1888. She died April 26, 1888. He married (second), ————.
Live in Choctaw nation, Oklahoma.
(2) Sarah, b. October 27, 1859. She died November 10, 1861.
(3) Charles W., b. February 12, 1863. He married Catharine Carter, March, 1893. He lives at Sweetwater, R. F. D. No. 1.
(4) Mary C., b. May 6, 1865. She married J. A. McCampbell April 15, 1899. They live at Knoxville, Tenn., R. F. D. No. 6.
(5) Elizabeth C., b. November 22, 1867. She married C. B. Tansy, January 22, 1890. They live at Chattanooga.

The children of Elizabeth Cunnyngham and C. B. Tansy are:

a Hoyt, b. April 20, 1893.

b Nita B., b. November 8, 1895.

(6) Hattie, b. September 9, 1870. She married J. W. McBroom August 14, 1912. They live at Leon, Okla.
(7) Jessie, b. May 30, 1877. She married Geo. C. Boutwell June 18, 1905. Mr. Boutwell died February, 1913. Mrs. Boutwell lives at Leon, Okla.

We have no history of John, Wiley and Wilkerson, brothers of Jesse. The four sisters were Polly, Jane, Betsey and Charlotte. They all married and settled in this section. Polly married Thornton C. Goddard in Knox County on February 3, 1817. Betsey married Johnathan Pickel, of Pond Creek Valley, 1821. Jane married William Patton, of Sweetwater Valley, June, 1823. Charlotte was the third wife of Samuel McSpadden. They lived on Dancing Branch seven miles south of Sweetwater.

The descendants of the Cunnynghams, wherever you trace them, are numerous. Those in McMinn, Monroe, Loudon and Roane counties are not exceptions to this rule. They are long-lived and retain their mental and physical vigor to ripe old age.

THE CUNNYNGHAMS.

It is a characteristic of the Cunnyngham posterity, wherever they have lived or whatever name known by, to be independent, free and untrammeled in politics, religion and personal habits. However there is little or nothing of the puritan in their make-up. There was never any disposition to persecute others for opinions sake. Their attitude to the outside world was: "You let me and my family alone and what does not concern you and I'll let you alone." They do not insist that others shall adopt their opinions and habits; which considering their number and influence is a "God's blessing." Not that what they do and the manner in which they do it may be wrong in itself, but some of them are idiosyncratic; have queer ways peculiar to themselves. One of these descendants I knew years ago said to a friend, who had criticised his actions: "I do and say what I please, when I please and where I please." This notwithstanding Solomon asserted: "There is a time for all things." So he proceeded in summer to go barefoot almost everywhere he went, except sometimes to church. This he did, not on account of the expense of boots and shoes, but he contended that it was more healthful and saved much time He lived, as we would now say, according to eugenics. He did not try to make others go barefoot but said that was his way and that was the way he was going to do as long as it violated no law of God or man. In simple matters of taste we should not dispute. No doubt it was just as uncomfortable for him to wear shoes in hot weather as it would be for a tenderfoot to walk over gravels without them. As to church predilections the Cunnynghams were nearly all Methodists, a few have been Presbyterians.

The Cunnynghams-Pattons.

We have already given the history of those branches of the Cunnyngham family which intermarried with Jonathan Pickel, T. C. Goddard and William Patton, of Sweetwater Valley. We now take up that branch of the Pattons, using largely as to remote ancestry information obtained from the late Wiley Patton, a former resident of Sweetwater but dying in Texas.

Hans Patton, evidently of German origin, settled in what is now Allegheny County, Pennsylvania, between the Allegheny and Monongahela rivers near the site of Pittsburgh. Fort Duquesne, located in the forks of above rivers, was in possession of the French and Indians until 1738. It is presumed from what is narrated hereafter, that he went there subsequent to that time and previous to 1776. Little is known of his history; when he died or what his wife's name was. He was the father of three sons, Robert, Frances and Jacob, and two daughters, Jane and Phoebe.

Robert was a Revolutionary soldier. His record is on file in the United States Pension Office, Washington, D. C. He was first a lieutenant and then a captain before the close of the war. His son, William Patton, was born in Allegheny County, Pa., April 22, 1792. After that time "he (Robert)," Wiley Patton wrote, "moving from there (Allegheny County, Pa.) to Kentucky, thence to Knox County, Tennessee, staying a few years in each state, and died in Knox County on the 4th day of September, 1815. He was about 65 years old." This would make the year of his birth 1750.

The maiden name of Robert's wife was Isabella Fraaser. From the use of the "aa" in the spelling of the name I would take it that she was a Hollander. She died in Knox County, October 18, 1822, at about the age of 59, making the year of her birth 1763.

William Patton was the son of Robert and Isabella Patton. If there were other children we are not informed.

WILLIAM PATTON.

William P. married Jane Cunnyngham, as has been stated, in Knox County, in June, 1823. Soon afterward they settled in Sweetwater Valley four miles south of where the town of Sweetwater now is, and one mile north of the low gap in Sweetwater ridge. He was a farmer and a mechanic. He paid considerable attention to stock raising. He was the first man if not the only man to have a track in the valley for the training of horses. It was on the quarter section on which he resided. It was a straight half-mile track and ran along near the public road. It was not inclosed and sometimes young bloods in this section who wanted to know who had the fastest horse went there to find out. The amount involved in the result was usually small and no great attention was attracted.

William Patton did everything with conscientious thoroughness. To illustrate. He was a fine mechanic. During the Civil War here in the south iron furnaces and foundries either were not running, or if they were they were engaged in the manufacture of arms and munitions of war for the Confederacy. Wood in many instances had to take the place of iron. At that time nearly every one who farmed at all raised a patch of sorghum. The cane was used for the manufacture of molasses and sugar, more largely the former. When sugar could not be obtained molasses was substituted for it; one was called "long sweetening" the other "short sweetening." In serving coffee or parched rye water (postum) it was sometimes asked which you preferred "long or short sweetening."

Cane mills were scarce in those days and very much needed. They were also considered difficult to make. My father, I. T. Lenoir, had tried several which had proved very unsatisfactory. It was a problem to find some one to make a good one. Mr. Patton learning of it told my father if he would furnish him a strong hand to turn the lathe and do whatever he wanted him to do that he would make him one that would work. My father told him that he would gladly do so and furnish any material that could be obtained. This I think was in the summer of 1861 or 1862. For a shop Mr. Patton had only a hand lathe under a shed in front of the house near the road. He had only a few tools.

True the machinery you might say was simple—two hard wood rollers with wooden cogs—the rollers placed upright in a frame and attached to a sweep or lever so a horse could turn them. The horse went in a circle and led himself around after he was started.

It was a very much mooted question in the neighborhood with the appliances at hand whether or not Mr. Patton could make a satisfactory machine. It was next in importance to whether the "yanks" or "rebs" would whip in the fight. It became a matter of neighborhood pride that he should be successful. I, a boy then, took great interest in the work, went along with the hand

and closely watched its progress. Mr. Patton took much pains and was very deliberate in his work. When the mill was finished we hauled it home with as much pride as if it had been the ark of the covenant. It worked like a charm; I would have been sorely disappointed if it had not. It lasted many years and proved a blessing also to the neighbors, who were free to use it. He was importuned to make other mills but refused; said that he made that one merely as a model to show what could be done; that he was getting too old for such work: He was then about 70. He had no idea then that his sorghum mill would be written of more than fifty years afterward or become historical.

The latter part of the war he resided with his son, J. H. Patton, of Sweetwater. He died there June 28, 1864. He was buried at Mount Lebanon Cemetery. His remains were removed and reinterred in the Wiley Patton lot in the old Sweetwater Cemetery.

His wife, Jane Cunnyngham Patton, was born February 9, 1798, and died October 28, 1857. Her remains lie in the old Presbyterian Cemetery at Philadelphia. They were both members of the Presbyterian church.

The children of William Patton and Jane Patton were eight:

(1) John Elbert, (2) James Harvey, (3) Elizabeth Ann, (4) Margaret Jane, (5) Alvin, (6) William H, (7) Wiley, (8) Thomas Wilkerson.

(1) J. E. Patton was b. July 22, 1824, d. February 23, 1852. Buried at cemetery at Philadelphia. He was never married.

(2) J. H. Patton was b. February 11, 1826; d. August 2, 1894. He was married to Margaret A. McSpadden, of New Market. Jefferson County. Tenn. She was b. October 3, 1836. She d. May 10, 1884.

In the latter part of 1853 or early in 1854 he came from his father's farm to Sweetwater. He formed a partnership in a general merchandise business with his cousin, John W. Goddard, who had been in business at Philadelphia. Mr. Patton purchased from I. T. Lenoir a lot on the corner of Depot Street and Wright's Alley, across the alley from the site now occupied by Guthrie, Bradley & Jones. In the old plan of the town, gotten up by I. T. Lenoir and as laid off by him, the street on the west part of the depot square was always called Depot Street and the street on the other side of the railroad opposite was Railroad Street and it was always written so in the early deeds to the town lots. Since then I have noticed in some of the deeds of late years to lots on Depot Street that street is called Railroad Street, and sometimes Main Street. I note this fact so that hereafter confusion in names and titles may be prevented.

In the fall of 1859 Wiley Patton, a brother of Harvey, bought out J. W. Goddard and became a partner of his brother J. H. The style of the firm was changed from Goddard and Patton to J. H. Patton & Brother, and this partnership continued until 1880. Mr. Patton and his wife first lived in a building back of his store, then in a residence next to where Mrs. Julia Stilman now resides, afterward in the house where William Patton, his son, now lives (1916).

His business affairs were various and he was eminently successful. He owned a quarter section of land one and a half miles west of Sweetwater. He occupied many positions of trust. He was elder in the Presbyterian Church at Sweetwater for fifteen years. He was secretary of the Sweetwater lodge F. & A. M. for more than that time. It was an exceedingly rare thing that he ever made a mistake in his accounts either in his personal business or in his offices of trust. Although not physically very strong he managed to transact a great amount of business. He was always known as a fine collector of debts due the lodge, the church or himself. Yet I have never known of his suing anybody or having a law suit or giving offense for asking for the payment of a debt. How this was accomplished I never understood.

He was always one of the moving spirits in his church and in all school affairs. He was particularly influential because of the confidence of the entire community in his good judgment and correctness. He was naturally very conservative and opposed change unless he was thoroughly convinced that the change would be greatly beneficial. However if he was out voted or anything was determined in opposition to his wishes, he generally strove for its success as much as if he had been in favor of it.

The married life of himself and his wife was an ideal one. He could not possibly have accomplished what he did in his varied business affairs had his wife been almost any other woman. They reared such a family of children as few people have ever been blessed with.

The children of J. H. Patton and Margaret Patton were:

1. Emma, b. October —, 1860. Married R. A. Tedford May 12, 1897. He was a druggist at Maryville, Tenn. He died in March, 1907.

2. Madge, b. June 3, 1863; d. June 28, 1908.

3. Alice, b. January 28, 1867.

These three sisters were educated mostly by Mrs. H. M. Cooke at Sweetwater. Alice was m. to J. A. Magill on January 11, 1894. James Alexander Magill was b. August 20, 1865. He was the son of Aurelius N. and Jane L. Wilson Magill. Died on Lookout Mountain on July 10, 1899. He was cashier of the Bank of Sweetwater from November, 1886, till January 5, 1897. He resigned the office on account of ill health. He organized the Mascot Knitting Mills at Sweetwater. He was a remarkable business man of his age. He was president of the Y. M. C. A., superintendent of the Presbyterian Sunday-school, and on May 1, 1897, he and W. G. Bogart were ordained deacons in the Presbyterian church.

Alice P. married (second) Rev. Wm. Bartlett, of Maryville, Tenn. He is the son of the late P. M. Bartlett, who at the time of his death was president of Maryville College. Mr. and Mrs. Bartlett now (1916) reside in Chattanooga.

4. William, b. June 29, 1872. Educated at Sweetwater. When a young man went to Dalton, Ga., as an employee of the Crown Cotton Mills of which his father was president. He married Francis McCuthen Bitting, daughter of John H. Bitting, of Dalton, Ga., on November 19, 1896, and they came to Sweetwater in that same month. They live in the J. H. Patton house, on Mayes Avenue, the third built by him in Sweetwater.

He is president of the Mascot Hosiery Mills.

5. James Patton, b. December 28, 1874. Educated at Sweetwater College under J. L. Bachman, D. D. He

married Bessie, second daughter of J. L. Bachman, on January 16, 1902. They reside on Mayes Avenue, Sweetwater. He is secretary and treasurer of the Mascot Hosiery Mills. In 1915 was chairman of the Monroe County Road Commission. James and Bessie Patton have one son, James Harvey, III, b. February 27, 1903.

(3) Elizabeth Ann Patton was born the 12th of September, 1828. She married B. M. Porter. He was born in McMinn County, January 14, 1831. After their marriage they resided in Knoxville for a short while and then in October, 1876, moved to Weatherford, Texas. They both died and were buried there. They had five children (1) Jane Amelia, (2) Boyd, (3) Benjamin Franklin, (4) William Harvey, (5) Maggie Elizabeth. Jane Amelia was married to O. K. Kidwell. Their postoffice is at Weatherford, Texas.

(4) Margaret Jane Patton was the fourth child of William Patton. She married A. H. Murray. They resided for many years in Sweetwater and vicinity. They reared a family. They moved to Ash Grove, Mo., exact date not known. They both died there.

(5) Alvin Patton died in infancy.

(6) William H. Patton was born in 1834. He moved to Texas two or three years before the Civil War. He joined the Texas Rangers and served throughout the war with them. A short time after his return home to Decatur, Texas, he died. He was never married.

(7) Wiley Patton was born in Monroe County on his father's farm on April 3, 1836. He clerked for S. J. Rowan a part of the year 1859; in the fall of this year he went into partnership with his brother, J. H. Patton. He joined the Confederate army January 2, 1862. He surrendered at Vicksburg, Miss., and was paroled. After his return from the war, he resumed business with his brother, J. H. Patton, and continued as his partner until 1880. On November 21, 1867, he was married to Julia A. Holston. She was born November 26, 1839, and died November 6, 1880. They had two children. Margaret Cunningham, born in Sweetwater 22nd of December, 1868, and died in Atlanta, Ga., on August 18, 1887.

(2) Ethel May. She was born July 27, 1875, in Sweetwater. Her residence is Weatherford, Texas. Married W. H. Arnett.

Wiley Patton was married the second time to Mrs. Sallie P. M. Taylor on the 1st day of February, 1887. She was born in Williamson County, Tenn., in 1852. He died at San Antonio, Texas, in 1915.

(8) Thomas Wilkerson Patton was the youngest of the children. He was born in 1838 or 1839. I went to the same school he did in the old log schoolhouse near the town of Sweetwater in 1856. There was so much excitement in the presidential political race that year that the scholars in the school, male and female, used to divide off in their games according to politics, the Whigs against the Democrats. Tom Patton was the largest scholar amongst the Whigs and Eagleton Ramsey the oldest of the Democrats. There was much rivalry, but so far as I remember, it was all good humored.

Wiley Patton says that he (Thomas) joined the Confederate army and was either killed or died during the war. He (Wiley P.), wrote me that he did not know his (Tom P.'s) history. He was not with him during the war.

The Cunnyngham-Pickels.

In the old family Bible of Jonathan Pickel he states that his parents were Christian Pickel and Katherine Pickel, formerly Pophanberg, and that they came from Germany. Entries are found showing that: Jonathan Pickel was born February 5, 1790. He died on September 20, 1854. His wife Betsy Cunnyngham was born March 17, 1796, and died July 12, 1877. The date of their marriage I think is not stated. It probably occurred in 1819. They are buried in the cemetery at County Line. They were the parents of nine children:

One. Rufus M., b. July 10, 1820; d. April 23, 1878.

Second. James Harvey, b. April 10, 1822; d. April 28, 1895.

Third. Jno. H., b. August 2, 1824; d. ―――

Fourth. Hugh Cunnyngham, b. October 28, 1826; d. ―――

Fifth. Jane Cunnyngham, b. September 3, 1828.

Sixth. L. Mitchell, b. August 30, 1830. L. M. P. m. Nancy Lowry, daughter of James L. on Eastanallee. They went first to Missouri, then to Boulder, Col. Both

dead. Children: Robert, Emma, Emmett, Carrie and Jane. Live at Boulder.
Seventh. Margaret S., b. November 23, 1832; m. H. B. Pennington, whom see.
Eighth. Sara M., b. August 8, 1836.
Ninth. Samuel Wilkerson, b. August 13, 1838.

* * * , *

One. Rufus M. Pickel was married to Emmeline Lotspeich, July 5, 1839. Rev. Ira Falls, officiating. She was born February 4, 1821, in Green County, Tenn. They moved first to Henry County, Mo. Afterwards they settled near Ottumwa, Ia.
He was a merchant and a farmer. He was a member of Board of Prisons for Henry County, Mo. He was collector of internal revenue from 1862-1867.
In 1871 or 1872 he moved to Ottumwa, Ia., and died there April 23, 1878. He died of dropsy. They were the parents of eleven children, only three of whom are now (1913) living. They are:
(1) Hugh Marion Pickel, b. December 23, 1841. Resides at Des Moines, Iowa.
(2) Maria Sophia Pickel, b. July 1, 1857. She married Jacob Pickle on ―――――. Their Post-office is Davenport, Washington.
(3) Emma Etter Pickel, b. November 25, 1858. She married Thos. H. Pickel. They reside at Ottumwa, Ia.

* * * , *

Second. James Harvey P. was married to Mary Jane Crump Browder, daughter of William and Elizabeth Browder on September 11, 1845. She was born May 17, 1827, and died April 25, 1872.
He was a farmer and resided three and a half miles west of Sweetwater. He met with an accident while plowing in the field. This accident caused internal injuries from which he died April 28, 1895. Although 73 years old at the time of his death he was very vigorous, and in the natural course of events he bade fair to live many years. He possessed in a large degree the Cunnyngham strenuousness of opinion, the Pickel industry

and in his home, the Browder hospitality. He especially resented being dictated to. He was a zealous worker in the Methodist church and the Masonic Lodge. He understood music well and enjoyed conducting singing at the church and camp meeting. He preferred the square note system of where each note in the octave was represented by a different shaped character. The pitch was regulated by a tuning fork. He did not look with favor on instrumental music in church. Being a man of a large family and a good citizen he took great interest in schools, and the cause of education generally.

He was a Union man during the Civil War and was a deputy marshal under Captain S. P. Evans in 1865. Although an efficient officer, there was no complaint made that he used his office unkindly, or subjected those arrested to indignities. In most cases he read the warrant to the party and told him to report at Knoxville. These were political not whiskey cases.

The children of J. H. and Sarah Pickel were eight in number. Their names were:
1. William Wilkerson.
2. Jonathan Asbury.
3. James Mitchell.
4. Elizabeth Ann.
5. Samuel Jefferson.
6. Sarah Jane.
7. Hester Ella.
8. Ada Baxter.

1. William W. was born September 5, 1846, and died August 15, 1913. He attended school at the Union Institute, now Baptist College, under Professors Ragsdale, Leyburn and Muller.

When a young man he learned the tinner's trade under Matt Carter at Sweetwater, and was with him until Mr. Carter's death. Working at his trade when a young man he got a fall from which he lay unconscious for several weeks and it was thought he would not recover, but a fine constitution brought him through. His death resulted from a fall of like nature. He never hesitated to go where his work called him and sometimes took chances which he should not have taken. He lost as few days from work in his business as any man that ever lived in Sweetwater. The taking of a holiday was almost unknown to him.

Although Wilkerson, his middle name, which ran through the Cunnynghams, the Pattons, the Goddards and the Pickels was a Methodist name, W. W. joined the Presbyterian Church in 1876 and was a faithful member. (Thos. Wilkerson was a noted Methodist preacher in Sevier County in early times.)

William Pickel resided all his life in the First Civil District of Monroe County, and since about 1870 until his death in the town of Sweetwater. He was at the time of his death the oldest resident of the First Civil District, having lived in it all of his life 67 years.

On April 24, 1878, he was married to Nancy Ann Cook, daughter of Adolphus M. Cook. She was born March 15, 1857. She still (1915) resides in Sweetwater. Their children were ten, viz:

(1) Frances Elizabeth, b. February 10, 1879. She married Robt. W. Johnston, June 28, 1911. He lives on Fork Creek. He is the son of Jno. H. and Sarah Gaines Johnston.

(2) Maude Ella, b. October 9, 1881.

(3) James Adolphus Pickel, b. January 21, 1883. He was married to Miss Annie Reece, October 12, 1910. They have one son, James Reece Pickel, b. ——

(4) Chas. Bates Pickel, b. February 10, 1885.

(5) Dora Pearl, b. February 5, 1887. She was married to Chas. N. Hulvey, June 8, 1909. Their children are: Frances Elizabeth (Dec.) Chas. Newton, Jr., b. ——. Col. Chas. N. Hulvey is president of T. M. Institute (1915).

(6) William Hugh, b. March 2, 1889.

(7) Mary Alice, b. July 23, 1891, d. October 22, 1893

(8) Robt. Lynn, b. February 28, 1894.

(9) Nellie May, b. February 8, 1897.

(10) Nancy Louise, b. August 28, 1900.

2. Jonathan Asbury Pickel, second son of J. H. Pickel, was born July 22, 1848; d. August 16, 1900. He married Sallie A. Thompson, May 26, 1875, who was born in Franklin County, Va., April 15, 1852. Died June 3, 1907. Both are interred in Westview cemetery. They moved

to Pilot Point, Texas, in August, 1881, and spent several years here, returning to Sweetwater, and lived here until their death. John, as he was usually called, took a great pride in raising fruit, vegetables and melons. When he was a boy thirteen or fourteen years old, in trying to protect his melon patch from Federal soldiers, he was shot through the body and came near dying from the wound. His pluck and determination to get well were all that saved him. After this occurrence no one ever again tried to steal his watermelons.

The children of Jonathan and Sallie Pickel are:

(1) Emma B., b. November 30, 1876, at Sweetwater, Tenn. Married Wm. Moser in November, 1899. They live in Chattanooga, Tenn.

(2) Berta May, b. in Sweetwater, January 20, 1879. Died at Pilot Point, Texas, September 12, 1881.

(3) James Samuel, b. September 25, 1882.

(4) Janey Lee, b. at Sweetwater, Tenn., October 26, 1886. She was married to B. A. Boone, October 26, 1911. Residence, Chattanooga.

(5) Edith Lillian, b. November 25, 1888, at Sweetwater, Tenn.

3. James Mitchell Pickel. He was born November 17, 1850. He went to Pilot Point, Texas in ———. Married Nannie E. Murray at that place, May 16, 1888. He is a merchant.

4. Elizabeth Anne was born January 6, 1853. She married Robert H. Locke, of Meigs County, September 4, 1879. Died March ———, 1909.

5. Sarah Jane, b. March 16, 1857.

6. Samuel Jefferson, b. April 5, 1855. Died February 12, 1911. Married Susan, daughter of Chas. Cannon, ——— ———. He was a merchant at Sweetwater. Children. Samuel J. b. ——— ———, (2).

7. Hester Ella was born August 31, 1859. She married Hon. Frank P. Dickey December 20, 1883. She died ——— ———. Dickey was a farmer in Pond Creek Valley. He and his wife were members of the M. E. Church, South. Dickey married a second time, Martha Washington Suddarth, of Harriman, November 20,

1907. One son, Franklin Pierce, was born to them November 4, 1908. They live at Harriman, Tenn.

8. Ada Baxter was born November 16, 1861. Married Frank L. Harmon of Germantown, Ky., on February 21, 1883. Their children are: Ethel, George, May and Ralph.

JOHN FINE.

From inscriptions on tomb stones we find that John Fine was born January 1, 1781, and died January 26, 1857. His wife, Nancy was born November 10, 1782, and died February 18, 1859; both arriving at the advanced age of more than 76 years.

It is very probable that they came here from Cocke County; they at least were originally from there. They came to this valley as soon as the Hiwassee District was open for settlement. The church records of Baptist Church on Sweetwater, show that they both helped to organize on Fork Creek what was afterward called the Baptist Church on Sweetwater, on the first Saturday in June, 1820. As has been stated heretofore this valley was not open to settlement till that year. The records also show that before the building of this meeting house the members met at the residence of John Fine on the first Saturday in August, 1821. It was the house above the springs where the city waterworks now get their supply. He paid for his land and obtained a grant, No. 686, from the State, dated September 7, 1827, and described as being the southwest quarter of section 34, township 2, range 1, east of the basis line. It corners in the road leading west to Pond Creek at the northwest corner of Mrs. Love's property. It runs thence south one-half mile (160 rods) and the same distance west, north and east to the beginning. The part on which the old house now (1914) stands is owned by the Charles Cannon heirs. The present Fair Ground is also on the tract.

In the days of the stage line the Fine house was a stage stand and stopping place. The stage road from Philadelphia to Athens went by there, the location of which was never much changed until the year 1913. Also the road from Madisonville west to Pond Creek Valley ran by there, leading almost straight from the Ramsey

(Waren) lane through the woods to the creek crossing near the house. The road from the McCroskey neighborhood on Fork Creek to the west took a turn at the Heiskell lane, led by the house and thence to Pond Creek. Thus from its natural location and the good accommodations obtained there by travelers, it was a well known stopping place. John Fine and his wife had been married and had a considerable family, when they came to Sweetwater Valley. They were in the prime and vigor of life, possessed of property and intelligence and consequently were an influential family. I have not found out the maiden name of Mrs. Fine. Mr. Fine was evidently interested in the cause of education, as the schoolhouse was located one-fourth of a mile south of his house on his land. This schoolhouse was built some time previous to 1834; for early in that year Baptist meetings are recorded to have been held in the Fine schoolhouse. The branch church here had authority to receive members for the old Sweetwater church. In the settlement of church difficulties and misunderstandings between neighbors John Fine was often called on to arbitrate. His fairness and sense of justice must have been generally recognized. His name sometimes occurs in he Circuit Court records on the jury lists. It was customary in the forties to summon men of the highest character and intelligence for that service. To be a juryman was then a badge of honor and it was not considered good citizenship to try to get relieved without some valid excuse.

There was until some years ago a Fine family burying ground, in which thirteen of the family were interred. This was situated on a hill north of the house. It was enclosed with a stone wall. The bodies there were removed and re-interred in West View Cemetery.

The children of Jno. and Nancy Fine were: John, Polly, Abraham, Sarah, Mahala, Minerva, Martha, and Nancy.

One. John, date of birth not known. He may or may not have been the oldest child. He enlisted in the Mexican war, fought through it, and on his return from Mexico took sick on board of a ship in the Gulf. He died and his body was consigned to the waves. This was probably in the year 1847, but the date is not known.

Two. Polly was born November 25, 1803. Died January 29, 1857. (Unmarried).

Three. Abraham, married Mary S. Haralson July 3, 1838. They moved to Missouri. History not known.

Four. Sarah was born November 29, 1809. Died December 25, 1870. She was married to Dr. Ira L. Hill, on April 5, 1832. He was born November 18, 1804. He died July 31, 1843. He lived in Sevier County. He was a physician. Their children were:

1. Mary M., b. in 1834. She died in Brownsville, Neb., in October, 1884. She married Jos. Marshall Owen, August 28, 1849. (See history of Owen family).

2. John was born in Sevier County, July 15, 1838. He moved to Sweetwater with his mother in the year, 1844 —not long after the death of Dr. Hill. She lived near the Fine residence on the hill above the spring. He married Isabelle Hotchkiss, daughter of Claiborne Hotchkiss, on January 17, 1871. They resided in Loudon County. He was a farmer. Isabella Hotchkiss was born in Roane (now Loudon County) April 16, 1848. She died January 8, 1902. John Hill died November 1, 1889, in Loudon County, and was buried in the New Providence graveyard.

They were the parents of eight children: Four girls and four boys:

(1) Sallie Abbott, age 43, Mineral Wells, Texas.
(2) C. H. Hill, age 41, Loudon, Tenn.
(3) Jno. W. Hill (age not given). Died in Texas.
(4) T. W. Hill, age 35, Loudon, Tenn.
(5) Mary Brazeal, died at the age of 32, in Loudon, Tenn.
(6) Ella Smith, age 28, Lenoir City.
(7) Sam Hill, age 25, Chattanooga.
(8)

This information was gotten from one of the family, I think C. H. Hill, in 1914. And the ages given refer to that date. He only speaks of three girls, Sallie, Mary and Ella, in listing the names.

3. Oliver Hazard Perry Hill was born in Sevier County July 15, 1840. During the Civil War, in 1861, he enlisted ——. Capt. Jno. A. Rowans, Co. of 43rd Reg., C. S. A. He was wounded at Chickamauga, on September

21, 1863. The lower portion of one arm was amputated and he was disabled from further service. On November 7, 1867, he married Mary Carter, daughter of Jno. Carter. She was one of 25 children.. They settled near Lenoirs, Tenn. He was a farmer. He died March 23, 1911. She died ——, (1914). They left children as follows:

(1) Sarah Fine, b. December 13, 1868. Married Jno. Heffner of Lenoir City ——.

(2) Ira Lee, b. November 10, 1870. Married Kate Miller ——, 1897.

(3) John W., b. October 15, 1872. Died October 11, 1889.

(4) Ambrose Parnell, b. August 15, 1874. St. Paul, Minn., is his address.

(5) Nancy Lucinda, b. April 1, 1877. Died in 1878.

(6) Martha E., b. June 8, 1879. Married Geo. O'Neal of Lenoir City, February 20, 1891. Their children are Levi, Paul, Cecil and Agnes.

(7) Marion M., b. September 17, 1883.

* * * * *

1, 2 and 3 of the Hill children, Mary, John and Perry, were all born in Sevier County, as to Ira, the fourth child, probably in Sweetwater Valley in 1844. He went to Minneapolis, Minn., after the Civil War and died there, not many years since. Not known to me whether he had a family or not. Mrs. Hill was married a second time to Welcome Beard, on December 29, 1859.

* * * * *

Five. Mahala was born February 18, 1814. She was married to N. G. Walker of Mo. ————. She died at the Fine residence while on a visit there on February 8, 1859.

Six. Minerva, b. ——. She married Jabin Snow Taylor of Pond Creek Valley, and brother of Elica A. Taylor on March 9, 1848. He was born in Grainger County, Tennessee, August 10, 1823. He died February 22, 1857.

Seven. Martha was born in 1828. She married J. C. Starrett on May 7, 1861. She died February 19, 1889.

He was born in Bradley County (date not given) and died September 14, 1874. Their children were:
1. Jno Starrett, b. October 27, 1864. Married Emma Boggs September 25, 1889, of Lenoir City. No children. He was married a second time. By this second marriage there were three children, Katharine Louis, in 1911, eight years old; Randall McKnight, in 1911, six years old; infant son, Jno. M., in 1911, three months old. Second child of J. C. and Martha Starrett, was Florence. She was born on October 12, 1868. She married Dr. J. T. Tillery, of Ebenezer, Knox County, on August 24, 1890. They had one son, Duncan E. Tillery.

Eight. Nancy E. Fine, b. October 15, 1836. Died April 9, 1857. From the time John Fine came to this country and built the old log house which now stands at the location mentioned, there were no deaths at that residence for about 37 years, although there was a large family. But from January to April, there were four deaths in 1857, viz: Jno. Fine, January 26, 1857; Polly, d. January 29, 1857; Jabin Snow Taylor, d. February 22, 1857; Nancy, d. April 9, 1857.

The disease which took them off was called pneumonia, but it occurs to me, or rather seems strange, that a whole family should have pneumonia, as I have never heard that it was a contagious or infectious disease. I believe that all of the family were attacked by some other disease and these four cases proved fatal. Now all the sons and daughters of Jno. Fine that were married in this country the Rev. Robt. Snead officiated at the ceremony with the exception of Martha, who married Starrett. She was married by Hughes W. Taylor, a brother of her brother-in-law, Jabin Taylor. None of the Fines or their descendants ever belonged to any other church, than the Baptist except Mrs. Starrett who joined the Presbyterian Church, with her husband after marriage.

Austin Fry

Was born in Monroe County and died at Sweetwater, at an advanced age, in January. 1880. He married Jane Brandon in 1833. He moved to McMinn County, near Reagan Station in 1839, and then to near the head of Conesauga Creek, in the 19th civil district. Not long after the Civil War he came to Sweetwater. He was the first recorder of the town after it was incorporated. He was buried in the old cemetery at Sweetwater. His children were:

1. Hugh, b. January 9, 1834; d. 1895. He was a mechanic and contractor, and was the editor and publisher of the first paper published in Sweetwater, called the "Sweetwater Forerunner." The first number of this paper was published September 21, 1867. He was married on November 8, 1855. Wife's name not known to me.

2. Sirena, b. 1835; 3. Kennedy, b. 1839; 5. Charlie, b. February 29, 1844; 6. Mary, b. August 6, 1846; 7. John, b. March 9, 1848. Married Sarah C. Young on September 12, 1881; 8. Emma, b. August 4, 1850; 9. Nancy, b. March 1857. Married — Rose. Address, Spring City, Tenn.

4. William, b. about 1842. He married Mary Caroline Orr on September 2, 1869. She was born August 28, 1848. He lives at Athens, Tenn. He is a mechanic. Their children are: 1. Minnie Laura, b. October, 1871; d. September 22, 1872; 2. Mary Etta, b. September 24, 1873; married H. A. McCambell, February 18, 1897; 3. Henry Mitten, b. April 6, 1876; d. January 19, 1877; 4. Willie Lee, b. March 27, 1878; married Agnes Underwood, of Legrande, Ala., in 1904; 5. Charles Austin, b. April 23, 1880; d. February 18, 1901; 6. Anna Lou, b. June 25, 1882; married Thos. Tidwell, of Dalton, Ga., September 15, 1909. Residence, Bonifay, Ga.

HENRY GLAZE

Came to Sweetwater Valley in 1824 from Washington County, Tennessee. In crossing the Tennessee River at Blair's Ferry, the ferry boat sank and his household goods were lost, together with his family Bible. It is therefore difficult to give exact dates as to himself and wife. His wife's name was Susan Wilhoite. He settled near Reagan's Station on a quarter section of land. Of that and two hundred and forty acres more, his descendants still hold possession. The Glazes have been and are excellent citizens, quiet and unassuming; their names do not figure in courts either as criminals or litigants.

Henry and Susan Glaze were the parents of ten children:

One. Anna, Married Wm. Cate, brother of Elijah Cate. They moved to Cleveland, Tenn.

Two. Jefferson, b. May 1820; d. July 11, 1910.

Three. Lucinda, married Henry Martin and moved to Texas.

Four. Henry, married Miss Martin and moved to Texas.

Five. Emmaline, married Dr. Crow of Athens, Tenn.

Six. Lizzie, married Jos. Neil, the brother of Wm. and Sterling Neil. Neil's wife died. He married again and now resides at Niota, Tenn. He was born February 20, 1828. Their children were:

1. James Polk, married Mollie Garrison.
2. John, married Miranda Rockwell.
3. Melvin, married Angelina Moore.
4. Laura, married Isaac Orr.
5. Sallie, married Noah Lybarger.

Seven. William, d. in infancy.

Eight. John, married Kirkpatrick and went to Cleveland, Tenn.

Nine. Ben, b. November 22, 1830; d. January 4, 1902. Married Lucy Reynolds of Chestua on August 20, 1856. She was born September 9, 1831; d. January 12, 1902. They had six children:

1. Marion J., b. September 7, 1857.
2. Mary, b. August 5, 1859.
3. James Henry, b. January 21, 1862. These three live on the Ben Glaze place and are unmarried.

Horace, Mattie and Hattie died in infancy.

Ten. Mary, married George Wilson, brother of Dot Wilson. He served in the Confederate army and died during the war.

Jefferson, second child of Henry Glaze, was married, first, to Miss Duggan. The children of first wife:

1. John, L., b. October 1, 1853; d. at Chattanooga about 1905 or 1906. He was married to Sarah J. Goddard, daughter of "Unc" Hugh Goddard, July 11, 1878. Their children were: Hugh, d. n 1896; Carter, Eugene and Ben.

2. Julia Miranda, married Homer Thompson, son of W. H. Thompson. They had one child. Homer Thompson died and she was married then to Wm. Malone. The second wife of Jefferson Glaze was Martha Jackson, whom he married October 32, 1865. She died September 17, 1902. Their children were:

1. Henry, b. November 16, 1866. He went to Kansas and was married there to June Orr, granddaughter of Wesley Orr.

2. Lura, b. July 17, 1870. She married December 12, 1905, Rev. D. M. Kerr of Greenback, Tenn. There was one daughter, born in 1907.

3. Horace, b. May 28, 1872. Married Edith Kratzer November 18, 1902. She was born August, 1880. They live on the farm adjoining James A. Reagan.

4. Grant, b. February 14, 1874. He married Mina Kratzer, who was born March 7, 1882. They were married September 28, 1904. Have one son, Carl Dean, born November 5, 1913.

5. Ella, b. September 22, 1876, d. June 20, 1896.

Thornton Goddard

Married Polly Cunnyngham in Knox County, Tenn., on February 3, 1817. Their children were:

One. William, H., b. December 17, 1817.

Two. Hugh, b. May 13, 1819; d. April 19, 1873.

Three. Elizabeth C., b. April 2, 1821; d. January 10, 1855.

Four. Jane M., b. April 3, 1823; d. August 4, 1859.

Five. John William, b. 13, 1825; d. October 5, 1896.

Six. Robert Avis, b. February 25, 1828; d. May 27, 1830.

Seven. Mary Ann, b. February 13, 1830; d. April 30, 1901.

Eight. Alvin, b. May 13, 1832; d. July 23, 1854.

Nine. Marcus Bearden, b. June 4, 1834; d. March, 1910.

Ten. Harriet Campbell, b. February 9, 1839; d. January 10, 1855.

One. William H. Goddard moved to Missouri. He died at Versailles, Morgan County, Mo.— His son, John J., lives at Clinton, Henry County, Mo.

Two. Hugh Goddard. There were several Hugh Goddards. This son, I think, first married Isabella Wilson, date not known. He afterwards married the widow Taylor, formerly Mary Ann Weathers, on August 5, 1857.

Three. Elizabeth, C., married W. F. Lenoir, whom see.

Four. Jane M., married George McCulley who lived near Charleston, Tenn.

Five. John W., married Margaret Bogart, daughter of Solomon Bogart, on December 23, 1852. He was a soldier in the Mexican war. In 1853 he was a partner in the mercantile business with his brother-in-law, W. F. Lenoir, at Philadelphia, Tenn. In 1854 he moved to Sweetwater and became a partner of J. H. Patton, under the firm name of Patton and Goddard. He was a first cousin of J. H. Patton. After the Civil War he did business with A. M. Dobbins as a partner, under the firm name of J. W. Goddard & Co.

He died at Dancing Branch, on a farm in the 6th Civil District of Monroe County. The children of J. W. and Margaret Bogart Goddard were:

1. Betty Cornelia, b. October 8, 1853. (See Mayes).

2. Susan Addie, b. June 4, 1857. On December 25, 1879, she was married to Joseph H. Dickey, who was the son of Samuel H. and Sarah Wright Dickey, formerly of Madisonville, Tenn. Joseph H. was born at Rhea Springs, Tenn., August 12, 1855. He came to Sweetwater January 1, 1874. Was in the employ of D. B. Childress for five years. He moved to Fort Worth, Texas, June 1, 1883, where he still resides. Their children are:

(1) Joe Hubert, b. in Sweetwater Valley, March 11, 1882; m. Rose M. Hardin of Fort Worth, November 12, 1902. They have two children, J. Hubert and Margaret.

(2) Nellie, b. at Fort Worth, January 8, 1889. She is unmarried. She lives with her parents and is a teacher of kindergarten.

(3) Anna Eva, the third child of J. W. and Margeret

Goddard, b. June 23, 1861. She married T. A. Frierson, of Chattanooga, October 23, 1884. She died —. They were the parents of four children whose names I do not know.

(4) John Newton, son of J. W. and Margeret Goddard, b. January 30, 1867. He married Mary Nicholson, of Atlanta. He is a broker with offices in the Equitable Building, Atlanta, Ga.

Seven. Mary Ann, daughter of T. C. and Polly Goddard, was married (first) to Solomon L. Stowe of McMinn County, in 1840. He died at Ellijay, Ga. Is buried there. Their children were:
1. Julia, b. October 26, 1847; 2. Florence, b. 1849; 3. Doss, b. 1851; 4. Frank, b. 1853. All of these dates, except Julia's, are approximated. Julia married A. Q. Orr on September 1, 1880. His first wife was a daughter of Hugh Goddard. She died June 12, 1880. Their children were: Hugh, b. March 1866; Florence, b. January 27, 1868; May, b. June 10, 1870, and Ida, b. November 25, 1872.

A. Q. Orr was the son of John W. Orr who came to this country from Virginia when a boy. His father entered land at the head of Sweetwater Creek. The children of A. Q. Orr and Julia, his second wife, were: Berta Leith, b. August 1, 1882; Dawson, b. February 28, 1884, and Irene, b. November 18, 1885. A. Q. Orr died at Chattanooga. Mrs. Julia Stowe Orr died at the residence of her daughter, Mrs. R. E. McLean, Longview, Texas, November 15, 1914. The other daughters, who are all married, reside in Texas. They are Mrs. H. B. Zigler, Houston, Texas. Mrs. F. C. Engall, Cooper, Texas; Mrs. A. J. Robinson, Houston, Texas, and Mrs. C. F. Windall, Longview, Texas. I cannot state which girls married these persons.

2. Florence Stowe, married J. W. D. Williams. Whom see.

3. Doss Stowe married Artie Hutsell. Their children were Harvey, Doss and Harry.

4. W. Frank m. Lucy Mattox, of Bristol, Tenn. Their children were: Pauline, Fred, Raymond and Beatrice. Do not know their residence or history.

Mary Ann Goddard Stowe was married (second) to

Archibald M. Dobbins on March 17, 1861. He was born in Knox County, May 30, 1831. He came to Sweetwater in 1856. He was first in the carriage business with Wm. McClung. Later he was a partner of his brother-in-law, Jno. W. Goddard, in the mercantile business in 1869. He moved to Knoxville in 1874. He now lives with his son-in-law, C. H. Gardner, who is a traveling man residing at 1213 West Landvale St., Baltimore, Md. The children of Mary Ann and A. M. Dobbins were:
1. Lula, m. James T. Cater; 2. Margaret, m. C. T. McClung; 3. Barbara, m. W. H. Lennon; 4. Henry, m. Mabel Willy; 5. Nina (first), m. — Fuller; second, m. G. H. Gardner; 6. Charles Henry.

Nine. Marcus Bearden Goddard married Clementine Amanda Hutsell on August 5, 1858. She was born December 15, 1839, the fifth child of Andrew Hutsell, b. January 2, 1805, and Polly Earheart, b. July 14, 1814. They resided near County Line and at Sweetwater until the year 1887, when they moved to Steptoe, Wash. Their children are:

1. Andrew Floyd, b. July 15, 1859; married Hattie Finley of Meigs County. Their children were Mary Cray, b. January, 1892; Andrew, b. June, 1894, and Dorothy. Andrew Floyd is a farmer living at Rosalia, Wash.

2. Hattie Goddard married Finley. He is a farmer and lives at Rosalia, Wash.

3. Mary Ellen, b. October 23, 1860; married J. W. Raymond November, 1892. They have one son, George, b. May, 1894. Mr. Raymond is a grain dealer. Address, Elm Flats, Spokane, Wash.

4. Robert Henry, b. April 2, 1863, unmarried. He is Claim Agent for the Northern Pacific Railroad and lives at Missoula, Mont.

5. Grace Ophelia, b. December 20, 1864, married John B. Finley, of Meigs County, March 4, 1891. Their children are: Rex Goddard, b. December, 1891, and Isaac Raymond, b. March, 1894. They own the Finley Islands, in the Tennessee River, near Decatur, Ala., which is their address.

6. Charles Avis, b. October 1, 1866; d. July 26, 1890.

7. Hutsell married Miss Mustard in Dayton, Wash.

They had two sons, one of whom, Charles was killed on a railroad and another born August, 1897.

8. Artie Isabella, youngest child of Marcus and Clementine Goddard, b. April 16, 1876. She married Cal F. Godfrey, capitalist, Roseland, Ill. Their children are: Maurine and John; the latter born January, 1908.

Ten. Harriet Goddard, the youngest child of Thornton C. and Polly Goddard, married LaFayette Osborne and, I think, moved to Missouri.

FEW HALL GREGORY, M. D.

Was born in Culpeper County, Va., October 4, 1781. He came to Philadelphia, Monroe County, Tenn., in 1820. He died August 18, 1872 in Sweetwater Valley at his home.

He married Martha Lynn Reynolds, June 1, 1841. She was the daughter of James Reynolds of Philadelphia. She was a member of the Baptist Church on Sweetwater. She died on February 2, 1884, in Marion County, Florida, on Lake Gregory.

Dr. Gregory enlisted in the war of 1812 from Virginia. He studied medicine in Petersburg, Va., Philadelphia, Penn. For 30 years he practised medicine and farmed. He was a legislator from Monroe County in 1839. He was a commissioned colonel of the State militia. He was called upon to act as Brig. Gen. Vol., in the Mexican war, but declined on account of his wife's health.

He was a member of the Methodist Church, South, at Bat Creek (Hiwassee College). He owned a large amount of land. The Eli Cleveland, Jr., place, and the H. E. Martin place. He was a wealthy man for his day and time.

Children of F. H. and M. L. Gregory were:

1. Susanna Virginia, b. May 13, 1842. P. O. 1913, Nashville.

2. Jas. Few, b. January 27, 1844; d. April 30, 1897 at Citra, Fla. Married to Georgia Dallas January 19, 1876.

3. Mary Elizabeth, b. February 1, 1846. Married to Daniel J. Fogg, January 19, 1885 at Lake Gregory. P. O. Belleview, Marion County, Fla.

4. William Richard, b. 1848. Died November, 1870, at Ocala, Fla.
5. Geo. Washington, b. January 12, 1851; d. February 3, 1855.
6. Martha Georgiana, b. January 17, 1857; d. in infancy.
7. Ann Eliza, b. October 15, 1858; d. an infant.
8. Cora Francis, b. January 1, 1861; d. December, 1887, at Livyville Fla. She married Wm. Brown January 1, 1885.

Jas. Few Gregory was a student at Hiwassee College when the Civil War began and enlisted from there in 1861, C. S. A. Daughters of James F. G.: Lula Lynn, b. October 26, 1876. P. O. (presumably) Citra, Fla.; George Dallas, b. February 21, 1878.

Children of James and Susanna Hilton. They were married in 1866.

(1) Robt. Reynolds H., b. April 25, 1868. Now in Colorado.
(2) Geo. Gregory, b. September 18, 1870. (Dead.)
(3) Wm. Andrew H., b. June 5, 1873. P. O., Nashville.

These children were all born in Sweetwater Valley. Above information was obtained from Mary E. Fogg, of Belleview, Marion County, Fla.

DANIEL HEISKELL.

We often hear mention of a family as being an "old family." Strictly speaking, if we are derived from a common ancestor whether we accept the Biblical or Darwinian theory, one family is just as old as another. It may sometimes mean one which has been for long years to the same manor born; oftener I take it to mean the majority of whose members have acted in such a manner as to bring credit to themselves and to the country where they reside. This can be of a truth said of the Heiskells. An interesting and instructive book could be written of them, but it is beyond our space and province to speak at any length except of those who had their home in our valley or moved from here to other sections. The history of the Heiskells so far as is known to us reaches back to the time of William the Conqueror, the Norman who invaded England and overcame King Harold of the Danish dynasty in the 11th century. After the battle of Hastings, which was fought in Sussex on the 14th day of October, 1066, William proceeded to partition out the island to his principal followers, or reward them in other ways and started new orders of dukes, lords, earls, barons, knights, et cet. Rouget Heiskell, rather a Frenchy kind of a name for a Heiskell, was a knight under that monarch, what we might term now a "soldier of fortune." He had a coat of arms which he was entitled to, being a knight. It is related that, during the hard fought and uncertain battle of Hastings, which raged incessantly from morning till evening, William complained much of thirst. There was an apple tree loaded with apples on the hill of Senlac within Harold's, the enemy's lines. Observing this Rouget true to the Heiskell motto, "Dread Shame; Love Loyalty," dashed through the lines and gathering the fruit in his helmet returned to William and relieved his suffering. For this act of valor he was allowed to add an apple tree to the crest of the coat of arms with the word "fructus" (Latin for fruit) engraved thereon. It is a tradition also that when William ate the apples, his strength was renewed and Fortune from that time on favored the Normans. So the eating of the fruit of that difficult, if not forbidden, tree, did not prove as unfortunate to posterity as the event in the Garden of Eden. It may have been the turning point in that decisive battle and settled the fate of the island; and what would England or for that matter our own America have been without the civilizing influence of the Normans.

Some of Rouget Heiskell's descendants afterward drifted back across the channel to Holland. From Amsterdam or Rotterdam, uncertain which, Christian Heiskell sailed and landed on our own shores in the year 1700. He married Katherine Hampton, grand aunt of Wade Hampton of South Carolina. He or some of his people lived and died at Hagerstown, Maryland, as a number of the Heiskells were buried in the Lutheran Churchyard, they being members of that church. This Christian Heiskell was the father of five sons, one of whom was named Frederic. This Frederic was also the father of five sons,

George, William, Frederic, Samuel and Daniel and four daughters. Three of these brothers, William, Frederic and Daniel finally came to Tennessee. The father Frederic moved to the Shenandoah Valley of Virginia, near Winchester, and died there.

Of the Heiskells who came to this State and their descendants many were prominent and well known public characters. Frederic, son of the Winchester Frederic, was one of pioneer newspaper men of our section, being editor and proprietor for years of the Knoxville Register, and was elected to the upper house of Tennessee Legislature in 1846. That same year William Heiskell was defeated in Monroe County by Col. John Ramsey for a seat in the lower house, an account of which has been given. Frederic Heiskell had distinguished sons, Joseph B. Heiskell and Carrick Heiskell. Joseph was a member of the Confederate Congress from the first district of Tennessee, elected in 1861. He was afterward Attorney General and Reporter for the State of Tennessee. Carrick is a distinguished lawyer and a judge in Memphis, Tenn. He, for a long time, has been prominent and influential there. "Ned," his son, was for a short time U. S. Senator from Arkansas.

Wm. Heiskell represented Monroe County in the Legislature and was prominent in politics. His son, S. G. (Samuel Gahagan) has been a Legislator and several times Mayor of Knoxville. He is a lawyer and one of the best known men in the State.

Pride of birth and inherited wealth when considered as a responsibility, and not as an asset to cause you to look down on your neighbors, is all well enough. If it is expected by the possessor that he be toadied to on that account he invites the fate of a haughty spirit. Even pride is not objectionable if it prevents one from doing a mean thing; otherwise it is contemptible. That one's ancestors were honored in the past is at least a satisfaction to the descendants. The Coat of Arms of the Heiskell's as mentioned above may be described as a helmet on a field of sable and argent between two leopards and surmounted by an apple tree with the word "fructus," aove and underneath the shield the motto (Norman French) "Craignez Houte, Aymez Loyaute." (Dread Shame, Love Loyalty).

Never do anything to be ashamed of and be loyal to your king or government. Daniel Heiskell was as far as any man from boasting of his ancestry. He was a simple citizen of the republic. He was born March 7, 1799, probably in the Shenandoah Valley near Winchester, Virginia. Exactly when he came to the State of Tennessee is not known but likely when he was a minor. Much to the disappointment of the members of the family, who chose rather the learned professions, he determined to learn the tanner's trade; deeming that this was a more certain avenue to competency than the learned professions. He never aspired to office as the many other Heiskells did. He was, however, Justice of the Peace for a number of years. I have heard it said that he did not pay strict attention to the code always if he thought justice pointed in another direction. For example he might give judgment in favor of the holder of a note, though out of date, if he was satisfied that the note was still unpaid and let the courts above on appeal correct the decision.

He married Elizabeth McBride near Greeneville, Tenn., on March 4, 1823, and came to the neighborhood of what is now Sweetwater, as one of her daughters has told me, when William M., the oldest child, was near a year old. He (William) was born May 2, 1824. This tract is the one on which Edgar Heiskell now resides, having been in the family now for ninety years. He did not purchase this land direct from Matthew Nelson, Treasurer for East Tennessee. He purchased from Robert Shaw. At the time Mr. Heiskell came to this section there were no saw mills except those using the up and down straight saw; consequently most of the houses first built were of hewed logs and in many instances the floor of puncheons. A few of these are still standing, one on the rise above the Sweetwater water works spring and another one and a half miles south of town on Mrs. Love's farm.

The Heiskell tan yard was just across the creek from where the Woolen Mill now stands. Mr. Heiskell also purchased some other tracts of land and was a successful farmer and tanner until his death, which was on July 23, 1875. He was interred in the Heiskell burying ground near his residence.

As has been stated the Heiskells in Maryland belonged mostly to the Lutheran Church. Daniel Heiskell was an ardent Cumberland Presbyterian. He may have joined that church on account of the absence of Lutheran churches in our valley and that was the nearest approach in doctrine to the Lutheran Church. This is rendered more probable from the fact that one of his sons was named Luther Melancthon, after the two great German reformers.

The Cumberland Presbyterian Church had its birth in the Cumberland Presbytery of Kentucky in 1810. In 1813 three Presbyteries resolved themselves into a synod and revised the Westminster Confession and excluded, as they claimed, the doctrines of fatalism and infant damnation. The passages they particularly objected to were: Chap. III. "God from all eternity did by the most wise and holy counsel of His own will, freely and unchangeably ordain whatsoever comes to pass." * * * * "By the decree of God, for the manifestation of his glory, some men and angels are predestinated unto everlasting life and others foreordanied to everlasting death."

"These men and angels thus predestinated and foreordained are particularly and unchangeably designed; and their number is so certain and definite that it cannot be increased or diminished."

RAPID INCREASE OF THE CUMBERLAND PRESBYTERIANS.

The C. P. Church increased rapidly in this section. There was a church of this order and a graveyard now mostly overgrown with considerable sized trees one and a half miles north east of Sweetwater at the corner of the Gaut, Young and Heiskell lands. The church there was called Mt. Lebanon. In about 1854, after the location of the E. T. & Ga. R. R. depot and the beginning of the town it was moved as being a more convenient location to the Heiskell land on a part of the lot now occupied by the Sweetwater Woolen Mill.

Mt. Lebanon Cumberland Presbyterian Church moved to Sweetwater when the Cumberland Presbyterian Church or, as our Baptist brethren insist, church house (a church being a number of organized baptized believers, and not a house) was moved from its former location 1 1-2 miles northeast to the town on the Heiskell land, it thereafter answered several purposes. The schoolhouse in the bend of the creek southwest of the town was too small to accommodate the increasing number of students, being only about 25 by 20 feet. The Cumberland Church, then the only church building in Sweetwater was about 35 by 30 ft. So it happened the first school taught in the town and the first I ever went to was in that building. I was between eight and nine years old at the time. I had been very much opposed to going to school because of what the school children I knew told me. I had come to believe that school was a place of confinement, punishment and torture, where the children spent the long summer day sighing for the open air. As they passed me trudging homeward, their talk was mostly of who had been whipped by the teacher and of who had unexpectedly managed to escape punishment. They carried no books home, as the studying they did was at the schoolhouse during the day. I dreaded going to school as much as the heretics the Spanish Inquisition. What I knew I learned from my father by asking questions. Usually when I questioned my mother she would say, "Go ask your Pa." And once in a while he would say, "Maybe you better ask Mr. Coffin that, if you think of it, next time you see him." Therefore I came to believe that if Mr. James Coffin did not answer a question the answer was unknown or that it ought not to be answered.

One summer day my father took me to the free (Public) school at the Cumberland Church. Instead of finding there some scolding ogre, armed with a large bunch of hickory switches ready for use as I expected, we found an intellectual, pleasant faced young woman, Miss Martha Stakely, daughter of Wm. M. Stakely, of Madisonville. She was the soul of goodness and kindness, a characteristic family trait. She welcomed us and I liked her at once, and was willing to remain at school. I have always remembered her with warm feelings of gratitude, not because of what I was taught by her from the blueback speller, for I did not learn very much, but because of her unvarying kindness to a sensitive boy. There were those of her scholars who could repeat their A-B-

C's forward and backward. This was to me an astonishing feat but was not to my taste. I did not see the sense in it. It was many months afterward when I began to like to go to school and became interested in my studies that I learned that letters formed words, words represented objects and ideas and that ideas could be translated into actions.

At that first school I used to watch from the window, near which I had a seat, the tan yard water wheel across the creek. It was an undershot wheel with cups attached, which as the wheel revolved dipped up the water and poured it into troughs that conducted the water into the vats in the tanyard. It was a never-failing source of pleasure to me to watch the wheel go round and see the streams of water sparkling in the sunshine. Miss Martha did not get angry with me for preferring this to my one book.

If she ever whipped anyone I do not recall it. She had reasonably good order without it. I have vividly in mind one escapade. I was in company with several boys larger than myself. Of course I was the dog tray of the crowd. A pot of greasy lamp black was found. It was suggested that we all black ourselves. It was agreed that it would be a fine joke, and so we all did. I used the blacking sparingly at the start, but they said it would not be a bit of fun unless we blacked up good and well. This was amusing enough until just before "books" we tried to wash it off. We stayed long enough to be sent for. Then we were given soap and sent back to the creek to stay till we were white again. But the black was like the smile on the face of "Sunny Jim," it wouldn't come off. When I reached home then more soap and water till I abhorred the very sight of them and a black mamma (as if I had not enough of black) was told to go along to assist in my ablutions. Pretty soon she said: "Mercy's sake! child, 'taint a bit of use trying to git this black off, you'll have 'sociate with niggers all yore born days." I jerked loose from her and looked for the dryest place I could find to meditate in. My thoughts were far from cheerful; there was a girl in the case.

But the gentle reader may ask what has this story to do with early history and what is the moral of it? It has not much to do with it and there is no moral to it. It is no Aesop's fable but a digression; and a digression does not have to have a moral. All truth is useful. At least I have been told so.

As has been remarked the Cumberland Presbyterian Church was a historic building. For the white people it answered the three fold purposes of a day school, church and a Sunday School building. The Sunday School carried on was a union, not a denominational one. After the new Cumberland Presbyterian Church was built the colored people used the old one for the same purposes. There were in the early days of the town, living in this section, quite an array of Cumberland preachers and effective ones too. Among others were Rev. Jas. Tate, Joseph Johnston, Jas. Blair and Jas. H. Fryer. During the week we were taught Webster's speller and reader, and in the same house on Sunday we heard the gospel expounded and the sacred desk pounded. In those days the conception of the Supreme Being as told was quite different from that presented now. Instead of preaching of love and giving entertaining lectures on the lands spoken of in the Bible, we were told in the vivid terms of the torments that awaited the unrepentant beyond the grave. The pictures drawn were truly awful. The Rev. Blair was quite an artist in that line. But however soul harrowing he may have been in the pulpit, he was pleasant and companionable in the family circle. He sometimes visited at my father's and was always a welcome guest. It is somewhat strange how, in the boyish mind, certain words and phrases are connected with certain public speakers and preachers. I never saw or thought of Mr. Blair without thinking at the same time of fire and brimstone. The Rev. Thos. Brown reminded me of the word "Faith;" Rev. Geo. Caldwell, then of Athens, of "Love;" Rev. Thos. R. Bradshaw of "dedicate and predestinate;" Rev. Jno. Scruggs of the Greek word of "Baptizo," which he was prone to explain meant "plunge or immerse" and could not by any implication or indirection in the remotest degree mean anything else. Of most of these things my ideas were of the vaguest nature, except about the brimstone. This I found by experiment smelt bad when cold and worse when burning. I was not anxious enough for knowledge to try the effect on my flesh. I connected Mr. Fryer with the word "freckwently" as he pronounced it. I became rather fond of the word and adopted it till my father told me if I used the word at all to pronounce it "free-quently." I then concluded not to use it at all, not being allowed to pronounce it as I wished.

We hear often now of old time honesty and "old time religion;" and many regret the changed conditions not only in church and state and schools, but even of the roads; for they say that in the last instance if we have pike and graded roads the automobiles traveling there will frighten the horses and make them run away.

It was also sinful in the minds of many to make places of worship comfortable, as by so doing you were listening to Satan's whispers and compromising with him. Services were twice as long then as now and the homes not so conveniently situated. Sunday to some children was made to appear as long as the rest of the week. Conscience did not make cowards of the people but it made them tyrants. Instrumental music in the church they thought a snare and a delusion of the devil. The favorite airs were heart-rending minors sung to such words as "Twas on that dark, that doleful night."

The place of torment was no figure of speech. The lake of fire and brimstone, the wailing and gnashing of teeth of the lost souls was made as realistic as possible, that its tortures were such as no words could picture.

As to the public school money in the forties, East Tennessee got the best of the other sections of the State.

The disbursements were made assording to scholastic population. The families were larger in this section of the State and the people poorer. Only about sufficient State taxes were collected in this end of the State to support the public schools. Middle Tennessee furnished the greater part of the money for the other State expenses.

The eastern part was looked down upon as poverty stricken and that it should ever amount to anything in wealth or resources was considered a remote possibility, which goes to show how provincial people were in those days, and how little was known of us in the other sections of the State.

As for the roads, they were built not for the purpose of transportation but for viewing the scenery and incidentally find out how much a yoke of oxen could pull up a thirty per cent. grade. They went straight up the hill and directly down to the hollow; they descended to the depths and rose to the heights; to wind and twist about was an unnecessary waste of energy. When they were muddy, Monroe County mud is about the muddiest mud of which I have any knowledge with the exception of Texas, whose weather behavior runs old probs crazy. If you happened to be traveling the road some night and saw something white in front of you, there was no occasion for alarm; it was no ghost but only the top of a North Carolina covered wagon, the rest of which was down below. All you had to do was to unhitch and leave your vehicle till tomorrow or next week as the case might be.

When you trudged home from school you would likely be greeted with the remark "Where in the world did you get so muddy?" "Where?" and the whole blooming world was mud over your boot tops. The town was little different from the country. When you went calling, after knocking you were allowed five minutes to clean your feet before the door was opened for your reception.

In 1873 and 1874 Daniel Heiskell, who had purchased a lot for that purpose, built the new Cumberland Presbyterian Church, where it now stands, across the railroad and east from the Southern passenger depot. He said he wanted to build the church as a monument to himself and, as he was amply able to build it, he would ask for no outside help, not even from the members of his own church. If they or others wished they could subscribe to the furnishing of the church and help to pay the salary of the pastor. He wanted to give the house and lot to the Cumberlands himself. Exactly what the church cost no one knew; when asked the question he replied that he did not know precisely and if he did know would not care to say. Not long after the church was finished, Mr. Heiskell executed a deed to the Cumberland Presbyterians. This deed was misplaced, lost or destroyed by fire. What the provisions in this deed were I have never been able to ascertain. Dr. R. F. Scruggs was confident it contained a reversionary clause, i. e. the property was to revert to the heirs unless used as specified for the Cumberland Presbyterian church. This deed was not placed of record on the Registers' Books of Monroe County, at Madisonville.

But even after the Cumberland Presbyterian Church determined in their assembly to unite with a branch of the Presbyterians, the Cumberlands here continued to use it and to claim that it belonged to the members at Sweetwater. There has been no suit entered to determine the question.

The first pastor of the church, if I remember correctly, was Rev. Solon McCroskey.

Some brief information about the older members of the Daniel Heiskell family:—

Daniel Heiskell was born near Winchester, Virginia, March 7, 1799. He died at Sweetwater on July 22, 1875. He married Elizabeth McBride near Greeneville, Tenn., March 4, 1823. She was born April 15, 1803; she died August 1, 1841.

The children of this marriage were:

One. Wm. McBride, b. May 2, 1824. Married Virginia Netherland, December 30, 1852.

Two. Eliza Adaline, b. January 20, 1827; d. July 14, 1906. Married Nathaniel Pope Hight, October 9, 1851, b. January 20, 1827; d. May 17, 1889.

Three. Luther Melancthon, b. June 8, 1829. Married Ellen Wright June 6, 1853.

Four. Hugh Brown, b. November 20, 1831; d. November 13, 1904.

Five. Sarah Catherine, b. September 25, 1834. She married John Patterson February 3, 1853. They moved to Springfield, Mo.

Six. Martha Isabella, b. November 13, 1836. She died in Missouri, April 21, 1861. She married N. W. Haun. Under the firm name of Haun & Stakely he was one of the first merchants in the town of Sweetwater.

Seven. Betsey (Elizabeth) Ramsey, b. November 5, 1839; married R. F. Scruggs February 14, 1860.

Daniel Heiskell married the second time Mary Wallace Montgomery on March 14, 1844. She was born January 1, 1819, and died June 4, 1888.

Children of this marriage were:

1. James Montgomery, b. January 30, 1845; d. March 26, 1898.

2. Margaret Caroline, b. August 19, 1847; married A. D. Scruggs May 1, 1867.

3. Dorcas Ann, b. April 5, 1850; d. January 14, 1854.

Most of those mentioned above were parents of large families. Daniel Heiskell's grandchildren and great-grandchildren are very numerous. From present indications, the Heiskell generation like the cause of popular government will not perish from the face of the earth.

WILLIAM MCBRIDE HEISKELL

Married Virginia Netherland. They had eleven children:

1. Ada Florence, b. November 2, 1853; married Isaac Johnson July 26, 1875. They had one daughter, Brucie Davis, who lives in Los Angeles, Cal.

2. Mary Lyde, b. February 3, 1855; married S. W. Flenniken, April 24, 1878. He died at Sweetwater, April 1902. She lives at Sweetwater.

3. James Netherland, b. July 20, 1856; married Elizabeth Browder, November 18, 1880. Their children are: Mamie Letitia; married J. W. Scott, September 19, 1914. Address, Sylvania, Ga.; John, married Lem Dickey June 15, 1910. Address Dallas, Texas; Loyd, married Maggie Fisher, October 27, 1900. Address Sweetwater; Samuel and Emmett, address Olustee, Okla., and Luther, address, Sweetwater.

4. Bettie Pendleton, b. April 16, 1858. Married Wilson Small, December 18, 1872. They had one child, Robert, who lives at Decatur, Tenn.

5. Myrtie, b. February 3, 1861. Married Mark Goddard, December 12, 1893. They live at Sweetwater and have two children, Willie and Hugh.

6. Ann Lipscomb, b. June 29, 1862. Married James Small September 3, 1878. They have three children, Willie, Henry and Thomas. They live at Niota.

7. Willie, b. October 28, 1863; d. September 2, 1870.

8. Virginia N., b. January 18, 1865. Married Wilson Small August 7, 1878. They had two sons, Isham and William, who live at Decatur.

9. Daniel, b. January 8, 1867; married Bertha Willis, October 6, 1901. Their children are: Earnest, Beulah, Grace, Mack, Anna and Tyler.

10. Cate, b. January 9, 1869; married John Ferguson, December 11, 1894. Their children are: Brucie (who married John Thomas, May 5, 1912), Earl, Charlie, Henry, Horace P. and Mary Alma.

Henry Lee Heiskell and Martha Neil were married January 29, 1898. They had one child, Elga, b. December 9, 1898. They live at Pilot Point, Texas.

Ada Heiskell Johnson, married second, T. J. Hinton, in 1894. They live in Knoxville. James N. Heiskell, owns and lives on the farm his father bought in 1852.

LUTHER MELANCTHON HEISKELL.

(The Melancthon is sometimes abbreviated to 'Ton'') was born June 8, 1829. He died at his residence near Spring City on September 16, 1909. He married Ellen Wright of Greenville, Tenn., January 6, 1853. She was born November 1, 1830, and died January 2, 1892. Soon after their marriage they moved to Missouri and from there to Rhea County, near the site of Spring City, in 1866. He was a farmer, being in a country where game abounded, he was very fond of hunting. Their children were seven in number:

(1) Martha Elizabeth, b. May 11, 1854; died October 24, 1887.
(2) Daniel, b. April 9, 1856.
(3) Pope, b. June 25, 1858; died September 14, 1871.
(4) John, b. March 26, 1860; died December 21, 1860.
(5) Emma Ada Bell, b. August 23, 1863; died September 12, 1894.
(6) Everett, b. March 13, 1866; d. August 28, 1867.
(7) Minnie.

* * * * *

Martha Elizabeth Heiskell was married to T. J. Robinson October 26, 1871. To them four children were born, two boys and two girls.

* * * * *

Daniel Heiskell married Belle Rose. To them were born five children.

* * * * *

Emma Ada Belle Heiskell was married to Jas. L. Hoyl October, 1882. To them were born two children, Ellen Hoyl and Barbara Hoyl.

* * * * *

Minnie Heiskell was married to S. E. Paul December 1, 1897. To them was born one child, Ellen Heiskell Paul, b. June 2, 1899.

HUGH BROWN HEISKELL

Was born in Sweetwater Valley, Monroe County, Tenn., November 30, 1831. He died at his residence in Rhea County, Tenn., November 13, 1904. He married Rhoda Farmer of Hillsville, Va., in 1856. She was born April 7, 1841, and died March 23, 1892. He moved to Rhea County in 1861. He was a farmer and stock raiser. He was Justice of the Peace for fifteen years. Their children were:

1. Florence, b. July 27, 1857; d. June 30, 1903; married R. M. Robinson of Rhea County on November 16, 1881.

2. Wade, b. October 21, 1858; married Lydia Ganett, of Alton, Mo., in the spring of 1891.

3. Frank, b. February 21, 1860; married Lucy Patterson of Bozeman, Montana, in November 1894.

4. Addie, b. July 21, 1861.

5. John, b. September 17, 1863; d. April 17, 1915. He was twice married; first to Eva Holloway, of Spring City, Tenn., on March 1, 1892. After her death in —— he married Kitty Caldwell, of Spring City, on October 17, 1906.

6. Hugh Brown, b. August 11, 1865; married Carrie Wallis, Spring City, on March 7, 1900.

7. Catherine, b. February 8, 1867; married D. C. Kemmer February 1, 1911.

8. Frederick, b. August 20, 1869; married Annie Smith, Bozeman, Mont., October 18, 1911.

9. Nellie May, b. May 2, 1871; d. August 13, 1898.

10. Richmond, b. September 2, 1873; married Etta Hart, of Spring City, on February 20, 1907.

SARAH HEISKELL PATTERSON.

Sarah Catherine Heiskell, b. September 5, 1834, was married March 30, 1853, to John A. Patterson, moving to Springfield, Mo., the same year. She joined the church at an early age and lived a faithful Christian life to the end of her more than four score years. To them were born ten children, all of whom were living and present when she died on June 16, 1916. Their names are as follows:

Bettie Y. Patterson, b. April 19, 1854.
Addie Isabell Patterson, b. March 23, 1856.
Virginia Ellen Patterson, b. May 13, 1858.
Joe Alma Kate Patterson, b. November 1, 1860.
Daniel Lewis Patterson, b. June 11, 1864.
Jessie Heiskell Patterson, b. December 15, 1866.
Hattie Amada Patterson, b. August 26, 1869.
John Hugh Rice Patterson, b. July 9, 1872.
Eva May Patterson, b. January 30, 1875.
Edward Tefft Patterson, b. July 25, 1878.

Bettie Y. Patterson, married W. E. Anderson, 1874; three children, Wm. Y. Anderson, Guy P. Anderson and Mary Heiskell Anderson (all living).

Addie I. Patterson married Wm. H. McCann, 1876; two children, John E. McCann, Fred Harrison McCann.

Virginia E. Patterson married Hugh M. Cowan, 1877. Children, Katherine, Bruce H., Wm. P., Edna, Aleen, Hugh.

Joe Alma Kate married Emory L. Hoke, 1886; two children, Clifford Hoke, Catherine E. Hoke.

Daniel L. Patterson married Allie Murden, 1892; three children, Dwight M., Louise, Frank.

Jessie Heiskell Patterson married Geo. D. Stateson, 1891; three children, Alberta, Salome, Ruth.

Hattie A. Patterson (single).

John H. R. Patterson married Elsie Moore, 1913, one child, Edward Moore Patterson.

Eva May Patterson married A. C. Jarrett, 1901; no children.

Edward T. Patterson married Marie Lagana, 1905; three children, Virginia Catherine, Bernice, Edward Raphael.

Mr. James Montgomery Heisnell,

Son of Daniel and Mary Heiskell, was born in Sweetwater, Tenn., January 30, 1845. Died March 26, 1898. Interred in West View Cemetery, Sweetwater. He was married to Miss Laura Jones on October 18, 1874. Her father was James Jones, her mother was Sarah Pugh Jones of Bertie County, N. C. She was born in Memphis Tenn., October 23, 1848. J. M. H. owned a very large farm and a number of houses and lots in Sweetwater. He was a Cumberland Presbyterian. The children of Jas. M. and L. J. Heiskell were:

Harry, b. August 27, 1875. Was married to Norah Jones on December 18, 1901. She was a daughter of Moulton and Sarah Cunningham Jones. He is a successful farmer and stock raiser and lives near Sweetwater. The children of Harry and Norah H. are: Lucille, King, Pauline, Harry Lee, Hugh Lynn and Annie Laurie.

Edgar, b. November 19, 1877. He married Annie Cleveland, daughter of Eli and Susan Martin Cleveland, January 16, 1908. He is a farmer and resides in the old Daniel Heiskell residence. Their children are: James Eli, Christine and Edgar Burton.

Maiden, b. October 4, 1880. She married D. C. Boykin June 15, 1902. He is a traveling passenger agent for the Southern R. R. Lives at Knoxville, Tenn. They have one child, Laura Elizabeth.

Margaret C. Heiskell Scruggs,

Of Knoxville, was born at Sweetwater on August 19, 1847. She was married to Dr. Abijah Scruggs on May 1, 1867, the Rev. Jas. Blair, officiating. Abijah was the son of the Rev. John Scruggs and brother of Dr. R. F. Scruggs. He was a physician and druggist. He moved from Knoxville to Niota in 1867 and from there to Cleveland, Tenn., in 1874. They resided there until September, 1889, when they moved to Knoxville. He died at Knoxville April 9, 1909, and was buried at Sweetwater April 11, 1909. The children of A. D. and M. H. Scruggs were:

1. Richard Francis, b. July 31, 1869; d. May, 1902.
2. Daniel Heiskell, b. September 15, 1874; d. July 11, 1909.

3. Mary Heiskell, b. in Cleveland, Tenn.
4. Bess, b. in Cleveland, Tenn.
5. Samuel, b. July 7, 1881; d. July 8, 1882.

Richard Francis married Geraldine Jackson of Nashville, Tenn., on January 24, 1895. She was the daughter of Dr. — Jackson, of Nashville. They had three children.

REV. JOSEPH JANEWAY

Was born in Claiborne County, Tenn., June 28, 1831. He moved to Sweetwater Valley, McMinn County, December, 1855, after having lived three years in Loudon, Tenn. He was educated in the literary course at Carson and Newman College at Mossy Creek, now Jefferson City, Tenn. He married Jane Helms of Claiborne County on February 12, 1852. She was a cousin of John Helms of Morristown, Tenn. She was born July 9, 1831. James Janeway's father was a minister and farmer. On the second Saturday of July, 1859, he was ordained at Mt. Harmony. He was pastor of the following churches in the order named: Cedar Fork, Post Oak, Stockton's Valley; Providence, in Roane County, Prospect, Philadelphia, Loudon; two churches in Knox County, Blair's Cross Roads and Mars Hill; Union (in McMinn); Goodfield, Decatur, Sewell, Mt. Harmony, County Line, Eastanalee, Hiwassee, New Friendship and others. His children were:

William Thomas, b. February 16, 1853; d. in infancy.

Nancy Jane, b. March 8, 1854; married S. K. Mountain. Address, New Tazewell, Tenn.

Elizabeth Ann, b. April 14, 1856; married H. M. Johnson, Bells, Texas.

Jno. Nelson, b. December 10, 1859; married Alice Mitchell of Pennsylvania in 1898. They have four children. He is in the transfer business at Edmonds, Puget Sound, Wash.

Prior Lee, b. July 14, 1862; married Etta Williams in Texas. They have seven children and live at Bonita, Texas.

James Patton, b. October 29, 1864; married Josie Bushong. Two children living, two dead. They live near County Line, Monroe County, Tenn.

Joseph Lung, b. March 13, 1867. Lives at the old Janeway place.

Franklin Berry, b. April 15, 1869, artist, portrait and landscape painter. Lives at Knoxville, Tenn.

Mary Josephine, b. September 30, 1871. She married Jno. Hansard. He died in 1871.

Mr. Janeway ceased ministerial work after his 70th birthday. He had read the Bible through more than fifty times. He was made a Mason at Loudon, Tenn., in 1861.

JOSEPH DYCHE JONES

Was born in Bedford County, Tennessee. Came to Philadelphia, Tenn., and lived there from the time of his marriage until his death. He was a cousin of the Rev. Eli Cleveland. He was a tanner by trade, and which in the early settlement of the valley was a very profitable one. He also owned a farm. Like many people of his time his house was always open to his friends whether on invitation or not.

He married Aley Mathis, daughter of Eli Cleveland, February 6, 1830. She was born May 7, 1813 and died May 30, 1855. He died in June 1883. They were members of the Baptist Church. The children by this marriage were:

1. Lodusky Caroline, b. October 6, 1834; d. June 30, 1862. (See Chas. Cannon).

2. Mary Louise, b. December 16, 1836. Married S. Y. B. Williams. (Whom see).

3. Aley Mathis, b. August 8, 1840; d. March 3, 1857.

4. Eli Cleveland, b. January 25, 1841; d. August 4, 1902.

5. James Chamberlain, b. August 26, 1844; d. October 5, 1872.

6. Joseph Morton, b. August 30, 1847.

7. Robert Augustus, b. April 3, 1849; d. in 1903 at Greenfield, Mo.

8. Jesse Franklin, b. June 1, 1851; d. by accident when a young man.

Eli Cleveland Jones was educated at Mossy Creek, Tenn., now Jefferson City. He entered the Confederate army, Co. F., 43rd Tenn. Regiment and was made captain of that company after the death of Captain Turner. He married (first) Emma Adkins, daughter of Eli Adkins, September 15, 1873, b. August 31, 1857. He was a merchant at Philadelphia, Tenn., for many years, and afterwards at Loudon, Tenn., until his death. His first wife died at Philadelphia, August 8, 1878. Children were:

1. Paul, b. June 10, 1874. Married Annie, daughter of Dr. William Harrison, of Loudon, Tenn., on July 31, 1907. He lives in Colorado. They have one child, Wm. Harrison, b. October 15, 1915.

2. Alma, b. May 5, 1876; d. June 14, 1903.

Captain E. C. J. was married (second) to Sarah, daughter of Rev. W. M. Kerr, minister of the M. E. Church, South, and formerly of Greene County, Tenn., January 25, 1882. She was born January 14, 1861. She resides in Loudon, Tenn. Their children are:

1. Earl C., b. January 19, 1883. Lives in Montana.

2. Edna, b. November 15, 1884. Married Frank Jones, son of Mat Jones, February 21, 1904. Live at Loudon Their children are: Jesse Franklin, b. June 15, 1908, Sarah Elizabeth, b. June 20, 1910.

3. Harriet, b. October 6, 1886. She married Ed., son of W. K. Blair, July 31, 1913. Two children: Jane, b. September 5, 1914; Corry, b. December 18, 1915.

4. Ann Mathis, b. February 28, 1889.

5. William Kerr ("Don"), b. September 5, 1891. Employee Bank of Loudon, Tenn.

6. Mary Katherine, b. January 1, 1894.

7. Margaret Bicknell, b. January 19, 1899.

James C., second son of Joseph D. Jones, m. Lou, daughter of Melvin Porter. They had one child, Sydney Lenoir, who died unmarried. After the death of her husband, James Jones, Mrs. J. married ———— McKnight and moved to Missouri where he died.

Joseph Morton, third son of J. D. Jones, married Louisa J., daughter of Eli S. Adkins, November 29, 1869. They moved to the state of Washington. They had one daughter, Joseph, who married Will, son of Philander McCroskey. Joseph M. J. died in Washington and his wife married again.

Robert Augustus, third son of J. D. Jones, married Nannie A., daughter of Thos. L. Upton, September 8, 1870. She was b. June 27, 1846; d. February 22, 1882. He was in the mercantile business, for a number of years, with his brother, E. C. Jones, at Philadelphia, Tenn. Their children were:

Joseph D., who died unmarried; Frank Upton and Thomas, both married and live in Missouri, and Hattie Cleveland, who died unmarried. Frank U. married Fannie, daughter of William Johnson, son-in-law of D. H. Cleveland. They have two daughters, teachers in Greenfield, Mo.

JESSE F. JONES

was a brother of J. D. Jones, of Philadelphia, Tenn. He was born August 9, 1808. He married Clarissa, daughter of the Rev. Eli Cleveland. She was born —————, 1815. She died March 11, 1880. They lived on the Philadelphia and Sweetwater road about half way between those places, on a farm adjoining those of F. H. Gregory and David H. Cleveland. Their children were:

1. Aley, m. W. H. H. Ragon January 26, 1865. They moved to the state of Washington. Their children were: Bettie, b. January 22, 1866; d. October 23, 1885. Dora, b. April 27, 1867; d. January 21, 1891. Sons Charles and —————

2. Matthew, m. November 21, 1875, Bettie Harrison, daughter of William Harrison, of Pond Creek Valley. She died in July, 1916. They had three sons and one daughter. One son is dead. One son, Frank, lives at Loudon and is postmaster. The youngest son, Robert, and his father live in Loudon, Tenn.

3. Florence, third child of Jesse F. and Aley Jones, was b. February 19, 1859, and d. June 1, 1876.

JOSIAH K. JOHNSTON.

There is an old burying ground where the Mt. Lebanon Cumberland Presbyterian Church used to stand. It occupies about two-thirds of an acre, one and one-half miles northeast of Sweetwater on a corner of the farm now owned by Harry Heiskell. Now it is almost entirely grown up in woods and undergrowth. There are many graves there judging from the rocks and footboards and from the remains of palings rotted down.

The Josiah K. Johnston enclosure, near the northwest corner of the graveyard is a solid brick wall about three feet high and about 30 by 13 feet in dimensions. Next to the north end of the cemetery is a monument bearing the inscription "Nancy P., wife of William E. Snead and daughter of J. K. and C. Johnson. Born April 3, 1833. Died December 31, 1863." There is also a monument near the centre of the enclosure, having on three sides of it these inscriptions:

"Josiah K. Johnston, born February 10, 1805. Died December 10, 1861. Clarissa, wife of Josiah K. Johnston. Born April 23, 1811. Died April 9, 1864. Sue, daughter of J. K. and Clarissa Johnston. Born December 15, 1845. Died August 8, 1864."

The enclosure to the Johnston lot is the only one in the graveyard which is well preserved.

Josiah K. Johnston came from Fork Creek Valley to the place on the Philadelphia road, one and one-half miles north of Sweetwater, where the Rufus Gaut family now reside. He purchased the land from W. M. Henderson. He had a fine body of land and, with slave labor, operated it successfully. He had a large family of daughters who were universally popular and, being of a hospitable nature, they entertained lavishly. Mr. Johnston was a Presbyterian. Mr. and Mrs. Johnston were the parents of six daughters and no sons. They were:

One. Nancy, b. April 3, 1833; d. December 31, 1863.
Two. Letitia, b. February 18, 1835.
Three. Sophronia, b. September 10, 1837.
Four. Callie, b. February 5, 1842.
Five. Josephine, b. February 22, 1844.
Susan, b. December 15, 1845; d. August 8, 1864.

One. Nancy was married to William E. Snead. They had one son, William E., who resides on the Madisonville road, three miles from Sweetwater.

Two. Letitia, the second daughter of J. K. Johnston was married to James A. Wright on March 13, 1855. James A. Wright was born in Wilkes County, N. C., in 1823. His father, Josiah Wright, came from England. His mother, Nancy Reynolds Wright was a native of North Carolina. Mr. Wright came to Monroe County, Tenn., in his boyhood. On the 25th of May, 1848, he married his first wife Emma Yoakum, of Philadelphia, Tenn. She died in 1854. They had one daughter, Mary, born at Madisonville in 1849. She married George H. Holliday, of Atlanta, in 1868.

About four years after his first marriage (second) to Miss L. Johnston, Mr. Wright bought the Bowman, now the Kilpatrick place, south of Sweetwater, and moved there. Mrs. Wright says he was the first postmaster of Sweetwater. He was a merchant in Sweetwater, belonging to one firm or another from the beginning of the town until after the commencement of the Civil War.

He moved to Tyner's Station in 1862, and in 1867 from there to Atlanta, Ga., where he became a member of the firm of Glenn, Wright and Carr, commission merchants. He died in Little Rock, Ark., where he then resided, on November 18, 1872, and was buried there in Oakland Cemetery. The children of James and L. Wright:

(1) Josiah J., b. February 16, 1856; m. Margaret Maude Horsfal on January 6, 1897. Their children are: Harry, b. April 16, 1898; Edith, b. December 14, 1910; Richard, b. April 16, 1911.

(2) Nannie, b. April 11, 1858; m. George A. Alexander in June, 1876. Their children are: Julia G.; Letitia J.; James A., and Florence Bell. Part (or all) of them reside in Washington, D. C.

(3) Benjamin B., third child of James A. Wright, was born April 6, 1860. He married Katie Ledwidge. They live at Little Rock, Ark. Their children are: Ben. B., Jr., b. June 26, 1892; Kathleen, b. October 15, 1891; Christopher L., b. February 18, 1898, and Edward L., b. July 16, 1903. They are Roman Catholics.

(4) Dicky L., fourth child of James A. Wright, was born December 12, 1867. She married Eli Richard Shipp December 12, 1889.

The children of Mary and George H. Holliday, mentioned above, Mary being the child of J. A. Wright's first wife Emma Yoakum are: Mabel, who married John Moody; Ethel m. Joseph Crenshaw, and George H. Holliday, Jr., of Atlanta, Ga.

Three. Sophronia, third daughter of Josiah K. Johnston, married Archibald Bacome on October 23, 1856. He was born in Sullivan County, Tenn., July 29, 1814. He died December 7, 1899, at his residence, one mile south of Philadelphia. He had lived on this place since

his father, James Bacome, moved there in 1819. During his lifetime he had bought and sold many valuable farms. The children of A. and Sophronia Bacome are:
1. Callie, b. October 21, 1858; m. W. C. Milligan October 15, 1893. Residence, Philadelphia.
2. Beulah, b. May 12, 1865.
3. Clara, m. S. J. Akin, of Cleveland, Tenn., November 11, 1898. He was a graduate of Annapolis and a lawyer at Cleveland. Their children are: Caroline, b. March 4, 1900; Sammie, dau., b. October 6, 1901. S. J. Akin died July 31, 1901.

Four. Caledonia, m. on October 4, 1865, H. C. Peake, a druggist of Warsaw, Ky. Their children were:
1. Clara, b. March 14, 1867; m. J. W. Evans February 11, 1885. They have three daughters, two of whom are married. Juliette, m. Henry Blanton; Sue m. J. T. Fowler and a third daughter, who is a school girl.
2. Josie, b. May 3, 1869. She married S. D. McDannold. Address, Tarrant, Texas. He has a large farm and makes a specialty of high grade horses and cattle.
3. Sue, b. December 20, 1876; m. E. F. Earnest January 9, 1909. Address, Douglas, Ariz.
4. Ben. b. September 26, 1879; m. May 7, 1910. He has been general manager of a large drug house for a number of years. They have one son of 4 years.
5. Nellie, fifth child of H. C. and C. Peake, was born January 25, 1886; m. E. Wolf June 6, 1903. He died June 20, 1904. She then married K. W. Goff, postoffice, Douglas.

Josephine, fifth daughter of J. K. and Clarissa Johnston, was married to Dr. J. B. Lackey July 20, 1865. They had two children: James Gilmer and Lizzie J. The latter married W. W. Holton, a son of Mrs. Lackey's second husband. Dr. Lackey practised his profession at Friendsville, Blount County, Tenn. He died on March 22, 1872. Mrs. Lackey married (second) John W. Holton, of Sparta, Ky., on April 5, 1876. He was a farmer and stock dealer. They had one son and two daughters. The son was drowned on January 1, 1897, at the age of 19 years. One of the daughters died at 2 years of age. The other daughter married Tilton Detheridge, a farmer living near Sanders, Ky.

Mrs. Josephine Holton is dead.

THE LENOIR FAMILY.

Our destiny and character are in a great measure determined by heredity and environment. No biography is complete therefore without an answer to the questions: "Who were your ancestors, where and when born, whence came you and why?" Nations, provinces and neighborhoods have their own particular racial instincts and proclivities, their prejudices, likes and dislikes. Families have their own peculiar characteristics. One distinguishing trait of the Lenoir family is impatience of dictation from others where personal, political or religious liberty is concerned. If you make the mistake of telling one of them he must or must not do something, which he thinks should concern only himself and not the public good, he thereupon resolves himself into a committee of one to devise ways and means to do or not to do that very thing. This pertains especially to such matters as amusements, food, drink and clothing, as he deems these are purely personal matters.

St. Paul said: "If meat make my brother to offend, I will eat no meat while the world standeth." A truly commendable spirit, considering the fact that he was once a persecutor "even unto strange cities."

I believe as a rule the Lenoirs have gone as far as they ought to relieve their fellow beings in distress, their time and money being at the disposal of their friends; but if one of them were asked, even by a friend or brother to refrain from something on account of some whim or fancy, I am afraid the answer would not be satisfactory. I have known few of them that would consent to regulate their diet according to the notions of another.

When Louis XIV in 1685 revoked the Edict of Nantes, the charter of religious liberty signed by Henry IV in 1598, a number of the Lenoirs left French soil forever. This they did not so much because they were enamored of the German, Martin Luther, or that the views of the gloomy and ascetic Calvin appealed to them, but because they resented the persecutions and tyranny then practiced by the Pope of Rome and Louis XIV.

When George III imposed a tax on the colonies they became ardent whigs and revolted, not that it would hurt them to pay the tax but because it was a violation of the Charter granted Carolina by King Charles II. Thus the spirit of Touchstone in "As You Like It": "If reasons were as plenty as blackberries, I give no man a reason on compulsion."

In 1861 the Lenoirs in all parts of the south wished to stay in the Union. But when Mr. Lincoln issued his call for troops to whip them in when and if they seceded, they unanimously, with one accord, to a man and to a woman, did their level best to get out and stay out and were sorry when they did not succeed. They were union men of their own volition but not on compulsion. Government should not be founded on the consent of those that govern.

In France the name Lenoir is not an uncommon one. It was first probably written Le Noir, then anglicized into Lenoir. The names Xavier and Cholmondeley have undergone still greater changes; now written in this country Sevier and Chumley. I have been told also that the Huguenots of the family even in France wrote the name "Lenoir" to distinguish themselves from the Catholics, who wrote it with a capital N. The Lenoirs in France so far as I have been able to ascertain were farmers, traders, merchants, manufacturers, explorers, and occasionally art collectors and bankers. They have never risen to celebrity as advocates, soldiers or professional men. Nearly the same has been the case in our own country. Farmers, merchants and manufacturers will include nearly all of them. I have known only one lawyer and one physician of the name in Tennessee and North Carolina, and they did not depend on the practice of their profession for a living. They have never been soldiers for pleasure, pay, plunder or glory. They have been under arms only when they were assured their country needed their services. Nor have they been statesmen, orators or politicians. If ever one was a preacher or could write "Rev." before his name I have never heard of it. They never had the gift of fluent speech nor were fond of exhibiting themselves to the public gaze. Few of them were so fixed in the belief of the tenets of any one church organization as to feel called to preach. Some of them have represented their counties and districts in the lower and upper houses of the Legislature of their states, as the saying goes, with credit to themselves and their constituents, but I believe that is about as far as they ever got or aspired to. They were not adepts at intrigue or swapping votes on public measures.

They have always taken prosperity and adversity with equal complacency; never boasted of the one or complained at the other or appealed to the public for sympathy. Their nonchalant disposition was illustrated by one of the Lenoirs who was an explorer in the deserts of northern Africa. Early one morning one of his companions came to his tent in great excitement and shouted: "Lenoir, the Bedouins are attacking us." "Tell the fools to wait; I'm shaving," was the answer. But the "fools" wouldn't wait. His dead body was found with the razor still in his hand.

Lenoir is a favorite name for the villain in melodrama and dime novels. Mrs. Southworth uses it in "The Hidden Hand." The adjective "noir" means black; and black in name, black by nature is assumed. Yet they are not always pictured as villains in the play but are sometimes given the place of the hero, coming out with flying colors.

I might as well give at the outset the authorities on which I rely for statements made below:

Wheeler's History of North Carolina.

Historic Homes of North Carolina Part III.

Homer D. L. Sweet's History of Avery Family of Croton. Published at Syracuse, N. Y.

The Unpublished History of the Lenoir Family by Miss Laura Norwood of Lenoir, North Carolina.

Public and Family Records and Letters. Personal Conversations and Knowledge. This will save footnotes and special quotations. Any of the family friends desiring more specific and lengthy information would do well to consult the above authorities.

There were four Lenoir brothers that came to America after the revocation of the Edict of Nantes by Louis XIV on May 2, 1685. One of these four brothers came across the ocean in his own vessel. He therefore was probably a resident of Nantes, as this has been a great commercial and shipping point from the time of the Roman occupation. He must have come almost directly to New York City. In the archives of the Old French Church is a Baptismal Record of which the following is a translation:

"Baptism Today, 6th October, 1696.

After the prayer of the evening has been baptized in this church, Isaac, son of Isaac Lenoir and of Anne, his father and mother, born on the 25th of last September and presented to his baptism by Auguste Grassot and Susanne Hulin, Godfather and Godmother, and baptized by M. Peiret, Minister."

(Signed)   I. LENOIR.
SUSANNE HULIN.

PEIRET, Minister.
AUGUSTE GRASSOT.

At this time New York was an English possession, having passed from the hands of the Dutch in 1674. New York City then included only the territory between the Battery and Wall Street.

In one of his voyages this Lenoir's vessel was lost "in a storm, carrying him to a seaman's grave." As however he was not heard from after his departure from New York this is mere conjecture. This was in the day of piracy, and he may have been captured by pirates. He was, I understand, the great grandfather of William Lenoir who settled in Wilkes County, N. C.

In what is now Caldwell County in the "Happy Valley" of the Yadkin River, surrounded by a grove of magnificent hemlocks and oaks, stands the colonial mansion of General William Lenoir, spoken of above. It was built by him after the Revolutionary War in 1785. Near this mansion is the family burying ground containing the remains of many of the Lenoir family. In this is a large monument of beautiful marble impressive in its silent majesty. It dominates the landscape and rises above the other monuments of children and grandchildren as his name and fame is above theirs. On this monument is the epitaph, which is almost an epitome of the history of his life. It is in a fine state of preservation, and reads as follows:

Here Lies
All That Is Mortal Of
WILLAM LENOIR
Born May 8th, 1751.
Died May 6th, 1839.

"In times that tried men's souls he was a genuine whig. As a lieutenant under Rutherford and Williams in 1776, and as a captain under Cleveland at King's Mountain he proved himself a brave soldier. Although a native of another state, yet North Carolina was proud of him as her adopted son. In her services he filled the several offices of major-general of militia, president of the Senate, first president of the Board of Trustees of the university, for sixty years justice of the peace and chairman of the court of Common Pleas. In all these high public trusts he was found faithful. In private life he was no less distinguished as an affectionate husband, a kind father and a warm hearted friend. The traveler will long remember his hospitality and the poor bless him as a benefactor."

The matter of the inscription, above quoted, was left to his friends and associates in public life. This is their estimate of him—their tribute to his memory.

In addition to the information heretofore given in regard to William Lenoir we give these facts: He was born in Brunswick County, Va. He married Anne Ballard, of Halifax, N. C., in 1771. In 1775 he moved to near where the site of Wilkesboro, then in Surry County, now stands. In 1785 he moved to his residence in Happy Valley, called by him Fort Defiance. There he died.

He served in the Indian campaigns against the Cherokees under Rutherford in 1776. From his account of the expedition against Ferguson and the Battle of King's Mountain I make the following excerpts:

"Ferguson had daily information of the advancement of the Whigs and was so on the alert that men on foot would not be able to overtake him; therefore orders were given that as many as had or could procure horses go in advance as mounted infantry, there not being a single dragoon in the Whig army. Whereupon about six hundred were prepared and marched off about sunrise on the sixth day of October, 1780, leaving the footmen, about 1,500 in number, encamped on Green River under the command of Major Joseph Herndon. They, the six hundred, marched all day to Cowpens, where they were joined by Colonel Williams with a few South Carolina militia. They started to camp but were ordered forward. They marched all night and in the morning joined the forces of Shelby, Sevier, Cleaveland and Campbell. They marched in four columns: Colonel Winston commanded the right-hand column, Cleaveland the left, and Shelby and Sevier the middle columns. As Colonel Campbell had come the greatest distance, from the State of Virginia, he was complimented with the command of the whole detachment."

(He then tells of the battle and highly important results. His own personal part in the engagement he relates as follows):

"I was captain of a company and left them at Green River, except six of them who procured horses and went with us. I went as a common soldier, and did not pretend to take command of those that belonged to my company, but fell in immediately behind Colonel Winston, in front of the right-hand column, which enabled me to give more particular account of the progress of that part of the army than any other. Before the battle Adjutant Jesse Franklin (afterward Governor of North Carolina), Captain Robert Cleaveland and myself agreed to stand together and support each other; but at the commencement of the battle enthusiastic zeal caused us all to separate. Each being anxious to effect the grand object, no one appeared to regard his own personal safety. As to my own part from where we dismounted, instead of going on to surround, I advanced the nearest way toward the enemy under a heavy fire, until I got within about thirty paces. * * * About that time I received a slight wound in my side and another in my left arm; and after that a bullet went through my hair, where it was tied, and my clothes were cut in several places. From the account I have given of the battle it will be understood that it was fought on our side by militia alone. By that victory many militia officers procured swords who could not possibly get any before; neither was it possible to procure a good supply of ammunition."

The above was written not to give a history of the battle but show what part William Lenoir, also the Clevelands, took in it. Rather than miss the fight he surrendered his position as captain and left his company at Green River and marched and fought as a private in the ranks. Thus he showed that he appreciated the sacrifices of the men who had come from beyond the great mountains, through pathless wilds almost, to their relief.

Until of late years the New England historians of the United States, notably in the school histories, gave little space and attached little importance to that expedition and battle. If they mentioned it at all they referred to it as a skirmish in which a few backwoodsmen under Campbell and Sevier captured several companies of tories under Ferguson. This Ferguson had been annoyings the whigs of North and South Carolina and the half dozen bullets he got in his carcass was very gratifying to them. After disposing of the expedition in this summary manner they would give several pages to the early life of General Israel Putnam. Oh there never was such a wolf as the one Putnam slew since the time of Romulus and Remus and the days of Red Riding Hood. He (or was it she?) ravaged the flocks and herds of the country around and left a pathway of blood and terror in its wake. Dogs could do nothing with it. When they attacked it they were torn to pieces. When closely pushed by men it fled to the caverns in the hills. But Putnam went into its lair and killed it and pulled it out with his naked hands. Then in the Revolution he rounded out a life of glorious deeds by galloping his horse down a flight of stone steps. When the British who were in pursuit, feared to attempt this feat he waved to them with all the grace of "Nolichucky Jack" leading a country dance.

But it has happened for a number of years that the Daughters of the Revolution have seen that the heroes of King's Mountain have received due meed of praise. Their names and fame have not been suffered to decay. In most histories now written they are given ample though tardy justice.

I have seen a little barnyard rooster that clucked and strutted and crowed around all day. He said in his chicken language: "No hen ever sat on the egg I was in; I am no high bred incubator chicken either; I was just hatched out in the sun; I pecked my way out of the egg all by myself; I was not raised, I just came up myself; not a single chicken ever did anything for me, they were all against me in the whole yard"—and then he flies up on the gatepost and flap, flap, flap, cock-a-doodle-doo —"what game rooster am I?" then the hens come running.

I have seen men like this little rooster, who virtually if not actually said: "I am strictly a self-made man; my father wasn't any account; he spent his money in liquor and gambling; my mother was barely respectable if that; she took in washing; they never gave me any clothes or sent me to school; they never taught me or left me anything; I was turned out just like a woods colt to graze in any pasture I could find;—but behold what I am now! I am owner of a bank or a railroad, or I've been to Congress, or a merchant prince or a copper king, and I've done it all myself, nobody helped me the least bit, everybody tried to hinder me, but just look what I've made out of myself'"

"Little Jack Horner sat in the corner
Eating his Christmas pie;
He put in his thumb and pulled out a plum
And said: 'What a great boy am I.'"

Some people admire a man who acts and talks in this way; it is their privilege so to do. You rest assured though that, however much others may admire him, it is not one-tenth as much as he admires himself.

It is of course unfortunate for a man to lack early advantages. In the majority of instances it is unnecessary for him to call attention to the fact. All honor to the man who rises above his heredity and environment and does more for the world than his father did before him. I do not wish to detract one iota from the credit due him. But let him not belittle his parents in order to place himself upon a pedestal: to put it mildly it is not in good taste.

On the other hand that one should be puffed up with pride or claim special privileges because some of his ancestors were rich or renowned is worse still—even odious.

I am led to make these remarks from the fact that, so far as I am aware, the Lenoirs have been well enough to do for the last 150 years in the United States to give their children a good education and a start in life. Few if any of them can claim that they were not given a chance in the world. If they did not succeed and become respected citizens they have no one to blame but themselves.

William Lenoir was a remarkable versatile man, excellently well equipped mentally and physically. It was thought by his relations that he could do anything almost except play on the fiddle and probably could have done that if he had tried. If only he had known how much satisfaction it was to be able to do so no doubt he would have added that to his other accomplishments.

He had a real genius for mechanics. My father told me that he (Wm. Lenoir), had already invented a cotton gin and had been a little slow in perfecting it when he found out that Mr. Whitney had patented something similar. It is not supposed that one borrowed from the other but that each was working independently. That I would have thought was in the nature of a family legend but for one fact: I have in my possession now a surveyor's compass which was made by him at home with apparently no other tools than a pocket knife, a hammer, a file and possibly a chisel. It is all of thoroughly seasoned wood except the tube that fits on top of the Jacob staff, the needle and its support, the cards with the degrees marked and the circular glass covering of the face. The copper tube and the needle support were once part of a copper kettle. The face is about six inches in diameter and has two compass cards, the one marking the degrees and the other the half degrees. The figures and lines are nearly perfect except the paper of the cards is slightly moth eaten. The circular glass covering the face is the least artistically done of any part of the compass. It was evidently not cut by a diamond but by some steel instrument. The edge is not smooth enough to have been cut by a diamond. The needle was made out of a piece of steel bearing the marks of having been filed. It was probably magnetized with a piece of magnetic iron ore. I have never tried to survey with this compass myself but my father said that it ran lines accurately.

I have never heard why he made the compass; whether he was unable to procure one when he needed it or merely to show what he could do. Whenever anything is badly wanted, whether needed or not, the inventive genius of the North Carolina mountaineer rarely fails to supply it.

* * * * * *

The Revolutionary War and the consequent loss of the colonies brought about a radical change of policy in

Great Britain in regard to the treatment of her dependencies. The idea of William Pitt (Lord Chatham) began to prevail: "That money or taxes should not be exacted from the colonies without their consent." From that time onward the success of the English in colonizing was remarkable, far beyond that of any other nation. The government at home felt a responsibility for the welfare of the colonies. They were not to be exploited, like the French and Spanish dependencies, for the benefit of the empire. Florida and Louisiana were made the football of kings and emperors to be kicked about at will and bought and sold like a piece of property. Well for the United States that they did not resist the change when bought by us.

The difference in the feeling of the soldiers of the colonies of the different countries can be seen in the European War from this circumstance: While those from the German colonies sing in camp and on the march "The Watch on the Rhine" the French the "Marsellaise," those from the English speaking colonies unite in singing "Home, Sweet Home," or "It is a Long, Long Way to Tipperary." "God save the King" is seldom heard.

* * * * * *

"A pebble in the streamlet cast
Has changed the course of many a river."

Here up comes the gentleman from Missouri and says, says he: "Point me to the river; show me the pebble;" or in legal phrasing, "produce the *corpus delicti.*" Get out of my sunshine, Missourian, you are a nuisance; you are obstructing the wheels of the gilded car of imagination; get thee hence to your mule infested bailiwick and hither return no more.

If hereafter I occasionally indulge in the "might have beens," though I may not attempt to make it rhyme with pen or pens, what harm is done? or if I choose to speculate (letting New York, Chicago alone) on the future or the past and call it speculation and not a sure thing who is hurt? What a dreary world this would prove without "ifs" or the magic enchantment of distant views of azure hued mountains. Let us determine not to let the grammarians abolish the subjunctive mood.

* * * * * *

There was once upon a time a vessel called the "Mayflower." I assume you have heard of it. It crossed the briny deep and anchored in Cape Cod Bay. (This is not a fish story.) This ship bore pilgrim fathers and pilgrim mothers, though little mention is made of the latter in history. They landed at or rather on Plymouth Rock in December, 1620. Some historians say there were just 100 of them. Many of them did not survive the winter but perished before the arrival of spring. They were reduced to such extremities that the allowance of food for each one was 15 grains of corn per day or 5 grains for each person at a meal. However some of them survived and being a prolific people their descendants are now as the stars in number—too many some have thought.

I have occasionally speculated that if some night a large rat had gnawed his way into the corn bin and eaten up the supply or the Commissionary General had carried it off in his coat pocket what would have been the consequence? and what would have been the effect on our civilization? We would then have no Rockefeller, consequently no Standard Oil Company; no Boston, no culture; no Sweetwater, no Beautiful Ladies City Improvement Association; where now the fountain plays in front of my window making ever vanishing rainbows in the summer sunshine, there might still have been the forests primeval.

You may ask what has the coming of the Mayflower to do with Sweetwater. This. One of the Averys or an ancestor was a passenger in the ship. Then the line of descent comes down to Waightstill Avery who came to North Carolina. His daughter, Elizabeth Avery, married William Ballard Lenoir who was the father of I. T. Lenoir, the founder of Sweetwater. But for the last named there would have been no town here. He was a stockholder in the E. T. & Ga. R. R.; also a director, a member of the county court, a former member of the Legislature, and he gave the seven and one-half acre plot on which the depot and railroad track stand. Then he evolved the plan of the town and laid off many lots.

WAIGHTSTILL AVERY.

The Avery family have been a noted one since the early settlement of the colonies. They have aspired to and held public office. Many of them have been lawyers and politicians. They have rather craved than avoided responsibility. They have characteristics directly opposite to the Lenoirs in this respect. They like "to read their history in the nation's eyes." They have rarely failed to fill the positions they sought with honor and credit. They have settled in almost every state in the Union. Of those who came south Waightstill Avery is best known and most distinguished. He was born in Norwich, Conn., in 1746 or 1747. He graduated at Princeton College in 1766 and was tutor there for a year. He studied law under Littleton Denis in Maryland. He emigrated to Mecklenburg County, North Carolina, and was licensed to practise law in 1769. He was a member of the Mecklenburg Convention and one of the signers of The Mecklenburg Declaration of Independence on the 20th of May, 1775. This document is credited to Ephraim Brevard but some of the Avery family think that Brevard got valuable assistance from Waightstill Avery. Many North Carolinians, with pardonable pride, are of the opinion that this paper is the equal in terseness and vigor to the Declaration written by Jefferson and passed by the Continental Congress, July 4, 1776. (The writer, however, does not share in that opinion.) Waightstill Avery was commissioned by Governor Martin together with Joseph McDowell and Sevier to treat with the Cherokee Indians in the early part of 1777. They accomplished nothing. But on the 20th of July, 1777, at Long Island on the Holston River, Avery, together with Wm. Sharpe, Joseph Winston and Robert Lanier, signed a treaty with the Cherokees. The signers on the Indian side (in mark) were Oconostota and many other head men of the tribe.

He was the first attorney general of the state in 1777. He married Mrs. Franks, of Jones County, in 1778.

His law office, books and papers were burned by Lord Cornwallis at Charlotte in 1781.

He moved to Burke County in 1781, Wheeler's History says "for his health."

Taking into consideration the depredations of Cornwallis and Tarleton and the still worse outrages of Pat. Ferguson and his gang of tories, one is not at all surprised at the unhealthfulness of the climate in eastern North Carolina at the time. We find this in Ramsey, page 274, taken from public records: "At a court of Oyer and Terminer and General Gaol Delivery for the counties of Washington and Sullivan, begun and held (at Jonesboro) on the 15th of August, 1782. Present Hon. Spruce McCay, Esq.— Waigtstill Avery, Esq., was appointed attorney general for the state and John Sevier, clerk."

He died in Burke County in 1821, then the patriarch of the North Carolina Bar.

There are three things in Tennessee history about which much speculation has been indulged and many accounts have been written, but the exact facts in regard to them will probably never be known. Those who could have told have long since passed away—their lips forever sealed. The occurrences referred to above are the challenge and meeting of Jackson and Avery near Jonesboro; the rescue of Sevier by Shelby and others when he was being tried for treason at Morganton, N. C., and what happened between Governor Sam Houston and his wife shortly after his marriage that caused him to resign the governorship and expatriate himself among the Indians. The tradition extant in the Avery family was somewhat different from the usually accepted version. My father told me that the real reason of Jackson's spite against Avery was not what Avery said in the courthouse. As Avery was then the most distinguished member then at the Bar in that district Jackson, hardly of age, began the study of law under him. Jackson had a share in those vices which were peculiarly distasteful to the conscience of the New Englander; betting on cards and horse races, whiskey drinking and a disposition to fight in any manner whatever for any fancied insult. Avery told him mildly that in his opinion his peculiar talents were not fitted for a legal career and advised him to adopt some other profession. Jackson's high strung temperament could not endure this reflection on his morality and intelligence and he sought an opportunity to wipe out the score. It occurred in the conduct of a case in the courthouse and accordingly Jackson sent his challenge. Avery accepted out of deference to public opinion. He had no animosity against Jackson and determined not to shoot or shoot up in the air. Jackson at the meeting held his fire as he sometimes did afterward in his duels and did not shoot. Avery also did not shoot. After he saw that Avery had no intention of injuring him, or even firing upon him, then they all, principals and seconds, returned and reported the difficulty as amicably settled.

William Ballard Lenoir, son of William Lenoir and father of I. T. Lenoir, was born in Wilkes County, N. C., September 1, 1775. In 1802 he married Elizabeth, daughter of Waightstill Avery. They settled in the Happy Valley of the Yadkin River, two and a half miles below Fort Defiance, the residence of General Wm. Lenoir. There were born to them four of their twelve children, Isaac Thomas Lenoir being the third. He was three years old in 1810 when his father came to Tennessee. In considerable travel through the states of our Union, I have known three valleys which seemed to excel all others in beauty and grandeur. They are rich in all the resources which go to make up a place where peace, prosperity and healthfulness reign supreme, "As happy a region as on this side of heaven." They are the Nacoochee Valley at the head of the Chattahoochee River in Habersham County, Georgia, the Valley River Valley in Cherokee County, N. C., and the Happy Valley of the Yadkin River in Caldwell County, N. C. The two first mentioned besides being exceedingly fertile, are immensely rich in mineral resources. They are all surrounded by grand and lofty mountains and nearby foothills, like steps ascending heavenward. In every season and weather they form an inspiring and pleasing prospect to the beholder. In speaking of these I am in no wise decrying the thousand charms of our own valley. However favored a spot of earth this may be, it is not unreasonable to suppose that there may be others that in the opinion of some one are still more favored. Of these vales spoken of I would, all things considered, give the palm to the Happy Valley on the Yadkin. In this valley in 1810 dwelt William Ballard Lenoir. He was happily married. He resided near many of his relations and in perfect amity with them. It would look as if he had everything to make life easy and pleasant. Yet "man never is but always to be blest."

Under such circumstances as these he chose to leave and come across the Blue Ridge and seek his fortune in a comparatively unknown and unsettled country. He built at the mouth of the Little Tennessee on the Holston (Hogoheechee) River. He may have been induced to do so by information obtained from his father-in-law, Waightstill Avery, who had previously visited this country as one of the commissioners of the state of North Carolina to treat with the Cherokee Indians. When he moved to where Lenoir City now stands he was 35 years of age and in the prime of physical and intellectual vigor. His mind had been informed by education and travel. His father had given him all the advantages possible in that day. Also he came not empty handed. He brought deeds to lands, wagons, horses and slaves. The negroes familiarly called him and his wife "Marse Billy and Mis' Betsy." He took his patrimony into a far country but not to spend it in riotous living, as the prodigal son, but to largely increase it and to make it a blessing to his family, his friends and his neighbors. What route they came from North Carolina I am not informed but it must have been down the Wautauga, and thence by Knoxville, as the way neither along the French Broad or the Little Tennessee rivers was then open. The land he acquired in and around what is now Lenoir City amounted to about 5,000 acres. He settled near the center of his possessions and never disposed of any of his real estate during his lifetime. The place and postoffice was called Lenoir's. There eight of his twelve children were born.

Isaac Thomas Lenoir when a young man visited the place of his birth in North Carolina. He was wonderfully pleased with that country. He asked his father how he had ever gotten the consent of his mind to leave such a place situated as he was. His father's answer was that a considerable portion of the valley was filled up with his own relatives and that when he went to church or public gatherings he met mostly his own kinspeople. Their relations towards each other were exceedingly cordial and agreeable, almost too much so he thought, so that they were liable to become clannish; by going to another section he could have numerous friendships and at the same time retain the love of his relations in North Carolina. His career in this country justified the wisdom of his choice.

William Ballard Lenoir was a very extensive farmer. The land that he cultivated consisted of river bottom lands, islands and fertile uplands. He was a manufacturer of cotton yarns and a miller and his house was a famous stopping place. His old residence is still standing north of the passenger depot at Lenoir City. He was also a land surveyor and acquired many tracts of land in McMinn, Monroe, Roane and Morgan counties. He was one of the surveyors for the state in the Hiwassee District. Just exactly what part of this territory he surveyed, I am not informed, but he must have surveyed a considerable part of Range One east of the basis line. The scheme of the survey of the Hiwassee district was to take as a starting point the junction of the Clinch and Tennessee rivers called southwest point and run what was called the basis line directly south to the Hiwassee River; then to run lines six miles distant from each other east and west of the basis line. The territory included between these lines was called a range. These ranges were surveyed into townships six miles square. These townships into sections, thirty-six in number, and the sections into quarter sections, one-half mile square, containing 160 acres. For these lots of land a grant could be obtained from the state by paying the stipulated price. The grant would read:

160 acres the .... Quarter Section of Section Number ...... Of Township .... In Range .... of the Hiwassee District of .... Date .... and signed by the Governor and Secretary of the state of Tennessee with the great seal

of the state attached. The county was sometimes given and sometimes not, but it was not necessary to do so to make a valid grant or a deed. The Hiwassee District whose boundary has heretofore been described was in the counties of Roane, Meigs, McMinn and Monroe. Sweetwater Valley was in the counties of McMinn, Monroe and Roane. The part that was in Roane County is now Loudon County.

Isaac Thomas Lenoir.

It was the policy of William Ballard Lenoir when any of his sons or daughters married not to have them settle around him in the same neighborhood but to seek other fields; he thought it better for them to do as he did. And even when they remained at home they ought to have a separate business and a responsibility of their own. His son, Isaac Thomas, engaged when a young man in the mercantile business at Lenoir's. In those days there were no drummers and no wholesale houses, not even in Knoxville, very few anywhere nearer than Baltimore, Philadelphia and New York. It was the custom then of the merchants to take a trip once or twice a year to one or more of those cities to purchase their supplies. The goods so purchased were hauled in wagons the greater part of the distance, competition then was not so great. Any reasonable business ability would insure success. In 1843 he was elected to the lower branch of the Legislature as a representative from Roane County. The county of Roane was then very close politically between the Whigs and Democrats. He was elected over Colonel Joel Hembree, by a majority of eight votes. In 1845 he was elected senator from the ———— Senatorial District comprising the counties of Roane, Anderson, Morgan and Campbell over Colonel Elbert Sevier. While in the Legislature he helped to secure favorable legislation in the amendment of charters for East Tennessee and Georgia Railroad, which insured the construction of that railroad from Dalton, Ga., to Knoxville, Tenn. As this railroad formerly under the name of Hiwassee Railroad, afterward under the name of E. T. & Ga. R. R. was graded in a great measure by the citizens along the route, it was done in small sections and at different times from 1837 to 1850.

And in some places notably between this section and Philadelphia, the graded right of way of the railroad was used as a road for vehicles between the time of the grading the road and equipping it with ties and rails. This was a fine object lesson for the advantage of graded roads, but the people were not thinking so much of getting good roads for their vehicles as securing a railroad for shipment of their farm products and many years had to elapse before the people were willing to submit to the proper expenditure for good roads.

While Mr. Lenoir was a member of the Legislature in Nashville, he met Miss Mary Caroline Hogg, formerly of Nashville, then of Rutherford County. They were married in Rutherford County February 10, 1846. In the latter part of that year or early in 1847 they moved to the old log house, which is still standing, one and a half miles south of Sweetwater. In 1851 he purchased from his father, W. B. Lenior, 1,240 acres of land in Sweetwater Valley. One of these was the N. W. Quarter of Section No. 2, in Township Third, Range one, East, on which part of the town of Sweetwater is now located. When the railroad was completed to the location of Sweetwater in 1852, the only towns in this section of the country were Philadelphia, Madisonville and Athens. Madisonville was nine miles distant or about that from the nearest point on the railroad. It was the county seat of the county and by far the most important place in the county; therefore Madisonville and the country tributary thereto must have a depot, as convenient as possible.

Great efforts were made at different places from Reagan's to Philadelphia to secure a proper location for a depot and a town. The nearest point to the railroad from Madisonville would have been one and three-fourths miles on the railroad southwest of where Sweetwater now stands, but that was in the center of the Lenoir farm, not so convenient for the neighborhood. It would have been somewhat difficult to secure good roads there too. Nor would the Heiskells, Fines, Biggs, Mayes, Johnstons, Owens, Sneads and others have so cheerfully contributed to the building up of the town; and Mr. Lenoir said: "Although a one-man town might be a financial success to the one man on whose land it was built, he much preferred for various reasons that this should not be that kind of a town."

Upon mature thought he came to the conclusion that the present location would be most fitting, and most convenient for this neighborhood and the adjacent valleys. Therefore to make certain it would be at its present location, he promised to give and did give the plot around the depot.

I have been asked many times within the last six months in regard to the exact status of the land thus conveyed. What rights the town, the public, had in said deeds. That is a legal question about which there has not been any completed litigation or decision in the courts and the deed might be construed in different ways. As a matter of information to the public it might be well enough to give the description contained in the deed and the main proviso therein. The deed is in Book Q, Page 150, Records of Monroe County. The date of the deed is August 12th, 1858. The deed is from I. T. Lenoir to E. T. & Ga. R. R. Co. The description is as follows: Commencing at a point on the center of the line of E. T. & Ga. R. R. at the center of the creek, at the bridge where the railroad crosses Sweetwater Creek at the town of Sweetwater, thence running at a right angle to the main track of said railroad, which passes the depot, northwestardly to a line 200 ft. from said track; thence parallel with said last main line, northeastwardly 975 feet more or less to the corner of Morris Street and Lot No. 27, thence southeastwardly at a right angle 200 feet. To the center of the main railroad track, thence north eastwardly 145 feet to the northeast line of McClung's Alley, thence at a right angle with the railroad 100 feet to the corner of Lot No. 31 and McClung's Alley, thence south westardly and parallel with railroad 1,120 feet more or less to the center of the creek. Thence 100 feet to the beginning, containing seven and one-half acres * * * The railroad company shall not use any portion of said land hereby conveyed for any purpose whatever, nor erect any buildings thereon, except such as shall be necessary for the purposes of said company.''

When this deed was made, this square had growing on it many forest trees and the farms next to the town were enclosed. A great many wagons came from long distances to haul farm products here and goods away. As there was not any other railroad in lower East Tennessee, the wagon trade here at that time was phenomenal. This was the shipping point of several counties in West North Carolina. It was absolutely necessary that the trade of the town and for the purposes of the railroad that there should be a camping place and a hitching place for wagons and horses coming from long distances. It was not unusual to see within this square twenty or thirty wagons at a time.

A large depot had been built which contained during the harvest season many thousand bushels of wheat and other farm products. Many farmers who hauled these products in also owned stock in the road and had helped to build it. They felt that they had a right to use their own grounds for their own purpose. These wagons, oxen, and horse wagons, had to wait sometimes a whole day or more before unloading their products and receiving the goods. In the busy seasons there was a scarcity of rolling stock on the railroad and freight trains, usually one a day each way had a limit of twenty cars each with an allowance of 16,000 pounds per car. The locomotives were small wood burners, as the coal fields had not then been tapped. When the railroad company could not furnish sufficient cars, they took care, so far as they could, of the wheat, corn, and meat brought in for shipment. Within any reasonable length of time the railroad company made no charge for storage and no damage was exacted for lack of cars for shipment. Perishable goods were rarely ever received except for short distances.

At that time there was a large territory contributing to the trade of this town and using this as a shipping point. It was a wonderful convenience to those coming here from a distance to be allowed to hitch their horses and rest under the shade of the trees.

The town was small then and in its beginnings. Then the town was not incorporated and conditions were far different from at present. It was almost a nightly scene to have the mountaineer campers get out their fiddles and have a jollification and dance in the grove. It furnished amusement to them and entertainment for the inhabitants. There was no grand rush in those days nor haste to be wealthy. Hundreds of people came here to camp to see a railroad train for the first time in their lives. There was little misbehavior and rarely such a thing as an arrest. It is useless to say that things are better now or worse; they are just different, and will be just as different from now twenty-five years hence. However one cannot help but regret the disappearance of the magnificent forest trees which were such an ornament to our town.

But the days of the picturesque and happy mountaineer and "Hill Billies" have passed. Should one regret it? That is owing to whether you knew them in the carefree olden days. Railroads more or less change habits and customs; and especially congestion of the population makes another people. What they once were, they are no longer, except in isolated locations. Many of these wagoners, I as a boy knew, and was fond of. Before I visited the mountains so frequently and almost became as one of them I have listened to their tales of adventure, hunting, fishing and the like with as vivid an interest as I read wild western scenes about "Daniel Boone" and "Sneak and Joe." I longed for the time when I could have an Indian pony and visit these mountains, hunt in them, and fish for speckled trout in their limpid streams. What cared they whether the air around the earth was one mile or one hundred miles high or if the sun was ninety-five or ninety-five million miles away. They were happy as long as turkey and deer were plentiful and there were chestnuts for the wild hogs.

As I heard a candidate for Legislature in one of the mountain counties say once, "Where was the log rolling and corn shucking that Old Sam was not there? Where was ever the cow in a mud hole or the hog in the crack that Sam didn't get it out? Elect me to the Legislature and I will take the dog days out of the almanac and make sang grow plentiful in all the mountain coves."

To know the mountaineer thoroughly you must see him when his foot is on his native heath. My heart has often been saddened to see them hunted down like wild beasts for some technical crime which was not intended to injure their fellowman. I have fished with them, traded and surveyed land with them and drank with them. Did one of them ever treat me otherwise than as a friend and brother? Emphatically no. Did one of them ever fail to return a loan which I had made him? Not that I recollect. Did one of them ever refuse to rise at any hour of the night and go where you wished, if you asked him? If so I do not remember it. When I went to the mountains to see them I did not think it at all necessary that I should wear my old clothes; I sometimes wore a $40.00 suit; but did I tell them that they ought to wear clothes like mine, and not butternut jeans and home-made shoes? I did not. Did I air my superior knowledge of college, books and cities and tell them they ought to go to college too? I did not. Did I say to them that they should pipe the water from the spring to the cabin and not carry it in buckets? By no means. Did I tell them it was necessary to their health to bathe at least once a month? I am not going around giving medical advice. Did I say to their wives and daughters that they ought to wear corsets and not dip snuff and chew tobacco? I failed to mention these things. Did I make myself obnoxious by pointing out to them that some other way of living was far better than theirs? By no means.

On the other hand, sometimes when I have told one good-bye I have said "John, come to see me, but I do not expect I can give you anything half so good as venison and wild turkey and the corn bread and potatoes and the wild sour wood honey which I have eaten with you. Nor can I furnish you water out of the gourd as pure as your mountain streams; nor brandy near so good as that made from the sun kissed native mountain apple. Nor is the air of our valley quite so invigorating as that of your hills. One thing I can do if you visit me, I can show you as good a fiddle as you ever drew a bow across. I have no bear dogs such as yours; but I think I have a dog or two that can interest you in a fox chase; I will take you driving behind a horse that you will long remember.''

Yes, I have drank with the mountaineer time and again, and I cannot honestly say that I am sorry for it; the result was apparently productive of none but the kindest feelings, and I have never been present when an altercation resulted therefrom. I have always felt safer in person and property when with the mountaineer than in any town I have ever been in. When I have spent the night in their cabins I have never put my pocketbook under my pillow, nor in my sock, nor in my shoe; I have always hung my pants on a chair by the fireplace, where they could steal my money if they wanted to. I have never lost a penny. The difficulty was to get them to charge anything for my entertainment. I am speaking now more of the mountaineer of the past than these of the present day; for they are beginning to learn the vices of the town without their corresponding benefits.

Do not understand me as apologizing for the evil effects of what is called whiskey and brandy now manufactured in the mountains, for they have become apt scholars in the art of adulteration. They are now not better products than those passed over the bar in our cities to the confiding customer, however palatable they may make them seem; and if there is an honest or kindly feeling in the drinks furnished by the bootleggers or received through the express office at our railroad stations, I have not felt it nor heard of it.

Exit the Mountaineer, enter the Ladies' City Beautiful League.

City Beautiful League.

There is or should be a kinship between those things which are physically and naturally beautiful and those which are morally beautiful—vice is naturally repulsive, goodness attractive. True, crimes are committed in palaces and villas adorned with paintings and statuary, yet we do not expect it so much as in the slums of our cities, offensive with refuse and garbage; just as a man wearing a silk hat or a flowered white vest is less liable to get into a street brawl than a tramp who has been riding on a coal car. It is an undeniable fact that harmonious sound and beautiful surroundings have more or less influence upon our conduct.

In all religions, in all times, amongst the different nations the place of punishment in the hereafter has always been described as dark and foul; and the place of reward whatever may be its name, has been described as one of beauty, life and light. Therefore anyone or any society which can make the home, the streets, or parks of the town more beautiful is increasing the happiness of humanity as much as the individual who makes two blades of grass grow where one grew before, and the persons who attempt this, even if they make a mistake in the place to be beautified will at least receive their reward from the reflex action upon themselves.

One little star, however bright it may shine, cannot make a lovely night, but the million stars that scintillate in the firmament will thrill us and elevate us by their united brilliancy. The violet may bloom in some secluded nook far from the sight of humanity, but can we even say then that its fragrance and beauty is lost and it existed for no purpose? Let no one, therefore, be deterred from making an effort because the whole world cannot be made beautiful at once.

The man of wealth who gives indiscriminately to every one that asks him may often make a mistake, but he cannot by any possible chance fail at some time to give relief to some form of human misery. If the work of the City Beautiful League proves evanescent and should be turned into the scrap heap the week following, some eye would be gladdened and some heart would be cheered by its influence. The loafer on the street corner may criticize, but has he ever turned over his hand to make a single object around him more beautiful? We sometimes travel 10,000 miles to see a painting or a piece of statuary which we never expect to behold again. What good does that do us if we come to our own town and neglect to make our own surroundings more attractive?

The last twenty years have wrought wonderful changes in the business conditions and needs of the town of Sweetwater. New railroads have been built; new villages sprung up in the territory which was once in the sphere of the business influence of this town. The wagon trade is nothing like what it used to be. Rural free delivery routes have had their influence in changing conditions.

In the plot of ground around the depot the forest trees which were not sufficiently protected have almost disappeared and conditions had been such that the surroundings were far from attractive to the eyes of the beholder, and produced a bad impression on those passing on the railroad. Some fifteen years ago the stockholders of the Sweetwater Hotel Association got permission from the railroad and from the city council of the town to enclose the plot of ground between the hotel and the railroad, sow grass in the enclosure, so as to protect the forest trees still there; when this was done it made the contrast between that part of the square and the remainder very marked. Those who preferred beauty to ugliness often commented on this difference and wondered why the other part of the plot was not made more attractive. About three or four years ago the ladies of Sweetwater and a few in the surrounding country took the matter up with the railroad authorities. Although the Southern Railroad Company seemed not unwilling to do their part in the matter, nothing definite was determined upon, or at least done.

About eighteen months ago Mrs. J. A. Reagan, Miss Nancy Jones, Mrs. W. D. Gilman, Mrs. H. T. Boyd and other ladies of the town, under an organization known as the City Beautiful League, after much correspondence and personal solicitation, induced Mr. R. E. Simpson, then superintendent of this division of the Southern Railroad Company, to do certain work in beautifying this ground on the west side of the depot. This was done. The work was started about April 1st, according to plans and suggestions furnished by the ladies' organization.

The finished work up to May 1, 1915, is as follows:

The concrete circle and basin for a fountain in front of the Scruggs' Realty Company's building, an enclosed park opposite the passenger depot, another enclosed park also between the freight depot and business houses, a concrete basin for fountain in the park started as spoken of some years ago in front of the Hyatt Hotel. South of this park is a hitching circle for horses, between the park and Sweetwater Creek.

The railroad has also leveled, rocked and filled in around the parks and fountains. The town commissioners have promised in perpetuity to furnish a reasonable amount of water for the two fountains. The City Beautiful League on their part engaged to sow in grass or plant in flowers the ground within the concrete circle around the fountain first mentioned and the parks between the two fountains and to do such other work as to make these places attractive as they can within their means and to fully equip the fountains they have purchased, and are now in place. They are tasty but not very expensive.

Mrs. F. A. Carter is now president of the City Beautiful League, and in charge of the improvements. I feel pretty well satisfied that after all the trouble the ladies have taken to get this work done that both their pride and inclination will cause them to do even more than promised; and the effective work they have done and caused to be done is strong proof that sometimes in the mouth of the truly beautiful the tongue is mightier than the vote.

I have heard some complaint from the country people and those living at a distance that these improvements are a diversion from the original intention of the donor. More than half a century ago he probably did not foresee this condition of affairs when there was a growth of forest trees upon the plot; yet since circumstances and conditions have been so changed, I doubt not, that if he were living today he would be heartily in accord with such a movement as has been instituted. I as his sole representative, am not inclined to put any obstacles in the way of them, but the opposite. It is much to my comfort, convenience, and pleasure to have things as they are or rather as will be ere long.

I am anxious to look out of my window, or sit under the shade of the trees and see the fountains play; the children laugh and sing; and the ladies promenading there and enjoying what they have so ardently labored for.

I. T. LENOIR, Synopsis.

Was born in Wilkes County, N. C., May 16, 1807. He came with his father to Tennessee in 1810. After he was grown he merchandised at Lenoir's and helped his father with his business until 1843, when he was elected to the Twenty-fifth General Assembly as representative from Roane County. In 1845 he was elected senator from the counties of Morgan, Campbell, Anderson and Roane to the Twenty-sixth General Assembly. He married Mary Caroline Hogg, then of Rutherford County, on February 10, 1846. They came to Sweetwater Valley late in 1846 or early in 1847. He was made a Mason at Madisonville. He was a charter member of Sweetwater Lodge No. 292, F. & A. M. He resided up to 1871 in the log house built by Sliger a mile and one-half southwest of Sweetwater. In 1871 he came to the town of Sweetwater and resided in the house where D. S. Bradley now lives. He died there of pneumonia on December 4, 1875. Besides being the founder of the town of Sweetwater and an owner of a large farm in Sweetwater Valley, he was a considerable owner of timber and coal lands in Roane, Morgan and Cumberland counties, Tenn., and, in connection with his brothers, part owner of many tracts in several counties of North Carolina bordering on Tennessee.

THE HOGG FAMILY IN NORTH CAROLINA.

(Quoted from records furnished by J. T. McGill, Ph. D., of Vanderbilt University to W. B. Lenoir.)

In colonial records of North Carolina it is said, Vol. IV, p. 8, that McNeal, McAlister and several other Scotch gentlemen arrived at the Cape Fear country with 350 Scotch people.

In Williams' History of Virginia we find that in 1747 McNeal came to New York from the western part of Scotland and visited the western part of Virginia and Pennsylvania. He purchased lands in North Carolina near Fayetteville.

McNeal arrived at Wilmington in 1749 with his family and 500 or 600 colonists. My opinion is that Richard Hogg was among the McNeal colonists. He died in 1768 or 1769. He left three sons: Robert, John and James. It may be that Thomas and Richard Hogg were brothers. Thomas Hogg (1) in 1735 got a patent for 316 acres in Craven County. He petitioned for a warrant for land in New Hanover in 1749 and in 1751 for land in Johnstone County. So I suppose that Thomas Hogg (revolutionary soldier) was born before 1751.

JOHN WEBB.

John Webb was a delegate from the town of Halifax to the Provincial Assembly, which met at Hillsboro, August 21, 1775. He married Rebecca Edwards in 1776. He died at Halifax in 1781.

Thomas Hogg (2) mar. the widow Webb (this lady I suppose) and it was she and not Mrs. Ashe (Wheeler's Hist., N. C., p. 186), according to Dr. Samuel Hogg, who replied to Colonel Tarleton when he said he would be happy to see Colonel Washington, "If you had looked behind you at the Battle of Cowpens, Colonel Tarleton, you would have had that pleasure."

THOMAS HOGG (2),

Son of Thomas H. (1), was one of four brothers. The others were: Richard of Richmond, Va., lieutenant in the navy; Captain Samuel H. of the Revolutionary army, and Robert Hogg. Thomas H. was 1st lieutenant of the first regiment raised by order of the Provincial Assembly, that met at Hillsboro August 21, 1775. This regiment was under Colonel Moore. Promoted to captaincy April 10, 1776. Was in South Carolina latter part of 1776 and first of 1777. Was with Washington at Trenton in July, 1777. In battle of Germantown October 4, 1777; promoted to be major 5th regiment October 19, 1777; wintered at Valley Forge. Joined Lincoln in 1779 and he and his brother, Captain Sam'l H. were captured when Lincoln's army surrendered at Charleston, S. C., on May 12, 1780.

Thomas H. lived in Halifax (or in the county) 1783-4, etc. He was elected by the Legislature in December,

1786, one of the commissioners to buy tobacco to pay the indebtedness of the state.

He was a member of the Society of Cincinnati. Was a member of the Royal White Hart Lodge, F. & A. M., at Halifax. The last meeting he attended was September 14, 1787. He died either in 1789 or 1790. He left two sons Samuel and John Baptist.

He received from the state of North Carolina 4,800 acres of land for military services. This land was located on the Big Harpeth River in Williamson County, Tenn. This was left to Sam'l, John B. and Elizabeth Hogg, his wife. Before November 1, 1805, Elizabeth H. married Wm. Killingsworth. February 12, 1825, Elizabeth Fisher, of Gibson County, Tenn., conveyed to her stepson, Samuel Hogg, all her remaining interest in these lands.

Dr. Samuel Hogg

Was born at Halifax, N. C., April 18, 1783. His father was Thomas Hogg; his mother was Rebecca Edwards, widow of ——— Webb. His mother died. His father then married Elizabeth ——— His father died before 1790. Samuel was educated at high school in Caswell County. Probably had an uncle Samuel, living in Granville County who was his guardian. This may have been Captain Samuel Hogg of 1st Va. Regt. (War of Revolution). For a short time had charge of school for boys. Studied medicine under Dr. Hare, whether of Granville, N. C., or Dr. Hare, professor in Jefferson Medical College, University of Pennsylvania, is uncertain. He came to Tennessee; first to Gallatin, where he remained a few months, and then settled in Lebanon. He married April 1, 1806, Polly Talbot, of Nashville, Tenn., a member of one of that city's oldest families.

He was one of the commissioners appointed by the General Assembly in 1807 for the regulation of the town of Lebanon. He was surgeon to the troops that descended the Mississippi to Natchez in 1813, and was in the campaign against the Creek nation. Went with the troops to New Orleans in the winter of 1814, and was present at the battle of January 8, 1815. "It is an interesting incident in his life," says Dr. Yandell, "that as he was about rising in the morning whilst the servant was handing him water to wash, the first cannon announced the opening of the conflict, and the servant was killed by a cannon ball, which carried away his head, scattering the brains in the doctor's face. (Dr. Y.'s account is found in Western Journal of Medical Surgery in Library of Nashville.)

Dr. Y. says Dr. H. was at one time a member of the Legislature. (I do not find his name on the journal, but those of 1806, 1807 and 1813 are missing.) He was a member of Congress 1817-1819.

While regularly engaged in the practice of medicine, he was for a number of years one of the proprietors of a drug store under various firm names, the last being that of Hogg & Young, in 1833, corner of Hendrick and Public Square. James Young mar. H.'s wife's sister, Ruth Rebecca Talbot.

Dr. Hogg was a stanch adherent of Andrew Jackson. He offered the resolutions on nullification at a meeting in Nashville in 1832. He named one of his sons Andrew Jackson (born August 20, 1825). He was a physician at the last illness of Mrs. Andrew Jackson. He removed to Nashville in 1828 (southeast corner of Cherry now Commerce, where his son, John W. was born May 13, 1828). Dr. H. removed to Natchez, Miss., in 1836. In 1838 was an invalid at Tyree Springs. May have returned to Nashville.

April 5, 1842, bought 224 acres of land on Nashville road and Stewart's Creek post-office, then Stewartsboro, near now Florence and Smyrna. He died there on his farm May 28, 1842. He was buried with Masonic honors in the city cemetery at Nashville. His monument is near that of Governor William Carroll, but the inscription is almost illegible. Dr. Hogg's character and work is given in Dr. Yandell's account of his life. He joined the Baptist church in 1838. The degree of M. D. was conferred upon him by the University of Maryland in 1818, and by Transylvania University some years later. He was appointed one of the censors for Middle Tennessee by the Medical Society of Tennessee on May 3, 1830. He was elected president of this society in 1840.

The will of Samuel Hogg was dated April 27, 1842. Mrs. Polly Hogg was executrix and "my good friends Joseph H. Talbot and Dr. James Young" were named as executors.

Mary (Polly) Talbot was born January 22, 1786. She died at the residence of her son-in-law, Hon. Allen A. Hall in Nashville, on December 13, 1860.

She joined the Baptist church on Sweetwater by letter on the fourth Saturday in May, 1851. Granted a letter of dismission the fourth Saturday in February, 1858. There were nine children of Samuel and Mary Hogg, three daughters and six sons. Mary Caroline was the third daughter and third child.

Mary Caroline Hogg Lenoir

Was born at Lebanon, Tenn., on January 18, 1812. She was the daughter of Samuel and Mary Talbot Hogg. Samuel Hogg was born April 18, 1783. Died ———. Mary Talbot was born January 22, 1786, probably at Nashville. She married Dr. Samuel Hogg April 1, 1806. She died April 1, 1860.

In the early thirties Dr. Hogg became financially embarrassed by security debts and moved from Nashville to Natchez, Miss., to repair his broken fortunes. Before many years, however, he returned to Tennessee, on account of his health, and settled at Stewartsboro in Rutherford County. He died there and was buried in the old cemetery at Nashville.

Mrs. Lenoir, when she and her husband moved to this valley, brought with her her piano, which was hauled from Nashville across the mountains. Fortunately care was taken and it was uninjured when it arrived. It was one of the first, if not the first piano ever brought to Sweetwater Valley. She was very accommodating about playing for others and it was very diverting to witness the delight of people who had never heard such an instrument. This piano had what was called an Aeolian attachment and was both a piano and a reed organ and these two could be played together.

Although she was reared in Nashville and accustomed to city life, and afterwards to aristocratic society in the wealthy town of Natchez, Miss., she was immensely popular with all classes of people in Monroe County. She came nearer treating everybody with equal consideration, whoever they were or wherever she might be, than any one I have ever known. I never learned fully the value of popularity, as an asset, until the turbulent times of the Civil War. She seemed to be safe in person and property, even from the most ruffianly of those who knew her.

Her church history is as follows: When a young woman she was received by baptism into the First Baptist Church at Nashville, Tenn., of which R. B. C. Howell was pastor. On the fourth Saturday in January, 1848, she was received by letter into the Baptist church on Sweetwater. On the first Saturday of August, 1860, when the Baptist church at Sweetwater was organized, she presented her letter from the Cleveland Baptist Church and was a member of the Baptist church in Sweetwater until the time of her death. She died at her then residence, in Sweetwater, on April 11, 1877. We make this short extract from the minutes of the church: "She evinced a deep interest in the youth of the community and her house was ever open for their entertainment when they desired to meet for innocent social amusement and recreation. The poor too, found in her, an abiding friend—no needy creature (whether deserving or not) was ever sent away from her door without relief. She was a lady of easy circumstances and was therefore enabled to gratify the desire of her heart in contributing to the support of the church at home and in sending the Gospel to regions abroad."

On her tombstone in the old Sweetwater Cemetery is this inscription: "Baptist in faith; all creeds in charity; she spent her life in giving." The word "charity" was here used in its broadest sense, meaning that in her conduct towards others she made little or no difference as to their denominational faith, and by "giving" is also meant, not only of money and means, but by doing everything in her power for the happiness of others. No trouble was considered too great for their gratification.

The children of I. T. and M. C. Lenoir were: William

Ballard Lenoir, born June 16, 1847. Samuel Hogg Lenoir, born December 27, 1850; died of scarlet fever May 19, 1854; buried in the Lenoir Cemetery, Lenoir City.

SOMETHING ABOUT THE AUTHOR.

I was born and reared in poor little Sweetwater Valley, in "Godforsaken" East Tennessee. I did not have anything to amuse myself with in my youth except fire-crackers, tops, kites, marbles, balls, blowguns, bows and arrows, red wagons, toy cannons, fiddles, banjoes, horns, dogs, ponies, guns, hunting, fishing, pet coons and squirrels, pigeons and other birds and wild animals. Some of them were sometimes ousted or slaughtered for malfeasance, but I always found others, I never had any goodies except cake, pie, preserves, candy, custard, lemonade, peaches, apples, strawberries, watermelons, muskmelons, canteloupes and peanuts. I never saw a railroad until I was five years of age, and never visited Washington and New York until I was eleven, and I never went to Europe at all. I never took a joy-ride in an automobile or sailed the air in an aeroplane, and never got to go to the movies. My father used to read to me about Moses and the Hebrew children; General Zach Taylor at Buena Vista; Milton about the war in heaven; Virgil about Aeneas and Dido; Cowper about John Gilpin's ride, and also parts of some plays of Shakespeare. I liked Macbeth, Julius Caesar and the Tempest, but I did not take to Hamlet, Othello and King Lear, although this last was my mother's favorite Shakespearian play. I never got to read fairy tales and wild Western scenes until I was ten, nor Robinson Crusoe till eleven, nor Cobb and E. D. E. N. Southworth until twelve, nor Scott until I was thirteen.

When sixteen I wanted to join the rebels. My father thought I would make a better plowman than a warrior, so in the summer of 1863 he put me to plowing in a stumpy new ground near the Fine schoolhouse. There was an epidemic of smallpox that summer in the town and the schoolhouse was used as a hospital for the girls and ladies of the town who took the disease. When plowing grew wearisome I would talk to the convalescing patients.

Mr. Guggenkutzenscheitpkeheimer, late of Germany, then of the Federal army, got the benefit of part of my summer's work. I soon became very fond of him. I was much touched with the kind and cultured method of his appropriations. I so much admired, too, the nobility of soul that caused him to travel three thousand miles across the Atlantic to fight for the "old flag" and save our distracted country from dissolution. How unselfish of him, also, in times of peace on Sunday afternoons to repair to the hilltops of our great cities and do his very best to "make Milwaukee famous"!

My father, to post me politically, used to take me to hear such speakers as T. A. R. Nelson, Haynes, Maynard, Temple, Brownlow, Bailey Peyton, Harris, Johnson, Hatton, Ben Hill, Zeb Vance, Bill Polk and John Hopkins, and he expected me to tell him what I thought of the speeches and why.

I was taken by my mother to hear preachers of all denominations, but sometimes, for fear I should be led away by any false doctrines, she would exhort me to particularly read the sixth chapter of Romans and about Philip and the eunuch in the Acts of the Apostles.

One sad mistake my parents made in my bringing up was that, when I attempted versification, they encouraged rather than discouraged me. You may possibly, but not probably, imagine my pride when, at the age of nine years, three months and two weeks, I became the author of these lines:

> "I had a little dog not as big as a hog,
> The only name he had was 'pup';
> He rold over and chast his tail,
> Also laid down and then jumpt up."

This is the unexpurgated edition. It was very much expurgated after my mother was through with it. However, I stuck to my original version. No poet worthy of the nam e will change his loveliest creations when criticised by any one, however respected. Afterward in my callow youth when I fell in love I used to write rhymes to the loved ones. It was always a mystery to me that while they liked my poetry fairly well they never loved the poet. But for this fatal error I might have married and lived happily ever afterward.

My school teachers were J. J. Sheldon, G. L. Leyburn, Oscar W. Muller, Mrs. Cooke, Alfred W. Wilson and the professors at the University of Virginia.

These prepared me for writing about the inhabitants of Sweetwater Valley. Had I been so fortunate as to get an education out of the spelling book and dictionary by a pine knot fire I might have written histories of such worthies as Chester Arthur, Dick Croker and Mark Hanna. But I will leave them for others and write of the people I know most about.

With all my faults in a varied career I cannot truly say that I have a great many regrets. I do not regret that I spent time and money to hear such violinists as Ole Bull, Camille Urso and Musin; such singers as Neilson, Gerster, Kellogg, Campanini and Carey; such actors and actresses as Booth, Barrett, Salvini, Forest, Jefferson, Bernhardt, Davenport and Maude Adams; such orchestras as Thomas and Damrosh's; such bands as the Seventh Regiment, Mexican, Gilmore's and Sousa's; nor do I regret the money I spent in travel.

I do regret that I ever gambled in any way, spent money for whiskey, or subscribed to party campaign funds and did not take more pains to find out and relieve the sufferings of humanity. Nor do I regret what I have spent in hospitality or for the pleasure of my friends.

I am proud of the fact that since I grew up I have never spoken a harsh word nor done an unkind act to a child in my life.

As to Slaves in Sweetwater Valley.

A history of this section would not be complete without some reference to the status of the slaves from 1820 to the time of their emancipation.

Nearly all the well-to-do farmers owning as much as a quarter or two-quarter sections of land also owned some slaves. They were not dependent entirely on slaves for their labor, for most of them supplemented their work with hired white labor. Very few of them had overseers, therefore the condition of slaves were better and more endurable than those of the cotton and sugar planters, owned in large numbers farther south. The owners themselves were more personally interested in the welfare of their slaves. The slaves had more privileges and were better satisfied than those of the cotton and sugar belts. The majority of the slave owners, unless in extra busy seasons, gave their negroes a half holiday on each Saturday, and most of the negro families had their own patches planted in melons or whatever they desired, to be sold by them for their own benefit, and they were encouraged to work them on half Saturdays and other odd times. The negroes spent the money thus obtained mostly on "Sunday" clothes—they were very fond of dressing up, going to church and visiting on Sunday. They were often allowed to take young horses, which were not at work during the week, and ride them during Sunday. This privilege was given to those who were more familiar with the care of young stock. Sometimes, also, they were permitted to take the work horses in a two-horse wagon and visit or go to church. It was a custom among the owners of the slaves, which was almost universally observed, to give the darkies a full week's holiday from Christmas to New Year's Day, they having to do during that period only such work as was absolutely necessary. This week they spent mostly in music, in visiting and in dancing. The dancing consisted of reels, danced singly and in couples, cake-walks, with an occasional square dance—this latter imitated from the whites. It was considered quite a feat for a darkey to get up a new step for a reel, and the one doing so was as proud of it as if he had invented a flying machine. The musical instruments used in their dances consisted of fiddles, banjoes and bones. The latter accomplishment is not so simple as it appears at first glance, and there were bone artists as well as fiddle and banjo artists. A good fiddler was a very noted and important character among the negroes, and when he was skillful enough to play for the white folk's dances he was inordinately proud. The music executed by the negroes was by ear—they had no use for notes. Their range was only about two and one-half octaves and very few of them practised shifts on the violin. The fiddlers and banjo pickers sometimes, in addition to reels, learned schottisches and some other kinds of music from hearing the white folks play on the piano. The plantation which had a good fiddler or banjo picker on it was considered particularly fortunate—they did not have to wait for the holidays to have their dances and walk-arounds. However, when fiddlers were scarce they executed their dance steps to the patting of their hands, called "juba." Where there were as many as ten or twelve negroes on a plantation hardly a night passed that there was not some form of music and dancing.

The negroes also had many weird songs, some of which I could never figure out whence they came, unless a survival handed down from their African ancestry. The negro ear seems to take particularly to minors and if they heard an air in the major key they often hummed or sang it in the minor. Unless the negroes were allowed some form of amusement they were very liable to be running around of nights and getting into some sort of mischief, and, as they sometimes observed, get "to plotting against the whites."

The negroes were perfect timists, and in a strain of music it was rare for them to put in too many or too few bars. Some of the quips and turns in their playing would have done credit to an artist.

Home Life of W. B. Lenoir, Jr.

My father, I. T. L., was not an advocate of starting children to school at very early age. They had things to learn of as much importance he said as spelling and arithmetic and far more interesting. My father used to take me with him about the farm and in the woodlands. He taught me the names of the different wild flowers, to distinguish the different kinds of trees by their leaves and bark, and what uses they could be put to. To observe and tell the various kinds of oak in Sweetwater Valley was a liberal education in itself. On his own farm there were these and more kinds of oak: black, red, chestnut, Spanish, spotted, post, white, willow and others; of course it was easy to tell the poplar tree when once pointed out or the walnut. It was not so easy to point out the different kinds of maple,—long before I could read I took pride in knowing the many kinds of trees in the valley, and was very much chagrinned when I made a mistake. He also told me particularly what weeds were most hurtful to the crops and what was the best method to destroy them. He taught me as an amusement chess, checkers and backgammon. My mother and father both taught me music and I had a supplemental education from the negroes on the fiddle and banjo. I used to own a dog that could with difficulty be kept out of the house when my mother was playing on the piano, but he liked lively music and did not take to the classical or solemn. I used to get insulted with him because he did not seem to care for the fiddle. I thought he was exhibiting very poor taste. However, he was too polite to howl but just went away.

My father did not like cards or any game of chance and when I got the best of him after a few years' training in chess and checkers he rather lost interest in these games. My mother never played a game of any kind, not on account of conscientious scruples but because she had no fondness for them and never learned them. I am not making an argument that it is the proper way to rear a boy to teach him games and music, but I do say that I could have a better time at home as a usual thing than I could away from home.

Facts About Hiwassee and East Tennessee and Ga. R. R.

In the history of General James H. Reagan it is related somewhat in detail how, when he was a member of the General Assemlby in 1836, a charter of an incorporation was obtained for the Hiwassee Railroad Co., for constructing a railroad through the Hiwassee district to the Southern boundary of the state; how the construction was commenced in 1837 and how in 1848 the charter was renewed under the name of East Tennessee and Georgia Railroad Co., and something of how the General Assembly of the state under the general head of Improvement Acts assisted in the construction of the railroad through our section.

In the Senate of 1846, Hon. I. T. Lenoir, then of Roane County, in a speech on the resolution directing the governor to issue the bonds of the state, claimed to be due the Hiwassee Railroad Co., in which, among other things, he says:

"The Hiwassee railroad, with the exception of about three miles, is graded from Blair's Ferry on the Tennessee River to the Georgia line, within twelve or fifteen miles of the place to which the Georgia Legislature has already made provision for completing the Western and Atlantic Railroad. A splendid bridge has been built across the Hiwassee; abutments and culverts have been made at the crossings of the creeks and branches, and the road might very soon, at comparatively small expense, be completed." And he further states: "Many of the goods for East Tennessee are now sent by the southern route, brought on the Georgia railroad to its terminus, and hauled right along the Hiwassee railroad grade in wagons. When the road is completed, almost all the goods for East Tennessee will pass over it; and large quantities of produce will in return be sent back upon it."

Thus, had the governor and others in whom the authority was vested refused to issue to the Hiwassee R. R. or its successors, the East Tennessee R. R., the bonds the whole work done would likely have been lost for want of capital to equip the railroad. There was, too, considerable opposition in the Legislature and many parts of the state to further bonding the state for this road. Some were actuated no doubt by selfish motives, and others for what they thought good reasons.

Mr. John Martin in a letter from Memphis, January 16, 1846, the Hon. I. T. Lenoir's brother-in-law, advised him to oppose the further issuance of state bonds of Hiwassee R. R., among other things he (Martin) said:

"In the first place the expenditure that it will require to finish can be much better appropriated by improving the river, the improvement of the river will be a much better improvement for all of East Tennessee than the road. You can take this argument in all its leanings and see if it is not correct; say that the river was navigable from Chattanooga to Knoxville for steam boats, the imports could be carried up the river much cheaper than on the road; while the river to take off the produce would be infinitely cheaper. It is clear that the river is tributary to the whole of East Tennessee, while the road would be partial in its benefits. The annual saving by the river instead of road transportation would be a great saving and consequently enrich the country. This is my candid view if the road could be completed for nothing, and the improvement of the river would cost $500,000. It would be economy in the east end of the state to improve the river and abandon the road."

The Athens Post at the time of its first publication, September 30, 1848, was the only paper so far as I am aware published between Knoxville and Chattanooga. From its columns, many of whose numbers were preserved by I. T. Lenoir for a number of years, we glean the following:

January 5, 1849.—Proceedings of stockholders E. T. G. R. R.: F. S. Heiskell, chairman; Jno. L. Hunt, secretary. The stockholders went into an election of directors for the year 1849, when the following gentlemen were elected, viz: Knox—Thos. C. Lyons, C. Wallace. Monroe—I. T. Lenoir, Jno. Stanfield. McMinn—T. Nixon Vandyke, A. D. Keyes, W. F. Keith, R. C. Morris. Bradley—Wm. Grant.

At that meeting a contract with Duff Green was entered into to build a railroad from Dalton to Knoxville.

The state directors appointed by the Governor for East Tennessee and Georgia R. R. for the year 1849 are: Jno. C. Gaut, S. A. Smith, J. C. Carlock, Jno. Hughes, Wm. Heiskell, J. G. M. Ramsey, S. B. Boyd, Jos. Jackson, Jno. Jarnagin.

* * * Persons along the line of railroad are notified by A. D. Keyes, president, to remove obstructions from right of way. * * * *

From "Dalton Eagle" June 12th. Account of ground broken at the Southern Terminal of E. T. & G. R. R. and ceremonies on that occasion.

Communication from A. D. Keyes of August 23rd. R. R. has succeeded in closing a contract with Messrs.

Bailey & Co., of England, for 8,000 tons of best quality Welsh iron improved pattern of the T rail to weigh about 57 pounds per lineal yard. Have also made arrangements for chairs and spikes, locomotives, passenger cars and other necessary appendages for furnishing and putting the road in operation at an early date to the Tennessee River.

September 27, 1850.—News has been received from England that the first thousand tons of iron rails for this road were shipped on the 17th of August and that two thousand more were manufactured and ready for shipment.

On October 25th. Acts of Georgia and Tennessee legislatures published authorizing East Tennessee and W. & A. R. R. to complete lines to junction and granting certain other privileges.

Call on the stockholders for $12.50 a share of all unpaid stock November 22, 1850.

January, 1851.—Meeting called for January. R. C. Jackson, secretary and treasurer. Notice signed by A. D. Keyes in the Post May 2nd, in which he says: "I have received a requisition dated April 24th signed by Messrs. Lyon Crozier and Wm. Lenoir directors, requiring me to convene the board of directors E. T. & G. R. R. Co. the third Monday of May for a purpose of reviewing action of the board in establishing shops for repairing engines, etc., meeting so called May 19th.

May 23rd.—At the said meeting of the directors at Athens, the permanent machine shops were located at Athens.

Ivins says referring to this: "McMinn has borne the brunt and burden of the contest (meaning a fight for the railroad) from first to last. Her citizens have suffered more and bled freer and there is no cause for any prejudice against us."

Nov. 7th.—Call on E. T. & G. R. R. stockholders $12.50 on each share of stock by E. D. Keyes, president.

From Athens Post for the year 1852, March 26th. Call by Thos. H. Calloway, president E. T. & G. R. R. $5.00 per share for stock.

From the best information obtainable it is probable that the track laying of the E. T. & G. R. R. reached

Sweetwater about April 1, 1852. A place for the "Y" to be used as a turn-table had already been graded. It occupied the place about where the circle of the northeast fountain now stands.

The depot also was under course of construction in anticipation of the arrival of the railroad. This building as I remember it was about 40x100 feet or more. This was considered a good sized depot for a place which was then only a dot on the map. Philadelphia had been a town then a number of years, Loudon was then known by the name of Blair's Ferry.

Mr. W. P. Jones, of Pond Creek Valley thinks that the laying of the track to Loudon proceeded at about the rate of 1-4 mile per day; that being the case the track laying must have reached the river near Blair's Ferry the latter part of May.

I find in the Athens Post of August 10, 1852, the following schedule:

Up Train	P. M.
Leave Dalton at	2:30
Varnell's	2:57
Red Clay	3:15
Blue Spring	3:42
Cleveland	3:54
Charleston	4:30
Riceville	4:51
Athens	5:15
Mouse Creek	5:35
Sweetwater	5:57
Philadelphia	6:15
Arrive at Loudon	6:35

Down Train	A. M.
Leave Loudon	4:00
Philadelphia	4:21
Sweetwater	4:59
Mouse Creek	5:03
Athens	5:21
Riceville	5:45
Charleston	6:06
Cleveland	6:42

Blue Spring 6:54
Red Clay 3:15
Varnell's 8:03
Arrive at Dalton 8:30

Thomas H. Calloway, president. (July 23, 1852.)

The railroad depot at Philadelphia was larger than the depot at Sweetwater and was built about the same time as the depot at Sweetwater. The depot at Sweetwater was burned by General Wheeler during the raid in 1864 on account of Federal supplies being contained in it.

The Loudon depot was first built at the riverside, a steep grade running down at the river from the railroad. The depot at the present location was not built until after the railroad bridge was finished at Loudon.

It may be interesting to note the following tables taken from the Loudon Free Press Saturday, January 15, 1853:

"We have been kindly furnished by Mr. Pritchard, chief engineer, with the following table of elevations of various points upon the line of the E. T. & G. R. R. above the level of the sea:

Dalton, Ga.	771 Ft.
Varnell's	828 "
Tennessee Line	837 "
Cleveland	778 "
Charleston	718 "
Low water, Hiwassee River...............	684 "
Athens	993 "
Mouse Creek Summit	1,023 "
Sweetwater	920 "
Philadelphia	871 "
Loudon	814 "
Low Waters of the Tennessee River.........	738 "
Lenoirs	786 "
Summit of Knox and Roane Line............	882 "
Turkey Creek	809 "
Water of Do.	778 "
Stones	834 "
Heiskell's	898 "

McClellan's Summit .... 972 "
Water of Second Creek...................... 870 "
Knoxville .... 898 "

The First Plan of the Town of Sweetwater

Was laid off by I. T. Lenoir entirely on his own land. This was a part of the northeast quarter of section 2, township 3, range 1, east of the basis line. The land that was included was as follows:

Commencing at a point in the centre of the E. T. & Ga. Railroad track perpendicularly above the north bank of Sweetwater Creek; thence down the creek along the bank to Daniel Heiskell's line; thence north with Heiskell's line to the middle of the Fork Creek Road; thence along Biggs' and Mayes' line crossing the railroad west to the Pond Creek Road; thence southeastwardly with that road to Monroe and High streets and the Athens Road; thence with the east side of that road 190 feet to a point on the south side of ———— street; thence in a direction parallel to Monroe Street southeasterly to Depot Street and the railroad lot; thence with that plot southwestwardly to corner of the same; then at a right angle with the line of railroad plot southeasterly to the centre of the creek directly under the middle of the railroad track; thence to the point of beginning.

The Plan of the Streets.

The streets in the first plan of the town ran parallel and at right angles to the general direction of the railway tract through the railroad plot, except Monroe Street. This last named street starting at the creek next to the bridge and Heiskell's line ran directly west to the railroad track, thence in a southwesterly direction the same as the other streets in the plan of the town. It was 66 feet wide. Most of the other streets were from 30 to 33 feet wide. The street on the east side of the railroad was called Railroad Street. That on the depot side of the railroad was named Depot Street. The next street west, running parallel with the railroad, was Oak Street, then High east of the Female College. Commencing at Monroe Street and going northeast the first street is Wright, then Walnut, then Morris running by the Trust and Savings Bank.

In this first plan of the town of Sweetwater I. T. Lenoir laid off 65 lots. Those fronting on Depot Street were intended and sold for business houses. The numbering of the lots was commenced on the corner of Oak and Morris. Number one was the lot now occupied by the J. A. Miller residence and the numbers ran southwesterly along Oak Street to twelve inclusive. Then from fifteen across from the Beard residence and going to twenty-eight northwardly along Depot Street to the post-office lot inclusive.

The number of the lots in the Lenoir tract were about equal on each side of the railroad.

The first recorded sale of any lot is that to N. W. Haun and William Stakely on the 14th of May, 1852. The number of the lot was 18 and was the location now occupied by the Sweetwater Pharmacy, the Ledbetter Store and the Cunningham Jewelry Store. It was 80 feet front on Depot Street, sometimes incorrectly called Main Street. The next sale was on September 30, 1852, to Wilson Parker of lots Nos. 11, 12, 15 and 16. These lots were located between the Sweetwater Hotel lot and the Sweetwater Creek, two of them fronting on Depot Street.

In about 1854 J. C. Vaughn purchased the property now occupied by the Hyatt Hotel and built a hotel and storehouse, and he resided there with his family until about the time of the Federal occupation of this country in 1863. The majority of these lots owned by I. T. Lenoir were sold previous to 1860, though in many instances deeds were not made for several years later on. He took great pains to sell only to those persons whom he knew to be responsible business men and good citizens, and some were sold with the proviso that no whiskey or intoxicants were to be sold on them.

From the country around came the Pattons, Rowans, Taylors, Robert and Bates Carter, the former of whom afterwards went to Texas. From Madisonville came S. Y. B. Williams, William McClung, Robert and Anderson Humphrey, the Clarks and James A. Wright, the last named being in business with James A. Coffin.

From Philadelphia came John W. Goddard, Frank Bogart and Charles Cannon. G. G. Stillmann and J. J. Sheldon came here from New York, and resided at this place to the time of their deaths. Thus the town of Sweetwater not only became noted on account of its location, but for the high class of its citizens. Names here mentioned are such as I recall to my mind at present—others moved here who made equally as good citizens.

WALTER FRANKLIN LENOIR,

Son of William Ballard and Elizabeth Avery Lenoir, of Lenoirs, Tenn., was born November 21, 1816. He died September 1, 1878. He first married Elizabeth Campbell Goddard, daughter of T. C. Goddard of County Line, Monroe County, on November 16, 1841. She was born April 2, 1821. She died January 10, 1855.

When a young man he entered into the mercantile business with his brother, I. T. Lenoir, at Lenoirs. About the time of his first marriage he came to Philadelphia, Tenn., and purchased land there. In 1853 and 1854, according to advertisements in the Loudon Free Press, he was in the mercantile business at Philadelphia, in partnership with his brother-in-law, John W. Goddard. He also owned and operated one of the few saw mills on Sweetwater Creek. He owned a large body of pine land east of Philadelphia from which he manufactured lumber. He built the brick residence in the grove just east of Philadelphia in 1853.

The children of W. F. and Elizabeth Goddard Lenoir were:

1. Julia Ann Campbell, b. September 6, 1842; d. May 22, 1848.
2. Walter Thomas, b. August 8, 1845.
3. William Goddard, b. August 23, 1847; d. March 21, 1915.
4. Thornton Pickens, b. July 23, 1851.

Walter Thomas Lenoir married Loua Edwards, of Little Rock, Ark. She was born September 30, 1851, the daughter of Richard and Susan Hilder Edwards. W. T. Lenoir was a student at Hiwassee College when the Civil War began. He left school when under 16 years of age, and joined the Confederate army. He was a member

Co. F, 43rd Regt. Tennessee volunteer infantry, under the command of Colonel Gillespie. He was in the siege of Vicksburg and was captured and paroled there. He was soon exchanged and served during the remainder of the war as a scout and as a member of the reorganized 43rd Tennessee Regiment. He was with the Confederate forces when Colonel Frank Wolford, commanding a brigade of Federal cavalry, was defeated on the morning of October 20, 1863, in what is known as the Battle of Philadelphia. Colonel Wolford was making his headquarters at the residence of W. F. Lenoir, father of W. T. Lenoir, at the time of the battle. W. T. Lenoir influenced the commander of the Confederate battery to so fire the guns, which were located on a hill about 600 yards distant, as not to do injury to the house or hurt any of the family. It was not a common experience in war for a man to be engaged in a real battle around his father's house. (For a more extended account of this engagement see another part of this book.) W. T. L. was with General Vaughn in the Shenandoah Valley campaign, and previously with him in upper east Tennessee. He surrendered and was paroled at Kingston, Ga., on May 12, 1865.

He located at Humboldt in the western part of the state in 1868, where he operated a hotel in the town, and a farm nearby. He was mayor of Humboldt in 1882. In 1886 he bought his grandfather's, T. C. Goddard's farm, in McMinn County near Reagan's Station. He moved his family there in 1887. While living in McMinn he was a member of the county court from 1888 to 1890, when he moved to Sweetwater. He was a member of the Monroe County Court 1893-1911. He was mayor of Sweetwater in 1915.

The children of W. T. and Loua E. Lenoir were:

(1) Frank, b. at Humboldt, Tenn., July 12, 1874. He married Annie Powell, of Atlanta, Ga., June 7, 1906. He is a manufacturer of tin and iron wares at Houston, Tex. Their children are: Louise and Frank, b. in 1907 and 1912.

(2) Caroline, b. in Humboldt, Tenn., July 4, 1876. She was married to Clarence, son of John S. and Theresa Young, on January 22, 1905. He is cashier of the Bank

of Sweetwater, Tenn. They reside near Sweetwater. Their children are: Lenoir, b. June 5, 1906; Katherine, b. March 1, 1908; Clarence E., Jr., b. November 22, 1909; Loua Theresa, b. March 5, 1913.

(3) Hattie, youngest daughter of W. T. and Loua E. Lenoir, b. September 5, 1879.

(4) Richard, their youngest son, b. August 14, 1881. He married Idelle May Waldrop, of Jonesboro, Ga., on April 10, 1916. They live in Sweetwater.

William Goddard Lenoir, second son of W. F. and Elizabeth G. Lenoir attended, in 1865, 1866 and 1867, school at the Dancing Branch Academy six miles south of Sweetwater. This school was under the charge of Prof. A. W. Wilson, afterward an M. A. of the University of Virginia at Charlottesville. Afterwards he was three years at the University of Virginia, from October, 1867 to July, 1870. He graduated there in several schools. In this university was developed that independence of thought and action which stood him in good stead throughout his life and contributed greatly to his success. After completing his education he taught school for two or three years at Johnson City, Tenn.

On October 14, 1871, he was married (first) to Alice Osborne, daughter of Thomas and Evaline Lackey Osborne, of Pond Creek Valley. She was born October 8, 1852, and died at Johnson City on June 20, 1874. She is buried at Stekee Cemetery near Loudon. There were two children, the youngest, a son, dying in infancy in 1874. Their daughter Lucy, born July 15, 1872, married R. H. Kizer, of Philadelphia. He was born in Blount County, Tenn., in 1858. They have three children: Lenoir, b. May 1, 1897; Alice, b. August 16, 1904, and John, b. February 13, 1913.

On September 5, 1876, W. G. L. was married (second) to Fannie Amelia, daughter of Eli and Elizabeth Childs Adkins. They resided principally at the old Lenoir homestead until 1884, when they moved to the Adkin residence near the spring in Philadelphia. They resided there at the time of his death in March, 1915.

He was a large real estate owner both in the country and in town, especially in Knoxville, and had a keen appreciation of their values. He was a dairyman and an extensive raiser of Register Jersey cattle. He was a justice of the peace and an influential member of the Loudon County Court from 1884 to 1912. He was a firm advocate and supporter of good schools and good roads. He always contended that they were worth more than they cost though they might not be economically carried on or constructed.

He was a joint representative from Knox and Loudon counties in the Fifty-sixth General Assembly, elected on the Fusion ticket. He was an ardent prohibitionist and voted and worked for all measures for the suppression of the whiskey traffic while he was a member of the Legislature. He was a great friend of the colored race, especially of the old Lenoir darkies. His hospitality to guests and visitors was recognized and remarked upon wherever he was known.

The children of W. G. and Fannie A. Lenoir were:

(1) Israel Pickens, b. September 14, 1877. He married Cate Willson (her mother was a Cate) on November 14, 1901. They reside in Phoenix, Ariz. Their children are: Mary Francis, b. October 7, 1902, and Avery Thornton, b. October 7, 1903.

(2) Emma Elizabeth, b. November 26, 1879. Married Robert Lee Mims on November 2, 1898. They live in Philadelphia. They have one child, Robert L., b. April 22, 1900.

(3) Walter Avery, b. November 13, 1883. Married Alice Comer, of Comer, Ga., October 23, 1909. She was born August 17, 1890. Four children have been born to them: William Alexander, b. April 18, 1911; Avery Comer, b. July 15, 1913; d. ————; Avery Fulcher, b. September 14, 1914; d. ————; and Francis Elizabeth, b. June 29, 1916. W. A. Lenoir is a planter and resides at Comer, Ga.

(4) Kate Lothrop, b. September 26, 1885. She was married to Edward Young, of Mitchell County, N. C., on May 25, 1908. He died on September 9, 1909. He left one child, Edward, born June 7, 1909.

(5) Eli Adkins, b. August 8, 1888. He married Eva Marler, of Lebanon, Tenn., on June 5, 1911. She was born at Murfreesboro, Tenn., on .September 3, 1890.

They have two children: E. A. Lenoir, Jr., b. April 3, 1913, and Barbara Francis, b. May 26, 1915.

(6) William Goddard, b. December 2, 1890. Lives at Philadelphia, Tenn.

(7) Charles Henry, b. September 26, 1892; d. November 14, 1896.

(8) Thomas Penland, b. February 16, 1895; d. January 17, 1901.

Thornton Pickens Lenoir, fourth child of W. F. and Elizabeth Goddard Lenoir, attended Emory and Henry College, where he graduated in 1874. In September of that year he went to Goliad, Texas, where he took up the study of law. Owing to a breakdown in health he gave up law and went into the cattle business at Refugio, Texas, where he was married in 187— to Lua McCampbell. Their children were: Thornton, who died in childhood, and Elizabeth, who married and died a few years afterwards leaving one child, a daughter. T. P. Lenoir lives at Victoria, Tex.

W. F. Lenoir married (second) Harriette Elizabeth Osborne, the daughter of John and Elizabeth Cathey Osborne (both formerly of Haywood County, N. C.), at Germantown, Tenn., on July 7, 1858. She was born at Asheville, N. C., on December 11, 1830. Died May 21, 1907, at her residence at Philadelphia, Tenn. This marriage was a remarkably happy one. Mrs. Hattie Lenoir, besides being a cultivated and accomplished woman, was one who drew many friends to her by the sincerity of her hospitality in a home from which no one was ever turned away without a gracious reception, and help, if in distress. She was a devoted member of the Presbyterian church while he was a zealous member of the Methodist Church, South; yet on that account there was never a jar or misunderstanding. Their house was ever a home for the ministers of both denominations. The Methodist church and parsonage at Philadelphia are monuments to his zeal and liberality. They had a beautiful home in a beautiful situation and lived a beautiful life. I know of no word that fitly expresses their relationship and conduct.

Her end was as serene as her life. She died while asleep without pain or struggle.

The children of W. F. and Harriette O. Lenoir were: Frank, Rose Summey, Henry and Earnest. These all died in childhood, except Henry L., who was born December 6, 1863. He married Annie Yoakum, daughter of William Cannon, May 23, 1888. They reside at the old Lenoir homestead one-fourth of a mile east of Philadelphia, Tenn. Their children are: Annie Lee, b. May 21, 1889; William Cannon, b. April 25, 1891; Frank Osborne, b. September 23, 1894; Susan Bogart, b. September 29, 1898, and Robert Henry, b. January 2, 1902.

THE LILLARD FAMILY.

William Lillard was a colonel in the Revolutionary War. His son William was born August 14, 1798. He died in Sweetwater Valley December 18, 1844. Louise, his sister, and daughter of Col. Lillard, married Benjamin Routh August 23, 1838. William Lillard, second, who lived near Philadelphia, in Sweetwater Valley, married Nancy Routh, who was born August 28, 1807. She died at her residence near Philadelphia, July 27, 1899. The children of William and Nancy Lillard were:

1. Andrew Jackson, b. on Island Creek, February 20, 1829.
2. Washington, dead.
3. Louisa Jane, m. Joseph Ragon, October 15, 1851.
4. Caroline, b. 1835. Lives at Philadelphia, Tenn.
5. Murrell, b. 1837.
6. Julia, m. Riley Burns. Died near Philadelphia in 1915.
7. Joseph B., b. 1843.

Andrew Jackson Lillard went to California in 1858. He went to the Indian Diggings and also to Brush Creek. He dug gold most of the time he was in California until he returned to Tennessee in 1865.

He married Samantha Taliaferro in 1867. She was the daughter of John Taliaferro. They moved to Fork Creek Valley. She died June 6, 1915, at the age of 67. He is a farmer. Their children are:

John, married in Colorado. Has four children. Lives in Farmington, N. M.

Murrell, lives in Atlanta and is in the employ of Rhodes & Co.

Nannie, m. Prof. W. T. Russell, Carson & Newman College, Jefferson City, Tenn. Mrs. Russell died about 1905 leaving two children.

Mollie, m. C. E. Harris, of Dandridge, Tenn.

Etta Lee, m. A. L. Burem, of Hawkins County. Address Burem, Tenn.

Murrell Lillard, son of William Lillard, joined the Confederate army and was afterwards captured at Piedmont, Va., and was taken to Camp Morton, Ind., where he died a prisoner of fever.

Joseph Lillard, youngest son of William Lillard, was a private in Co. D 11th Regt. Tenn. Cav., U. S. A., during the Civil War, serving twenty months. He is a farmer and lives one mile from Philadelphia. He married Maggie J. Harrison, of Pond Creek Valley, on March 31, 1885. Their children are:

William F., b. August 2, 1886.
Minnie L., b. April 17, 1890.
Hattie E., b. November 8, 1892.
Joseph Murrell, b. July 24, 1896.

JOHN LOTSPEICH

Was born in Greene County, Tenn., November 9, 1762. He moved to Sweetwater about 1820. He married Mary Ann Earnest of Greene County, on February 18, 1806. She died January 27, 1878 or 1879. She was born December 23, 1789. Mr. Lotspeich was a farmer and built a brick house and settled on the southwest and southeast quarters of section 3 and the northwest and northeast quarters of section 4, township 3 and range 1, east. He was a member of the Methodist church. He died at his residence on April 19, 1825. He and his wife are both buried at County Line Cemetery. Their children were:

1. Ralph, b. September 6, 1807.
2. Henry L., b. February 10, 1810.
3. Samuel T., b. March 5, 1812; d. April 2, 1847. 6. Christopher Marion, b. October 15, 1815. 10. Amanda, b. Sept. 29, 1827.

4. Felix, was born in Greene County, Tenn., and married Eliza, a daughter of William Neal. They were members of the Methodist church; he was a farmer.

They moved to Green (afterwards Henry) County, Mo.

5. Mary Ann Lotspeich was born in Greene County, Tenn. She married Wm. Robertson, who was born on Pond Creek, in Monroe County, Tenn. They moved to Green County, Mo., where he died.

6. Christopher Marion Lotspeich married Susan Shearl, who died about 1873-4. He was a farmer and settled near Ottumwa, Iowa. He was drowned in the Iowa River May 26, 1852. Their children were: Nannie, Henry and Julia.

7. Emmeline Lotspeich married Rufus Pickel. (See Pickels.)

8. John W. Lotspeich married Nancy Ann Baker on December 7, 1856. She was born December 26, 1857. Died March 13, 1874, and was buried at Sweetwater Cemetery. He was a farmer. They moved to Weatherford, Texas. He died at Abilene, Tex., March 4, 1894. Their children are:

Mollie, b. December 19, 1857; m. R. W. Ellis.

Florence, b. April, 1859; m. Benton.

Addie, b. April, 1861; m. L. Dempsey; d. Marshall, Tex., in 1911.

Carrie, b. April, 1866. Married Chas. Waters. She is a ranchwoman near Abilene, Texas.

9. Elizabeth J. married J. J. Browder (whom see).

10. Amanda Lotspeich married Francis Y. Jameson on April 29, 1854. They moved to Gentry County, Mo.

11. Chas. W. Lotspeich was born at the Lotspeich residence, near Sweetwater. He married Mary Smith, daughter of Bryant Smith, of Meigs County, in November, 1871. She was born May 24, 1847, and died July, 1877. Interred in Sweetwater Cemetery. He was a farmer. In 1883 he moved to Texas, and in 1886 he located in Jones County, where he died, and was buried near Hawley, October 4, 1907. Their children were:

(1) Bryant, b. 1872, in Sweetwater Valley. Address Hawley, Tex., R. F. D. No. 1.

(2) Thomas J., b. in Sweetwater Valley July 17, 1875. Lives at Hawley, Tex.

(3 & 4) Died in infancy and were buried at Sweetwater, Tenn.

Henry Mayes.

Birds sing and flowers bloom and shed their fragrance on the summer air. This is but natural; it is expected; as Josh Billings would say it is their business. There are people, now and then, so constituted that they have no desire or appetite to do wrong or take any pleasure in straying into forbidden paths. Their instincts point as sensitively to right and justice as the needle to the magnetic pole. If they veer from the straight path at all it is but a circumstance of the moment and not to be reckoned in the great trend of life. Kindness, liberality and hospitality are as much a part of their nature as for the flowers to bloom or the birds to sing. Of such a character was Henry Mayes. He traveled along the even tenor of his way without attracting any great attention. He did nothing startling. The only thing he could have done startling was to have gone very wrong. Though a man of ability and deservedly popular, particularly with the young people of the neighborhood, he would never consent to take the lead or aspire to any office. You always knew where to place him even if he would not allow himself to be pushed to the front. He was always ready to assist in every good work and work for the bettering of the town and community. To be honest and truthful came to him as natural as to breathe the breath of life. A man of that kind would not hold his own financially in the fierce business competition of today. That is one change that we can not help but regret. The ideals and ethics of business are different. Many things have changed for the better but not that.

Henry Mayes had as few faults as any man in the valley and his virtues were by no means all negative. Yet if any man had called him good to his face he would have been much astonished. "Why callest thou me good?" he would have thought. For never in public or private life or when he took the journey to the Great Beyond did he for a single instant pose for effect. Some might have regretted that he said nothing of seeing angels or hearing music as he passed through the portals of death.

Mr. Mayes died as he had lived, simply. He who has lived theatrically often dies so.

Henry Mayes' death was calm and peaceful. There was no posing. It was merely the last incident of a well spent life. Every thing he ever did was done quietly and in order.

I have thus emphasized his distinguishing characteristic, the disinclination to be the central figure, because he did more to make Sweetwater the town it is than any man who ever lived in it except one, and that one was his most particular friend and with him in business matters he always consulted.

Henry Mayes was married to Nancy Maginnis at Thorn Hill, near Bean's Station, Grainger County, Tenn., April, 1837. As he was born at Bean's Station on April 15, 1817, he was just 20 years old. They soon thereafter moved to Sweetwater Valley and settled on the southwest quarter of section 35, township 2, range 1, east. He afterwards acquired from the Chancery Court of Grainger County two other tracts of 160 acres each, the southeast and northwest quarters of section 34 of the same range and township. He built a two-story frame house, then rather scarce in this part of the valley. They were usually either log or brick, mostly log. The reason for this was that at that time steam engines were very expensive and in this immediate section and Sweetwater Creek did not have sufficient fall in its course to furnish water power for sawmills. This house was near the site now occupied by the residence of J. H. McCaslin in the town of Sweetwater. The stage road ran directly by the house and this was a popular and convenient feeding and stopping place. The stage drivers were well known characters. They had regular schedules and ran pretty well on time. When the bugle sounded for the stopping places those in the neighborhood would collect to hear the news and see if there were any distinguished passengers on board. Rube Crabtree and Andy Davis were popular drivers.

The nearest neighbors of Mayes were Owen, Biggs, Heiskell, Ramsey, Fine, Bunch, Henderson, Snead and Fryer. The tract on which he lived joined Owen, Biggs, Lenoir, Fine, and on the west another Mayes tract. At that time the site of the town of Sweetwater was timber lands and virgin soil.

Thus Henry Mayes being married to a lovely, attractive and domestic woman, living at an ideal situation, surrounded by agreeable neighbors the future seemed exceptionally bright; he was blessed according to his deserts.

True, church and school privileges were not all that could be desired. The school-house was a small log affair one-half mile southwest in the bend of the creek, and there was teaching only from three to four months in the year. The Cumberland Presbyterian Church, named Mt. Lebanon, of which Mr. Mayes and his wife were members, was located one mile to the northeast. This as has already been related was afterward moved to the town. The children of this union were:

Letitia, born in 1838, and died in infancy.

James H., born 1840; died at Atlanta, Ga., 1867.

Mary Louise, born 1843; died at Sweetwater 1859.

Noble I., born May 6, 1845. Now living in Chattanooga.

E. Virginia, born 1854 and died at Knoxville on October 10, 1910.

Mrs. Nancy Mayes died at Sweetwater 1857 and was buried at Mt. Lebanon.

The Mayes place was a lovely one to visit even in those early times. They had enough slaves to do the house and farm work and it was a rare thing that they sat down to a meal without some one present other than the members of the family. Those were times when people felt free to go to see each other garbed as they happened to be at the time, whether in store or home-made clothes did not matter. The fashions remained much the same from year to year till the coming of the railroad.

The Mayes family were fond of music and innocent amusements. Mrs. Mayes herself played the old time music on the fiddle. She did not play often but only for particular friends, as some of the "unco guid" thought it not exactly in form. Dancing too was frowned upon as now but was not considered one of the unpardonable sins.

The family were looked upon as a particularly fortunate and happy one. Ignorance of sanitation by one who should have known better was the cause of much trouble. Sometimes an unforeseen circumstance, call it luck, fate, Providence or what you will, can materially change the whole outlook of a family.

Dr. M. C. Parker, about the time of the first settlement of Sweetwater, built him an office and started in the practice of medicine. He might have known the common practice then recommended by the old practitioners but that would be thought antiquated now.

He became afflicted with tuberculosis, which afterward proved fatal. He was boarding before and during his sickness with the Mayes family. They waited on him with great care throughout his illness.

Thus was sown the germs of the disease and was the cause of much sickness and some fatalities. It was not a well established fact at the time that this disease was communicable. Instead of living and sleeping in the open air as much as possible and leaving the windows of the sick room open it was thought best for the patient to be confined in a close room and so as to prevent taking further cold,—thus causing him to breathe over and over again the same vitiated atmosphere. This hastened his disease and made it much more dangerous for any one waiting on the tuberculosis patient.

The practice here when I was a boy was as far wrong in case of fevers as in tuberculosis. When I was six or seven years old there was an epidemic of scarlet fever in the Valley. Several of the Bowmans, our nearest neighbors, died of it. I took it. My father was absent from home in the mountains of North Carolina. My mother sent for Dr. Parker. He promptly proceeded to bleed me freely. He prescribed the most nauseating compounds for me to take; he left particular instructions that I should have very little water to drink, and under no circumstances cold applications. Owing to my violent rebellion against such methods the instructions were not strictly carried out.

My longing for my father to return, the intolerable thirst from bleeding and high fever is a fearsome thing for me to contemplate even to this day. I grew rapidly worse. The third or fourth day my father got back. I was truly happy. In about three minutes I had plenty of cold water to drink and a pitcherful or two was poured on my head. Had he been delayed many more hours "little Willie" would not be here now trying to write the history of Sweetwater Valley people. I resolved there and then I would never allow any one to suffer as I had those three or four days if I could prevent it. It seemed to me greatly worse than natural thirst. I have told this to show what unnecessary tortures ignorance can inflict on humanity. The doctor did only what the books he happened to have told him to do. My mother, whose father was a physician, did not dare to disobey instructions. She had a reverence for tradition. He (her father) bled his patients sometimes and charged five dollars for it too. This was the price for that service (?) during the thirties in Nashville.

A friend of mine once told me that a man told him that Dr. W. G. E. Cunningham, a former missionary to China and well known educator and editor of Sunday-school literature, is reported to have said that the manner of employing physicians in China was radically different from what it is in this country. There the doctor is hired and paid to keep you well and see that your household does not disobey the laws of health. If you get sick he is obligated to give you his medical services free of charge and, in addition to this, to pay you a reasonable sum for loss of time during the illness. Thus the M. D. resolved himself into a medical aid, sick benefit, accident insurance and benevolent society and sanitary commission all in one. This custom, if adopted here, would revolutionize the method of procedure in the United States. This statement of Dr. Cunningham, if he made such, might have been true of the Mandarins and the higher class Chinese, but that it is generally a fact, applying to the common millions, there is much reason to doubt. Dr. Hattie Love, a medical missionary of the Methodist Episcopal Church, South, at Soochow, makes no mention of such a state of affairs in her letters home.

I am not able to qualify as an expert on Chinese customs, yet I have seen enough of them in my travels in this country to form and express an opinion. I was an honorary member of the order of the Sons of Confucius at college; I have looked on in the Rue Royal at New Orleans, where a great many Chinamen were playing "keno" (this is a game somewhat similar to baseball; the one gambols on the green and the other gambles on the "green"; one is sward and the other cloth). I have in my possession a receipt, written in the Chinese characters, for clothes washed in Chicago; I have seen the "yellow perils" shoveling sand off the railroad track in the deserts of Nevada; I passed the time of day with a "Chink" at Portland, Oregon (I asked him what time it was and he passed on without a word); a quarter of a century ago I walked along several of the streets of Chinatown in San Francisco and I saw enough in the daytime from the outside to know that I did not wish to visit their opium dens and sinks of iniquity at night; I left that for the "slummers" and the philanthropists. From the knowledge obtained as above, I am positive that the Chinese resident here is not controlled by any medical director, and that there is nothing sanitary about him from his queue to the soles of his wooden shoes; whatever may be his condition in his own Celestial Kingdom, or, as they call it now, republic.

There is no profession, the members of which have half the temptations and opportunities to deceive and fake as the medical. The physician thrives on the ills of humanity; it is money in his pocket for people to stay sick. When he prevents epidemics and diseases he is taking the bread out of his own and his children's mouths. He is the depositary, too, of more people's secrets than any one except a Roman Catholic priest. Thus a physician is usually the best and most unselfish or the very worst of men. His opportunities for good and evil are incalculable. In my experience I could point to many instances both ways, but to much more in the way of good. It is rare that he abuses his professional knowledge or intentionally lengthens illness to obtain a fee. When he varies from the truth it is when he thinks it is for the good of the patient. I believe this is the rule and not the exception. "Skin for skin, yea, all that a man has will be given for his life." Many a man since Job's time has cursed the day on which he was born on account of bodily afflictions. Then it is not hard for the designing to make capital out of his circumstances. I thus apparently digress to pay a deserved tribute to the medical fraternity, as some things I have said heretofore might be taken as a reflection upon them. I do this also more cheerfully for the additional reason that among the most reputable physicians medical ethics does not allow one of them to say anything about himself in public print, except in the medical journals, which are not read by the general public. In these days of advertisement, when so many blow their own trumpets or hire it done, this is an anomalous position, however fortunate it may be for the patent medicine vender.

Destruction of New Mayes Residence by Fire.

In the destruction of the new Mayes residence by fire, I think in about the year 1870, the family records were partially destroyed; therefore, it is difficult now, in some instances, to arrive at the exact dates of births, deaths and marriages. Under the circumstances we can only approximate. We have to rely on our own memory and that of the living members of the family. The Athens Post for many years was the nearest newspaper published anywhere in this section of the country. Then, too, the personal happenings and neighborhood affairs were not considered important enough for publication. In the early days I doubt if the passing through of President Polk on the stage line would have been chronicled unless it had some political significance. From the year 1875 forward should be easy sailing to write the history of our Valley, provided one have access to the daily and weekly papers.

In say about 1856 there had scarcely been a death in the Owen, Biggs or Mayes families. The Mayes house was up on the top of the hill; the Biggs at the foot of the hill near the large spring and north of The Mascot Hosiery Mills. The brick is a very old house and is still standing. The meadow land near was practically a swamp overgrown with calamus, watercress and bushes. The overflow of the creek also was much more than at present, there being many more obstructions in the bed of the stream. The Owen residence was in a low place near a large green pond and not far from the bank of the creek. From the situation it would appear that the site of the Mayes house was the most healthful of the three. After results did not prove this to be so.

Mayes Family in 1856.

In 1856 the family consisted of Mr. and Mrs. Mayes, a son, James H., aged 16, very much resembling his father in looks and disposition; a daughter, Mary L., who bade fair to be a handsome and accomplished woman, at that time 14 years or more old; a son Noble of 11, and Virginia, an infant of 1 year. They were a happy family and very much respected and loved. Mr. Mayes was a serious minded man and rarely ever joked, but he was not one of the "killjoy" kind; he could forget his own troubles to try to give pleasure to you.

In 1857 Mrs. Mayes died of tuberculosis, supposed to have been acquired waiting on Dr. M. C. Parker during his illness. In 1859 the daughter Mary died of the same disease.

James Hamilton Mayes was a railroad man. He died at Atlanta, Ga., July 7, 1870.

He m. Leila Viola Stoy, of Atlanta, October 20, 1868. They had a son, James Herbert, who was b. June 13, 1870; d. in Augusta, Ga., in 1906. He m. Ellen Roach April 11, 1894. Their children were:

Lelia, b. May 10, 1895; Francis, b. February 7, 1898; John Herbert, b. April 10, 1901.

Noble Irving Maginnis, second son of H. and N. Mayes was b. at Sweetwater May 6, 1845; m. Bettie Cornelia Goddard, oldest child of J. W. G. (whom see). They resided in Sweetwater for several years and then moved to Plainville, Ga. In 1885 they moved to Chattanooga. Mrs. Mayes died in Chattanooga on November 18, 1915. Children of N. I. and Bettie C. Mayes were:

1. Belle Goddard, b. September 24, 1872; m. Wm. G. Hartley July 31, 1901.

2. Margaret Bland, b. June 8, 1874. She is a D. D. S. Formerly worked in Dr. S. B. Cook's office, Chattanooga.

3. James Henry, b. at Chattanooga, January 20, 1877. Was killed in a railroad accident on December 6, 1889.

4. Mildred Louise, b. August 25, 1889; m. Thos. W. Miller, of Columbia, S. C., on November 12, 1913.

The fifth child of H. and N. M. Mayes was E. Virginia; m. Captain J. P. Edmondson (then) of Blount County, September 5, 1885. He was b. October 16, 1844. Was sheriff of Blount County August 1872-6. Department U. S. revenue collector 1880-5. Postmaster at Maryville 1890-4. Moved to Knoxville 1901. Residence, 1319 Highland Avenue. His wife E. V. E. d. at residence October

10, 1910; buried old Gray Cemetery. One child Irene d. January 5, 1914; aged 16 years and 5 months.

HENRY MAYES' SECOND MARRIAGE.

Mr. Mayes' second wife was Mrs. Ada Treadway. They were married at Athens, Tenn., April 6, 1860. She was the daughter of Peter Reagan, a half brother of General J. H. Reagan's father. (See J. H. Reagan Sketches.)

Henry Mayes was particularly fortunate in both his marriages. When he married Mrs. Treadway, he had been deprived by disease of his first wife and eldest daughter, Mary, who had gotten to be of an age when she could have been a great help and comfort to him. He had a family who sorely needed a mother and the second Mrs. Mayes filled the place as well as any one could. True he had slaves at the time who could do the house and farm work but even then there were rumors of war and insurrections that caused a feeling of uneasiness through the South as regards that kind of property. John Brown had already made his raid on Harper's Ferry, been captured by Colonel Lee, been tried, disposed of and was being sung about. As has been stated in 1860 Mr. Mayes married Mrs. Treadway. She was such a capable, lovely woman as rendered the conditions during the Civil War and the reconstruction period much more tolerable to him. He was a rebel or southern sympathizer, but was exceedingly prudent in his conversation and conduct. He did not fall out with others for a difference of opinion. He desired that the Union men should be protected in life and property during the occupancy of the country by the Confederate army. To keep free of malice and passion was no easy thing to do when this section was occupied by first one and then another and continually fought over.

The feeling was sometimes stronger between the noncombatants at home than between the soldiers in the army. The rancor became so great in some sections of East Tennessee that it amounted to a system of reprisal and extermination. This however was happily not the case in the town of Sweetwater and the country immediately surrounding. At the breaking out of the war the town had about 400 inhabitants. It remained about the same during the war. When the hostilities of armies were practically over the troubles of rebels were by no means ended. Then came the reconstruction period. Then none but men of approved loyalty were allowed to vote or sit on juries. The administration of justice was a one-sided affair. Even Mr. Mayes, whose well-known Christian spirit did not suffer him at any time willingly to give offense to others, was harassed by damage suits in the courts. Nor had he or any of his family ever engaged actively in the rebellion. What partially saved him from being broken up was not this, but the fact that the plaintiffs in the causes never had had anything to be taken by rebel raiders, and in many instances the cases were put off until there was a change in the complexion of affairs. The real horror of war is that when the fighting is done the evil results last for a century.

Henry Mayes, I understood, was not a highly educated man but there was nothing rough about his conversation or manners. He would not have attempted to discuss the binomial theorem, or solve examples by logarithm or compute the age of the world by its geological formations; but he never used such expressions as "I taken," "I seen," "me and him" did so and so, please "set down," though it is possible he may have said "ain't;" fairly well educated people do that sometimes.

He was a remarkably close observer of animals, plants and weather conditions, and had a retentive memory. I recollect distinctly of his explaining to me the meaning of the passage in Ecclesiastes: "The wind goeth toward the south and turneth about unto the north; it whirleth about continually; and the wind returneth again according to his circuit." The explanation was that the wind turns to the right like the hands of a clock and goes from the south to the north by way of the west and then to the south by the east. It usually travels the half circuit from the north to the south more quickly than that from the south to the north. If the direction of the wind is from the west, it is almost certain to come from the north before coming from the east. He also called my attention to the fact that whirlwinds and whirlpools gyrate in the same manner. Such things as these, not then found in books, was what he frequently told me and interested me much.

MUCH OF SWEETWATER ON MAYES' LAND.

The town Sweetwater is built, much of it, on the Mayes land. A line drawn from the middle of the Heiskell lane on the east side of town to the middle of the public road, going west toward Pond Creek, would show the division line between the Mayes and Lenoir lands. Henry Mayes died at Sweetwater on August 13, 1873.

MRS. ADA REAGAN MAYES.

Miss Ada Reagan was born at Rome, Ga., December 1, 1828. She married Thos. J. Treadway, January 23, 1851. He died November 3, 1856. Mrs. Treadway married Henry Mayes on April 10, 1860. She died at Asheville, N. C., on May 5, 1901.

Cuba Treadway was born February 8, 1855. He was a railroad man. He died August 20, 1885.

Oscar Reagan Mayes was born April 10, 1861. His post-office is Hurst, Ill.

Carrie Lee Mayes was born at Sweetwater on September 16, 1863. She married John H. Weaver, of Asheville, N. C., November 22, 1888. Dr. E. E. Wiley officiating. Mr. Weaver, formerly of Weaverville, is a prominent merchant of Asheville, N. C. Their residence is 119 Cumberland Avenue.

The children of Jno. H. and Carrie Lee Weaver are:
1. Eugene Mayes Weaver, b. March 22, 1891; m. Mrs. Lillian Daniels Dryser.

    (1) By this marriage one child, Oliver Dryser. He died and she m. E. Mayes W. Children of this marriage are:

        (1) Constance Alene, b. March, 1914.
        (2) Lillian Doris, ——————— 1916.

2. Henry Cedric, b. November 24, 1894. In mailing department New York Times.
3. Mary Adalena, b. November 28, 1897.
4. Carrie Lee, b. September 15, 1900.

The Taylors.

Hughes and Betsey Cannon Taylor, his wife, came from Virginia and settled in Grainger County. They reared a family of twelve children: H. Woodson, Elika Adams, Mrs. Emma Witt, Grant, Mrs. Eliza Boatwright, Jabin Snow (see Fine), Mrs. Rachel Witt, Mrs. Amanda Patton (see Francis A. Patton), Thomas, Elbert E., Mrs. Edna ——— (name of husband not known to writer).

Elika Adams, second son of Hughes and Betsy Cannon Taylor, was born in Grainger County, Tenn., July 30, 1811. He married Elizabeth Mayes, March 30, 1830, in Grainger County, who was born February 4, 1813; died February 26, 1889. Her father was James Mayes. Her mother's maiden name was Jane Howel. Mrs. E. Taylor was a sister of Henry Mayes, of Sweetwater.

They moved from Grainger County to Pond Creek Valley in the first civil district of Monroe County in 1839 or 1840. He resided there until his death on May 10, 1903, in the 92nd year of his age.

There is a deed of record at Madisonville, Book "NK," p. 487, of a purchase of 80 acres of land from John Glaze by E. A. Taylor, the same having been bought by him (Glaze) of Lindsay Roberts. The date of the deed is January 27, 1840.

In September, 1842, E. A. Taylor and wife Elizabeth, were received by experience into the Baptist church on Pond Creek. This church was located about one mile south of the Taylor residence. The membership of this church afterward met in the town of Sweetwater and the name was changed to the "First Baptist Church at Sweetwater."

It is related in the church records of the then Pond Creek Baptist Church that they were baptized in Sweetwater Creek near John Fine's. Presumably the rite was performed by Rev. Robt. Snead as he was acting as pastor of the church at the time. The reason the baptism took place in Sweetwater Creek was that there was not "much water" in Pond Creek especially at that time of the year.

In March, 1845, E. A. Taylor became clerk and was

clerk of the church until October, 1860, when his son, William H. Taylor, was elected church clerk in his place.

In June, 1854, the church decided to build a house of worship in the town of Sweetwater, which was then beginning to be a place of some importance, hoping thereby to largely increase their membership. Mr. Taylor was one of the active members in bringing about this change. However, the church house was not completed until the fall of 1860. The first record of meeting in it was the first Saturday in December, 1861. At this meeting Thos. D. and Martha L. Taylor joined the church and Wm. H. Taylor was church clerk.

In the year 1861 at the outbreak of the Civil War Elder Hughes Taylor, of Beach Spring in Grainger County, was pastor; his brother, E. A. Taylor, was a deacon. Wm. H. Taylor was church clerk and Elizabeth, Woodson, Thos. D., Martha L., and Minerva Taylor, were members of the church. There joined the church afterward of the Taylors—James H., Mrs. Emily S., Zachary, Eliza, Sarah, Elizabeth and William.

E. A. Taylor as a clerk kept the books of the church neatly, correctly and in good diction. The same was the case of two sons who afterward were also clerks, viz: Wm. H. and James H.

E. A. Taylor was an educated man in this sense, that education consists more in the ability to apply what you know to the duties and circumstances of life than the amount of knowledge acquired. When he (E. A. Taylor) knew anything, he knew it as well as anybody could know it. He could converse on the Bible as interestingly as any one I have ever known. He was an authority on Baptist doctrine. He was also one of the most progressive farmers in all this section of country. Being a reader and having a receptive mind he could not help but be versed in the political history of the nation. He was a fluent talker and was never at a loss for a word. He was always enthusiastic in the advocacy of what he believed. He was always anxious for others to believe as he did. Usually one who wears himself out in the reformation or service of others does not attain to old age. He is a notable exception to this rule.

In the presidential election of 1896 he came to Sweetwater three and one-half miles to vote. He remarked at the polls that the first ballot he ever cast was for William Henry Harrison and that he took great pleasure in casting the last ballot he ever expected to cast for Wm. J. Bryan. He was then more than 86 years of age. I told him I hoped that he would live to cast a ballot for Mr. Bryan again. This he did and when he came to the polls in 1900 I reminded him of what he said four years previous. But he did not live to vote for Bryan the third time.

He was a teetotaller by practice and none of his five sons ever drank at all except one and he very rarely. Yet I do not think I ever heard him discuss the question of prohibition. However he preferred charges against one of the members of his church for being intoxicated. The member was excluded and his quotation of the passage "Eat, drink and be merry for tomorrow ye die" did not save him. The church did not interpret the Scripture as the offending brother interpreted it.

The children of E. A. and Elizabeth Taylor were:

One. James Hughes, born March 21, 1831; died in the summer of 1876.

Two. Woodson, born September 22, 1833; died March —, 1912.

Three. William Henry, born February 4, 1836; died June 26, 1914.

Four. Thomas Daniel, born September 29, 1838; died October 6, 1902.

Five. Martha Louisa, born April 6, 1841.

Six. Mary Elizabeth, born February 4, 1844.

Seven. Zachary ———, born November 14, 1849; died August 9, 1914.

Eight. Eliza, born December 28, 1859.

Two. Woodson Taylor m. Emily Palmer, then of Sweetwater May 8, 1867. Rev. Snead Minister. She was a younger sister of Mrs. W. L. Clark and was born in New York.

Woodson T. was a farmer. He went to Grainger County on Holston River soon after marriage. His wife died October, 1915. Their children were:

Mrs. Mary Sheldon (dead), of Kentucky; William

Elika, Frank Palmer, Geo. Elbert, Elizabeth Cleveland, and Ernest. A daughter, the youngest, died in infancy. Mary married a distant relative, Claude Taylor. The Taylor home is at Jefferson City, where Frank and Elizabeth still live.

One. James Hughes Taylor was first married to Sarah Warren of Iowa, who died leaving two children, Mrs. Lizzie McAmis, of Ash Grove, Mo., and William H., of Columbus, Miss. His second wife was Mary Minnis, of Madisonville, Tenn. Died at Elika Taylor's home September 12, 1915. Left two children: Mrs. Fannie Arendall and John Quincy, both of Atlanta, Ga.

William Henry Taylor came to Sweetwater and went into the mercantile business with Joseph Boyd, brother of Mrs. J. C. Vaughn in a part of the old hotel building in 1854 or 1855. He married F———— Adelia Bradshaw of Towns County, Ga., on July 5, 1859, A. H. Barkley, minister. After the Civil War he did business in Atlanta, Ga., as a commission merchant. He came back to Tennessee. He was a farmer in Grainger County. He went to Paris, Texas, in the year ———— He died in Paris, Texas, and was interred there. She was a Methodist. She was a sister of Lieutenant Nicholas Bradshaw who married Miss Sallie Brown, daughter of Judge Geo. Brown of Madisonville.

The children of Wm. H. and F. A. Taylor were:
Frank, Charles, Robert, Bettie, Flora, Edward, Pearl, Libby, Hugh, Henry and Lucy. Bettie married John J. Browder, son of J. M. Browder (whom see).

Martha Louisa married Hugh C. McCammon, of Boulder, Col., on April 21, 1874. He was born in Knox County. After moving to Colorado he was a miner and farmer and was a member of the Legislature at one time. He died at Boulder. Their children were:

Blanche, who married Seth M. Thomas, of Boulder, and Anna, who married Horace Griffin of that place. Their son, Hugh, lives at Black Hawk, Col. Their third daughter was named Olive.

Mary Elizabeth was b. February 4, 1844; m. Sam M. Thomas on February 18, 1869. He was the son of ———————— of Kentucky, and was a brother of Mrs.

Sterling Neil. They moved first to Trenton, Tenn., then to Collins County, Texas, finally to San Saba County. Post-office, Brownwood, Texas. There are two children now (1915) living: Welin, post-office, Denver, Col., and Gardner.

Eight. Eliza m. Will Thomas, son of John L. Thomas, December 10, 1890. He (W. T.) was b. in McMinn County, March, 1866; d. December 3, 1915. He was a very zealous and efficient member of the First Baptist Church, Sweetwater, and was a noted teacher in the Sunday-school. He and his wife resided during married life at the old E. A. Taylor place. He farmed the land as intelligently and industriously as his father-in-law. Children five in number: Harold, b. January 12, 1893; Jennie Valeria, b. September 10, 1894, d. September 3, 1897; Blanche Elizabeth, b. December 21, 1896; Ruby and Ruth were twins, b. August 3, 1898.

Mrs. Eliza Brewster

Was the daughter of James and Jane Howel Mayes, of Grainger County, Tenn. She was born April 8, 1838. She was a sister of Henry Mayes and of Mrs. E. A. Taylor. She married John Brewster from her home October 15, 1857.

He was b. in Virginia, February 7, 1828. He was a stock trader. He was supposed to have been lost in a steamboat disaster on the Mississippi River. She moved to Sweetwater from Grainger County early in 1867. Their children were:

(1) Ora was born in Grainger County, November 15, 1858. She was a noted piano player and music teacher. She taught at Thomasville and at Shelby, N. C. She had the gift of absolute pitch. She could tell instantly what note was struck on any instrument. On a piano that she was accustomed to and in good tune she could tell by ear and name each note without seeing the piano as many as eight notes struck simultaneously, whether chords or dischords. She was an accomplished sight reader of music and also could reproduce any short piece of music that she heard if allowed to go to the piano at once, but nothing like the lengthy productions Blind Tom could.

She played for Blind Tom once at a performance. In playing the piece after her probably as much as five minutes long she said that he made a good many changes especially in the cadenzas but that some of them might have been just as good as the author's idea. The tempo of the piece as played by Blind Tom was slightly more rapid than Miss Brewster's. I have heard him I think as many as four times and he was more successful in reproducing Miss Brewster's piece than that of any other.

At Shelby, N. C., while teaching there Miss B. got acquainted with Charles C. Blanton and they were married in Sweetwater July 15, 1885. She died in Atlanta, January 17, 1890. He is a resident of Shelby, N. C.

(2) Mary Brewster was born in Grainger County, Tenn., May 14, 1861. She died in Sweetwater, February 7, 1873.

(3) Valeria (Vallie) was b. in Grainger County, July 31, 1865. She married A. R. Melendy, D. D. S. of the firm of Cook & Melendy, June 30, 1884. Parents of one son, Melville B. Melendy, who was born in Sweetwater, August 21, 1886. Dr. and Mrs. Melendy moved to Knoxville. She died there November 16, 1910.

M. B. Melendy married Miss Eleanor Darcy, of New York City.

Mrs. Brewster resides in Shelby, N. C.

THE MANIS FAMILY.

The information below was gotten from James Harvey Manis in Sweetwater, in 1912. He had no records with him and the information is from his memory:

Ephraim Manis, father of John, Harvey and George and those given, came from Hawkins County to this section about 1819. He died at the age of 87 years. His children were:

William, b. 1822. Went to California in 1849. Lives in Oregon.

John, b. 1824. Married ——— Randolph.

Sarah Ann, b. 1826. Married ——— Cooper.

George, b. 1832. Lives at Gudger. Married. Has large family. Served as a soldier in the Confederate army.

James Harvey, b. January 15, 1836.
Esther, b. 1838. Married John Pryor. Lives in McMinn County, Tenn.
Joseph, b. 1840; d. 1909.
James Harvey Manis married Lucinda Randolph February 15, 1867. He had served through the war in the Confederate army. He was a farmer. Their children were: Isham G. Harris, b. December, 1867. Lives in Oklahoma; Bettie and Callie died young; Dosia married Alex McAmis, lives in McMinn; Sallie, married ——— Tallent; Mary, married ——— Duncan, lives in Oklahoma; Mattie, married ——— McCosh, lives in Oklahoma; Joe, lives in the first district of McMinn County; Annie, dead; Harriette, married Connor and lives in Oklahoma; James Harvey, died in youth.

THE MARTINS.

John Martin was born June 29, 1779; d. November 29, 1841. His son, Hugh E., was born February 25, 1809, and died January 3, 1857. He married Mary Griffitts of Blount County, a sister of Mrs. John Ramsey. Mary Griffitts was born April 17, 1819, and died February 28, 1907. They are both buried at Philadelphia.

Hugh E. Martin owned a large farm about midway between Philadelphia and Sweetwater. Their children were:

1. William Edward, who died at Vicksburg, Miss., in 1863.

2. James G., d. near Chattanooga in 1913. He was a soldier in the Confederate army during the Civil War. He married Mary McPherson of Meigs County. Their children were: Annie, Jennie and Margaret, who died in early life; Hugh, lives at Evansville, Tenn., m. McPherson. They have nine sons. Joe, Jack and Bertie (Mrs. Johnson) live in Chattanooga; Georgia, lives at Tasso, Tenn., where he is agent for the Southern Railway Company., and is a merchant. He married Maude Woods, of Concord, Tenn. They have three children, Elizabeth, George C., Jr., and Catherine.

3. Margaret, daughter of Hugh E.; m. Thomas Harris, who was a carpenter and farmer. Their children were: William Ramsey, d; Mary Elizabeth, d; Hugh

Alexander and Charles M., who live in Chattanooga, Tenn.

4. Elizabeth, b. September 12, 1851; m. Dr. Thomas Arrants, of Decatur, Tenn., on August 29, 1876. Their children were: Artie, b. 1879. W. H., b. November 18, 1881. He took a literary course at the University of Tennessee and a medical course at the University of Nashville. He married Hulah Cowan, of Covington, Tex. He is a practising physician at Sweetwater, Tenn. Sam. H., third child of Elizabeth Arrants, b. October 18, 1884; is a farmer in Meigs County. Lizzie Crate, fourth child of Elizabeth Arrants, b. February 24, 1888.

5. Susan, fifth child of Hugh E. Martin; m. Eli Cleveland. See Clevelands.

6. Harle, d. about 1908. Unmarried.

7. George, b. December 3, 1853; m. Mary Davis. Address, 1313 Indiana Avenue, Spokane, Wash.

8. Hugh, died in early manhood.

THOMAS J. MOORE

Was born at Kingston, Tenn., January 9, 1824, the son of John Moore and Susan Moore. (This Susan Moore was the sister of Ann Moore who married Solomon Bogart, whom see.) Thomas J. Moore, married (first) Elizabeth Martin Cannon, b. June 11, 1822, daughter of Robert and Ann Galbraith Cannon, of Philadelphia, Tenn., in about 1846. He moved to that place when a young man. After the completion of the East Tennessee and Georgia Railroad he was agent there for that company for a number of years. After that he worked in the general offices of railroad company at Knoxville almost up to the time of his death. In 1871 he moved to Sweetwater, where he purchased a part of the Chas. Cannon farm, just southwest of the town. He died there on March 2, 1875, and was buried at Philadelphia. The children of T. J. and Elizabeth C. Moore were:

Octavia, b. November 8, 1847; d. July 8, 1886, and was buried at Philadelphia.

Ann, b. June 20, 1850.

Robert Cannon, b. November 24, 1853. Unmarried. Lives at Sweetwater, Tenn.

J. Charles, b. May 5, 1856.

Ann Moore married George McKnight at Sweetwater on November 16, 1885. He was born June 12, 1844. He was depot agent at Sweetwater for a great number of years for the Southern Railway and its predecessors. He afterwards bought the Biggs farm near there. In May, 1905, he purchased a farm three miles west of Charleston, Tenn., and moved there. He sold this place in August, 1912, and moved to Cleveland, Tenn., where he now lives. Their children were:

George M., b. August 21, 1886; d. January 15, 1915.

Robert Cannon, b. August 19, 1888. He is a pharmacist living at Los Angeles, Cal.

J. Charles Moore, married Sarah Bachman, daughter of Nathan and Sarah Cunningham Bachman, on June 15, 1893, the Rev. Nathan Bachman, officiating. Charles Moore is a member of the Presbyterian church. He is a certified public accountant and auditor. The children of Charles and Sarah Moore are:

Charles Bachman, b. April 5, 1894; Nathan Thomas, b. May 31, 1896; Laurence, b. August 6, 1902, and Robert Cannon, b. October 25, 1907.

J. Charles Moore lives at Knoxville, Tenn.

Thomas J. Moore, married (second) Rowena Brown, the daughter of the Rev. Thos. Brown, of Philadelphia, Tenn. Thomas Brown, M. G. Their children were:

Susan, b. March 31, 1869, at Philadelphia, Tenn.

Thomas J., b. October 21, 1874, at Sweetwater, Tenn.

Susan Moore was married to J. B. Sizer at Sweetwater March 8, 1888. He was born at Newark, N. J., on April 12, 1861. He is a lawyer and first practised in Sweetwater. In the year of 1890 he moved to Chattanooga and became a member of the firm of Pritchard & Sizer. After the death of Mr. Robert Pritchard he became a partner of Mr. Chambliss. He has a very lucrative practice. The children of J. B. and Susan Sizer are:

Margaret Moore, b. January 8, 1889; Rowena Brown, b. June 1, 1891; Hilda Wade, b. October 13, 1893; Mary Helen, b. October 12, 1896; James Burnett, b. March 9, 1899; Octavia, b. June 26, 1901, and Anthony DeSosieur, b. March 10, 1909.

Margaret Moore Sizer was married to Alexander

Chambliss, of Chattanooga, on January 5, 1910. He is a lawyer. They reside at Chattanooga.

Thomas J., youngest son of Thomas J. and Rowena Moore, was born October 21, 1874. On July 10, 1912, he married Helen Swalm, of Colorado Springs, Col. She died at Chattanooga January 6, 1915. He is a manufacturer in Chattanooga.

HON. MATTHEW NELSON.

The following was taken from a sketch of his life in possession of Mr. M. M. Nelson, of. Knoxville, Tenn. It was written by his grandmother, the wife of Matthew Nelson. She was, if I mistake not, a sister of Robt. Cannon of Roane County, who lived the latter part of his life near Philadelphia on what is still known as the Cannon place. She was born April 19, 1784, and died April 26, 1862. She and her husband were both buried in the Presbyterian cemetery near Philadelphia. The sketch referred to is so well written that it is copied almost entire.

Matthew Nelson, Sr., was born in Rockbridge County, Virginia, October 17, 1778. His father migrated to (what was afterward) this State whilst it was a territory and was a sharer, first, in the Revolutionary War and then in the Indian war. (Note—He was too young to have fought in the Revolution, but remembered it as a spectator.) He was the oldest of a family of eight children and was taught the rudiments of learning by an old maiden aunt, who had become much attached to him on account of his aptness to learn. Slates being scarce in those hard times, she procured a piece of slate-stone and with a pencil of the same material she set copies for him. She used to say to her sister in her good old Scotch-Irish dialect: "Matthew is a fine boy and shows signs of talents." He never was at school but three months, yet notwithstanding his disadvantages he had so far advanced as to be employed to teach a small school at the age of seventeen years. About the year 1799 or 1800 he went to Kingston, where he worked at his trade (that of carpenter), and resided in Roane County until his marriage (to Miss Martha Cannon) on the 20th of August, 1803. Shortly afterward they settled in Kingston, where, by his honest labors and moral habits, he gained the confidence of all who knew him.

In 1813 he was elected representative (to the General Assembly) from Roane County. During the session he was made treasurer of East Tennessee. He then moved to Knoxville. He entered upon the duties of his office January 13, 1814. These duties he discharged with scrupulous care and fidelity for fourteen years. About 1816 he went into partnership in the mercantile line with the late worthy James Campbell, of Knoxville. At the close of the term of partnership, he continued the business alone for a number of years. During his term of office as treasurer, the public lands in the Hiwassee District were subjected to sale, and the treasurer was required to superintend the sale. For this service the law allowed him two per cent commission on the gross proceeds of the sale, and all the emoluments and perquisites of his office instead of a stated salary. The land sales were large, and in one year his commission amounted to six or seven thousand dollars. He believed that the Legislature contemplated no such large compensation to the treasurer, and acting upon this conviction he paid over to the treasury all but fifteen hundred dollars, which he reserved to himself as an honest compensation.

Honesty in theory is no rarity among men; but we see here the man that acted it out in practice in its length thereof and in its breadth thereof.

On the 25th of December, 1828, he left Knoxville with his family and arrived at Philadelphia on the 1st of December, 1829, and settled on his farm to spend the remainder of his days in peace and quietness, but his public course was not finished. He was shortly made justice of the peace, giving satisfaction to all parties in all cases of law. His motto was law and justice. In 1844 he was elected treasurer of the State of Tennessee. He went to Nashville with the determination to know nothing among them but truth and honesty. During his residence in Nashville the Lord wrought a good and gracious work in his soul, and on the 11th of March, 1845, he joined the Second Presbyterian church of that city, which was under the pastoral care of Dr. Lapsley.

On the 5th of November, 1845, he was voted out of office, and gave it up with as much ease as David laid aside Saul's armor, believing it to be a bar to his spiritual interest.

On April 2, 1846, he left Nashville, and, on the 7th, arrived at his residence in Philadelphia. He was invited by his friends to resume his seat as justice of the peace, which had been vacant for two years. He held this office from that time until his death, which occurred on December 1, 1852.

DOMESTIC HABITS.

He never was an early riser; generally lay until called up by the breakfast bell. Owing, I suppose, to his having both legs broken when young and which remained painful at times all his life. His temper was rather rough of a morning, but a cup of coffee generally brought on a sweet calm. He paid but little attention to what he ate. He seldom could tell an hour after meal what he had eaten. He was rather slovenly in his dress. Candor and punctuality marked his way. His family generally knew where he was and what he was about. He never aspired after a great name, but if honesty and sound piety make a part of great men he had a large share of the best kind of wisdom. The path of the just is as a shining light "that shines more and more until the perfect day." For the last few years of his life his Bible and family altar were to him as the precious dews of heaven. He never neglected these until worn out by age and affliction. His last illness was long and painful, but he bore his suffering with Job-like patience.

His long and useful life closed on the 1st of December, 1852. "Mark the perfect man and behold the upright, for the end of that man is peace."

From this sketch, which I believe is truthful, it is evident that the Hon. Matthew Nelson was a very remarkable and exceptional man. He was a warm personal and political friend of my father, I. T. Lenoir. They both were whigs. I. T. Lenoir was a member from Roane County in the twenty-fourth and twenty-fifth General Assemblies of the state. Mr. Nelson was a representative from the same county in 1813. Mr. Lenoir was an ardent and influential supporter of Mr. Nelson for state treasurer and was among the first to suggest his making the race. He had a very high opinion of Mr. Nelson's ability and integrity. He made as good a treasurer as the state ever had. Mrs. Nelson's saying "that he was voted out of office" (treasurer) merely means that the complexion of the Legislature had changed from whig in 1843 to democratic in 1845. Aaron V. Brown, Democrat, had also beaten Foster, whig, for governor. Therefore Nelson failed of re-election as treasurer. He had been as accurate in his accounts as state treasurer as he had been for the sale of lands in East Tennessee, and as well prepared to settle and vacate. In conducting the land sales in East Tennessee he could have made himself immensely wealthy, not only by collecting the fees allowed him, but agreeing with the purchasers to turn over to him the lands so bought for stipulated sums, erecting a man of straw as a go-between, practically thus purchasing the lands he desired from himself at his own price. Our modern financiers of the Guggenheimer type would not have asked for a better chance. But he came out of it all rather a poor man and bought not as much probably as he would otherwise have done.

It has been related under the caption of General James H. Reagan, that he was one of the first in this section to grant a right of way to the E. T. & G. R. R. Co., when after a description according to grant, he adds: "The land upon which I now reside and on which the town of Philadelphia is located."

Taking his career as an example it may well be doubted whether ideal "honesty is the best policy" to pursue to accumulate wealth or for a successful financial career. Mr. Nelson had almost unlimited opportunities inside the law to become rich but he failed to take advantage of them. No doubt resisting temptation to do what he considered would be wrong gave him greater satisfaction than to be able to draw a valid check for many thousands acquired dishonestly or in ways to which suspicion might attach. His policy of "letting his family know where he was and what he was about" no doubt in his case was a peacemaker and a worry-saver; but adopted by the average husband would be about as likely to cause trouble as to prevent it. Would it not be better sometimes to use a little diplomacy in the matter?

Mrs. Nelson's tribute to the beneficent influence of a cup of coffee upon the feelings and temper of her husband would have been quite a blow to the postum business had there been any such at the time. But how the coffee men would have relished it! And pray why should not the coffee berry boiled in water produce as healthful and palatable a beverage as the rye and wheat berry?

It will be interesting to note that the old house which Mr. Nelson built and resided in till his death is still standing. Its location is across the branch from W. C. Cannon's residence.

The children of Matthew and Martha Nelson were:

1. Lawrence, married Louisa Cannon (see Cannon). He died ———

2. Caroline, married John O. Cannon. John O. C., Jr., their son, was reared by Matthew Nelson.

3. Sydney C., married Robert Cleveland (see Clevelands).

4. Eliza, married Dr. Blackburn, of New Market. One son, David B., who went to Oregon.

5. Matthew, married ——— McGaughey, of Athens, Tenn. He is dead. She is still (1916) living in Knoxville. One son, Matthew N., merchant and accountant, Knoxville, Tenn.

6. John D. He must have been something of a humorist. He obtained a license at Madisonville, Tenn., on the 1st of February, 1839, to marry Polly Maddy. They did not marry and he made the return: "No property found in my county, J. D. Nelson, sheriff." However, next time he had better luck. On the 20th of August, 1844, he obtained a license to marry Sarah D. Taliaferro. They were duly married and moved to Texas.

7. William Cannon, was born at Knoxville, Tenn., September 16, 1821. He married Caroline Jones, born May

26, 1826, daughter of Hardy Jones. He was a farmer and also conducted a tanyard. He lived in or near Philadelphia most of his life. He died at Greeneville, Tenn. Their children were:

1. Martha, b. November 24, 1843. Married Harris Tipton, of Morganton, Tenn., on September 29, 1867. He was the son of John B. Tipton and Louisiana Tipton. Their children were: Sydney, John B. (dead), Hope, Nelson, Lawrence and Bessie.

2. Sydney Caroline, b. May 29, 1846; d. July 21, 1861.

3. David, b. June 2, 1848. Died in the west about 1912. He married Ida Shrader, of Loudon, Tenn., who died in the west a short time before her husband. David Nelson was a lawyer and was a member of the Forty-sixth General Assembly, sixth senatorial district. He had an only daughter who is dead.

4. Bettie Nelson, b. July 4, 1856. Married Charles Howard, of Greeneville, Tenn., on October 17, 1882. Lives at Ocmulgee, Okla.

5. John, b. June 29, 1858. Died in Oklahoma about 1905.

6. Annie, b. April 6, 1860. She married (first) Cicero Haynes, September 30, 1883. They had one daughter, Bessie Roe, married Howard. Mrs. Haynes married (second) Dr. C. Stearns. Two children, both dead.

8. David, the youngest child of Matthew Nelson died while his father was state treasurer.

STERLING NEIL.

The parents of Sterling Neil came from Virginia to this country. Sterling Neil was born in McMinn County on November 14, 1823. He married Miss Sallie Thomas, of Thompkinsville, Ky. She was born in West Tennessee. Her parents were Samuel and Sallie Thomas. She died in 1880 at Fort Valley, Ga.

Sterling Neil moved from McMinn County to his farm on the Athens road, one and one-half miles from Sweetwater, in 1849. They moved to Fort Valley, Ga., in 1863. He left his farm in Sweetwater Valley in charge of his father-in-law when he went south on account of the Federal occupation. Owing to the absence of the real owner, the farm and house suffered more from dep-

redation than it otherwise would. At Fort Valley he was a farmer and banker. He and his wife were both members of the Christian church. Their children were:
1. Stella, b. August 11, 1852.
2. John R., b. March, 1855. Lives at Fort Valley, Ga.
3. Mary, b. December 13, 1858.
4. Alice, b. December 24, 1861; d. at Athens, Tenn.
5. Sam Thomas, b. February 6, 1864; m. Stella Harris. He died in January, 1869.

1. Stella married J. C. Slappey, who was born December 10, 1842, on December 14, 1859. They live at Fort Valley, Ga. Their children are:

(1) George A. Slappey, b. April 27, 1871. He m. Fannie Harris in 1891, who lived only a year. Eight years later he married Clara Visscher. They live at Fort Valley, Ga.

(2) Beulah, b. December 22, 1872; m. W. H. Harris May 16, 1894. Address, Fort Valley, Ga.

(3) Alice, b. October 17, 1874; m. W. C. Black, November 29, 1893. Address, Tampa, Fla.

(4) Neil, b. September 18, 1876. Lives at Fort Valley, Ga.

(5) Ruby, b. January 3, 1879; m. H. L. Harris, January 10, 1898; d. Sparta, Ga., February 1, 1914.

(6) Sterling, b. January 4, 1881; m. Elmer Green, June 14, 1904. Address, Fort Valley, Ga.

(7) Maude, b. October 27, 1888; m. R. C. Suder, April 9, 1913. Address, Macon, Ga.

(8) Gladys, b. January 23, 1895.

2. Mary, second child of Sterling and Sallie Neil, was born near Sweetwater. She married Will C. Wester, of Chattanooga, Tenn., December 16, 1879. He was born on Half Moon Island, Tenn., November 27, 1854. He is a fire insurance man. They have one child, Earl Neil Wester, who married Lucille Gerstle.

CHARLES OWEN.

A cosmopolitan population makes a prosperous section and community, when there are not more "undesirable citizens" as immigrants than can be readily assimilated. The lessons of history, if I read them aright, inform us that, without the infusion of new blood into a nation, it degenerates and finally gives place to, or is overcome by, some other that is stronger or more aggressive. Our own section of country was peopled by those differing in customs and, in a measure, religion and descended from varied national ancestry. Those settling in our valley, so far as the states were concerned, came from Pennsylvania, Virginia, North Carolina and a few from each of the states of Maryland, Kentucky and South Carolina. As regards remoter ancestry we have the German Lotspeich, Pickel, Patton, Fry and Fryer; the English Cannon, Cleveland, Johnston, Mayes, Nelson and Yearwood; the Scotch Gregory, Neil, Ramsey and Wallis; the French Bogart, Berry, Fine, Goddard, Julian, Lenoir and Rowan; the Irish Moore, Ragon, Reagan, Sligo and Scruggs; the Welch Jones and Owen; the Norman-Dutch Heiskell, the Scotch-Irish McGuire.

Most of the families did not come to this valley direct from the mother countries, but had undergone a process of fusion in other states before settling here. To this no doubt is attributed the absence of friction between citizens and neighbors. It has rarely happened that there has been a feud perpetuated in our immediate section. No Jews, Russians or Italians at first came to our valley. You find in the records no names of people ending in "io," "ini," "ani," "off," or "sky." There were no "steins" or "bergs" or "schmidts" but however there were a few plain Smiths.

Those early settlers had no use for people who divided the world into just two classes: those of their own tribe and kindred and the others, the Gentiles, whom they thought the Lord did not consider his children and who were of the opinion that Moses was greater than Jesus Christ. They, the pioneers, had just as little use for those who took orders from any foreign potentate temporal or spiritual. They were all Protestants in religion and mostly belonged to one of three churches: Baptist, Methodist or Presbyterian. By Presbyterian we mean any branch of that great body.

Thus the elements (the inhabitants) were so mingled as to make a palatable state of affairs. Like the Frenchman's drink, which he named a "dim contradiction," it contained various ingredients:

"A little lemon to make it sour,
A little sugar to make it sweet,
A little (?) liquor to make it strong,
A little water to make it weak."

The difference there was in manners, religion, political opinions and customs served only to make social conditions more pleasant and agreeable.

OWEN OWEN.

Owen Owen, of Northampton County, Penn., was the great grandfather of Charles Owen, of Sweetwater Valley. Owen Owen had a son, David Owen, who was born March 13, 1713. His will is of record at Easton Pennsylvania. His wife, Sarah, was born March 1, 1724. They were parents of ten children. Joseph Owen was the fifth son. He married Susan B. Hartsell July 24, 1771. They had seven children of whom Charles Owen, who came to Sweetwater Valley, was the second.

Jesse Owen, brother of Charles Owen above, had a daughter, Sarah Wallace, born January 20, 1831. She married Samuel F. Hurt, of Abingdon, Va., on April 12, 1859. Her daughter, Rosa Lee, born December 23, 1868, married James W. Bell, of Abingdon, Va., April 14, 1892. He is president of the First National Bank of Abingdon, Va.

The eldest daughter of David Owen, was named Rachel, who married Samuel Bachman. It was thought she was the first of the Owens to move South. Samuel Bachman settled in upper East Tennessee.

Joseph Owen came to Tennessee between 1793 and 1795. These facts about Charles Owen's ancestry were obtained from Mrs. James W. Bell, of Abingdon, Va.

Charles Owen was born in Allegheny County, Penn., on December 29, 1793. He died at his residence near Sweetwater on September 6, 1873.

Louisa Berry, his wife, was born in Sullivan County, Tenn., on March 22, 1798. She died January 8, 1867. They both were buried in the old cemetery on the hill west of the town of Philadelphia, where the old Presbyterian church once stood.

They were married in Sullivan County on May 7, 1818.

The exact date they came to Sweetwater Valley is not known to me. The records both at Athens and Madisonville show that he was a purchaser and made sales of lands as early as 1827. At Madisonville in Book "A," page 93, is found this conveyance: "Chas. Matlock to Charles Owen 100 acres, part of tract, the northwest quarter of section 35, township 2, range 1, east. The residence he built on this tract is a brick house at the fork of the Pond Creek and Philadelphia roads, and south of the Tennessee Military Institute. This last named building is also on the Owen tract. This date (1827), without going back any further makes Charles Owen one of the pioneer settlers.

The following record is found in the state archives at Nashville, Tenn.

"In conformity to an act passed by the General Assembly of the State of Tennessee at Nashville, 3rd December, 1835, entitled an Act to provide for the laying off the several counties in this State into districts of convenient size, within which constables and justices of the peace shall be elected; and for other purposes, and also in conformity with a resolution appointing commissioners for the several counties, we, William Bayless, John Callaway, Sr., Thomas L. Toomy and Jesse Cunningham, four of the commissioners appointed for Monroe County by said resolution, met at Madisonville, January 16, 1836, and after being sworn, as said act directs, by Joseph Marshall, one of the acting justices of the peace for said county, proceeded to lay off said county into districts as directed by said act, beg leave to report seventeen districts in accordance with the sixth section of said act."

(Boundaries of the First Civil District.)
"No. 1 District. Beginning at the northwest corner of Monroe County, thence running with the line of Monroe and Roane Counties, to include Thomas Vernon, Esq.; thence a direct course to Dr. Gregory's mill on Sweetwater Creek; thence to Morganton road, leading by the farm of William Dillard; thence with the road leading from Dillard's to Gregory's Gap till you come within about two hundred yards of the Boiling Spring; thence a direct course to the county line between Monroe and McMinn Counties, passing between the dwelling house of E. Moore and James Axley, and between John Lotspeich and William Neil; thence with the county line to the corner of Monroe County the beginning of the First District. Election Ground, Charles Owens."

He was an elder in the Presbyterian church at Sweetwater when it was built. He was a farmer but was known more as a money loaner and broker (called "note shaver" in those days) than as a farmer. He was considered a good financier.

It was well known that he was an anti-slavery man and thought it wrong to own slaves. The work on the farm was done by himself and family and sometimes with the aid of white hired help. Although his farm was not a very fertile one for this valley, he reared in comfort and educated one of the largest families in the section. Who his descendants were and what became of them we will give some account later on.

Politically previous to the Civil War Charles Owen was a Democrat. One might have expected that from his views on the slavery question he would have allied himself with the whigs; for Henry Clay through the greater part of his political career was a gradual emancipationist. There was then no Republican party in the South.

He was a man of probity and strong character. Whatever views he held political or religious he had no hesitation in expressing them. He was a Union man during the Civil War.

CHARLES AND LOUISA OWEN

were the parents of fourteen children as follows:

1. Sarah White Owen was born August 2, 1819. She married Hugh Lawson White Patton, December 12, 1837. They moved to Gentry County, Mo. While they were on a visit here he died on November 29, 1852. Charles O. Patton, of Albany, Mo., is a son of theirs.

2. James White Owen was born January 22, 1822. He married Ann Amelia Kirkpatrick, October 4, 1842. They had a daughter, Margaret, who was born near Sweetwater, August 14, 1846. She married Charles Cunnyngham, then of McMinn County, Tenn., but now of Albany, Mo., on May 9, 1867. They have a large family of children and grandchildren.

Some time after the death of his first wife, J. W. Owen married Mary Jane Patton on June 4, 1856. They resided in Gentry County, Mo. He was county treasurer of that county four years and postmaster at Albany, Mo., for four years. He died in Dewey County, Oklahoma, July 15, 1906. There were four children of this second marriage, and each one of them has a Charles Owen in the family. Charles Owen, a son, resides at Independence, Okla.

3. Susanna Owen was born January 10, 1824, and died July 6, 1839.

4. Joseph Marshall Owen was born in Sweetwater Valley, September 1, 1825. He married Mary M. Hill, granddaughter of John Fine, on August 28, 1849. There was one son, Charles LaFayette, who resides at Independence, Neb., on a Mexican war claim given his father by Charles Owen, the grandfather. J. M. Owen died in Gentry County, Mo., in 1851.

Charles L. Owen is the father of six children.

Mary M. Hill Owen was born in 1834. She died in Brownsville, Neb., in October, 1884. In 1856 she was married a second time. Wm. H. Lorance, who was born in Monroe County, Tenn., became her husband. To this union were born twelve children, six sons and three daughters of whom are still living (1914).

6. Charles Lilburn Owen was born July 5, 1829. He married Mary Patton, daughter of Francis A. Patton and sister of Horace Patton and a half sister of Frank, James and Ann Patton whose mother was Amanda Taylor Patton. This Frank Patton, the father of Mary Patton, resided near County Line where C. D. Browder now lives. I do not know the maiden name of Frank Patton's first wife, but his last wife, Amanda Taylor, was a sister of the late E. A. Taylor. C. L. Owen and wife went to Gentry County, Mo., where so many sought homes from this valley. They have a son, Charles, who, resides there.

7. Louisa Owen was born April 6, 1831. She died May 13, 1908. She married Horace H. Morris on November 18, 1852. He died February 14, 1909. They resided, during their married life, one mile east of Reagan's Station in McMinn County.

They reared a family of eight children, four sons and four daughters.

Children of H. H. and Louisa Morris:

Josephine, m. J. L. Lowe. She is dead.

Hattie Florence married James Forrest Yearwood, September 11, 1879. She was born September 13, 1857. She resides at 419 Chicamauga Avenue, Lincoln Park, Knoxville, Tenn.

Charles A., married Janie Dillingham, of Travis County, Texas. He lives in Austin.

Nannie Louise married Joseph Bogle. They live in Chattanooga.

Walter L. married Elizabeth Forrest of Niota. Reside in Austin, Texas.

Edward married Dora Blanton. Live at Soddy, Tenn.

Owen married Victoria Shell. They live in Knoxville.

8. Jesse Franklin Owen was born April 4, 1833, and died November 7, 1895. He married Sarah P. Taylor on November 25, 1861. When a young man he went with W. L. Clark and others to California during the excitement about gold in that state. He returned previous to the Civil War. In the conflict between the states he took the Union side and came out of the war a lieutenant.

He was elected as representative from Monroe County to the Thirty-sixth General Assembly of the state of Tennessee. He was voted for and elected partly by the Democrats as a compromise candidate. He had announced himself as being opposed to the wholesale disfranchisement of "rebels" and their sympathizers, which state of affairs existed from the close of the war up to the state election in that year, 1869. He was known as a Senter Republican as opposed the more radical whig of the party, which had up to that time had control of affairs in the state. He was postmaster at Sweetwater under Grant, during his last administration, and also under Hayes and Harrison, occupying that office in all twelve years.

As one would naturally expect he was a Presbyterian. He was a member of Lodge No. 292, F. and A. M., and Chapter No. 57.

The children of J. F. and S. P. Owen were seven in number: Jessie E., Fred Winton, Fred, Ross, Kate, Charles and Hugh. Only three of the children are now living: Ross, Kate and Hugh. Kate, in October, 1898, married Henry Adkins, formerly of Philadelphia, Tenn., but now of Pony, Mont. Ross married Anne Scruggs, daughter of the late Dr. R. F. Scruggs. Charles married a short time previous to his death.

The first two children "Jessie E." and "Fred Winton," died in infancy. "Fred was not born until after the death of "Fred Winton."

9. Harriet Owen was born February 9, 1835. She married George L. Beavers, then living at Sweetwater, on March 5, 1857. They went to Louisville, Texas. He was a farmer. They both resided at Louisville till their death. He died October 5, she September 21, 1910.

Their children were five in number: William H., Fronie, George H., Charles F. and Ruth E. These are all living, are married and all have families and constitute quite a colony of themselves, having its origin in Sweetwater.

10. Solomon Hartsell Owen was born February 21, 1837; he died October 23, 1861.

11. Wm. Francis. Born and died October 1, 1838.

12. Susan Adeline, was born October 11, 1839. Her post-office is Maryville, Tenn.

13. Emily Caroline Owen was born February 20, 1842. She died March 30, 1874. She married William Jordan Clayton June 14, 1860. He was born in Knox County, August 31, 1835. He lives in Knoxville. Their children were six in number, three boys and three girls. They are now all married and have families. Their places of residence are scattered from Tennessee to Texas. Their names are: Louise Elizabeth Butler, Houston, Texas; Jessie May Richard, Knoxville, Tenn.; Wm. Graham Clayton, Knoxville, Tenn.; Robt. Owen Clayton, Birmingham, Ala.; Frank Crawford Clayton, Jackson, Tenn.; Helen Adaline McNutt, Knoxville, Tenn.

14. Mary Haseltine Owen was born November 11, 1843. She married John C. Winton of Loudon County, April 15, 1875. He died on February 21, 1901. Mrs. Winton now resides with her daughter, Mrs. Alice Winton Hensley, who married B. F. Hensley, a florist of Knightstown, Ind.

CHARLES OWEN'S CHARACTERISTICS.

Success to the individual consists largely in getting what you want when you want it and in getting rid of what you do not want. This is not a Websterian but a chimney corner definition, but it is sufficient for our purpose. This has reference to a man's subjective attitude towards his own achievements. The end striven for may be worthy or unworthy. There is also an objective point of view: the light in which others regard what you have done. Most people who think they know you well and often others too, can tell precisely where you failed of achieving success; or how your success would have been much greater had you followed a certain line of conduct, which they advised or could have laid down for you had you consulted them. Like the bed of Procrustes they have an invariable standard to fit you to, and lop you off if you prove too long and stretch you to the proper length if too short. This tendency of humanity is expressed in the wise saw of the mountaineer: "Measuring my corn with your half bushel."

What Charles Owen's ideal was I have no satisfactory means of knowing. I think he never spoke to me more than a dozen words in his life and he was loath to express himself in public assemblages.

When I was a boy I attributed his not noticing me to his disapproval of a youth who played checkers, ball and the fiddle and ran about the country hunting with a dog, a pony and a gun. I think now he was scarcely aware of my habits and that this was merely indifference. However this might have been, I was careful not to cross his line in my hunts and when Brer' rabbit got on the Owen land he was as safe from me as if he had fled to another county. But I cared little for this since I could go to any other place I wished. There were no wire fences in the valley then to tear my clothes or bar my way. I was not told at home nor by Mr. Owen not to go on his territory, but I much preferred to take no chances of a rebuff with a man who usually ignored me, neither smiled, sang nor looked pleasant even at church. There was an added reason to this; there was a green pond of considerable size in one corner of the yard at Mr. Owen's, on whose margin grew a large weeping willow tree with long drooping branches. In the depths of the pond lived a colony of water moccasins, that on sunny days lazily stretched themselves out on the rocks with which the pond was lined. These things gave the landscape a dreary appearance and taken together had a depressing effect on the spirits. I did not have to be warned to stay away from them. I always treated Mr. Owen with marked respect, for besides being a little afraid of him, it had been time and again impressed upon me by my mother and father, with methods more effective than Scripture quotations, that I should have a special regard for the feelings of old people and under no circumstances whatever misbehave at church or in the schoolroom, and that if I must cut any extra shines to do so at home. I was rarely, if ever, a visitor at the Owen residence, during his lifetime. In referring to myself in these notes, it is not to inject into them the personal equation, but merely to show that if I have given or shall give more space to him and his people than most others, it is not due to any extra partiality to him or what he stood for, but to record essential facts such as go to the making up of a truthful and instructive history.

Gilbert Parker in one of his books relates that, during the war between the British and the Boers in South Africa, there was a soldier from New Zealand in one of the regiments. He was a very fine one and never shirked a duty. He always carried a set of chessmen with him. In a fierce charge up a steep hill (kopje), from which the Boers were driven, he was mortally wounded. He was not found until after his death. He had adopted this means of sending a message to his comrades: He had taken from his set of chessmen a pawn (a piece the most numerous and of least value in the game) and placed it on a stone at his head. This was to tell them that he considered himself only an insignificant private in the game of war and that it was inevitable that many should meet such a fate and he was contented to be one of the number. Just this.

It would not have suited Charles Owen to have been so small a factor in affairs; he was too positive a character; but he would have fought just as hard as the New Zealander. He pursued methods of his own and resented dictation from others.

When he wished to be emphatic in his language, his preface or by-word was "I say," which if unnecessary is at least more scriptural than some in too common use. If he had been writing instead of Francis Scott Key, who wrote the words:

"O! say can you see in the dawn's early light,
What so proudly we hailed at twilight's last gleaming?"

He would probably have said:

"I say, I can see in this broad land of ours,
By Faith the Presbyterian Banner still waving."

He was the ancestor of a score who were named for him. He lived to see many of his children and grandchildren grow up to be useful and honored citizens. In most instances his numerous descendants, wherever dispersed about the west, south and southwest, have been ingrained with Presbyterianism. When the question was asked: "What church did he or she belong to," the almost invariable answer was "The Presbyterian" (written with a capital P).

If success consists in perpetuating the family name and Presbyterian principles then, measured by that standard, Charles Owen was an eminently successful man and I have no doubt these were facts highly gratifying to him.

If half the Presbyterians had been like the Owens and as devoted to their principles, there would, in a few generations, be room for no denominations other than the Presbyterian. For, from Cromwell down they have been fighters and you find them marching solidly toward the enemy when according to the doctrine of chances, you would expect to see them facing the other way. But in the lexicon of the Presbyterians there is no such word as "chance."

As a matter of convenience I append a few facts about Gentry County, Mo., where so many of the Owens and others from this immediate section have made their homes. It is situated in the northwest part of the state about 100 miles north of Kansas City. It is in a rich agricultural country. It contains 490 square miles to our county's 673. The population by the census of 1900 and 1910 were, respectively, 20,554 and 16,820, to Monroe's 18,595 and 20,716. So the last census does not make a favorable showing for Gentry county as compared with our own.

Albany, the county site of Gentry County, contains

about the same number of inhabitants as Sweetwater and is about the same elevation above the sea level.

In the presidential election of 1912, Gentry county voted 4,060 and Monroe 2,336. Wilson carried Gentry County by 1,000 votes. It appears they pay more attention to politics there than we do. Evidently a much larger proportion of the voters went to the polls.

IRBY ORR

Was born September 9, 1821; d. in Sweetwater, April 10, 1904. He came from the head of Sweetwater Creek to Sweetwater about the time the E. T. & Ga. R. R. depot was built. He was among the first settlers of the town. He was married (first) to Nancy Ann Weathers on December 4, 1840. She was born March 18, 1825. She died June 24, 1862. Their children were:

1. Sarah Jane, b. March 16, 1844; m. James G. Forkner, December 1, 1866. They moved to Oklahoma about 1892, where she died in 1912.

2. Julia Ann, March 14, 1846; m. James F. Nichols, June 16, 1864, and moved to Decatur, Ala., where he died.

3. Mary Caroline, b. August 28, 1848; m. William Fry on September 2, 1869. (See Fry.)

4. John Willson, b. September 8, 1850; m. Mollie E. Young, August 28, 1875. They went to Texas and from there to Arkansas. They had five children, names not known.

5. Samuel Rowan, b. October 30, 1852; (first) m. Miss Rogers, of Decatur, Ala. She died April 11, 1902. He died in Nashville and was buried at the Sweetwater Cemetery. They had three children: Walter, Samuel and Irma. He married (second) Miss Smith. Two children.

6. William, b. September 22, 1854. Went to Texas in 1892; married there. History not known.

7. James, b. December 3, 1856; d. January 28, 1890. He was a stock trader. Unmarried.

8. Robert Jackson, b. March 7, 1859; m. Nannie Eddy of Meigs County. She died and he afterwards married Ella Pratt. He was a locomotive engineer in the employ of the L. & N. Railroad in Birmingham, Ala.

9. Nancy Lenoir, b. July 13, 1861; d. June 24, 1862.

Irby Orr was married (second) to Mrs. Chaney S. Barrett on March 10, 1863. She was formerly Chaney Nichols, of Pittsylvania County, Va. Her parents were John and Elizabeth Shelton Nichols. Their children were:

10. Charles W., b. May 10, 1868; m. Miss Love. They had one child, b. May 14, 1903.

11. Lillian, b. March 2, 1874; m. Reece Lowry June, 1907. He is an insurance agent living in Chattanooga, Tenn.

FRANCIS A. PATTON

Was born in North Carolina. He came to Monroe County, Tenn. He married a Miss Rose. They had two children, Horace and Mary. Mary m. Charles L. Owen (whom see). Horace joined the Confederate army and was captured at Vicksburg. After the war was over he married Mary E. Cleveland on December 28, 1865. Jos. Janeway, minister. Mary was the daughter of Robt. and Elizabeth Cleveland and a sister of Wm. Cleveland. Their subsequent history is not known to the writer.

After the death of his first wife, Francis A. Patton married Amanda A. Taylor, sister of E. A. Taylor in the latter part of 1841. He died at his residence where C. D. Browder now lives, in 1845. Their children were: Frank T. He was born in 1842. He was in the Civil War and was captured at Vicksburg. Soon after the Civil War he went to Georgia and afterwards to the southern part of Missouri. He was elected to the Legislature from one of the counties there. He died on September 13, 1901.

Anne E., b. January 12, 1844; d. March 18, 1890. Married T. E. Snead (whom see).

James F., born in the latter part of 1846. Married Callie Ferguson, formerly of Monroe County, Tenn., in 1868. They reside at Alva, Okla. Their children are: Mary F., Elizabeth A., Will E., Preston C., Sallie A., Carrie E., Amy L., Horace F. and Ora J. All married except the two youngest, Horace and Ora. Horace is a minister in Rhode Island. Was educated at theological seminary in Boston, Mass.

Francis A. Patton died in 1845. Mrs. Amanda Patton was married (second) to Thomas L. Brickell on January 3, 1850. They had one daughter, Emma, born the latter part of 1850, who married Joseph Traylor in 1870. She is dead. He lives in White County, Ark.

STEPHEN PARSHLEY

Was born March 11, 1811, in Middletown, Conn. He came to Lenoir's, Tenn., in 1832, where he was employed for some years in the cotton factory. Moved to Philadelphia, Tenn., in 1845. Married Martha Stewart Brock, in 1839, in Stockton valley. She was born in Virginia, September 25, 1816. Died at Philadelphia, November 18, 1882, and was buried there. Stephen Parshley, in the latter years of his life, was a stock trader. He was a Methodist. Died at Philadelphia in February, 1851. Interred in Stekee Cemetery, near Loudon. His children were:

Sarah, b. June 27, 1840. Married Harvey Porter.

E. Sophia, b. June 22, 1846. Married Thomas H. Grieb, of Joplin, Mo.

Mary Virginia, b. January 23, 1849. Married Milton Bayless, of Chestua, McMinn County, who was a farmer. She died near Gudger, Tenn., March 27, 1914. He died there in 1915.

Stephen, b. June 4, 1851. He went to Ashland, Kan., about 1880, and was a lawyer and prosecuting attorney while there. He went from Kansas to Park City, Utah, and from there to Lawton, Okla., where he was married to Mrs. Kate Whitney. He afterwards moved to Denver, Col., where he now (1916) lives.

WASHINGTON LAFAYETTE PRICE

Was the son of Addison and Julia Loughlin Price. He was born at Philadelphia, Tenn., on December 8, 1830. He died there on May 28, 1890, and was buried at the old cemetery. His wife, Mary Jane, was the daughter of John and Mary Holston. John Holston was born November 29, 1800. Mary Jane Holston Price was born June 5, 1834, and died at Johnson City at the home of her granddaughter, Mrs. Kate Burbage, on January 11, 1913. She was buried at Stekee Cemetery near Loudon, Tenn.

W. L. Price was express agent at Loudon during the Civil War and was also postmaster until he came to Sweetwater in 1864 and engaged in the general mercantile business. He was a member of Sweetwater Lodge No. 292 F. & A. M., and also of Chapter No. 57 R. A. M. He lived at Sweetwater until 1872 when he sold out his business there and moved to California. Later he returned to Tennessee and made Knoxville his home for many years.

The children of W. L. and M. J. Price were three, one daughter, Mary Julia, was born at Loudon July 16, 1854. Died there February 16, 1859.

William B., his oldest son, was born at Loudon December 3, 1859. He took up the study of music under Mrs. H. M. Cooke, at Sweetwater, and also under his father, both of whom had a thorough understanding of music. William B. was organist at the Episcopal church at Cleveland, Tenn., and afterwards organist in Chicago. He is now president of the Price-Teeple Piano Company of Chicago, Ill. Their business is the manufacture of pianos and player pianos. Mr. Price presented a fine piano to the H. M. Cooke Memorial Library Association at Sweetwater, Tenn. William B. Price has been twice married. He married, first, Lucie A. Smith, of Rogersville, Tenn., and second Natalie Whitted, of Chicago, Ill.

Albert F. Price, son of first marriage, was born in Knoxville, Tenn., on January 9, 1883. He is general wholesale representative of the Price-Teeple Company.

Kate, daughter of the first marriage, was born in Knoxville, August 11, 1884. She married Henry J. Burbage. He resides at Johnson City, Tenn., where he is engaged in the wholesale produce business.

Charles, the second son of W. L. and M. J. Price, was born at Sweetwater on September 27, 1868. Unmarried. He is the eastern representative of the Price-Teeple Piano Co.

The ancestors of W. L. and Mary J. Price were among

the early settlers of America and fought under Washington in the Revolutionary War.

WILLIAM PENNINGTON

Was born in Ashe County, N. C., December 13, 1777; d. in Sweetwater Valley, April 22, 1838. His wife, Elizabeth Eller, was born in North Carolina in October, 1776; d. December 7, 1844. He moved to Sweetwater Valley and settled on the Jesse Martin (Presley Cleveland) place. He sold his interest there to Presley Cleveland and moved to what was afterwards the Riley Burns farm and there reared his family. They had one son,

John Pennington, who was born in Ashe County, N. C., October 27, 1801. He came with his father, first to Knox County, and then to Sweetwater Valley in 1820. He married Alpha Davis, of Somerset, Ken. She was born in 1802 and died in 1872. She was buried at Cleveland Cemetery. The children of John and Alpha Pennington were:

One. Lucinda Elizabeth, b. July 4, 1823; d. December 9, 1828.

Two. Hiram B., b. 1825; m. Margaret Pickel, daughter of Jonathan Pickel, in 1848. He died in Gentry County, Mo. (at the age of 58), where they had previously moved. Their children were:

1. ("Big") John, lives at Salem, Ore. He is now (1916) 61 years of age.
2. Alpha, m. ―――― Easterly. Lives in Missouri.
3. Eliza, m. ―――― Robinson. Lives in Gentry County, Mo.

Three. Emeline, b. 1827; m. Eli Mathew, son of Eli Cleveland (whom see).

Four. William Jasper, b. April 10, 1829; d. October, 1852. Baptized July, 1851. Unmarried.

Five. John Calloway, b. July 31, 1831. His father, John Pennington and John Calloway, who lived near Cleveland church, were cousins. He was baptized October, 1856. He married Esther Caroline Bryant, March 20, 1855. She was the daughter of A. P. Bryant, of McMinn County, Tenn. She was born January 9, 1836; d. June 4, 1905. Their children were:

1. Addie Frances, b. December 25, 1855; d. May, 1905. She married S. S. Caldwell of Alabama. They moved to Dodd, Fannin County, Texas. They were the parents of seven children, six boys and one daughter. They mostly live in the section of Texas named above.

2. Alpha Ann, second daughter of John Calloway Pennington, was born October 4, 1857; m. James Richeson of Pond Creek Valley in 1884. They moved to Fannin County, Texas, in 1888. They are the parents of six children, four daughters and two sons. Bertie and Gertie were twins and were born in Pond Creek Valley in 1886. They were married in Texas. The other children, except the youngest daughter, are also married and several of them have families.

3. Aley, b. February, 1860; d. June, 1913; m. James A. Cook, brother of Dr. S. B. Cook, late of Chattanooga. She died in 1877. They resided on Paint Rock Creek. Their children were:

(1) Lena, now (1916) 33 or 34 years of age; m. B. F. Kyle, of Anniston, Ala.

(2) John, now (1916), aged 30.

(3) May, married. Resides at Anniston, Ala.

(4) Charles Bates, b. 1888 or 1889. Lives at Anniston, Ala.

4. Mary, daughter of John Calloway Pennington, b. October, 1862; d. 1882. Unmarried.

5. Emma, b. February 22, 1865; d. 1890; m. Robert Pardue, brother of Rev. H. Clay Pardue, in 1884. Their children are John, b. 1885, and William, b. 1887.

6. John Bryant, b. June 7, 1868; m. Margaret, sister of W. Y. Wilson, on March 29, 1891. He was elected county court clerk of Monroe County in August, 1910, and re-elected in 1914. Children are: Carl, b. January 19, 1894; Janie Esther, b. October, 1896; Callie, b. February 9, 1898; Nannie, b. March 13, 1901; Eliza, b. January 29, 1904; Margaret, b. April 21, 1906.

7. William Horace, seventh child of John Calloway Pennington, b. July 2, 1870. Married Zada Lloyd in Springfield, Mo. Was killed October 16, 1915, in Interurban Railroad accident. Four children, one boy and three girls were born to them.

8. Charles Edward, eighth child of John Calloway Pennington, b. October 2, 1872. Married Belle Pope, a niece of James Pope, who was county court clerk of Roane County for thirty years. Charles Pennington is a R. F. D. carrier. Their children are: James Clifford, b. April 15, 1894; Essie, b. February, 1896; Annie Belle, b. 1898; John, b. 1901; Lizzie, b. 1903; Mattie Lee, b. 1904; Emma, b. 1907; Charles, b. 1911.

Sixth. Mary Ann, sixth child of Jno. and Alpha Pennington, b. November 10, 1833; d. 1913; m. Harvey H. Cleveland (whom see).

Seven. Francis Marion, seventh child of John and Alpha Davis Pennington, was born in 1836. Baptized May, 1860; m. Virginia, daughter of Dan Lowry, of McMinn County, Tenn. He died at Athens, Tenn., at the age of 52. Their children are:

1. John B. Lives in Chattanooga, Tenn.
2. William, killed in a street car wreck in Chattanooga, on October 18, 1909.
3. Susie, m. Frank Page. Both dead. Three children: Mabel, Buell and Annie.
4. Callie, m. Wm. Cass, his second wife. Children: Carl, 23; Fred, 19; Claude, 13.
5. Maggie, m. Bedow. They had one daughter, Fannie, who m. Mills of Chattanooga.
1. John B. m. Corda Coltharp, daughter of Ham. Coltharp. She d. 1908. Six children:
(1) John Tedford, m. Nellie Roberts. Two children. Live at East Chattanooga.
(2) Ola Virginia, unmarried.
(3) Myrtle, m. McGloffin.
(4) Willie, b. 1897.
(5) Hubert, b. 1911.

6. Francis M., son of F. M. P.; b. February 20, 1883. Unmarried. His address is 535 Dodson Avenue, Chattanooga.

Eight. Robert Snead Pennington, b. 1840; d. unmarried.

Nine. Lodusky Caroline, b. 1842. Baptized September, 1855; m. Louis Bryant, son A. D. Bryant, who went to Gentry County, Mo. Mrs. B. is living; Mr. B. is dead.

Col. John Ramsey.

If a man bore the name of Ramsey, was a Presbyterian, revered his Maker, loved his country, stood by his section, was true to his party, was steadfast and immovable in every principle he advocated, was clannish to a degree and would never desert his people till the last sad act in the drama of life, was fearless in demeanor, keen of eye, long, lank and lean of form, would it take a Sherlock Holmes to figure out where he sprung from? One would not have to decipher cryptograms and make microscopical examinations to ascertain. Any intelligent schoolboy could tell you. That his ancestors at some time dwelt in the highlands of Scotland would be self-evident.

The Ramsey form was built for speed and endurance and not for grace. They leaped from crag to crag as they chased the wild deer over the brow of Ben Nevis; they waded the firths as they followed the trails in the fastnesses; they collected their clan as the torches flashed their code signals from mountain top to mountain top. They marched over the peaks to the music of the bagpipe or the shrill notes of the pibroch. With a Moray (Murray) or McGregor, claymore in hand, they made fierce forays into the lowlands. Many were the head of cattle they captured and drove northward to supplement their scant supply of "razor backs" on the Grampian Hills. Yet in "ye olden times" they did not always have things their own way; notably when Culloden "reeked with the blood of the brave." They were unconquerable, however, on their native heath.

How they would have laughed at the build of a Dutch Stuyvesant, five feet high and four feet broad; or was it four feet high and five feet broad? What a contempt those mountaineers would have had for the stein and the long stemmed pipe. When they drank strong drink at all it was usquebaugh unmixed even with the water of their own pure mountain rills.

> When clan met clan then came the tug of war,
> When Dutch met Dutch then came the lager beer.

In the middle of the eighteenth century there lived a wealthy planter by the name of Stovall in Bedford County, Va. He owned much land and slaves and a large stock of family pride; in other words he was what might be termed an aristocrat. He had a beautiful daughter who was born on January 8, 1757.

He had in his employ an overseer named McBride. McBride died while in his service and he (Stovall), charged his family in spite of the difference in station and circumstances always to treat the McBrides with kindness and consideration in their bereavement. Overseer McBride had a son not a great deal older than Elizabeth Stovall. She fell in love with and married him contrary to her parents' wishes. Although Mr. Stovall had exhorted his children to treat the McBrides kindly, he considered that this was kindness run mad. He sent word to his daughter that he never more wished to see her, her husband or his kinspeople and that he would forgive her in case she stayed away and never called on him or his for anything in the future. Thus Elizabeth Stovall early realized how sharper than a serpent's tooth it is to have a thankless father. Soon after the marriage with McBride the Revolutionary War came on and McBride joined the Virginia troops and came out of the war with the rank of colonel. Yet that made no difference and her parents were no more reconciled to her than before. McBride died not long after the war was over and she not a great while a widow married Major Jno: Ramsey who was also a Revolutionary soldier. They moved to Iredell County, N. C., where John Ramsey, the subject of this sketch was born May 5, 1797. While he was yet an infant John Ramsey senior moved to Greene County, Tenn., where he died. John Ramsey, Jr., came to Sweetwater Valley somewhere about the year 1820 when the Hiwassee District had been surveyed and the different tracts were for sale by the state. He made arrangements to purchase what was known as the Bunch tract, being the northwest quarter of section 35, township 2, range 1, east of the Basis Line. On a part of this tract now stands the T. M. I. College and the surrounding buildings. He however gave this up or disposed of it and finally settled, where J. C. Waren and wife, daughter of John Ramsey, now (1914) reside, one-half mile south of Sweetwater.

Colonel John Ramsey's mother resided with her son many of the last years of her life. She died on October 4, 1854, reaching the advanced age of nearly 98 years. She is said to have retained her mental and physical faculties to the last in a remarkable degree. She was known for years in the neighborhood on account of advanced age as "Granny" Ramsey.

COL. JOHN RAMSEY IN THE LEGISLATURE.

They say it was a great race for the Legislature in Monroe County, between Colonel John Ramsey and William Heiskell. The political state of the nation and also the state of Tennessee and the personality of the contestants made it so. At that time in 1847, James K. Polk, of Tennessee, was president of the United States. He had been elected by a narrow margin over Henry Clay on account of the latter's oppositions to the Mexican War. At that time also Aaron V. Brown and Neil S. Brown were opposing candidates on the Democratic and whig tickets. The parties in Tennessee were on a balance and it was impossible to say beforehand which should be successful, and the complexion of the Legislature whether whig or democratic was just as hard to predetermine as the aggregate vote of all the counties. Each seat in the General Assembly both in the lower and upper house was hotly contested.

Col. John Ramsey was the democratic candidate from Monroe County for the Legislature; William Heiskell was the whig candidate. Besides the personalities of the candidates themselves, various issues made the canvass exciting. On the one hand it was charged that William Heiskell was an aristocrat. That he had to have a negro valet to help him dress himself. That he was too proud to wear the ordinary jeans clothes woven by the people of the county; that he wore store clothes and otherwise conducted himself as an aristocrat. It is true that he took his toddy and was fond of music and played the fiddle in Old Virginia style. On the other hand it was charged among the common people that Colonel Ramsey was somewhat effected by the prohibitionist ideas of Lorenzo Dow, who had made a canvass through this country. Furthermore it is charged against Colonel John Ramsey that he was not at all in sympathy with the southern ideas of the institution of slavery and did not believe in its moral right. Ramsey was in favor of the Mexican War and acquisition of territory resulting therefrom. Heiskell was opposed to this.

But the result of the canvass really turned on this, whether what was termed as the "one gallus copperas breeches Democrat" or the rich man should elect their representative to the county. As nearly always happens in such instances, what might be termed as the common people were in the majority, and Colonel John Ramsey was triumphantly elected.

Although William Heiskell was defeated by Colonel John Ramsey for the Legislature, yet his brother, F. S. Heiskell was elected senator from Knox County. This gave the majority to the whigs, the upper house of the Legislature being composed of thirteen whigs and twelve Democrats. The house was almost equally as close. In the year 1847 John Bell, who was then a member of the Legislature, was elected United States senator, receiving 51 out of 90 votes on joint ballot. John Bell was afterwards a whig candidate for the President of the United States in the year 1860. That was when Lincoln was elected.

In the governor's race in 1847, Neil S. Brown, the whig candidate, defeated Aaron V. Brown, who was elected governor two years before. This was one of the last successes that the whigs ever had in the state of Tennessee. The Legislature of 1847 was composed mostly of farmers and young men. John Bell and John Ramsey were the oldest members of the house, each being, according to the published roster, 60 years of age. Before Ramsey went to the Legislature the charter of the Hiwassee Railroad from Dalton to Knoxville had been abandoned and given place to the charter of the E. T. & Ga. Railroad. Colonel John Ramsey had always been in favor of internal improvements and was a friend to the railroad. He did what he could in expediting the building of the railroad. From that time on there was little doubt that the railroad would be built, and before many years it was finished.

We will hereafter give something of the history of when the railroad was graded through Sweetwater Valley and how this was accomplished. The railroad was built partly by help of the state, lending its aid by bond issues, which constituted first mortgage on the roadbed, and by the citizens along the line of the railroad subscribing money and doing work on the grading, for which they received stock of the E. T. & Ga. Railroad. The railroad from Dalton to Knoxville was built entirely without the aid of foreign or out-of-state capital.

Colonel John Ramsey was by no means a highly educated man nor a man of extraordinary ability, but few men in the county have had more to do with its success and prosperity than he. This was owing to his honesty and integrity and his rare common sense, and men of all parties and religions recognized the existence in him of these sterling qualities.

This shows that a man has neither to be rich nor great nor highly educated nor have extravagant opportunities to have great influence in a community. I know of no man among early settlers whose example could be imitated with more profit by the rising generation.

William Griffitts, of Blount County, Tenn., was born in Virginia, July 13, 1781. His wife was born September 26, 1779. She died at Unitia, Blount County, Tenn. These were the parents of Susanna Griffitts Ramsey, wife of Colonel John Ramsey. She was born at Unitia, Blount County, Tenn., February 12, 1802. She married Jno. Ramsey, February 28, 1822. She died at the Ramsey residence January 6, 1881. Jno. Ramsey died April 28, 1872. (For further history see Presbyterian church.) The children of Jno. and S. G. Ramsey were:

One. Mary, born October 19, 1828. Died March 7, 1863. On April 8, 1856, she married Frank Rowan and lived on Fork Creek, near Christianburg Church. They had one daughter, Bettie, who was born February 23, 1863. She married Jno. Moon, of Hamilton County, November 29, 1905. They now (1915) reside at the old Ramsey residence. (1916) He looks after large estate of Mrs. Waren.

Two. William Griffitts R., born March 29, 1835; d. February 22, 1850.
Three. Elizabeth Emmeline R., born March 25, 1837; d. October 19, 1862. Two and Three never married. buried in the Philadelphia Cemetery.
Four. John Eagleton R., born September 27, 1839; married Martha E. Smith of Jonesboro, November 6, 1866. He served in the Confederate army in Co. ——— Regt., Tenn. Vol., C. S. A. He moved to Bridgeport, Wise County, Texas. The children of J. E. and Martha E. were 11 in number. Six of whom now (1913) living and none married. They are:
James, Charles, George, Mary, Katie, Alice.
Four. Martha R., daughter of J. and S. Ramsey, born July 17, 1842.

CAPTAIN JACOB CATHEY WAREN.

His mother was Mary Cathey, daughter of George Cathey, of Haywood County, N. C. She was married twice, first to Sherwood Osborne, one of eleven brothers in Haywood County. They had no sisters. Sherwood, Thomas and Joseph, came to East Tennessee. Sherwood Osborne died leaving several children, one of whom was, afterwards, Captain Tom Osborne, of the Confederate army. Mrs. Osborne married, a second time, to Jacob Waren, who came from Virginia in 1788, locating in Roane County, what is now Loudon. Jacob Cathey Waren, her son, was born in Roane County, December 25, 1842. On July 27, 1861, he enlisted in Captain John A. Rowan's company, afterwards known as Co. G, Ashby's 2nd Tenn. Cav., Ashby's brig. Hume's Dis., Wheeler's army corps, Army of Tennessee (Confederate).

In the archives of the General John C. Vaughn, Chapter No. 1244, U. D. C., is a history of his career as a Confederate soldier, prepared by Mrs. Myra Love Lowry. It is too lengthy for us to reproduce in this work.

A great part of the time during the war he served as an independent scout under General Jo. Wheeler.

Soon after the war he came to Sweetwater and commenced business. He married Martha E. Ramsey on December 10, 1873.

He was for two terms, sheriff of Monroe County, and in 1882 was elected trustee of the county. In 1902 he was elected to the Fifty-sixth General Assembly as the representative from Monroe County. When he was elected to the Legislature he was living in the old Ramsey residence, where Colonel John Ramsey lived when he was elected to the Twenty-seventh General Assembly. Captain Waren was a very fine business man. He owned several large farms, besides the one on which he lived, and much property in the town of Sweetwater. He died suddenly of heart failure, near his home, on May 11, 1915, and was interred in Westview Cemetery, His wife, Martha E., is the beneficiary and executrix under his will.

REYNOLDS ALLEN RAMSEY

Was born in Knox County, Tenn., near the present site of Concord, November 13, 1799. He first lived at Ross' Landing. In 1840 moved to Catoosa County, Ga. He married (first) Anne Campbell Roane, who died in a short time, leaving one child, Mary Roane Ramsey. She married James A. Corry. She died leaving two sons, Allen Corry and Robert Corry.

James Corry married (second) about 1861 Carrie, daughter of John Y. and Leah Lenoir Smith. They had one child, Thomas Avery. He was born February 22, 1862. He was educated mostly at Sweetwater. By profession he is a civil engineer. He married Laura Montgomery of Roane County, Tenn. They moved to the city of Mexico. He was chief engineer of railroad running from the city of Mexico to Vera Cruz for a number of years. About 1911 he went to Arequipa, Peru, where he is chief engineer, constructing the ——— railroad. They have two daughters, Margaret, born ——— and Elizabeth born ———

Reynolds A. Ramsey married (second) Louisa Caroline Lenoir. She was born in Wilkes County, N. C., in 1805, the second child of Wm. B. Lenoir. She died in Catoosa County, Ga., August 11, 1841. Their children were:

William Lenoir, b. April —, 1829; d. at Knoxville 1896.

Samuel A., b. September —, 1830; d. June, 1839.
Waightstill Avery, b. January, 1832; d. at Lenoir's, Tenn., August, 1866.
Elizabeth Fleming, b. October, 1883. Married N. A. Patterson, then of Kingston, Tenn. Her daughter, Mrs. Cora A. Hardin, lives at Olustee, Okla.
Thomas Isaac, b. October, 1835. Living in San Antonio, Texas. Married Amelia Boyd about 1870. They were the parents of seven children, five of whom are living. One son, Reynolds A., lives at Waycross, Ga. J. G. M. married June Burdett 1913. One daughter of T. I. Ramsey Lenoir, married a missionary and lives in Africa.

The seventh child of R. A. and Louisa Ramsey was Julia Ann Campbell, born December, 1839. She died at Austin, Texas, in 1915. Married Gideon B. Caldwell, in Monroe County, Tenn., January 19, 1863. They were the parents of six children, most of whom are married and are living in Texas. Their names are: Allen R., Catherine C., Louisa L., Mary Lizzie, James Harvey and Addie Ellen.

Colonel Ramsey married (third) Mrs. Ann B. McGhee, nee McLin, of Maryville, Tenn., in February, 1845. She was born February 3, 1814; d. February 15, 1882. He died at Dalton, Ga., June 23, 1884. Both are buried in the old Sweetwater cemetery. They came to Pond Creek Valley, near Sweetwater, in 1858. They belonged to the Presbyterian church at Sweetwater, in which church he was a ruling elder. Their only child, Emmett Alexander, was born December, 1849, died in 1898. He married Miss Lena Wilhoite, of Shelbyville, Tenn., in 1894. He was a Presbyterian minister of fine attainments and was a pastor of a church in Memphis, Tenn., at the time of his death in January, 1898.

WILLIAM RUTHERFORD

Was born in Grayson County, Va., on April 11, 1797, and came to Sweetwater Valley, first living near Reagan Station until 1864. During the remainder of the war he lived at the old Bowman (Benson) place. He died on June 25, 1870, and was buried at County Line Cemetery. He married Celia Hale, who was born in Gray-

son County, Va. She moved to Kaufman County, Texas, in 1877, and died there and was buried at College Mound, Texas. Their children were:
1. Rufus.
2. John F.
3. George, b. September 28, 1848. Died January 5, 1883. Married Mary Miles in Chattanooga. Died in Texas.
4. James. Post-office, Cartersville, Ga. Married Miss Oliver.
5. Cynthia, b. October 11, 1822. Married Phillip Cole. Lives in Texas.
6. Elizabeth. Dead.
7. Parmelia Jane, b. February 11, 1827; d. June 19, 1855. Married Jake Williams. Dead.
8. Samuel, b. May 1, 1825. Died in Missouri. Married Mick Ann Richardson.
9. Julia, b. April 29, 1828. Married Jake Patton, and lives at Miami, Texas.
10. Felan Louis, b. February 1, 1830. Married in Misrouri. Dead.
11. Rosamond Caroline, b. December 2, 1834. Dead. Married Wm. McCaslin.
12. Margaret, b. April 9, 1839. Married John Billingsly.

RUFUS RUTHERFORD

Was born in McMinn County, Tenn., March 8, 1832. Married Elizabeth Fender, May 18, 1855. She was born June 15, 1831, in Roane County, Tenn. Died January 27, 1905, and was interred at Bell Springs, Texas.

Rufus Rutherford lived for five years, in the old I. T. Lenoir residence, until he moved to Texas, in 1877. He was a farmer and was a member of the Cumberland Presbyterian Church. Served in the Confederate army, until the close of the war, as a member of Captain W. L. Clark's company, 2nd Tennessee Calvary. He is now a farmer and banker at Hillsboro, Texas. His children are:

Mrs. Maggie Kyle, Hillsboro, Texas.
William H., Rockwood, Texas.
Mrs. Cynthia Parks, Hillsboro, Texas.

Mrs. Mary Parks, Hillsboro, Texas.
Mrs. Julia McClure, Hillsboro, Texas.
Mrs. Celia Whitlock, Lockney, Texas.
Rufus W., Claude, Texas.
Mrs. Bettie McCarty, Hillsboro, Texas.

JOHN F. RUTHERFORD

Was the son of Wm. Rutherford, and was born in Sweetwater Valley, October 30, 1837. Married Malinda J. Williams, daughter of John Williams, September 16, 1873, by the Rev. G. W. Butler. She was born March 7, 1856. John F. Rutherford was a farmer. He served in the Confederate army as a private in Co. B, 5th Reg. Vol., Tenn. Cav., from 1862 to 1865. He moved from Sweetwater Valley to Jalapa, Tenn. They had eight children, six of whom are living:
1. Inez, b. 1875. Lives in Texas.
2. Clifton, b. 1878. Was a ranchman in Idaho. Now lives at Tellico, Tenn.
3. King. Dead.
4. Daisy. Dead. Married John Tate.
5. Key, b. 1883. Lives in Idaho.
6. Rankin, b. 1888. Lives in Idaho.
7. Creed, b. 1895. Lives in Idaho.
8. Fred., b. 1898. Lives in Idaho.

S. J. ROWAN

Was a brother of Jno. A. Rowan who lived on Fork Creek, and who was a colonel in the C. S. A., during the Civil War. He married Jane Carter, a sister of Robert Carter and F. B. Carter. They lived in Sweetwater some time during the Civil War. He (Rowan) owned a large farm at County Line, on the Athens road. In June, 1857, for the consideration of $13,000, he conveyed his holdings there to J. M. Brett, formerly of Georgia. He moved to Sweetwater and engaged in the mercantile business. He was postmaster during Buchanan's administration. Some time in 1868 he moved to Waco, Texas. At a session of the Presbyterian church at Sweetwater, March 22, 1869, Samuel J. and Jane Rowan, his wife, were granted a letter to join the Presbyterian church at Waco. Their children were: Miranda, Carter and Crockett Rowan. Miranda married Dr. ——— Parshall. They were the parents of several children, names and number not known. Some of them live in Hillsboro, Texas. One of them married Burt Barnett, who lives on Lamar Street, Fort Worth, Texas. He is a wealthy cotton broker. Mr. Rufus Rutherford, of Hillsboro, Texas, says that now, 1916, Carter and Crockett are both dead; that Crockett married and reared a family, but that he did not know their address or history.

Mr. and Mrs. J. T. Rowland.

Mr. J. T. Rowland came from Georgia. He married Miss Louisa Keith, a sister of Judge Charles Keith, who resigned his position after being judge for thirty-four years. Mr. and Mrs. Rowland purchased land in Sweetwater Valley from William Wallis on the 10th of September, 1855. This was a part of the northwest quarter of section 15, township 3, range 1, east. Consideration, $3,000. This land lay between the Browder and Yearwood places. They lived at this place until some time during the Civil War, when they moved away. Rowland died, and in 1865 Mrs. Rowland with her two sons moved back to the farm. She soon sold out, however, and moved away. She was a brilliant and gifted woman and not only was a contributor to the magazines but was also a musical composer. She gave my mother one of her compositions in reply to, "I have just been learning a lesson of life," which was thought to have been better than the other. Her two children were: John T., an accomplished musician, who died when a young man, and Charles K., now a broker and real estate dealer of Atlanta, Ga.

General James H. Reagan.

Some sixty-five years ago Reagan's station consisted of a very large pond, having an area of 5 or 6 acres, a flourishing apple orchard or two, the Reagan boys, the big house, the negro cabins, various brier patches, the store, the United States Post-office, the E. T. & Ga.

Railroad Depot and water tank and the cribs and barn. These resources are intended to be mentioned in the order of their relative importance in the boyish mind. The pond, placed there by a beneficent Providence, who seemingly watches over the safety of good and bad boys alike, could be and was used for the threefold purpose of swimming in, fishing in and rowing and sailing boats over. The apple orchards were both food and drink. Their products were a source of ever recurring enjoyment from their first bloom in April through the red June, the mellow fall, the rough winter and until the return of spring again. What would a home be without a swimming hole, red June apples and sweet cider? And echo answers: "Nothin' doin'." And what would be the use of such things without boys to revel in them and satiate their appetites? The "big house" was to eat in and sleep in; otherwise of no special importance. The negro cabin was a mecca when at night some noted negro fiddler or banjo picker was playing for a dance. Life in those boyhood days would not have been wholly satisfactory without brier patches. The blackberries were watched with interest through all their stages of developments, green, red and black. When the berries had come and gone the brier thickets became the favorite warren and home of the rabbit; then "ho" for the chase of the nimble cotton tail. The store was the source of supply of candy, tops, balls and marbles. These were very much a part of boyish equipment, far more important then than anything that came through the post-office which frequently occupied a portion of country store. Few articles at that time came by parcels post. The railroad depot was a very flimsy affair and the water tank, capable of containing only about 2,500 gallons, was filled by a chain pump from a spring. The barns were useful as places to play in on rainy days.

On Sunday our privileges were somewhat abridged. After reading a chapter in the Bible and hearing it explained we were allowed quietly to go out to play with a few parting injunctions; not to go in swimming, not to hunt rabbits and not to get into a fuss or fight with the neighbor boys. No, we wont go in swimming in the pond, we'll just wade round the shallow places near the bank unless some one pushes us into deep water and then we'll have to swim; no, we won't hunt rabbits or indulge in any unseemly merriment on Sunday; but sometimes we can't slip off from the dogs and they will follow us and we hate to rock them back home; we mustn't be cruel to animals, for once there was a boy in the second reader and he was bad; he used to stick pins in flies instead of swattin' 'em and throw stones at dogs and when he grew up to be a man he got to be a monopolist and had to appear before the Congressional Committee or something just as dreadful happened to him; no, we won't impose on the neighbor boys; but they mustn't muddy our swimming hole, they mustn't climb our apple trees, they mustn't run our rabbits or "sic" their dogs on our dogs and they mustn't call us names or irritate us any way; we are peaceable but we can't bear to be irritated—and—we are not bound to tell everything that takes place.

Old folks have such queer ideas about what they want boys to learn and spend their time on. Who was Publius Virgilius Naso, and why didn't he write in plain English? Nix on that stuff about the Trojan horse as big as a mountain (*instar montis*). What difference does it make if Queen Dido did stand on the beach in the moonlight and wave with her willow wand for her recreant lover to come again to Carthage? He never came, did he? And what if Tityrus, at ease under the shade of a beech tree, did elect during the summer day to pipe his pæans to the charms of the beautiful Amaryllis; did that make his corn grow any better? That was his business. What Johnnie wants to know is: "Why spend five days out of seven in acquiring this information, when the fish are fairly itching to bite and the call of the wild is sounding in his ears and especially when his high school nine is straining every nerve to win the pennant in the B. U. M. Baseball League?" Up, comrades, and at them! Progress is here; get out of the way or you will get run over by the automobile! Lincoln struck the shackles from the slaves but Ty Cobb still holds the batting record!

But now the pond, mentioned in the outset of this article, is about dried up, the apple trees have died of old age; the war rendered the negro cabins useless and they were torn down; few now living know that there ever was a store there and that S. Y. B. Williams clerked in it; there is not a stick or stone remaining to show where the barn stood; even the depot and water tank are gone and have never been rebuilt; "Facility," the post-office, has long since been abolished by the government and absorbed by Sweetwater and Dan. Scruggs of Route No. 2 is now "it;" most of those living there in the fifties have passed to the great beyond. The old residence, though somewhat dilapidated, is yet standing; some magnificent old oak in a grove near the railway, still lend a majestic attraction to the scene.

I am happy to state that the girl, who used to play the piano for us and give us pies and cakes between times, is a much loved and respected grandmother in the town of Sweetwater.

One of the Reagan family is now living at the station. He was called "James" by his mother, "Avery" by his father, "Jeems" by the darkeys, "Jim" by the neighbors, "Legs" by his intimates, Reagan by his collegemates, is called Major by the road men, Judge by the lawyers and his former associates in the county court.

He married about a quarter of a century ago (1889). He is still married, but with this difference: For many years of their married life Mrs. Lizzie Reagan was known as the wife of Judge James Avery Reagan; J. A. Reagan, Esq., is now known in several states of the union, as the husband of Mrs. Elizabeth Buchanan Reagan and I have not heard of his objecting to it. The writer of this often revisits these scenes of his boyhood days in imagination, and sometimes in person. He still remains to bear testimony to the fact that in the times before the war at Reagan's, when two or three or more of us were gathered together, there would be enough ideas in our midst to cause somethin' to be doin' in pretty short order.

James Hayes Reagan was born February 12, 1800. I am unable to say now exactly where. In 1822 or 1823 he started to go west. However on his way he chanced to stop at the house of the Rev. Irby Holt, who then lived about one-half mile west of where Reagan's Station now is. This determined his future life. He went into the mercantile business with Mr. Holt. The nearest stores then were at Athens, Madisonville and Philadelphia. Before many years a United States post-office was needed, as there were none nearer than the places mentioned; and it was petitioned for and obtained. In the rapid settling up of the new country there was need for everything in the way of household goods and sales were easily made at good profit.

He married Elizabeth, daughter of Rev. Irby Holt, on April 22, 1824.

General Reagan was an all-round business man; he prospered as a merchant, a farmer and a banker and became one of the wealthiest men in East Tennessee in his day. He was also popular with the people and was considerable of a politician. He was a strong Jackson and Polk man. He was known as an uncompromising Democrat. In 1836 he was elected as senator from the counties of McMinn and Monroe to represent these counties in the General Assembly of the state. In the History of Tennessee by Garrett and Goodpasture on page 257, section 463, under the head of "First Railroad Construction" we find this: "Through the influence of Senator James H. Reagan, afterward a distinguished citizen of Texas, the Legislature granted a charter of incorporation to the Hiwassee Railroad Company, in 1836, for the purpose of constructing a railroad through the Hiwassee District to the southern boundary of the state. The road was surveyed and ground broken in 1837, being the first work ever done on a railroad in this state. In 1848 the charter was renewed and the name of the corporation changed to the East Tennessee and Georgia Railroad Company. The road was not completed (to Knoxville) until 1856."

This is all perfectly correct history, except that John H. Reagan, postmaster general, C. S. A., Governor of Texas and U. S. Senator from that state was not the Reagan spoken of and was never a member of the Tennessee Legislature but a cousin of his, James H. Reagan, who was a citizen of McMinn County for more than forty years and who again in 1853 represented Monroe and McMinn in the Legislature.

Major W. B. L. Reagan, son of J. H. Reagan, is responsible for the following statement: "Father was a brigadier general of militia. When the Mexican War came up he was making every arrangement in his business to go to Mexico. General Caswell of Knox also wanted to go, and then governor of the state (Aaron V. Brown) had them to "cast lots" for it. Caswell "drew the long straw," much to father's disappointment."

G. and G.'s History of Tennessee says: "Upon the requisition of the War Department, on the 26th of May, 1847, Governor Brown called for three regiments of volunteers, numbering in all 2,800 men. In answer to this call, 30,000 volunteers promptly tendered their services. So eager were they all for services that it became necessary to adopt some mode of selection. Accordingly the governor directed the four major generals of the state to decide by ballot, according to rules laid down, the companies to be received from their respective divisions."

This shows how the men were selected but not how the commanders were chosen. What sort of hocus pocus was resorted to determine this I have not been able to find out. As General Reagan was totally ignorant of, and averse to, all forms of gambling perhaps he did not get a square deal. What would have been his future career had he gone to Mexico can be only a matter of conjecture. No doubt it would have made a great difference in his after life. The battle of Beuna Vista, and not such a great battle after all, made two presidents, Zachary Taylor, President of U. S. A., and Jefferson Davis, his son-in-law, President of the C. S. A.

Aaron V. Brown, a very eloquent and powerful man on the stump, was governor. He was afterwards postmaster general under President Buchanan. He was defeated in his next race for governor by Neill S. Brown. His defeat is not unlikely due the fact that so many got mad at him because they wanted to fight and did not get to fight. We have now so much advanced in civilization that those whose voices are loudest for war with Mexico now, will be the "most afraid" of bullets when the war is really upon us.

General J. H. Reagan's Railroad Record.

In these days of railway construction and immense fortunes it is a comparatively simple matter to build a railroad, when once a proper charter is obtained from the state. Not so in those days. A standard oil magnate can run his cars into the sounding deep, as Flagler did along the Florida keys, easier than the people of Georgia and Tennessee then could through the mountains. They can do now with money and scientific appliances what was not even dreamed of in the "Arabian Nights." When General Reagan had gotten the charter from the Tennessee Legislature his work had not fairly begun. Money at that time could not be borrowed in New York for the purpose. If the railroad was built at all, it must be done by the people along the line in the Hiwassee and Ocoee Districts. Many of these had not as yet finished paying for the tracts of land which they had purchased from the state. In many instances work was done and material furnished and stock in the railroad was taken in payment therefor.

Thus the very men who used the railroad as a common carrier were the ones who owned the stock in it.

W. B. L. Reagan (son of James H.) says: "The controlling officers of the road induced General Reagan to take charge of the work of building the road as superintendent and to use his own discretion in all matters. He was very successful. When he got it finished to near Cleveland, he applied to the company to release him, as his own business matters were suffering seriously for want of attention. They endeavored to get him to continue as general superintendent, but he declined. They then offered him the position as president. He told them that it would be impossible for him to assume the responsibility as his own private business would need all his time. He was made a life director and served as such faithfully with much profit to the company.

"He loaned the company (The Hiwassee Railroad Co., and its successor the E. T. & Ga. R. R. Co.) $150,000."

Previous to the breaking out of the Civil War from 1831 to 1854 the General Assembly of the state passed various acts, coming under the general head of Internal Improvement Acts, to assist the construction of railroads. The one proving most effective was that of 1852. "Under this act (History of Tenn., G. & G.) when any railroad company with bona fide subscription to grade, bridge and prepare the whole extent of its main line for iron rails, had prepared a certain extent of its roadbed, it was entitled to receive $8,000 (per mile) of the 6 per cent. bonds of the state, to be used in ironing and equipping the road. These bonds were to have the force and effect of a first lien or mortgage on the road, its franchises and equipments. Under this act and its subsequent amendments, about $14,000,000 of bonds were issued, prior to the Civil War, making the total issue to railroads up to this time about 15 millions."

One of the first deeds to right of way in Monroe County to E. T. & Ga. R. R. Co. was from Matthew Nelson of Philadelphia, at one time treasurer of the State. For the consideration of 9 shares of the capital stock of the E. T. & Ga. R. R. Co. he conveys, to-wit: "The right of way through his lands in Monroe County, Tenn., where said road is now located, to include such width as is necessary for the working and proper construction of said road; said land being the southeast quarter of section 5, township 1, range 2, Hiwassee District, it being the land upon which he now resides and upon which the town of Philadelphia is located." (Still located on that tract in 1914.) The date of the deed is November 22, 1850. The witnesses to Nelson's signature are D. H. Jones, I. T. Lenoir and John Stanfield.

I think at that time (1850) the road was graded through the greater part of Sweetwater Valley; for the reason that the right of way grade was used in some places as a public road between the neighborhood where Sweetwater now is and Philadelphia. Mr. J. A. Reagan is authority for the statement that construction reached the location of Mouse Creek (Niota) early in February, 1852. Not a great while thereafter cars were running to Sweetwater. Here a "Y" or a turn switch was made among the timber close to where the new Scruggs brick building is being erected. For some time this place became the terminus of the road. However in about six months the railroad was constructed to Loudon, where it hung up for nearly two years awaiting the completion of the bridge across the Tennessee River. Loudon was on a boom and predictions were frequent that it would be many, many years before trains would be running to Knoxville, if they ever were.

In considering the location of the railroad, the question is sometimes asked by the more observant; why the road went up the hill (Sweetwater ridge) at Athens just to get to come down again. The question is easily answered. When the railroad was being built Athens (as its name might imply) was by far the most important town in lower East Tennessee, more so than even Chattanooga. There was a bank there of which General Reagan was president. The sentiments of the town could not be disregarded. The railroad must come to them if it did have to climb a ridge to do so. I am inclined to the opinion that one reason of General Reagan's resignation as superintendent of construction was that he knew that question of location would come up and being a politician and also a large creditor of the company, he did not wish it even suspected that he used his official position to determine the location. Few of late years would hesitate to use official influence for private gain. However the way is not so smooth and easy as it was a few years since.

Second Marriage.

On September 3, 1835, General Reagan married his second wife, Myra Ann Lenoir. She was magnificently endowed mentally and morally and had received all the advantages of education which our southern country could bestow. She was the daughter of William Ballard Lenoir of Roane County. She was eminently fitted to be the wife of such a man. She had the noble and beautiful impulses of the woman, combined with the sound sense and logical acumen of the sterner sex. When General Reagan was absent attending to his varied business affairs there was no fear in his mind that those at home and on the farm would not be looked after. From the time of their marriage till 1861 everything of theirs prospered. The sky of life was cloudless; there were no gloomy days.

The situation at the outbreak of the Civil War briefly told was this: They had 2,000 acres of land in Sweetwater Valley, a considerable portion of this in a high state of cultivation, and in as healthful a location as in this or any other country; there were $75,000 still due him from the East Tennessee & Ga. Railroad Company, and equally that much from individuals, which heretofore he had never had a lawsuit to collect any of; he was president of a bank and owned large stock therein; he was deservedly popular and could have gotten almost any office he desired; they had a family of children of which any parents ought to have been proud; also he had forty or more negroes who were well fed and clothed, not overworked and apparently satisfied with their lot; thus from a southerner's point of view the condition was ideal.

But what startling and almost unbelievable changes can "man's inhumanity to man" bring about!

The poets sometimes write beautifully of war, expressing sentiments such as:

"Oh if there be, on this earthly sphere,
A boon, an offering heaven holds dear,
'Tis the last libration liberty draws
From the heart that bleeds and breaks
   in her cause."

But had the war of 1861-5 anything to do with liberty? Lincoln solemnly affirmed, time and again, that he was not fighting to free the negroes. It might have been then to free us from the toil and trouble of taking care of the negroes. The white folks did not wish to be liberated; however, as Kipling says: "That is another story."

Some of the things that happened to General Reagan and family were: $75,000 due from the E. T. & Ga. R. R. Co. that were paid in bonds of the Confederate States of America, forced upon General Reagan by the company, became worthless. This debt could have been collected after the war but the heirs refused to take any steps in that direction. The debts due from individuals were nearly all lost through inability or unwillingness to pay. The negroes instead of being property became our masters at the ballot box.

But we will let Mrs. Reagan tell her own story (which explains itself) in letters written at the time. Being a careful, prudent woman the picture was underdrawn rather than overdrawn. The letter that follows was not in any envelope but the two sheets were folded in the old fashioned way. Thus only three pages could be used in the body of the lettter and the other was outside with the address upon it. The letter was sealed with a wafer and a seal. The seal had a rough surface with no monogram upon it. Reagan's was at the time of the writing of the letter in the rebel lines while Memphis was held by the Federal forces. The address was: Mrs. Eliza M. Martin, Memphis, Tenn. There was no postage stamp on the letter nor were there any marks to show methods of transportation or date of delivery. There must have been an "underground mail" system. This was called so because carried on without the knowledge of the military. Any one caught carrying these letters was in danger of being executed as a spy.

McMinn County, E. Tenn.,
Oct. 28, —'63.

Dear Sister Eliza:

It has been a long time since I have had the pleasure of a letter from you, or had the chance of writing to you. Dr. Green, a resident of your place (Memphis), who is in Cheatham's Division, told me to-day that he would send a letter for me. I will try to give you a few items, though surrounding circumstances are not favorable for writing anything like a connected letter. Cheatham's Division are camped here and it would be hard to imagine the annoyance and confusion. East Tennessee is thronged with soldiers now, both Federal and Confederate, and Sweetwater Valley seems destined to experience the horrors of war. Several skirmishes have occurred between here and Loudon—more about Philadelphia than any other place. Yesterday week the Rebels surprised Wolford's brigade, which were encamped around W. F. L.'s (Lenoir's) house, completely routing them and taking some four or five hundred prisoners, some sixty vehicles, tents and everything they had there. There were not a great many casualties. Since that there have been some cannonading and picket fighting. Since that troops of infantry have come in and appearances indicate that there will be heavy fighting, or retreating by one side or the other. Two large armies cannot long subsist here with communications cut off. This Valley begins to show the footprints of the armies. We have had both to camp here. The Federals injured us in one stay—taking all of our hay, fodder and oats—wasting probably four times as much as they consumed, as it was a wet time. Much fencing and some other things were burned and a great deal of corn wasted, fields turned out and so forth—too tedious to mention—hogs, sheep, turkeys and chickens killed—some hogs shot that died afterward. Since the Yankees came we have been closely at home and know certainly but little that is transpiring among our friends. When we hear anything, we do not know how much of it is true. * * * It is distressing times here and I am afraid it will still be worse. What is to become of us our heavenly Father only knows. Soldiers, bushrangers and robbers! Everything in confusion and tending to disorganization! We hope our enemies will not remain much longer, but we cannot tell what the future will reveal. (Here follows news of the relatives not of general interest.) * * *

Catherine's (widow of A. S. Lenoir) folks were well a short time since. Robbers (bushwhackers) took $1,000 from her and such things as they wanted out of the house. Frank Welcker's (son-in-law of General Reagan by deceased wife) house was robbed of everything, even to the bed that Mrs. Welcker was lying on and the furniture hauled away. W. F. L.'s (Lenoir's) house was visited; guns, blankets and clothing taken. (Done by bushwhackers claiming to be Unionists.) Many others have suffered in the same way. * * * Many Southern men have left home. Some have returned; others are waiting for things to become more settled. Many Union men leave home when the Rebels are in the ascendant, and so they have it in turn. * * * Mr. Reagan's health is bad; worse for the last year than before. * * * Lenoir and James (her sons) have been at home for a few days. They were in the fight at Philadelphia.

James left home when Loudon was evacuated (by Rebels). I have heard from Julia (afterward Mrs. Love), we are all here but her. She is well but anxious to come home. Cousin Thomas Lenoir (of Haywood County, N. C.) thinks she had better remain there until the Yankees are driven out of East Tennessee. We have been talking of sending for her, thinking she would rather be at home and suffer with the balance of us. * * * A good many negro men and some women have gone to the Yankees; some four or five of ours. It is getting bedtime and I do not expect to have a chance of writing in the morning, as it keeps me busy to talk to and wait upon the soldiers. If we never meet again in this world may we meet in a better.

Affectionately your sister,

M. A. R.

29th, 9 A. M. The Yankees have evacuated Loudon and the division is under marching orders. Will fold this ready for sending. May heaven's choicest blessings rest on you and yours.

M. A. R. (M. A. Reagan).

In continuation of these sketches about the Reagan family I can not see how I can do better than to give the contents of another letter from Mrs. Reagan to her sister, Mrs. Martin, of Memphis, Tenn. The former letter was dated October 28, 1863.

This was shortly after the battle of Philadelphia. At that time all the family were at home except her daughter, Julia, afterward Mrs. Love, who was in North Carolina. Lenoir and James A. were soldiers in the rebel army. They shortly afterward went with Longstreet to the siege of Knoxville. John, then a boy of 15, remained at home with his father and mother. Lenoir and James were with Vaughn in the upper East Tennessee campaign and also in Early's campaign in the Shenandoah Valley. Lenoir Reagan was wounded near Winchester, Va., on July 24, 1864, and for many weeks lay at the point of death a prisoner of war. On July 25, General Reagan was arrested at home and taken to Knoxville. All East Tennessee was then in possession of the Federal forces. We will now let Mrs. Reagan tell to her sister, Mrs. Martin, some things that happened:

At Home, Dec. 5th, 1864.
Dear Sister E.:
* * * You will probably have heard before this of the death of Mr. Reagan. He died in Knoxville on the morning of the 15th of October. He was taken there the 25th of July as a hostage for a man of this county, who was carried South last fall. He (Mr. Reagan) was taken there (to Knoxville) on the 25th of July. The last that man's friends heard of him, he was sick in a hospital last winter, and it is believed that he died, and it is also thought that he was held as a prisoner of war as he told the men that arrested him that he was a Federal soldier. It is said that he joined a company but had never been mustered into service. His father's and his father-in-law's families were all acquaintances and friends of Mr. Reagan's, and his wife petitioned that he be permitted to come home on parole; but the Provo Marshal at A. (Athens) thought he had not been sufficiently punished for opinion's sake (they could make no charge against him) and would not fully endorse it. After a new Provo was appointed, another petition was gotten up and signed and sent up a few days before Mr. Reagan's death, which procured an order for his release, and he was to have been sent home on Sunday, the 16th. Instead of his coming home to enjoy the comforts of his own fireside, his lifeless remains were sent—to rest a few hours in his once loved home and then to rest beside our departed son's body till the morning of the resurrection. Mr. Reagan had been a great sufferer for years and could not bear confinement. I made his condition known to the authorities soon after his arrest, and my belief that he could not survive a prison life. I entreated them if they could not permit him to come home, to let him have the liberty of the town and board at a private house. His many friends seemed willing and anxious to do anything they could for his release, but it seems they could not effect it in time. He is done with the troubles of this world, and I have an assuring hope that he has gone where troubles and sorrows will never be permitted to enter. * * * I did not see him during his imprisonment. He would not agree for me to go up, as I would be allowed to see him but a few minutes at a time in the presence of a guard, and he did not wish to see me subjected to the treatment I might have to receive, and I was not apprised of his last illness in time to go. He was taken to the hospital four days before his death. The

disease was said to be jaundice, which his appearance indicated. A kind friend procured a metalic burial case and suitable clothing, and another friend accompanied the remains home.

Excerpts from letters from Mrs. Reagan to Mrs. Martin, her sister, heretofore given, graphically and concisely describe some of the events in our valley in the sixties. From these we can form some idea of the horrors of war. What happened to the Reagan family could be truthfully written of numerous others in our section. Yet here we did not get the worst of it. There were few if any houses burned and outrages committed by the regular troops on either side, as was the case in Georgia in Sherman's March to Sea or in the Shenandoah Valley and Manassas plains of Virginia. The mere recital of the dead and wounded in battle shows but a small fraction of the evils of war—Its resultants are debts, demoralization, disease, famine and an enduring crop of personal feuds and national hatreds.

One hundred years ago a war lord was a captive in the isle of Elba. As a person he was supposed to be eliminated from the list of European monarchs. Yet one year later he was the central figure in a war of nations in Belgium, now the theatre of a conflict beside which, the loss of life and property at Waterloo will appear insignificant. No time now for "beauty and chivalry" to gather in Belgium's capital; for the happening there will be of lightning like rapidity. The gatherings there will be all warlike. The pity of it is that that little nation had nothing to do with bringing on the conflict and not one of her inhabitants wanted to fight. Whatever the result, she will be ground to powder between the upper and nether millstones. What to her is the "pomp and circumstance of glorious war!" What a spectacle to the heathen of ten million trained soldiers of Christian nations, preaching the Gospel of Peace, using all their ingenuity and energies in destroying each other!

As a writer has said: "It is the twilight of the gods." Our human understanding can but faintly illumine the clouds of providential gloom that now lower on the European horizon. Napoleon had his Waterloo and St. Helena; William, the "war lord," today the most forceful (1915) personality on the face of the globe, may have his inglorious defeats and his rock bound island captivity.

* * * * * *

The following beautiful tribute is taken from an obituary written for the Nashville Christian Advocate by L. L. H. Carlock, D. D.:

"Departed this life, at the residence of her son-in-law, Colonel James R. Love, near Sweetwater, Tenn., on March 8, 1879, Mrs. Mira A. Reagan. in the 69th year of her age. * * *
She had been a member of the Church from early life, at which time she made a profession of religion and joined the M. E. Church, South. * * *
Her character was perfect in its proportions; not rugged nor erratic, but harmonious, symmetrical and unobtrusive; yielding its fruit not by paroxysms, but regularly and constantly; moulded not after Wesley or Fletcher or Watson, but after the pattern shown her "in the mount," where she had communed with Him and grown into His likeness. For her a personal, present Saviour was the only one who could solve the enigma of life—the Sun of righteousness, the only infallible standard by which to set your timepieces for eternity. * * *
Her religious life was convincing; not demonstrative, but demonstrating."

WILLIAM BALLARD LENOIR REAGAN.

He was the oldest son of General James H. and Mira A. Reagan. He was born in Sweetwater Valley, McMinn County, Tenn., May 31, 1838; died at Terrell, Texas, September 1, 1913.

When a boy he received such education as the public schools afforded at the time and also went a year to Prof. Aldehoff's private school at Kingston, Tenn. When quite a youth he went into a branch bank of the state at Athens, as assistant cashier to David Cleage, who was cashier, and his father the president. He remained in that position until the beginning of the Civil War, executing his duties with exactness and fidelity.

He first went into the war as a member of the cornet band of Colonel J. C. Vaughn's 3rd Tennessee regiment, of which G. R. Knabe, afterward of Knoxville, was the leader. However, he did not remain long a member of the band as he wished to be in the thick of the fight. He served first in Colonel Vaughn's regiment in Virginia, and afterward served as first lieutenant and adjutant in

Colonel John R. Neil's Sixteenth battalion, Tennessee cavalry, Rucker's legion, Pegram's brigade, under General Bragg in Kentucky and Tennessee. He was under General Forest in the battle of Chickamauga, and afterward served in General Vaughn's mounted infantry brigade in the valley of Virginia and Maryland campaigns and was in the battles in which his command was engaged up to the time he was wounded near Winchester, Va., July 24, 1864, where he lost his leg. Soon after that date he was captured and sent to prison, where he remained until June, 1865.

The General J. C. Vaughn, Chapter No. 1224 of the United Daughters of the Confederacy, at Sweetwater, conferred upon him a cross of honor in January, 1910. Lenoir Reagan had a very minute and accurate recollection of the events of the Civil War in which he was engaged, and was fond of talking of them. He related reminiscences in a very interesting manner. It was never his intention to exploit himself and his own part came in frequently, only by implication. In one of his stories he said: "Once I was with the rear guard in coming from Kentucky, near Point Burnside. The Cumberland river was at flood tide and the army was slow in crossing. A mile or so from the river, being very weary and having lost much sleep, I lay down in a cabin and told an old darky to wake me up when all the rebel soldiers had passed. Several hours afterward the old negro shook me and said: 'Boss, your men are all gone. If you don't mind, the Yankees will git you.' I got on my horse and galloped to the river. The last boat had gotten some distance from the shore. I hailed them and told them to come back and take me over. The officer in command said it was impossible to do so, that they would be captured, and ordered the men to proceed. Some of the soldiers on the boat, knowing my voice, disregarded the orders of the officer and forced those rowing the boat to come back and take me aboard, and all got over to safety."

This is told to show the regard and esteem in which he was held by his comrades, who saved him from capture even at the risk of being shot for disobedience of orders.

The late Judge J. M. King, of Knoxville, was one of

his comrades in prison at Fort Delaware. After his return from prison, Mr. Reagan engaged in farming at the old farm on which he was born. He remained there until a few years ago, when he moved to Texas. He was a member of the J. E. B. Stuart Camp, No. 45, U. C. V., at Terrell, Texas. Members of this camp helped to care for him and relieve his sufferings in his last illness.

Fort Delaware was on an island in the northern part of Delaware Bay, a few miles out from Delaware City. It was used during the Civil War mostly as a prison for captured officers of the Confederate army. The prisoners were allowed to receive boxes and money from friends inside of the Federal lines. They were also allowed to write and receive a certain number of letters of prescribed length and contents. A prisoner could write a letter to friends every two weeks on one side of a sheet furnished by the prison quartermaster. This sheet was not so large as the common letter paper but larger than the ordinary note. Of course all letters were strictly censored and contraband information and recondite meanings were looked for. If they contained any objectionable matter they were never delivered or sent. Cipher of any kind was not allowed and only such abbreviations the meaning of which was plain; as "&" for "and," "tho" for "though," "recd." for "received." Reagan wrote a very plain, neat hand not smaller than the ordinary business scrip. With this explanation I append in full one of his letters. This letter dated at Fort Delaware May 14, 1865, was post-marked at Delaware City, May 16, thus giving time for censoring, and arrived at Memphis, Tenn., on the 22nd.

> Fort Delaware, Div. 25,
> May 14, 1865.
>
> Miss Bettie Martin,
>   Memphis, Tenn.
>
> My Dear Cousin:
>   Yours of the 6th instant came to hand yesterday evening. It was surely a welcome visitor and one that I had been daily expecting. Now that you have recovered from your fever I am glad I had not heard of the attack before, for I would have suffered from constant and painful anxiety, without the power to help ward off the blows of merciless enemy, or even being cognizant of the progress of the struggle. I hope you have fully recovered your health and spirits, though to do the latter will certainly require an extraordinary effort— that is, I feel it an almost impossibility for those with feelings sym-

pathetic with my own to enjoy their wonted cheerfulness and hope. As to us prisoners being offered our release on the terms granted General Lee and army, is something we had not the least cause to expect. I do not suppose, my dear cousin, there is one among us who intends to live in the States, but what entertains very little hope of getting his release on terms less than what we are made to understand will at some time be offered us—that of taking the oath of allegiance to the government we propose to live under. Some few are even fearful that those terms will not be granted. Others, by special application, are leaving daily. As much as I desire to be released, and knowing that so long as I remain here I can be of service to no one, an increasing injury to my health, and a source of uneasiness to my best friends, I will never do anything to escape these evils that I consider in the least dishonorable. I will bide my time, trusting soon to be released. Give my love to all, and please write at once.

Affectionately your cousin,

L. REAGAN.

When the Confederates under General Early evacuated Winchester, W. Va., Reagan was unable to be moved; consequently he was captured by the Federals. Later on he was transferred to the old Capitol Prison at Washington, D. C. In November, 1864, he was taken to Fort Delaware, from which place the above letter was written. The journey now by rail would be only a matter of hours; then it occupied perhaps a week or more. It was made with a number of other prisoners on a prison ship. The route was down the Potomac River to the Chesapeake Bay; thence down that bay by Fortress Monroe through Hampton Roads to the Atlantic; thence up the coast of Virginia to the mouth of Delaware Bay; thence north up the bay to the fort, making a journey of many hundreds of miles. The weather at the time was very bleak and stormy. The sufferings of the wounded prisoners were terrible. Reagan had undergone a double amputation at Winchester and was from loss of blood in a very weakened condition. He was exposed to the cold winds on the upper deck without sufficient clothing. The officer in charge of the prisoners was asked to allow him to be moved to a more comfortable place or to furnish covering for him. His refusal was very brutal and positive. A companion, who was almost unknown to Reagan, then took off his own coat and spread it over him, thereby as he (Reagan) thinks saving his life. Owing to this kindly act he himself took pneumonia which terminated fatally. So it often happens that war and suffering bring out the best as well as the worst qualities in humanity. Conditions were not much improved on arrival at the prison. One might think from reading some of the prisoners' letters that the stay there was rather pleasant than otherwise and that they were in no hurry to get away; but that was far from being the case. No criticism of guards or officers was allowed in any correspondence. Complaints of bad treatment to occasional inspectors only intensified the rigors of their prison life. The food furnished by the government often did not reach them. It was "grafted" and sold. Money and boxes sent prisoners by friends were partially or wholly appropriated. They had no remedy. Fort Delaware from accounts of those who were there was one of the worst of the Federal prisons. The guards were short term men or foreigners who could scarcely speak English so as to be understood, and thought they would be commended for cruel treatment of prisoners.

Reagan did not have to take the oath of allegiance but was finally released on parole.

I have written the above not with the purpose of making any comparison between Fort Delaware and Andersonville and Libby. Conditions in the last may have been, and probably were, just as bad, as in the northern prisons, barring the severity of the winters in the northern climate. What I wish to emphasize as strongly as possible is that prison life under the most favorable conditions either in war or peace is horrible to any human being whether inflicted by an enemy or by a jury of peers. As cruelty exasperated the prisoners during the Civil War, so will undue severity make the inmates of our state penitentiaries the greater enemies to society. Deprivation of liberty and the companionship of our fellowmen are terrible punishments in themselves.

THE ANCESTORS OF GENERAL JAMES H. REAGAN.

The information below given about the Reagan family up to General James H. Reagan was obtained from W. M. Sweeney of 126 Franklin Street, Astoria, Long Island, N. Y., who has gone to great trouble and expense to trace the genealogy of the different branches of the

Reagan family. His investigations have been very painstaking and thorough. Out of the material, which he has allowed me to use, I give these facts.

The O'Regans were an ancient Catholic family in Ireland and about the year 1729 a number of them emigrated to Pennsylvania. It seems that after coming to this country that they dropped the O in their name and spelled the last part in a variety of ways.

According to the first Federal census of the state of Pennsylvania of 1790, there were seven heads of families of the name living in the state, viz: James Reagin, Weldin Reagan, Reason Reagan, Stephen Regan, John Regan, George Ragon and Phillip Ragin. I also have the military record of two Revolutionary soldiers from Pennsylvania, who served in the 2nd Pennsylvania regiment. They are James Reagan and Michael Reagan. James was killed October 4, 1777, at the Battle of Germantown. They were both engaged in the Battle of Brandywine, where Senator Reagan's great grandfather was wounded. They were both probably his relatives. This is taken from a letter of W. M. Sweeney to W. B. Lenoir dated November 15, 1915. In the same letter he gives these additional facts:

I have just returned from a trip to Guilford County, N. C., where I made an examination of the records of that county to find traces of the Reagans, and thinking that the result of my investigations might interest you I write to inform you of the result.

Under date of March 22, 1772, I find a deed from John Reagan and Mary, his wife, conveying 200 acres of land on the south side of the Dan River, to John and Samuel Henderson for a consideration of £150. (Deed Book 1, page 96.)

I also find a marriage bond dated March 28, 1776, signed by Thomas Cook and John Reagan, in which Thomas Cook agrees to marry Elizabeth Reagan (daughter of John and Mary Reagan?). This Thomas Cook, who served in the Revolution as captain of the Independent Company, Light Horse, North Carolina Militia, in Continental service, was a brother of Nancy Cook, who married James Reagan, Sr., who died near Knoxville, Tenn., in 1827. I think it is most likely that James Reagan, Sr., was a son of John and Mary Reagan.

A Deed dated May 22, 1782, from John Reagan to Francis Cook (the father of Captain Thomas Cook), conveying "156 acres of land, part of a tract of 640 acres of land granted to the said John Reagan December 16, 1778." (Deed Book 2, page 200.)

A grant (No. 835) of land from the state of North Carolina to James Reagan, dated October 14, 1783, conveying 179 acres of land. (Deed Book 1, page 116.)

Another Grant (No. 833) of land from the state of North Carolina to James Reagan, dated October 14, 1783, conveying 150 acres of land. (Deed Book 1, page 116.)

A deed dated January 1, 1783, from Samuel Parks to James Reagan, conveying 120 acres of land, consideration, £120.

A deed dated September 12, 1785, from William Wilson to James Reagan conveying 400 acres of land, consideration, £100. (Deed Book 4, page 30.)

As the names of John and James Reagan are found in the first Federal census of the state of North Carolina, 1790, it shows with the deeds that they were both residents of Guilford County from 1772 to 1790, at least.

I do not find any record of John as a resident of Guilford County prior to 1772 nor of James prior to 1770, when his son, John (who died in East Tennessee in 1857), was born there. Mr. Sweeney adds:

I wrote to Senator Reagan some years ago and his reply was as follows:

"My greatgrandfather, Timothy Reagan, was a native of Ireland, but came to this country before the American Revolution; lived in Pennsylvania, was a soldier of the Pennsylvania Line in the War of the Revolution, and was dangerously wounded at the battle of Brandywine. He subsequently moved to that part of North Carolina which was west of the Alleghany Mountains, and is now East Tennessee. He helped to build Lawson's Fort, the first fort built in what is now Sevier County, but which was then occupied by the Cherokee Indians. The name of my grandfather was Richard Reagan. He and the wife of Major James Porter were the first two white children born in the territory of what is now Sevier County, Tennessee, and they were born on the same day, but I do not know the date. My father, Timothy R. Reagan, was born in the same county, in 1797. I was born in the same county, 1818.

"My greatgrandfather had a numerous family, mostly sons, and their descendants are scattered through the Southern and Western States, and are very numerous, though I know but little of them.

"I knew General James Reagan, of East Tennessee, and we called each other cousin, and, while we understood that we were of the same family, we did not know the precise relationship between us.

"Very respectfully,

"JOHN H. REAGAN."

"Mr. W. M. Sweeny,
"Astoria, N. Y."

From a letter from Joseph Reagan (a grandson of James Reagan, Sr.), to William M. Sweeney, of Astoria, Long Island, N. Y., we make the following extracts:

"Conyers, Ga., April 8, 1895.

"My Dear Nephew:
"My grandfather (James Reagan) I never saw, but have heard that he was a man of fine and discriminate judgment. He accumulated quite a good fortune in the way of land and negroes. I can recollect that when I was a boy ten or eleven years old he sent for all his children to come to see him. Some of them were living in Georgia. My father (James R.) was one of them, and one brother, Charles Reagan, and one sister went. They rode horseback from Georgia over the mountains of North Carolina and Georgia into Tennessee, two or three hundred miles. He divided out his negro property among all his children; I recollect my father brought home one of the largest horses I thought I ever saw and two likely negroes as his part. My grandfather kept enough to live comfortably on, but in less than a year afterward he died. In the year 1837 I made a trip into Tennessee, above Knoxville, near where he had lived. Uncle John Reagan, my father's oldest brother, lived there. I saw the old family Bible, in which I saw the record that grandfather had married three times and had fifteen children. Some of them I have never seen. One of them, Peter, came to Georgia and settled in upper Georgia at Rome. The youngest, William, went to Texas, and died there some years ago. Brother Thomas was well acquainted with him. He left a large family. My grandmother was named Cook. Grandfather married her (his second wife) in North Carolina before he moved to Tennessee.
"When she died my father and his brother, Charles, and his sister, Frances, were grown and they came to Georgia.
"My grandfather Morrison (his mother's father) was named Joseph Higginbotham Morrison. You see, quite a long name. It is said that there were as many letters in his name as in the alphabet, and so there were."

James Raggon made a will of date July 23, 1821. The subscribing witnesses were John Rigney and John Calloway. He died sometime late in the year 1827. The will was admitted to probate in the Knox County Court in July, 1828. John, Peter and William Reagan, were the three executors to the will—"The undernamed, ten of my children" were mentioned as devisees in the will: John, May, Ann, James, Charles, Franky, Peter,

Rachel, Rebekah and William, and one nephew, Havern Raggon to whom he bequeathed a 42-acre tract of land. After disposing of a few items of personal property, he directs that the balance of the realty and personalty be sold and the proceeds divided equally among the ten children; from the parts of certain ones were to be deducted specified sums which he had charged to them. From Peter's part was to be taken the sum of $370. As this will was made in 1821, the father likely gave this in money or its equivalent when he went to Sweetwater Valley. Peter came here and married Miss Cunnyngham.

It appears from this will and from precious gifts to children mentioned by James Reagan, of Conyers, Ga., that James Raggon of Guilford County, was an eminently successful business man. Who the other five of the fifteen children set down in the John Reagan Bible and whether living or not at the writing of the will is not known.

EXTRACTS FROM AN OBITUARY OF JOHN REAGAN, PUBLISHED IN KNOX COUNTY.

"Died on Jan. 25, 1857, at the residence of his son-in-law, Mr. Thomas McMilland, Knox County, Tennessee, Mr. John Reagan in his 87th year. The deceased was born in Rockingham County, North Carolina (then Guilford) May 24, 1770. He emigrated and lived in South Carolina and afterwards to Kentucky and later to Knox County, Tenn., where he resided since 1910."

(Note:—Thus any one of three states, North Carolina, Georgia or Kentucky might have been the birthplace of James Hays Reagan, his son.)

The obituary continues: "In his extreme old age, though nearly blind, he retained in a remarkable degree, his vivacity, his cheerfulness and his quaint humor. Age never chilled the ardor of his friendship; infirmity never impaired the exercise of his good nature and cordial feelings; debility never blunted the keen edge of his wit. He was without avarice, envy, ostentation or malice. He never had an enemy; never owed anybody anything but good will. Interment was at Lebanon churchyard, where repose the remains of a former wife whom he has survived thirty-four years."

REAGAN GENEALOGICAL TABLE.

A John Reagan came from Pennsylvania and settled in Guilford County, N. C. His wife's name was Mary.

One son, James, b. ———; d. in 1827. James m. three times: (first) Miss Hays; (second) Nancy, daughter of

Francis and Betty Cook; (third) unknown. Children of James R., whose names are known are:
1. John, by first wife; 2. James; 3. Charles; 4. Frances (m. Narremore); 5. Peter; 6. William, Rebekah by second wife; May (m. Whitter), Ann (m. Hamlin), Rachel (m. McCall).

1. John had a son (1) James Hays and (2) a daughter Sarah, who married Thomas McMillan, of Knox County, Tenn.

5. Peter m. Nancy, daughter of Jesse Cunnyngham of Monroe County. He went to Rome, Ga., where he died. Children were Carrie and Addie. (See Mayes.)

7. Rebekah m. Wm. Burns, a merchant of Athens, Tenn.

2. James, son of James and Nancy R.

James, b. Guilford County, N. C., July 2, 1780; d. Pike County, Ga., December 27, 1855; m. in Elbert County, Ga., January 8, 1805, Mary Dandridge Morrison, daughter of Joseph Higginbotham Morrison and Francis Higginbotham. Mary D. Morrison was b. in Virginia, ————, 1784; d. in Elbert County, Ga., September 8, 1839. Children of James and Mary D. M. Reagan:

William Morrison, b. January 10, 1806; d. February 25, 1858.

John, b. January 28, 1808; d. June 22, 1862.

Martha, b. May 31, 1810; d. July 28, 1828.

Nancy A., b. May 15, 1813; d. August 6, 1872.

Charles, b. May 13, 1815; d. October 8, 1874.

Joseph, b. March 29, 1817; d. February 28, 1904.

James, b. July 26, 1819; d. September 5, 1896.

Francis W. Reagan, b. August 21, 1821; d. May 25, 1865; m. December 14, 1845, Sarah C. Refo. Child, Eugenia Octavia, b. October 17, 1846; m. September 30, 1867, Thomas W. Sweeney. Children: Thomas Francis, b. July 14, 1868; William Montgomery, b. August 29, 1871.

Mary Dandridge, b. October 8, 1823; d. January 22, 1902.

Sarah Elizabeth, b. August 6, 1825; d. October 30, 1854.

Thomas Jefferson, b. March 21, 1828; d. May 9, 1887.

Mrs. J. R. Love.

Mrs. Julia Reagan Love, the second child of J. H. and Mira Reagan, was born September 4, 1843. She went to school to Mrs. H. M. Cooke at Athens, Tenn., also to Asheville, N. C.

On November 18, 1868, m. Colonel James R. Love. He was born in Jackson County, N. C., August 19, 1832. Died at his residence near Sweetwater, Tenn., on November 10, 1885. His father was John Bell Love and his mother, Margaret Coman Love. They lived three miles from Webster, N. C.

James R. Love took the B. A. degree at Emory and Henry College 1858. He then studied law under Colonel Nicholas Woodfin at Asheville, N. C. At the beginning of the war he enlisted in the 16th North Carolina, (C. S. A.) Regiment. He was elected lieutenant-colonel in the 69th North Carolina Regiment, which was organized in September, 1862, and he was made colonel of the regiment before the close of the Civil War. Not long after which he was elected to the lower house of the North Carolina Legislature. He was a member of the North Carolina Constitutional Convention and in 1873 was elected to the state senate. After marriage he lived in Webster, N. C., where he practised law. He moved to Tennessee in November, 1876, having purchased part of the I. T. Lenoir farm. In 1884 he was elected representative from Monroe County to the Forty-fourth General Assembly, of which he was a member when he died. He was a member of the M. E. C., South. The children of James R. and Julia Love were:

1. Son, d. infancy.
2. Mira Lenoir, b. June 19, 1872. Educated at Centenary College, Cleveland, Tenn., and graduate of Asheville (N. C.) Female College. On May 8, 1902, she married J. W. Lowry, son of J. H. and Mary Caroline Lowry, of Sweetwater, Tenn. Her children are: Joseph Walker, Jr., b. August 27, 1903; Julia Love, b. May 8, 1906; James Robert Love, b. November 16, 1907.
3. Margaret Bell, b. August 4, 1874, at Webster, N. C.; d. January, 1885.
4. Julia Burgwin, b. March 30, 1876, at Webster, N. C. Was educated at Price's School, Nashville, Tenn. She

was married November, 1894 to Frank B. St. John, of Johnson City, Tenn., who was born June 16, 1870. His father was George W. St. John, of Virginia. His mother was Martha Blair, of Loudon County, Tenn. George W. St. J. settled near Watauga, Tenn. Frank B. St. J. is engaged in real estate business. Their children are: Frank Love, b. November 11, 1895. Louise Avery, b. July 5, 1893. Julia Love, b. December 18, 1910.

5. James Reagan Love, b. September 3, 1877. Farmer, Sweetwater.

6. Elizabeth Avery, b. September 3, 1879. Educated at Randolph-Macon Woman's College, Lynchburg, Va. Teacher, Sweetwater and Madisonville, Tenn.; Jalapa, Mexico; Edmonds, Wash. Went to Soochow, China, September, 1914, where she teaches in Laura Hagwood School.

7. Robert John, b. September 19, 1881. Graduate of the University of Tennessee. Profession, civil engineer. Worked in the state of Sonora, Mex., in Peru, for the Southern Railway in Mississippi, Georgia and North Carolina. For the past three years has been doing engineering on county roads of Monroe and Loudon counties. He married Lillian Dee Worrell, on July 3, 1915. Her father is Charles B. Worrell, of Clayton, Ind. One child, Robert John Love, Jr., born at Madisonville, Tenn., on September 5, 1916.

8. Hattie Frank, b. February 6, 1884. Graduate of Randolph-Macon Woman's College, Lynchburg, Va., and of Woman's Medical College, Philadelphia, Pa. Was interne at Worchester Memorial Hospital, Worchester, Mass., and studied at Scarritt Bible and Training School, Kansas City, Mo. Went to Soochow, China, in September, 1913, as medical missionary. She is dean of the medical school at Soochow, and practises in Mary Black Hospital.

* * * * * *

James Avery Reagan, third child of J. H. and Mira Reagan, was born at the old Reagan homestead, at which Callahan now (1914) lives, on January 7, 1846. Went to school to Prof. Aldehoff on Lookout Mountain in 1861 and 1862. In August 1863 he enlisted as a private in Co. B (Captain Maston), 16th battalion Confederate cavalry, Lieutenant Jno. R. Neal, commander, and served continuously and principally in Tennessee, also in Virginia, Maryland, South Carolina and Georgia, until the surrender at Washington, Ga., in 1865. He was fortunate enough to be paid there before the surrender $28.25 dollars in silver out of the Confederate treasury. From 1865-7 he was a student at Dinwiddie's School at Greenwood, Va. He was a student at the University of Virginia four years 1867-71. Took there the degrees C. E., M. E. and B. S.

Worked under Major Ruhl in the location of the Cincinnati Southern Railway.

Was resident engineer in construction on the section near Robbins, Tenn., including the tunnel.

Worked for the Union Pacific in Wyoming one or two years.

Was the engineer in charge of location and superintendent of construction northern end of the Mexican National Railroad for several years. He was superintendent of the Lenoir Manufacturing Co., Lenoir's Tenn., after the death of W. A. Lenoir until the sale of the property to Brice, Sanford and others.

He was married to Miss Elizabeth Buchanan, of Abingdon, Va., on June 25, 1889. They came to Reagan's Station in the fall of 1891, where he owned a large farm. Miss Elizabeth Buchanan was born July 12, 1867. He was a member of the McMinn County Court for fourteen years, and was chairman of that body four terms. Was chairman of the Road Commission of that county for several years. He was engineer of road location and construction, for Loudon County 1911-1915, inclusive.

Mrs. J. A. Reagan was a daughter of Prof. John L. Buchanan and a granddaughter of president E. E. Wiley of Emory and Henry College, Virginia. Prof. Buchanan has been teacher of languages at Emory and Henry and Vanderbilt University; president at Agricultural and Mechanical College, Blacksburg, Va., and president of the University of Arkansas at Fayetteville. Mrs. Reagan, coming from intellectual ancestry on both sides, preserves the reputation of her people for accomplishments and popularity. She has been quite in demand as a speaker on selected subjects at farmers conventions and meetings. She has been a demonstrator on certain lines of home improvement work. She and her neighbor, Mrs. C. O. Browder, have acquired almost a national reputation as original dialogue and dialect entertainers.

The children of J. A. and E. B. Reagan are: Frank, b. May 31, 1890; Julia, b. July 25, 1892; Margaret, b. October 24, 1894; d. April 11, 1896; Elizabeth Avery, b. March 13, 1897; Myra, b. November 27, 1898, and James Avery, b. September 24, 1907.

4. John Martin, fourth child of J. H. and Mira Reagan, b. February 20, 1848; d. July 17, 1870. He was the second person and the first adult buried at the old Sweetwater cemetery. He attended school at the University of Virginia, for three years, in the academic department. He was pursuing a law course at Lebanon, Tenn., when disease overtook him. I have heard that tuberculosis, which was fatal to him, was brought on in this way: one very cold night there was a fire in Lebanon and he became overheated in his efforts to help put it out. By accident a bucket of water was poured upon him. This brought on sickness which terminated in tuberculosis. This soon resulted fatally. He died at the old Reagan residence. He was a fine student. He was courteous, handsome, unselfish and manly, and therefore was immensely popular. There never was a young man passed away in Sweetwater Valley whose death was more regretted by his neighbors and schoolmates.

Frank Reagan, the fifth child of J. H. and Mira Reagan, b. July 15, 1851; d. November 30, 1862.

RICHARD FRANCIS SCRUGGS

Was born at Warrensburg, Tenn., February 1, 1834. He died of pneumonia at his residence in Sweetwater on December 28, 1903.

He was the son of Rev. John Scruggs and Theresa Newell Carter Scruggs. They were the parents of fourteen children, of whom R. F. was the —— th. Elder Jno. S. was the second son of Richard and Eliza McMahon Scruggs. He was born in Grayson County, Va., March 14, 1797. He was a graduate of Tusculum College in

Greene County which was founded by Samuel Doak in 1794.

J. and T. N. C. Scruggs were married on September 7, 1824. She was the third daughter of Francis Jackson and Esther Crockett Carter and was a first cousin of the celebrated Davy Crockett. She was born near Newport in Cocke County, October 8, 1806. F. J. C. and E. C. were married on February 16, 17—. F. J. C. was the son of John Carter, one of the first settlers of Hawkins County. He established a store which was conducted under the firm name of Carter and Parker. They were robbed by a band of Cherokee Indians. When the Henderson treaty was made with the Cherokees C. and P. demanded compensation. The lands of Carter's Valley from Cloud Creek to Chimney Top Mountain were granted them, on the payment of a small sum of money. This was advanced by Robert Lucas, who thus became a partner of Carter and Parker. This firm leased their lands to settlers much after the manner of the patrons in the early history of New York.

In 1771 J. C. settled one-half mile north of Elizabethton, Tenn. He was a member of two constitutional conventions of North Carolina. His son, Landon Carter, was prominent in the Tennessee Constitutional Convention of 1796. His grandson was the chairman of the Constitutional Convention of 1834. His great grandson, also named Wm. Bates Carter was an active participant of the Constitutional Convention of 1870. All these men represented the same constituency and the last named Wm. Bates Carter was a Democrat chosen in a strong Republican district. James Robertson, Landon Carter and others laid the foundation of the Watauga settlement which was first mainly in Carter County.

After the death of F. J. C. in 1857, his wife E. C. C., went to Monroe County to reside with her daughter, Theresa N. Scruggs, whose husband John S. had purchased a large body of land on Chestua Creek in Monroe County and had moved there in 1833. She died July 9, 1870, and was buried in the churchyard of the church house erected on the farm of J. S. Here lie also J. S., who died November 11, 1867, his wife T. N. S., d. November 9, 1888, and also seven of his children and many of his grandchildren. J. S. was a preacher, farmer, stock-raiser and slave owner. For many years he was pastor of the Chestua, Mt. Harmony and Madisonville Baptist churches. He made no charge for his services.

R. F. Scruggs, after completing his academical education at Mossy Creek, now Carson and Newman College, became a physician. He obtained his medical diploma from Jefferson Medical College at Philadelphia, Pa. He commenced the practice of medicine in Sweetwater in the year 1855. He occupied the office made vacant by the death of Dr. Parker, who was the first physician coming to Sweetwater. On the 14th of February, 1860, he married Elizabeth Ramsey Heiskell. He erected the residence on Oak Street now occupied by Mrs. Scruggs.

He built up a very large practice for a young physician, previous to the Civil War.

Soon after the war ended he became a partner with his brother-in-law, N. P. Hight, in the mercantile and produce business. N. P. Hight was the husband of Addie Heiskell.

This firm also acquired numerous holdings and lots in the town of Sweetwater. They erected the brick buildings at the corner of Monroe and Depot streets and the brick hotel opposite, now the Hotel Hyatt, and various houses for rent in different parts of the town.

Dr. Scruggs was an extensive druggist as well as physician and sold drugs in the store now occupied by the Sweetwater Pharmacy.

He was most of the time during his business career treasurer of the Sweetwater Masonic Lodge No. 292, from the obtainment of its charter till his death.

He was also administrator of several large estates and was noted for his good judgment in business and the strict honesty and accuracy of his accounts.

Notwithstanding the multiplicity of his business relations, when not necessarily occupied he was a genial and interesting companion and conversationalist. His information was accurate and varied and was by no means confined to his profession. He found time in some way to read many books, managed to get at and understand the main points in them. Anything that touched humanity even outside of his own profession, met with his intelligent and considerate attention. He was consulted by more people about more different subjects than any man in town and his advice was rarely disregarded.

His knowledge of locations and people in this section and their history was little less than phenomenal.

The children of R. F. and E. R. Scruggs were:

One. Martha, b. October 21, 1861; d. in infancy.
Two. Frank Heiskell, b. September 5, 1862; d. July 8, 1895.
Three. John Frederick, b. May 6, 1865.
Four. Daniel Pope, b. June 19, 1867.
Five. Arthur Bruce, b. September 24, 1869.
Six. Susan Newman, b. September 13, 1871; d. November 6, 1890.
Seven. Joseph.
Eight. Katherine, b. August 27, 1876.
Nine. Annie Nelson, b. January 2, 1878.
Ten. Richard Abijah, b. March 10, 1884.

Five. Arthur Bruce, the fourth son of R. F. and married to Annie C., daughter of William and Margaret Edwards Lowry. He was a bookseller and stationer in Sweetwater. He was also editor and proprietor of the Sweetwater News, which began its publication in the year 1886. In 1891 he bought of W. B. Lenoir the Monroe Democrat and published his paper under the name of The Democrat-News until his death in the year 1895.

The children of Frank and Margaret Scruggs were:

Margaret, b. May, 1890; Elizabeth, b. January 25, 1893; Frank H., b. December 3, 1894.

Three. John Frederick, the second son of R. F. and E. R. S., was married to Maggie May Williams, daughter of J. B. and M. T. Williams on June 3, 1891. Their children are: John Henry, b. January 25, 1893; Richard F., b. June 11, 1895; Wm. Thomas, b. September 28, 1903.

Four. Daniel Pope, third son of R. F. and E. R. S. was married to Eva Dulaney Rogers on November 13, 1887. She was born at Blountville, Tenn., July 7, 1867. He is the carrier on rural route No. 2. Their children are:

1. Edgar Browne, b. August 25, 1888; d. ———
2. Richard Francis, b. February 7, 1890; d. ———
3. Ellen Marie, b. November 1, 1891.
4. Louis Eugene, b. January 12, 1894.

5. Lela, b. August 27, 1895; d. ———
6. Bertha Barrow, b. February 19, 1897.
7. Hugh Rogers, b. April 15, 1899; d. ———
8 and 9. Robert Maynard, James Jefferson, b. August 2, 1901; d. ———

Five. Arthur Bruce, the fourth son of of R. F. and E. R. S. married Belle, daughter of David and Laurena Heabler, on November 25, 1890. She was born in West Lodi, O., on April 10, 1871. His business is that of stock trader and joint administrator with his brother, J. F. S., in his father's estate. The children of A. B. and B. Scruggs are: Edith, b. February 6, 1893; Joe Heabler, b. February 24, 1895; Mabel, b. November 19, 1896; d. November 29, 1900; Earnest Carleton, b. January 5, 1901; David Richard, b. March 29, 1906.

Eight. Katherine was born August 27, 1876. She married Henry Hardey, of Tulsa, Ind. Ter., on August 27, 1902. He was born in Knob Noster, Mo., July 17, 1878. Went to Tulsa, Ind. Ter. in 1895. Clerked in a store there seven years. Met there Katherine Scruggs whom he married. They moved to Rocky Ford, Col., in August, 1904, where they now reside. He is a merchant. Their children are: Gordon Stakely, born August 12, 1903; Henry Francis, born September 13, 1906.

Nine. Annie Nelson Scruggs was born January 2, 1888. She married Ross Owen, son of J. F. Owen. He was born February 3, 1869. He is an R. F. D. mail carrier from Erie, Tenn.

JAMES J. SHELDON.

I have several times spoken of the cosmopolitan population of Sweetwater. Of course to make a town where there is no town, the people have to come from somewhere. But in a mere commercial town like Sweetwater was in the beginning, neither a manufacturing or a mining town, depending wholly for its support on the agricultural products around, the population was more varied than usual.

In the early settlement of the place, there came from New York, Mr. and Mrs. James J. Sheldon, Miss Emily Palmer, Mr. H. G. Cooke, Mrs. Helen M. Cooke, Miss

Bland E. Smith, and from Massachusetts Mr. George G. Stillman.

They soon became identified with our people and showed a wonderful adaptability. They had a much greater influence upon our community endeavoring to be one of us, than if they had made themselves conspicuous in criticising our institutions or customs.

First of these to come here were Mr. and Mrs. James J. Sheldon. He was born in Dutchess County, New York, July 4, 1829. He married Miss Mary E. Palmer in 1855. She was born August 24, 1834, in Columbia County, New York. They came to Sweetwater soon after their marriage, probably for the reason that they were related to Mr. Spencer of Fork Creek.

They taught school in 1856, in the old school house near the bend of the creek called the Fine School-house. He was a successful teacher and a versatile man. He was a fine scribe, as the expression went in those days, which was considered of prime importance. Also being a good musician and fond of music, he taught the school children to sing together various simple songs. Up to the time of his coming to this country the note books used in the singing in the churches were printed in what is called the square note system, each note of the tonic scale was of a different shape, which made it somewhat easier for beginners to learn simple music.

He introduced and taught what was called in contradistinction to the other, the round note system, which had before been used for instruments and the pitch depended wholly upon the position of the note.

"Mason's Harp and Carmina Sacra" were two of the books used by him and taught in the neighborhood. All the farm houses around were glad to have the young and sometimes the old people too, to meet and take part in these singings.

The song book published at Madisonville, name not now remembered, square note system, was soon discarded. After teaching several years, he discontinued on account of his health. He was employed in several stores in Sweetwater, mostly as an accountant and bookkeeper. The credit system was in vogue in those days and needed a careful accountant.

He was a member of the Baptist church and was clerk

at the time of his death. In the year 1857 he purchased a lot from I. T. Lenoir on Oak Street. He died in Sweetwater, at his residence January 18, 1868. He was buried at the Daniel Heiskell Cemetery.

Mr. and Mrs. Sheldon had one daughter, who was born January 20, 1856, died December 28, 1868.

CHRISTIAN SHELL.

He was a contemporary of General James H. Reagan and lived on an adjoining place. From the information at hand his children were as follows:

1. Emmaline, m. ——— Phillips; second to ——— Floyd.
2. Paris Montgomery. Lives in Knox County, Tenn.
3. J. Will.
4. Sarah Landonia. Married James Gibbs, U. S. mail agent on the Southern Railway. Their children, two sons, John and Ludlow, and a daughter, Iola, who married ——— Houk, son of L. C. Houk.
5. Ella. Unmarried.
6. James R. Married Mary J. Thomas, February 13, 1879. Died about 1913. They were the parents of twelve children. He was a promoter.
7. Lou Emma. Married Captain John Anderson, of Pond Creek Valley.
8. Victoria. Married Owen Morris, son of H. H. Morris.

GEORGE G. STILLMAN.

It is a tradition in the Stillman family that in the early settlement of Massachusetts, there came three brothers. It was supposed they fled from England on account of political or religious persecutions, and probably for fear of other persecution even after coming to this country they failed or refused to tell their name or history. Therefore they were nick-named Stillman or (Stillmen). This name clung to them so that it was adopted as a surname. One of them was William C. who was the father of George G. about whom this sketch is written.

George G. was born February 9, 1828, in North Egremont, Berkshire County, Massachusetts. He married Cynthia B. Robbins April 8, 1852, at Thomas Stillman's. Ella, their daughter was born March 9, 1853. Mrs. Stillman died soon afterward. Ella, is now a teacher in Massachusetts. Mr. Stillman came South shortly before the Civil War, he visited Mr. James J. Sheldon. He decided to remain here. He was an accurate and natural bookkeeper. His great knowledge of Masonry commended him to the brethren.

In 1861 he was a member of Prof. Wagstaff's Sweetwater Brass Band. The other members were A. M. Dobbins, Wiley Patton, Carter and Crockett Rowan, ——— Monfi, William McClung, S. McKinney Walker and W. C. Browning. It was considered a fine band for that day and time.

Some time in May in the year 1861 this band was employed to go to Hawkins County, Tenn., to a secession rally. Mr. Stillman was with them. The band took supper with Mr. A. Buckner, a brother-in-law of Mrs. Stillman, who was then Miss Julia Craft. They became acquainted. They were married about three months afterwards, on the 27th of August, 1861.

Mr. Stillman was a conscientious Baptist. He was thoroughly posted in many degrees of Masonry, including the Knight Templars. True to his name he was a very prudent man in his conduct during the Civil War and though a Union man, he endeavored to protect the Southern sympathizers, after the Federal occupation during the Civil War. He purchased the property where Mrs. Stillman now lives, across the street from the telephone building. He resided there until the time of his death, which occurred on July 29, 1872.

I take the following from the preamble and resolutions adopted at the August meeting of Lodge 292, F. and A. M.:

* * * * * * "Some years previous to the war our brother G. G. Stillman came among us a stranger. He did not long remain so. His native worth and intelligence were soon known and appreciated and caused him to be recognized as a friend and a brother. He was a pleasant and agreeable companion, kind and affectionate in his family, a true friend, a good and useful cit-

izen, a devoted Christian. He was also a bright and honored member of the fraternity." * * * * * *

These and many other things were truly said by the committee, not in a perfunctory way but because they believed them. The committee were W. B. Lenoir, W. W. Morrison, and A. M. Dobbins.

Julia H. Craft Stillman was born at the old homestead in Sullivan County on October 7, 1840. Her father was ─────── Her grandparents on her father's side were Thomas. A. Craft and Mary Acuff Craft. Her great grandfather was Timothy Acuff. He was a Revolutionary soldier and acquired land from the United States government on account of his services. He was a slave owner.

The mother of Mrs. Stillman was formerly Mary A. Wilson. She was a sister of Anna Wilson, who was the mother of the late John M. Jones, Sweetwater, Tenn. Mrs. Stillman is a noted Sunday-school and church worker, with the vigor of her intellect (now 1915) undimmed.

George Rowan Stillman (named for Samuel J. Rowan) son of G. G. and Julia Stillman was born May 17, 1863. He is a trusted employee of the First National Bank of Chattanooga, with which he has been for the past twenty-nine years.

He married Cora Stallis of Missouri, in October, 1885.

REV. ROBERT SNEAD

Was born in Rockbridge County, Va., April 20, 1801. He came to Sweetwater Valley in 1824. He married Frances Henley soon afterwards. His first recorded purchase of land was from William Dillard in May, 1831. The deed is for eighty acres, east half of the northeast quarter, section 36, township 2, range 1, east. He afterwards acquired other tracts and at the time of his death owned a very large farm on the public road between Philadelphia and Sweetwater. This farm was divided and sold in 1915. Mr. Snead was one of the most versatile men in this section of the country; whatever he was called on to do he always rose to the occasion. He was a brick-mason, farmer, minister of the Gospel, railroad director and capitalist. He was chairman of the committee appointed for the construction of the Cleveland Baptist Church, and his knowledge of building is shown by that church edifice. In the old Sweetwater cemetery in the grave of John Reagan is a brick vault which was erected by Mr. Snead, purely as a matter of accommodation and because no one else understood how to do it. This is the only one constructed in that cemetery. During the time he was minister he officiated at the marriage ceremony of more people than any other minister in the valley or county. He was a fine presiding officer and was moderator during the active term of his life of a great many associations. Whenever he was in a Baptist association he was nearly always called upon to perform that duty. In his sermons he was more logical than eloquent; he appealed to the reason more than the emotions. He and his wife Frances joined the Baptist church of Sweetwater, sometimes called the Cleveland church, on the fourth Saturday in July, 1826. He was clerk of that church during the years 1831 and 1832. He was ordained by that church to preach the Gospel on the fourth Saturday of February, 1833. He was considered an authority, in the Sweetwater association on Baptist doctrine and parliamentary ruling. He probably had more influence with the churches of Sweetwater Association than any one belonging to it. He, like Elder Eli Cleveland, never charged or accepted anything for his pastoral services; not on account of any conscientious scruples in the matter, but because he thought they could use the money more judiciously in other ways.

He was one of the best and most successful farmers in our valley. In a field across the railway from his residence in 1857, he raised more than forty-one bushels of wheat to the acre; this he did without the use of any fertilizer except such as came from his own barnyard.

He served two terms as director of the East Tennessee and Georgia Railroad.

He moved to Knoxville from his farm, in November, 1874, where he resided until his death on March 29, 1878, and was buried in old Sweetwater cemetery.

During the Civil War he was considered a Union man

but was opposed to any discussion of it, or prayers for either combatant in church meetings, and rarely could he be induced to express an opinion about the war in private conversation. This is by no means strange, as he had two sons in the Confederate army and one in the Federal.

The children of his first marriage were as follows:
1. Martha A., born August 22, 1825. Died 1906.
2. William E., born December 11, 1827. Died August 28, 1875.
3. Elizabeth, born ——————— Died July, 1875.
4. Virginia A., born July 17, 1834. Died ———
5. Mary L., born February 23, 1839. Died ———
6. Lilburn, born March 22, 1841. Died ———
7. Thomas E., born October 26, 1843.

Martha A., married Jacob Kimbrough in 1846 and died at Mesquite, Texas. J. C. Kimbrough was a talented member of the Baptist church; he was a farmer and lived near Madisonville, Tenn. Their children were Robert, Jacob and Spencer, the two latter dying in early manhood. Robert moved to Mesquite, Texas, when a young man. He died in 1906 at about 45 years of age. In business he was quite successful; was a merchant, a president of two banks and had large land holdings.

William E. Snead was married to Nancy Prater Johnston, daughter of Josiah K. Johnston. He joined the Confederate army soon after commencement of hostilities. He held the rank of major in the 43rd Tennessee volunteer infantry, serving through the entire war period. After the war he was accountant and salesman for the firm of Hight and Scruggs until incapacitated by disease. He had one son, William Prater Snead, who was born December 31, 1852, and resides on Fork Creek.

3. Elizabeth married Robert Cleveland on June 4, 1840. For her family history (see Presley Cleveland).

Virginia A. married Richard Jarnagin, September 29, 1852. They settled at Clinton, Anderson County, Tenn. She died there and was buried at that place. Their children were:
(1) Minnie, married ——————— Coward.
(2) Richard.
(3) W. J., who lives at Coal Creek, Tenn.

4. Mary L., married A. S. Worrell, December 14, 1859,

who was a Baptist minister. She died in Minneapolis, Minn., 1903. Their children were:
(1) Martha.
(2) Mary.
(3) Albert.

Two daughters are married: married names and post-offices not known.

6. Lilburn, enlisted in the Federal army at the age of 20. He was captain of Co. ——, —— regiment, Tennessee volunteer infantry. He was called the "boy captain." He died at Nashville, Tenn., of wounds received at the Battle of Shiloh.

7. Thomas E. served in the Confederate army from August, 1861 to April 23, 1863, in Co. G, —— regiment Tennessee volunteers.

He married Anne E. Patton, daughter of Francis A. and Amanda A. Patton on August 27, 1863. His wife, Anne Patton was born January 16, 1844, in Monroe County, Tenn. For fifteen years or more after he married Thomas E. Snead was a farmer in Monroe County, going west after that and living in Texas, Indian Territory, Missouri and Washington. In the year 1898 he settled at Hinsdale, Mont., which is now (1915) his present residence. Their children are:

Robert Snead, born December 20, 1864.

Fannie A. McLean, born —— 16, 1867. Post-office, Kerman, Cal.

Dick T., born December 31, 1869. Post-office, Hinsdale, Mont.

Minta L. Wilson, born August 10, 1874.

Charles H., born July 19, 1871.

Addie E., born April 20, 1877.

Thomas, born September 6, 1879. Post-office, Hinsdale, Mont.

Fannie A., married Edwin McLean in 1894.

Dick T., married Annie M. Riley in 1904.

Minta L., married Frank Wilson in 1891. Post-office, Placerville, Cal.

Charles H., married Ida Mooney in 1892. Post-office, Colfax, Wash.

Addie E., married Edward Kelso in 1896. Post-office, Albion, Wash.

Thomas B., married Nettie Ballke in 1906. Post-office, Hinsdale, Mont.

* * * * * *

Robert Snead's second wife was Samantha Ann McReynolds, to whom he was married on the 17th of September, 1852. She was born in Tazewell, Tenn., April 28, 1815. She died at Sweetwater, Tenn., January 12, 1897, and was buried in the old Sweetwater cemetery. They resided at the Snead farm, near Sweetwater, after their marriage, until they moved to Knoxville, in 1874. They had one daughter, Laura F., born December 20, 1857, who married Sam Epps Young, a Knoxville lawyer, September 5, 1878. Their children are:
1. Stella, who married Henry T. Boyd of Sweetwater, on June 10, 1903. Their children are Sam Young Boyd and Frances Boyd.
2. Robert Snead, born ─── He was educated at the University of Tennessee and afterwards studied law under his father, Colonel S. E. Young. He located in Knoxville in ─── He married Lillian, daughter of Hon. H. B. Lindsay, on October 14, 1908. Their children are: Elizabeth, Robert and Lindsay.
3. Frances.
4. Anna.
5. Sam Epps. Lawyer in Knoxville, Tenn.

COLONEL SAM EPPS YOUNG

Was born near Clinton, Tenn., the son of the Rev. J. H. Young, a Methodist minister, and a nephew of Judge D. K. Young, an eminent lawyer and jurist, of Anderson County. He attended the University of Tennessee, and graduated there in 1878. He was captain of Co. B in the military department there the year of his graduation. He studied law under ─── at ─── He was admitted to the bar in ─── and began the practice of law at Knoxville. He came to Sweetwater in 1880 and opened an office here. However, in the earlier part of his career, a large part of his practice was in the mountain counties of Morgan, Scott, Fentress and Cumberland. There he made quite a reputation as a jury lawyer, which, before a great while extended to the counties around where he resided. He was not only a successful jury lawyer but I heard Judge T. M. McConnell say he was one of the best chancery lawyers that practised before his bar. He cultivated most successfully a large farm of more than 1,000 acres. Notwithstanding his extensive law practice in other counties he found time to operate it. It was while on his way to his farm June 22, 1914, that he collapsed, while in his buggy, from heart failure.

While a man of a most social disposition, he never sought office though he was often spoken of as a candidate for various positions. Though a strong party man he rarely attended political meetings or conventions. He was a member of the M. E. Church, South, and when not absent in the practice of his profession, nearly always attended Sunday-school and often made interesting talks, which he had the ability to do without extensive preparation. Some of the best speeches I have heard him make were when he was called upon unexpectedly to him. He was a member of the Sweetwater Masonic Lodge. He was always prominent in whatever body or assembly he attended.

General John Crawford Vaughn.

In the estimation of most persons who know his history, it might well be said that he was Sweetwater's most distinguished citizen. His varied career, his chivalry, commanding presence, and magnetic personality would make him the hero of the novelist as well as a favorite character of the historian.

A painting of him hangs in the H. M. Cooke Memorial Library.

He was in turn captain in the Mexican War, gold seeker in California, high sheriff of Monroe County. Hotel man, brigadier general in the C. S. A., broker in New York, speaker of the Senate in Tennessee and extensive planter in Georgia.

He was the son of James Vaughn and Mary Jane Crawford Vaughn. He was born at Madisonville, February 24, 1824. He married Nancy Ann Boyd in 1847 at Mt. Vernon, Tenn. She died in New York City, November 13, 1869.

Mr. Ross Young, who was a soldier in the Mexican War, also a Confederate soldier in the Civil War, says that Jno. C. Vaughn was captain of Co. C, 5th Reg. of Tennessee volunteer infantry in the Mexican War, commanded by Colonel McClellan. Ross Young was a private in Co. F and volunteered from Maryville, Blount County, Tenn.

In a letter written from San Juan, dated February 12, 1848, to E. E. Griffith, Esq., and published in the Madisonville Democrat of April 15, 1909, we make the following extracts:

"I will write you a letter this morning. I got up this morning with the sun, had my breakfast and put on a light colored shirt. Then I read several chapters in the Bible, which I do nearly every day. Then I seated myself by the side of a long dining table which Santa Anna used before the Yankees entered Vera Cruz and drove him from this place. Lieut. Brown and I use it to write on during the day and at night we use it to sleep on, and I think it a great thing in the sleeping line.

* * * * We are all far from home and all that is dear to us, but there is not the same number of men in Mexico that enjoy themselves better than the gallant company from Monroe does. We all love each other. We can think of home but that is all. We live in hope of seeing you all again, but we may not. There may not be one-fourth of us live to see Tennessee again. To look around at Companies that came here one hundred strong and now number only forty and none killed in battle, and some that number only twenty-five when, six months ago, they numbered one hundred twenty-five; this is enough to make us all doubtful of our lives. We wish the prayers of our friends at home." (I have not the date at hand to know when the company returned to Monroe County.)

Being of an adventurous disposition in 1850 he went to California by the New York and Panama route. A letter from J. C. Vaughn and E. C. Harris from Panama City June 4, 1850, which appeared in the Athens Post July 19, 1850, contains some very interesting data; the more so on account of the completion of the isthmus canal and the exposition celebrating the event in San Francisco, Cal.

Some time since a letter appeared in The Sweetwater Telephone from Tyler Heiskell to his father, William Heiskell, recounting the dangers and expense of a trip across the plains to California. From what these reports say there seems to have been little choice as to the two routes. Greater personal danger from Indians by the plains route, and far greater danger from disease by the Panama route. We deem the extracts below very interesting:

"We left Chagres, on the 24th of May in canoes for Cruces up the Chagres river, a distance of 80 miles. These canoes being large enough to accommodate from 5 to 10 passengers, owned and made by the natives generally for which we paid $13.00 each (finding ourselves). The first night at 10 o'clock P. M. we hauled up for the night where we found something similar to a shack of an American camping ground, only about one-third as large, which was covered with canvas in place of boards, where we found something in the way of refreshments.

A cup of coffee for .05c, a small piece of bread for .10c. and a small apple pie for three dimes; and we were also accommodated with berths upon the ground for two dimes; each furnishing his own blanket. We engaged passage to Cruces, though from the fact that our yawls or canoes could not navigate further than Gorgono, on account of shallow water, we were compelled to stop at the last named place. We arrived at Gorgono on the 25th. of May, where we found about four hundred small ranches scattered about in every direction, inhabited by Spaniards and Natives, with one American house whose sign was the Panama Railroad Hotel, where a meal could be had for an Isthmus Dollar (eight dimes) and lodging on the floor for five dimes, finding your own blankets; we tarried here for one night only. On the 27th, we hired Natives to pack our baggage across for $8.00 per hundred on mules and their own backs, a distance called by inhabitants twenty-five miles. After two days we arrived at the great city of Panama, situated on the coast of the Pacific on a small point of land which extends far out into Panama Bay, distinguished principally for being a great port of entrance, for being surrounded by a huge stone wall, for its numerous number of Catholic Cathedrals, whose tall spires loom up to the clouds in really majestic splendor, for its mixed population of Spanish and Native (Negro), for the universal want of energy amongst its ignorant and stupid inhabitants, and distinguished generally for being one of the most completely worn out and decayed cities this side of Hindoostan.

Though Monte and Faro banks flourish here while almost every thing else is held in low repute except commercial operations, which is a source of grand speculation here, and in confirmation of this we will give you an instance; on our arrival here we found that tickets on steamers could not be had for less than $400.00 in the steerage, and from six to nine hundred dollars in the cabin to San Francisco, while the same tickets were purchased in New York from two to four hundred dollars each, and held, offered, and sold here on speculation, at those advances, governed entirely by the number of emigrants here, waiting transportation to the much sought 'El Dorado.'

Those prices are eagerly given here, while the number and names of the steamers now plying between this place and San Francisco are as follows: The California, Oregon, Panama, Tennessee, Carolina, Unicorn, Gold Hunter, Sarah Sands, Isthmus and Columbus, 'making in all ten, which leave this port universally crowded, even at those extravagant prices, and there are soon expected here via Cape Horn, to go on the same route, the steamers New Orleans, New World, Northerner, West Point, William G. Pease, Republic and Duncan C.

Pell, which will complete the entire number of seventeen steamships.' In discussing the case of going from East Tennessee to San Francisco without experiencing any delays which can seldom be avoided, the cheapest possible taking sail vessel would be $350.00 and to take steamer from New Orleans to San Francisco it would cost $365.00 on deck and in the cabin $750.00, never less, and a chance for it to be higher.

Taking these statements as correct, all who are thinking of the perilous adventure can now make up their minds as to the amount they would feel safe in leaving home with, knowing at the same time that if it should fall short that it would be where they would be surrounded by the mongrel population of the whole earth. This is the amount, to say nothing of the expenses up the Sacramento river to Sacramento City, a distance of 125 miles and then some 80 miles by land out into the diggings. * * * *

Without a through ticket a person stands no chance for a passage aboard a steamer from this port, as they are always filled to a disagreeable number by persons owning through tickets or those who have the funds to pay a heavy advance on second-handed tickets, and we have seen them sold during our stay here second-handed for from six to eleven hundred dollars, and while on this subject we would remark, that the shaving and swindling system is carried on here to scientific perfection, at the expense of the poor emigrants from the states, and the great wheel is turned, not by foreigners, but by American citizens.

This city numbers a population of about ten thousand, inclusive, within and without the walls, with at present a transient population of about three thousand, principally emigrants. The major portion of its inhabitants are Spaniards, one-third we suppose are natives, as black as the ace of spades, though all speak universally the Spanish language, which language we are in a fair way to learn 'Pocotiempo.'

This city is surrounded by the most sublime and majestic natural scenery upon which the eye of curiosity ever rested, almost entirely surrounded by Panama Bay, completely decorated with little island mountains, whose beautifully green peaked tops pierce the sullen and heavy clouds, which almost constantly enshroud them at this season; while the approach by land is similarly adorned with here and there, small round capped summits, intervening occasionally beautiful narrow and level valleys, which appear to groan under the abundance of the rich tropical fruits of the forest, which are to be seen and obtained at all seasons, from the luscious Isthmus peach through the innumerable varieties of tropical fruits down to the delicious pineapple, which, in some degree, perfume the air with their rich fragrance.

* * * * We cannot conclude without giving a few brief statements relative to the incidents connected with our two days' travel across the Isthmus. From Gorgono to this place we were never out of sight at one time of the vast continued train of mules and natives packing baggage to and from this city, during which time we very frequently met with numbers of American ladies dressed entirely in gentlemen's attire and universally riding astride, which odd custom they are compelled to adopt in order to travel at all, except they walk, as there is no such thing here as a vehicle of any sort, and during our travel across and the eight days we have been here, amongst all the travelling we have seen but bare one side saddle.

We arrived at this city on the 28th of May, where we have remained for some eight days, awaiting the published day for the sailing of the ship Cacholot, aboard of which we have engaged our passage to San Francisco. We have purchased our tickets for which we paid

$150.00 each in the steerage and she positively sails tomorrow, the 5th of this inst., which port she promises to make in thirty-five or forty days.

Here we saw numerous 'East Tennesseeans, who all meet like endeared relatives and amongst the many we have had the pleasure of meeting with. and listening to a very able sermon delivered by one Mr. Horn, from Knoxville, who has formerly resided in Athens, E. Tenn.'

In the Athens Post of Dec. 20th, 1850, we find this editorial reference: 'we received last week the Polynesian of Sat., July 20th, printed at Honolulu, a town on one of the Sandwich Islands. It was sent by Mr. E. C. Harris, who belonged to the company that started to California from this country some time since. The ship on which they embarked at Panama (June 5th), put into Honolulu on account of stress of weather and was expected to set sail again in a few days."

It would seem they must have been disappointed in reaching San Francisco at the expected time—thirty-five or forty days. For sailing from Panama on June 5th, they were still at Honolulu on July 20th. If I am not mistaken it is about 2,800 miles from Honolulu to San Francisco. What time General Vaughn reached San Francisco and how long he remained in California I have not the information at hand, however think he did not succeed in obtaining very much gold, or was not among the lucky prospectors.

In the files of the Athens Post in my possession I do not find any other letters from either Harris or Vaughn, but I lack considerably in having the papers for the year 1850-1. In about 1854, General Vaughn built a hotel in Sweetwater in which was a store-house on the site now occupied by the Hyatt Hotel. William H. Taylor and Joseph Boyd, brother-in-law of General Vaughn, were of the first that did business in that store-house. I think others too at different times sold goods there. General Vaughn was elected sheriff in 1859. I do not remember whether this was his first or second term.

When the Civil War came up he raised the first company in Monroe County, of which he became captain, that with other companies formed the first regiment raised in Tennessee for the Southern Confederacy. He was elected colonel of this regiment. Although this was the first regiment raised in the state, it was the third mustered in by the Confederacy at Lynchburg, Va. Owing to a railroad accident between Knoxville and Lynchburg they were delayed and two other regiments, I think Turney's and Hatton's, got ahead of them. Thus

Vaughn's regiment instead of being the first as it should have been became the 3rd Tennessee Regiment, Volunteer Infantry.

Colonel Vaughn's command captured the first pieces of artillery taken in the war at the bridge in Romney, Va., June, 1861. He was engaged in numerous battles in many parts of the Confederacy during the Civil War from the first Battle of Manassas until the end in 1865 when he was promoted to the rank of brigadier general.

General Vaughn was in command of the cavalry escorting President Davis to Washington, Ga., and was the last organized body of cavalry of the C. S. A. to surrender.

A part of the treasure belonging to the Confederacy was divided among his soldiers. Daughters of the Confederacy here at Sweetwater have considerable of General Vaughn's war history. It is very voluminous. I give the following from a letter by Mrs. Lua Nixon, now deceased of 733 Peachtree Street, Atlanta, Ga., dated July 9, 1913. Mrs. General Jno. C. Vaughn, her father-in-law, James C. Vaughn and three daughters, Margaret, Lua and Mary, were arrested (at their home in Sweetwater) June, 1864, by order of General Sherman. The original order is in possession of Mrs. Nixon and reads as follows:

"Headquarters Military division of the Mississippi, Nashville, Tenn., July 27th, 1854. Special order No. 91. It appearing to the satisfaction of the Maj. Gen. commanding that the following named persons are implicated in corresponding with the enemy beyond our lines, it is hereby ordered that they be sent to Jeffersonville, Ind., there to remain in the care of the Provost Marshal under Military surveillance during the continuance of the present war, the quarter master department will furnish the transportation necessary to carry out this order. By order of Maj. Gen. Sherman. M. Rochester, assistant adjutant general."

The same day the family of Judge T. Nixon VanDyke were arrested and joined General Vaughn's family. They were taken to Nashville in a box car, the prisoners Mrs. Vaughn and Mrs. VanDyke, and the seven children were confined in one small room for days awaiting their orders. During the time of their confinement every effort was being put forth by influential Union friends and friends in the North, through Governor

Johnson (then military governor) of Tennessee and President Lincoln to have the order changed. Judge VanDyke's family were allowed to give bond and they were released but the original order was carried out as to General Vaughn's family. Several months later General Vaughn sent scouts to arrest the family of a Federal general in Kentucky and held them as hostages till arrangements were made for exchange. Everywhere the family were held as prisoners in Louisville, Cincinnati and Baltimore, they found friends and sympathizers with the Confederacy who gave them aid and alleviated the condition of their confinement. Later the family were confined in Fortress Monroe awaiting exchange. President Davis made every arrangement that General Vaughn's family be received and cared for by the exchange commissioners Major Ould, and Captain Hatch, and also in Richmond until joined by General Vaughn.

After the Civil War General Vaughn, following the example of the Inmans and R. T. Wilson, formerly of Loudon, and many other East Tennesseans moved to New York City to go into business. Some of the East Tennesseans who went there were eminently successful, and became very wealthy; but General Vaughn was more fitted for work in the open with the musket and the sword, than to contend for commercial supremacy among the trained business men of Wall Street; he knew nothing of their methods.

Soon after the death of his wife in 1869, he returned to Tennessee. Being very popular he engaged in politics. He received the democratic nomination for senator in 1871 from the Seventh Senatorial District: comprising the counties of Meigs, McMinn, Polk and Monroe. He was elected by a large majority and became senator from this district in the Thirty-seventh General Assembly of the state, which began its session in Nashville, October 1, 1871. Although he had never been legislator before he was elected speaker of the senate. He probably could have gotten almost any office he sought in the political field but about this time he was married a second time to Miss Florence Jones, of Thomasville, Ga., and settled there. He preferred the quiet of a planter's life to the scramble for office.

As a military commander his bravery was unquestioned, he was almost too fearless. He preferred to lead rather than direct. He considered it was his business to fight the enemy wherever he met them. General Forrest's motto was "To get there first with the most men." General Vaughn did not seem to regard numbers; he rarely waited to see whether he or the enemy were the more numerous and the way he found out whether he could whip them or not was to fight.

In the various offices and positions he held he was actuated by a high sense of duty and love of his country and his fellowman. Of him it might be said slightly changing the phraseology of a Confederate commander, "he seen his duty and he done his damndest." He, himself, was modest and would have been far from saying anything of the kind. He was intensely reverent in his turn of mind as shown by his letters from Mexico and during the Civil War.

He was a member of the Cumberland Presbyterian Church, but toward the last of his life he belonged to the Methodist Episcopal Church, South. He was one of the few born leaders of men. He never had the slightest trouble in arresting a criminal, or being obeyed by those under him.

Before he returned from the Civil War many rough characters who wanted to make themselves conspicuous made their threats of what they would do if he ever came in their neighborhoods. After he returned, he having heard of these threats, seemed to take pleasure in meeting these very fellows alone, and probably unarmed. He was never insulted and the very ones who had threatened him were the first ones to welcome him. They probably voted for him when he ran for office.

These Jacksonian qualities of the eagle eye and dauntless personality overawed them. They forgot he was the man they had started out to humiliate. The children of General and Nancy Vaughn were:

Margaret, b. 1848. Died in 1873. Married Timothy Gibson, of Athens, Tenn., at Thomasville, Ga., September, 1866. They then lived four years in Bainbridge, Ga., coming back to Athens, Tenn., in 1871. He was born in Gerard County, Ky., April 30, 1834. Was one of a family of fifteen children, he being the seventh.

His father, the Rev. Elias Gibson, came to Columbus, on the Hiwassee River in 1844. Margaret and Timothy Gibson had one child, Mary Lua, who was born at Bainbridge, Ga., on December 5, 1867. She married the Hon. W. B. Miller, at Athens, Tenn., who is a noted lawyer of Chattanooga, residing on Lookout Mountain. They are the parents of four children, two living and two dead; the living (1916) are Burkett Miller, practising law in Chattanooga, and Vaughn Miller, studying law at Harvard College.

The second daughter of General Vaughn was Lua, who married W. M. Nixon, formerly of Ohio. They resided in Athens, Tenn., until 1895, when they moved to Atlanta, Ga. He is president of the Atlanta Woolen Mills. Their son, Vaughn, was born September 14, 1878. Mrs. Nixon died December 23, 1914.

Mary Vaughn was born March 6, 1855. She married Frank B. McElwee of McMinn County. He was born in Meigs County on March 12, 1844. He was the son of Thomas B. McElwee. He was a manufacturer of cotton yarns. He resides (1915) in California—postoffice, Stockton. Mrs. McElwee died at Athens, Tenn., on July 30, 1891. Their children were:

1. Lua, born February 16, 1878.
2. Florence, b. March 31, 1879. Died March 5, 1903.
3. Mattie, b. October 16, 1880; d. February 5, 1904.
4. Mary, b. August 25, 1885.
5. Frank, b. April 4, 1882.
6. Vaughn, b. October 6, 1883. He is a civil engineer at Los Angeles, and is unmarried.
7. Thomas, b. June 19, 1888. Married Martha Martinke, at Los Angeles January, 1915.

1. Lua McElwee married Charles D. Chandler, of Rockford, Tenn., December 28, 1898, now (1915) a merchant at Maryville. One daughter, Margaret McElwee Chandler, b. January 30, 1901.

3. Mattie McElwee married John L. Anderson January, 1898. Their children are:
Mildred M., b. March, 1899.
Larnard, b. November, 1900.
Thomas, b. May, 1903.

5. Frank McElwee is in the real estate business at San Diego, Cal.

4. Mary McElwee married C. P. Griggs, of Stockton, Cal., on October 20, 1906. He died March 6, 1913. She lives at Manteca, Cal. They had one daughter, Mamie, b. July 12, 1907.

General Vaughn's second wife was Florence Jones, of Thomasville, Ga., whom he married in 1871. One daughter, Mrs. E. A. Armand. Mrs. Florence Vaughn died at Savannah, Ga., in 1890.

General Vaughn died on plantation near Thomasville, Ga., on ———, 187—.

THOMAS L. UPTON.

Three brothers, William A.. Thomas L., and Joseph Upton, came from Blount to Monroe County. William A. settled on Four Mile Branch, Dr. Joseph Upton in Madisonville, and Thomas L. in Sweetwater Valley. The latter resided in the old Sliger house where I. T. Lenoir afterwards lived. He moved from there to what was afterwards known as the Upton place on Pond Creek, one mile from the Cumberland Presbyterian camp ground.

On the 24th of February, 1854, he conveyed to I. T. Lenoir, for the consideration of $2,000, the northwest quarter of section 11, township 3, range 1, east, to which deed Jno. C. Vaughn and N. W. Haun were the subscribing witnesses. Thomas Upton's wife was Anne Yearout. Their children were:

1. Bettie; 2. Thomas L.; 3. William A., and 4. Nancy.

Bettie married James Blair, who was a physician in Sweetwater in the first beginning of the town. They had several children, number not known to me, but the oldest one was named Annie, and younger than she were twin girls, one named Inez. About the beginning of the Civil War he moved to Corsicana, and then to Henderson, Rusk County, Texas.

William A. married Mrs. Ballard of Pond Creek, who was the daughter of Reps Jones. Some time in the eighties she came to Sweetwater and he went to Texas. For some time she was proprietress of the Upton Inn, now the Hyatt Hotel. Their children were: Byrd, Thomas, William and Mamie.

Nancy Upton, fourth child of Thomas L. and Anne Upton, married Robert, son of J. D. Jones (whom see).

David Caldwell married ——— Yearout. He was a farmer and lived on a farm adjoining Thomas Upton. They had one daughter, Bettie, who married Charles H. Jones, son of Reps Jones. Helen Graham, whose mother was also a Yearout, resided with Mr. Caldwell. She married Charles Cannon of Sweetwater (whom see).

HON. JOSEPH WALKER.

He was the third son and sixth child of Joseph and Mary Howard Walker, who were married in 1797. Joseph Walker, Sr., moved to this county perhaps in the late twenties and settled in Fork Creek Valley, the old homestead being on the west side of the creek in the meadow between what is now the Vineyard farm and the old Kile place. Here they reared a large family, one of their children dying in childhood. The children were:

1. Elizabeth Caroline, m. Nicholas Vineyard.
2. Caswell Lincoln, moved to Georgia.
3. David Perkins, was a farmer living in Fork Creek Valley.
4. Nancy, m. James Harvey Johnston. They lived on a farm, now the Howard place, three miles southeast of Sweetwater.
5. Sarah, m. Cunningham.
6. Joseph, b. in Grainger County, September 10, 1813.
7. Nicholas Grant.
8. John Horn, d. on the plains en route to California, August 22, 1849.
9. Stirling Creed, d. when a child.
10. Mary Anna, m. Colonel John A. Rowan.

The family largely settled about the father's home and at one time the sons and sons-in-law owned contiguous farms from Christiansburg church to the Davy Walker farm near Glenloch.

Joseph, the sixth child of Mary and Joseph Walker, Sr., was three times married.

First to Caroline Cleveland, daughter of Rev. Eli Cleveland on March 1, 1838, Robert Snead, M. G. She died August 28, 1840.

Second, he married on July 22, 1845, Elizabeth Jane Prater, R. Snead, M. G. She died on January 14, 1846.

Third, he married Lodusky Jones, the sister of Joseph D. and Jesse Jones, on February 2, 1848, the Rev. R. Snead again officiating. Her death occurred on September 25, 1875.

Mr. Walker was a member of the Baptist church and of the F. A. Masons. Like a great many of the old line whigs he was a Union man and opposed to secession until the state voted to secede and then he cast his lot with the state. In August, 1861, he was elected representative from Monroe County to the General Assembly, and was a member of Governor Harris' Legislature at the time it left Nashville, because of the occupation of that part of the state by Federal troops. Mr. Walker was noted in his community for the generous help to young men starting for themselves in life. A few years ago when Squire William Sample died, in tribute to his memory, his son wrote how his father's early start in life had been due to Mr. Walker's help, in tools, farming implements and opportunities secured by the latter's aid.

Joseph Walker left four daughters, all children of his last wife. These daughters have all been teachers.

(1) Mary Caroline, m. J. Harrison Lowry August 16, 1871. They lived at the old homestead on Fork Creek until 1882 when they came to Sweetwater. He has been a merchant, traveling man and recorder of Sweetwater in turn. He is a Presbyterian and she a Baptist. Mrs. Lowry has been a teacher in the public schools of Sweetwater since 1895 and still is in 1916. J. Harrison Lowry died on September 25, 1916. Their children are:

Carl Jones, b. January 29, 1875; m. Helen Gardner, of Charleston, S. C., October 1, 1905. They have one son, Carl J., Jr., b. September 5, 1907. Carl J., Sr., is now (1916) an accountant in the railway office at Hattiesburg, Miss.

Cleveland Morton, b. October 31, 1881; m. Schiller Ferguson in 1908. He is a railway clerk at Hattiesburg, Miss.

Helen, is a music teacher.

Emmett Ramsey, b. April 11, 1885. is a railway clerk

at Meridian, Miss. He married Pearl Ten, of Mobile, Miss., on January 29, 1913.

(2) Elizabeth Jane, second daughter of Joseph and Lodusky Walker, was born on Fork Creek. She taught in country, near Philadelphia, until she went to Chicago in 1882. She graduated in Colonel Francis A. Parker's Cook County Normal. She then taught twenty-four years in the public schools of Chicago, where she now (1916) lives.

(3) Emma Alice, was born in Fork Creek Valley. She was teacher at Dallas, Texas, from 1882 until June 1, 1904, when she married Colonel Joseph F. Swords. He resides at Dallas.

(4) Laura Eugenia, b. on Fork Creek. She moved to Dallas, Texas, where she taught some years in the city schools. She is now (1916), and has been for ten years, Sunday-school visitor and pastor's assistant in the First Baptist Church of Dallas, of which the Rev. George Truett is pastor.

S. Y. B. WILLIAMS.

Information not known to the writer was obtained mostly from Taylor Williams at Chattanooga, Tenn.

Subject of this sketch was born in Madisonville, Tenn., March 30, 1830. His father was William Williams of Madisonville, one of the first settlers of that town. His mother was Polly Cline, a cousin of Jacob Cline who lived near Loudon, Tenn.

When but a boy he went to Reagans and clerked for J. A. and C. W. Coffin.

When Sweetwater began to be a town, this store was moved here, and he became a partner of J. A. Coffin. At different times he was in partnership with J. A. Wright, A. C. Humphreys, W. H. Taylor.

During the Civil War he purchased from James A. Wright a farm one and a half miles from Sweetwater, now the Kilpatrick farm, which he afterwards sold to Isaac Benson. During the latter part of the Civil War he acted as agent for the East Tennessee and Georgia Railroad at Sweetwater.

After the Civil War he went to Knoxville and was

chief clerk of the East Tennessee and Georgia Railroad; after the consolidation of this road with the East Tennessee and Virginia Railroad, he was sent to Bristol in the same capacity. Later he was made general agent, which place he filled for nearly twenty years. After he left Bristol and the railroad employment he went to Chattanooga and engaged in wholesale and retail coal business; this he carried on there until his death, which occurred January 19, 1908. He was buried in Forest Hill Cemetery.

He was a member of the Presbyterian church and a Mason. He was universally popular and was a fine business man. He did much in the early days to build up the trade of Sweetwater. He was a liberal giver to all benevolent purposes.

He was twice married, first to Mary L. Jones, daughter of J. D. Jones, of Philadelphia, on October 30, 1856. She lived only a few years. They had one son, Charles Williams, who died when a young man.

His second wife was Barbara Bogart, daughter of Solomon Bogart, also of Philadelphia. They were married in February, 1860. She died July 22, 1866, at the age of 29 years and 9 months. She was the mother of three children who all died in infancy.

J. W. D. WILLIAMS

Was born at Madisonville, January 9, 1841. His father was William Williams. His mother was Sarah Steele of Madisonville. He was therefore a half brother to S. Y. B. Williams. He went to Sweetwater at the close of the Civil War, entered the produce business with William Calfee.

He married Florence Stowe, granddaughter of Thornton C. Goddard. He moved to Knoxville afterwards and was in the railroad business. He died in Chattanooga December, 1910. Their living children are: Lillian (Mrs. Albert Welcker), St. Elmo; McChesney Williams, Chattanooga; James, also Chattanooga, and Ruby.

The Yearwoods.

There are families some members of which from generation to generation are leading and distinguished men renowned alike in war and peace; who tower above the great majority of their fellow citizens through long periods. Such were the Lees of Virginia, the Harrisons of Virginia, Illinois and Indiana, and the Adams of Massachusetts. There are certain individuals of families that stand alone or who are distinguished far above any of the name, whose parentage gave no promise of renown and whose name in a measure died with them. Of such were Abraham Lincoln and Patrick Henry.

There are others called in England the great middle class. They are well educated, industrious, thrifty and hospitable. They are law abiding citizens, well enough to do to practise the amenities and courtesies of civilized life, brave and patriotic enough to answer to the call of their country when menaced by foes foreign or domestic. These have been the backbone and bulwarks of our states and nation. They may not furnish presidents and governors in times of peace, nor generals in war times, but in war they are the men behind the guns and in peace stand for law and order, morality and education. Such a family have been the Yearwoods. Some of them came here in colonial times. It is but natural that long residence and ancestral traditions should intensify a love for home and country. The native, other things being equal, is more patriotic and has a greater desire for the prosperity of his state than a late arrival from the fatherland whether it is Italy, Germany or Russia. Being educated here he better understands the genius of our government. The colonists mostly came from England, they of course spoke the English language and their customs and laws were taken therefrom. Therefore an English immigrant actuated by a love of freedom was almost one of us before he arrived here. For these reasons we feel it not inapt to speak of the ancestors of the Yearwoods that came to Sweetwater Valley.

Wm. Yearwood, whom we call the first, that is the first who settled in this country of the Yearwood family, came from England. The approximate date even is not known but likely somewhere from 1730 to 1740 and made his home in Charleston, S. C. He there reared a family. He lived to be 90 years of age. This was remarkable as at that time Charleston and the country round were very much subject to yellow and miasmatic fevers which often proved fatal.

He was an extremely expert fencing master and taught the youth of his city that art. To know how to use the sword was part of a liberal education. It was a day when an insult was wiped out with blood on the field of honor. To fight a duel was not contrary to law and many a one was fought with swords as weapons.

When the Revolutionary began Wm. Yearwood, the I, was likely of too advanced an age to stand hardships of a campaign, or from his profession he would have become a soldier. No mention is made of his enlisting.

However his son, Wm. Yearwood, whom for convenience we will call the II, was a member of Captain Wm. Alexander's company and served under General Wm. Sumpter during the Revolutionary War. He was wounded in the arm at the Battle of Ramsours Mill Pond and Mrs. Ramsour cut the bullet out with her husband's razor. He was the ancestor of Wm. Yearwood who lived in Sweetwater Valley.

WM. YEARWOOD, III.

This Wm. Yearwood was born in Charleston, S. C., on January 8, 1780. He had three brothers and two sisters. He was educated and grew to manhood in Charleston. He volunteered in the war of 1812. He was in Captain Sublett's company in a regiment led by Colonel Wm. Henderson and served under General Jackson. He was in service all through the war and when it ended was honorably discharged. At the age of 25 he married at Charleston. His wife lived only a few years, dying in 1818. One son, Elijah, was born April 13, 1807. Not a great while after her death he married Martha Neely on January 24, 1809. She was born October 24, 1789. She was the daughter of John and Martha Dickson Neely. He (Neely) was 1st lieutenant under General Nathaniel Greene in the

Revolutionary War. He was wounded at the Battle of Eutaw Springs and was lamed for life. Wm. Yearwood soon after his second marriage moved to Buncombe County, N. C., remaining there for a few years. From there he went to Dutch Bottoms on the French Broad River in Cocke County, Tenn. In 1814 he bought a farm in Rutherford County, Tenn., near Murfreesboro. He engaged in general farming and the raising of thoroughbred horses. In 1824 he sold out in Rutherford County and came to Sweetwater Valley, contracted or bought part of what has been known for a number of years as the Robt. Snead farm and moved his family there. About 1836 he bought the J. H. Pickel farm (now known as that) where he resided for several years. He sold again and purchased a farm in McMinn County, near Reagan's. He lived there until the time of his death which occurred August 5, 1865, at the age of 85 years and seven months. His wife Martha Neely Yearwood died on February 14, 1867, aged 78 years and 4 months. They were both buried in Netherland Cemetery near Mount Harmony Church in McMinn County.

It is said that in the war of 1812 he belonged to Captain Sublett's company in a regiment led by Colonel Wm. Henderson under command of General Jackson. If so he must have volunteered from either Buncombe County, N. C., or Cocke County, Tenn., because he was not in South Carolina, if the dates given heretofore are right and he did not return there. Wm. Yearwood was in the Seminole War, volunteering with his son, Thomas in 1835, in Captain Thomas Prigmore's company; regimental officer Colonel McClelland, under General Newton Cannon. He was sociable, hospitable, fond of amusements, fiddling and dancing. He taught all of his children both girls and boys, who showed any talent that way, to play the fiddle.

Changing an old rhyme somewhat it might be said of him:

> He shot the musket, he swung the sword
> Fiddler and fighter through,
> Champion of lady, hater of lord
> Dancer and farmer too,

Being quite versatile in his accomplishments.

Wm. Yearwood, III, and Martha Neeley Yearwood, second wife, had seven children: four sons and three daughters.

Child of first wife was Elijah Yearwood, born April 13, 1807, Charleston, S. C. He married one Prudence Morrow and went to Arkansas.

Children of second wife:

Thomas Yearwood, born April 2, 1810, in Buncombe County, N. C.; Nancy Neeley Yearwood, July 24, 1814, in Rutherford County, Tenn.; William Yearwood, born December 24, 1816, in Rutherford County, Tenn.; Horace Burton Yearwood, born March 3, 1820, in Rutherford County, Tenn.; Sarah Dickson Yearwood, born May 26, 1823, in Rutherford County, Tenn.; James Morrow Yearwood, born February 5, 1825, died January 12, 1863, in Monroe County, Tenn.; Martha Jane Yearwood, born July 24, 1829, in Monroe County, Tenn.

COLONEL HORACE BURTON YEARWOOD

Was born at Murfreesboro, Rutherford County, Tenn., March 13, 1820. He died at his residence near County Line two and one-half miles southwest of Sweetwater, on June 17, 1897. He was buried in old Sweetwater cemetery. He married Elizabeth Esther Scruggs, daughter of Elder John Scruggs, September 30, 1847, Robert Snead, M. G., officiating. She died October 25, 1905. He was a member of Co. "H" (Captain Jno. D. Lowry) 2nd Reg. Tenn. Vol. Inf. in the Mexican War, joining in 1845. He was colonel in the state militia.

At the beginning of the Civil War he was quartermaster with the rank of colonel in C. S. A. under General Beauregard and stationed at Augusta, Ga. He was a charter member of Sweetwater Lodge, No. 292, F. & A. M. He was a member of the Baptist church at County Line. He was president of the Fair Association which held its meetings at Madisonville for a number of years. He was the president and moving spirit in the Sweetwater Fair Association, whose grounds and track were one mile west of Sweetwater. Being an authority on all kinds of stock, especially horses, he was in great demand at all the fairs in East Tennessee, and also for the reasons that he was fair and impartial in his decisions. He wrote frequently for the Sweetwater papers a series of articles which he called "Horse Talk." He was a farmer. He with his brother William, purchased school land in 1845. H. B. obtained the grant from the state No. 4836 of date April 19, 1855, signed by Governor Andrew Johnson. At different times he bought small parcels to add to it from F. A. Patton, J. J. Browder and S. J. Rowan. He was the first man on this line of road to place windows in his barn, saying that horses needed light as well as food and other attentions. Some who laughed at him afterward followed his example.

He was genial, jovial and popular and was always a welcome visitor to the town. He was tall and of imposing presence and showed to a great advantage on horseback, being a natural born horseman. He was therefore solicited and led many processions both masonic and political and was always equal to the occasion.

The information contained in these sketches not personally known to the writer was obtained from Miss Miranda E. and Daniel Bone Yearwood, to whom acknowledgment is hereby made.

His children were:

1. William Cerro Gordo, b. July 12, 1848. Unmarried and lives at Sweetwater.

2. John Scruggs, b. January 12, 1850; d. August 1, 1903, at Riceville, Tenn.

3. Richard J., b. August 8, 1853.

4. Lavinia Ida, b. June 12, 1856; d. December 10, 1890.

5. Horace Burton, b. January 12, 1860. Railway conductor in Mexico for fifteen years. Now lives at San Antonio, Texas.

6. Daniel Boone, b. March 3, 1862. Farmer living at Riceville, Tenn.

7. James Bennie, b. October 2, 1863. Was drowned June 9, 1873.

8. Francis Carter, b. October 27, 1864. Telegrapher in the employ of railroad company for twenty-nine years (1916). Lives at Sweetwater, Tenn.

9. Charlie, b. December 27, 1867; d. January, 1868.

10. Hugh, b. December 19, 1868; d. August 21, 1889.

John Scruggs Yearwood was first a railroad employee and then editor of the Monroe Democrat and was postmaster at Sweetwater under Cleveland's first administration. He was married to Mary Belle Fitzgerald, daughter of the Rev. J. B. Fitzgerald, at Fullen's Station (now Chucky City, Tenn.), December 27, 1876. Their children are:

Pearl, b. December 30, 1877; d. January 1, 1878.

Ida Zoe, b. at Euchee, Tenn., April 7, 1879. Lives with Boone Yearwood.

Sadie Ethel, b. at Euchee, Tenn., March 15, 1881; d. February 4, 1889.

James Horace, b. at Sweetwater, June 3, 1885. Lives at Knoxville, Tenn.

Ella Hortense, b. Sweetwater, June 2, 1885. Lives at Knoxville.

Mack Fitzgerald, b. Sweetwater, May 26, 1887. Resides in Knoxville.

Hugh Gaines, b. Oaksdale, Wash. Lives at Knoxville.

Mrs. J. S. Yearwood was born at Waynesville, N. C., August 8, 1853. She died at Sweetwater, January 4, 1904.

Richard Jarnagin Yearwood married Jennie Walker, January 10, 1883. (See D. H. Cleveland.)

Francis Carter Yearwood married Mattie Moulton, February 10, 1891. She was born November 7, 1867, in Meigs County, the daughter of Jno. P. Moulton, who was a soldier in the Confederate army. Her mother's name was Brady. Their children were: Esther, d. in infancy; Francis C., Jr., b. November 1, 1896. Student at Carson and Newman College, Jefferson City, Tenn.

WM. YEARWOOD, IV (Mexican War Veteran).

In 1845 he and his brother H. B., purchased a farm near County Line in Monroe County. Soon after when the call for volunteers for the Mexican War came, he with his brothers, Thomas and H. B., enlisted in Co. H 2nd Reg. Tenn. Vol. Inf. The officers of the company were: John D. Lowry, captain; Wm. Yearwood, 1st lieutenant; John Willson, second lieutenant; and James Forrest, third lieutenant. They were ordered to assemble at Memphis, Tenn., and there in June, 1846, they were sworn into service. The officers of the Second Regiment were: J. E. Thomas, colonel; R. D. Allison, lieutentant-colonel; Richard Waterhouse, major. From Memphis they took steamers to New Orleans, La., and embarked in ships and arrived on the Brazos River early in July, 1846. He participated in the capture of Monterey, Mex., in the following August. After the capitulation of Monterey there followed a four months' armistice. The second regiment was placed under the command of General Scott. They marched to Tampico and from there sailed for Vera Cruz, where they landed in December. The siege guns opened fire on the city which continued for several days. To the second regiment was assigned the task of assaulting the barricade which defended the Maderine Bridge. It was taken. After a siege of seven days the city surrendered, the castle of San Juan Ulloa on the 29th of December. After the conquest of Vera Cruz General Scott soon began his triumphant march to the city of Mexico. At the assault of Cerro Gordo on April 18, 1847, the second regiment was left on the line. The assault was very vigorous. The second regiment became entangled in the chapparal in front of the Mexican fortifications and suffered terribly—their loss being seventy-one. Here while in command of his company Lieutenant Wm. Yearwood fell mortally wounded in the shoulder and side. He lived for six days, dying on April 24. After the expiration of his term of enlistment his brother, Thomas Yearwood, brought his body home to McMinn County and the remains were interred in the cemetery at Athens.

THOMAS YEARWOOD

Was born in Buncombe County, N. C., April 2, 1810. Died May 24, 1889, at his farm two and one-half miles southeast of Sweetwater, buried in old Sweetwater Cemetery. He lived with his father, Wm. Yearwood, until the Seminole War. He volunteered with his father in that war. He was in the 1st Tenn. Reg. under Colonel McClelland.

He volunteered again in the Mexican War, in 1846, joining with his brothers, Wm. and H. B. Yearwood, Co. H 2nd Tenn. Reg. Vol. Inf. They rendezvoused in

Knoxville. Went from Knoxville to Memphis on the steamboats "Knoxville" and "Harry Hill." Then they went to New Orleans from Memphis. At New Orleans they embarked on the ships Sevia, Virginia and Endora for the Brazos River. He was at the capture of Monterey, Mexico., in August. The climate and water were unhealthful and many got sick and died, even more than were killed by the bullets of the Mexicans. Thomas Yearwood, though suffering and weakened from dysentery, refused sick leave and was with General Scott and participated in all the engagements of the company. He returned after his period of enlistment expired bringing home the body of his brother, William, who was killed at Cerro Gordo. On September 8, 1835, he was married to Lavenia Walker Scruggs, daughter of Rev. John Scruggs. on Chestua.

In 1854 he purchased the farm two and one-half miles southeast of Sweetwater now owned by his sons, T. A. and R. S. Yearwood, where he resided at the time of his death, May 24, 1889. His wife was born February 3, 1832, and died August 4, 1899. They are both buried in old Sweetwater Cemetery.

Thomas Yearwood was an honest, fearless, outspoken man. He hated all shams and hypocrisy. He was an ardent whig and was a Union man during the war and not afraid to aver it even during Confederate occupation. He said he could not stultify himself by holding against the flag under which he had fought through two wars. Besides being a farmer he was a contractor and builder. He is said to have built one of the first if not the first house in the town. It was the house used as his office and shop by Dr. M. C. Parker. It stood near where the Hyatt Hotel now stands. It is now part of the old building standing on the west side of the hotel lot. There is some conflict of opinion as to the first house built in the town, as several were commenced nearly at the same time, when it was found where the depot was to be located. I am inclined to the one expressed above.

Thomas Yearwood was a slave owner and a successful farmer and a good neighbor. He was always considered impulsive and eccentric. He possessed little of what is known as "policy." He did not hesitate to speak his mind on any and all occasions, and did not mince matters. He never pretended to be what he was not. No one ever accused him of being a hypocrite. Is it not better to err on the side of too plain speaking than to lack boldness to tell the truth?

The children of Thomas and Lavinia Yearwood were:

1. James Forrest, b. June 16, 1854; m. Harriette Florence, daughter of H. H. Morris of McMinn County, September 11, 1879. He died at Butler, Bates County, Mo., January 12, 1887, and was buried there, as also were his son Paul and daughter Inez, both of whom died at early age. His widow resides at Knoxville, Tenn.

2. Martha Theresa, b. July 11, 1857. She married John Scott Young of Monroe County, on December 17, 1876. He was a druggist in Sweetwater. She lives in Sweetwater. Their children were: Clarence E. (See W. T. Lenoir.) Earl, b. August 9, 1880.

3. John Francis, b. October 30, 1859. Married Ella Coffee, daughter of Colonel Coffee of Georgetown, February 4, 1892.

4. William Frederick, b. March 27, 1862. Lives at Sweetwater.

5. Thomas Abijah, b. August 2, 1865. Farmer.

6. Miranda Elizabeth, b. January 26, 1868.

7. Robert Snead, b. December 23, 1870. Farmer.

8. Lora May, b. June 30, 1875; d. at Sweetwater, June 4, 1900.

The other children of Wm. Yearwood, III, and Nancy Neeley Yearwood were:

Nancy Neeley Yearwood (second) married Robert L. Johnson, June 12, 1838.

Sarah D. Yearwood married Frank A. Holt, October 26, 1845.

James M. Yearwood married twice, first to Susan Lowry, November 20, 1853, and second to Carnelia Netherland, to whom one son was born. He lived near Cleveland, Tenn.

Martha Jane Yearwood married S. B. Haines. Two children: Sam Y. and ―――――.

HENRY BRADLEY

Was born on Ball Play Creek, Monroe County, February 8, 1827. He, while a young man, was in the employ of C. M. McGhee, who owned what was afterward the Calloway farm on Little Tennessee River. He married Margaret Williams on January 26, 1859. (C. M. McGhee, J. P.) She was born March 29, 1834. He was a farmer. He came to Sweetwater in 1865. He first lived on the lot afterward the electric light property; then on lot No. 58 back of the C. P. church. After that he bought fifty acres of land from W. B. Lenoir and moved to the I. T. Lenoir residence. He died there on March 14, 1897. His wife died June 6, 1909. Their children were: 1. Nannie, d. in infancy; 2. Matt, b. October 11, 1862, d. July 29, 1900; 3. Andrew R., d. June 17, 1908; 4. D. S.; 5. Sarah, September 29, 1872; 6. Luke; 7. John.

3. Andrew, married Amanda Jane Heabler, January 11, 1892. She was born December 13, 1867. Their children were: (1) Henry, electrician in the navy; (2) Lorena Margaret, b. August 31, 1894. She is a trained nurse in Atlanta; (3) Carrie, b. December 14, 1896, is a graduate of Clinton, S. C. High School; (5) Frank Russell, b. February 14, 1906, died in infancy; (4) Hugh Carleton, b. August 25, 1904.

4. D. S. married Myrtle Kratzer, June 19, 1909. He is a farmer. Their children are Robert, William and Sarah Rose.

5. Sarah, married W. T. McGuire, of Jellico, Tenn., June 16, 1893. He d. March, 1904.

6. Luke, married Rose Ewry, of Lafayette, Ind. They live in Houston, Texas. Their children are Elizabeth, Walter and Jane.

7. John, b. June 12, 1873; married Beulah Sue, daughter of Gideon B. and Elizabeth Johnson, on December 16, 1903. He is a member of the firm of Guthrie, Bradley and Jones, Sweetwater, Tenn. He is a Democrat, a Mason and a Presbyterian. They have one child, Margaret Elizabeth.

MATT CARTER

Was born in Greenville, S. C. on December 15, 1829. He came to Jonesboro, Tenn., when a young man and there married Mary Emma Brown (Rev. David Sullins, M. G.). She was a school teacher and the daughter of Captain Enoch Brown of Jonesboro. (Bishop E. E. Hoss of the M. E. Church, South, attended the first school she taught.) They moved to Cleveland, Tenn., in 1857. He there joined the M. E. Church, South, in 1859. They moved to Sweetwater in the spring of 1865. He was first a manufacturer of tinware and was, for years before his death, a produce merchant. He was made a Master Mason in Sweetwater Lodge No. 292, on April 17, 1867.

In old Sweetwater cemetery are monuments bearing these inscriptions: "In memory of my dear husband, Matt Carter, born in Greenville, S. C., December 15, 1829. Died April 28, 1885. 'The Noblest Work of God, an Honest Man.'

In memory of our dear mother, Mary Brown Carter, born at Jonesboro, Tenn., October 17, 1831. Died May 29, 1906. 'Life is Richer, Heaven is Sweeter Because of Mother."

The children of Matt and Mary Brown Carter were:

1. Edgar V., b. ————— He graduated at Emory and Henry College, Va., where he obtained the orator's medal. After graduation there he studied law. He married Kate, the daughter of A. C. Robeson, of Athens, Tenn. He went to Atlanta, Ga., where he began the practice of law as a member of the firm of Mynatt and Howell. He is now of the firm of E. V. Carter and sons, who are one of the leading ones of the city. Office in the Atlanta National Bank Building. Residence, 141 Lee Street, West End. The children of E. V. and Kate Carter are: Robeson, b. —————; E. V. Jr., b. —————; Frank, b. —————; Katherine May, b.

2. Robert LaFayette, married Viola Cleveland. (See Clevelands.)

3. Andrew P., married (first) Pauline Gray, of Atlanta, Ga. One child, A. P. Jr. He married (second) Eva Wintersmith, of Louisville, Ky. One child, Richard.

4. Walter Bland, married Pearl Linch, of Atlanta, Ga. Their children are: Afton W., Walter and Pearl Corrie.

5. Fred. A., b. October 14, 1870. He was educated at Sweetwater College. He married (first) Josephine King, daughter of A. S. and Laura J. King, of Atlanta,

Ga., on November 14, 1895. She died May 27, 1903. Their children are:
Josephine, b. at Atlanta, June 16, 1897. Student at Martha Washington College, Va.; Mary Craig, b. April 3, 1899.

F. A. Carter was in the employ of the Sweetwater Woolen Mills as bookkeeper and then as secretary and treasurer. He is now president of the American Textile Woolen Company. He married (second) Belle, daughter of the late John M. Jones, on June 14, 1905. She is president of the City Beautiful League and choir leader of the Methodist Church, South, and Mr. Carter is superintendant of the Sunday-school, the largest and most progressive in Sweetwater with an average attendance of about 375 for the year 1916. The church is now building a Sunday-school annex.

6. May, the youngest child of Matt and Mary Carter, was born June 30, 1872. Was educated at Centenary College, Cleveland, Tenn., and Price's College, Nashville, Tenn. She married Frank Y. Jackson. He joined the Holston Conference, M. E. C., South, in 1890. He is a noted revivalist. He is now (1916) in charge of Marion, Va. church. The children of Mary and Frank Y. Jackson are: Mary, Frank Y., Margaret and Mansfield.

MARY ISABELLA MAGILL MONTGOMERY.

The following sketch is taken by permission of R. E. Magill, of Richmond, Va., from the "Magill Family Record" book:

Mary Isabella Magill (daughter of Nathaniel and Jane Rankin Magill), born April 20, 1829; died March 10, 1906, at the home of her sister, Penelope, Mrs. J. R. Russell; buried at Madisonville. Married to James Harvey Montgomery, at the home of her father, October 19, 1849. (J. H. Montgomery, born February 7, 1825. Died at their home, in Sweetwater, Tenn., May 26, 1888; buried on Fork Creek.)

The subject of this sketch was a woman loved by everybody who knew her; of a bright, sunny, cheerful, self-sacrificing, loving disposition, she scattered sunshine wherever she went. Ever ready to lend a helping hand. "None knew her but to love her." Their first home was in Fork Creek Valley, near Glenloch, Tenn. Her husband was a tanner. Selling out his business, after a number of years, they moved to Sweetwater. In 1866 they went to California and lived about eight years at San Jose, and followed the dairy business. Returning to Sweetwater they kept a private boarding house and also a meat market. After the death of her husband, she went to live at the home of her sister, Mrs. J. R. Russell, near Madisonville. Always ready to go to the bedside of the sick with her help and cheering words, everybody was always and everywhere glad to welcome "Aunt Mary." Her very presence was a blessing, and her exalted Christian character will always be remembered as a high ideal by all who were privileged to know her."

(I endorse unreservedly all the statements made as to the beauty and goodness of her character. I boarded with her for seven years and rented her house for an additional seven. I knew her for more than forty years. W. B. L.)

The Misses Coffin.

In the fall of 1872 there came to Sweetwater five sisters, none of them then married. The eldest of them was 30 years of age and the youngest about 16. They had lost one brother in 1862 of fever taken at Manassas during the Civil War. They had also lost both father and mother, the latter about a year previous. They had a lovely home in the country. They had numerous relatives and a host of friends. Their father previous to his decease had advised them however not to attempt to live in the old home but to select some town on the railroad in which to reside. They had been left with ample means and had a wealthy brother-in-law in New York, and the whole country was before them to choose. They were importuned by their friends in various towns and cities to select or build a home in their midst, and the advantages of each location were placed before them and many inducements were offered. It may have been for sentimental reasons, as they had all been born and reared in Monroe County, that they chose Sweetwater for their home; this too when our town lacked the advantages it could offer now. I think they never regretted their choice. The citizens of the town were more than delighted to have them.

Their ancestors on their father's side came from Massachusetts and had the New England culture and attainments and the New England conscience. On the mother's side came wealth, southern geniality and hospitality. The young ladies were so everything that was admirable and lovely that it has been said more than once that to have known the family, that alone would have made one's life worth living. The majority of the people here were convinced that what any one of them did was the right and proper thing to do. No one was jealous of their almost unbounded influence. They gave with such cheerful and ungrudging hand that the receivers never felt the obligation weigh upon them. Notwithstanding they were sisters and were rarely separated from each other for long at a time, they were yet unlike and differed from each other "as one star differeth from another in glory." The eldest sister had an intimate knowledge of most business transactions and values and yet was a womanly woman. Before her father's death for some years she had been his main stay in business and was amply able to have charge of a large estate. In the early days of the corporation of Sweetwater they paid one-third of the municipal taxes. It would have been very easy for them to have become tax dodgers, as a large part of their wealth consisted of notes, stocks and bonds, but that was not their way of doing business. They received from the taxes paid, as far as they were concerned, little benefit. The corporation imperfectly macadamized the street in front of their lot for seventy-five feet; yet a corrupted voter who sold his vote for a few drinks or a dollar had more to say as to who should be mayor and aldermen of the town than they. One would have expected they would have been advocates of female suffrage, but Miss Sue Coffin always contended that woman's influence would not be best exercised that way.

It has already been told, in the account of the building of the new Presbyterian church and parsonage, that they contributed about half. Miss Sue said that they would not mind building the church themselves but thought that would be very impolitic. What people strive for and sacrifice for they take more interest in than what comes to them easy, and nothing is truer than this. Nor did she want to build a very expensive church for the purpose of outshining other denominations in a spirit of rivalry. Nor should they build such a church as would strain the resources of the members to keep up, and starve the pastor, to keep up a show for the public. They were great church workers and they all, except the youngest, were teachers in the Sunday-school.

Through their influence with their brother-in-law, John H. Inman, a passenger depot was built here, which was very sadly needed.

The Coffins had an abiding faith in their church, their town, their friends and kinfolks. Their effort was always to help and build up not to tear down. Whatsoever was deserving received their earnest and loyal support.

One J. L. Bachman, formerly a soldier in the C. S. A., married Miss Fannie Rogan, a relative of theirs. He was then comparatively unknown to fortune and to fame. The trustees of the Union Institute were looking for a competent teacher. Owing to the Coffin influence, as much as anything else, the position was given to him. They did not then know much about him but knew intimately his wife, and that was enough for them. When he once came to Sweetwater from Hawkins County, the citizens here would not let him go. He is here yet and has been since 1874, nearly forty-two years. We are not going to write his history; for that would take a book in itself—to tell of the thousands of young men he has taught, the hundreds of couples he has united in bonds of matrimony, the tens of thousands to whom he has preached, the sick he has visited, the numerous funeral services at which he has been speaker and comforter, the addresses he has delivered on social occasions, to give his masonic history, to mention his home life—these and many other things future historians will delight to relate, but I shall not undertake it. Even were his coming to this section within the limit (1820-1865) I have set for myself, I would dislike to make so many of the dead, about whom I have written, appear small by comparison.

Nor shall I give a history of the Coffins more than as follows:

James A. Coffin, son of Charles Coffin, D. D., b. November 5, 1806; d. September 27, 1871. His wife was Margaret Martin, b. January 29, 1812; d. March 14, 1865. Children were:

Hugh M., b. August 7, 1840; d. December 5, 1861.
Sue E., b. December 1, 1842; d. September 11, 1890.
Sarah, b. January 8, 1846; d. January 16, 1899.
Margaret, b. ————; m. John H. Inman June 8, 1870; d. ————
Nancy, b. September 1, 1850; d. June 5, 1879.
Mary Ella, b. June 17, 1853; d. December 14, 1898.
Julia Ayer, b. ————; m. James W. Harle, October 23, 1878.

The Misses Coffin built and lived in the house where S. T. Jones now resides.

THE BAPTIST CHURCH ON SWEETWATER.

A Baptist church is an association of baptized believers organized for the salvation of sinners, the good of the community and its members and for the spread of its own peculiar beliefs. Denominationally there is no such thing as "The Baptist Church." Each church is an entire, separate, independent and sovereign democracy. Each member, male or female, has equal rights and there are no special privileges. One has just as much power (not influence) as another. Even the pastor or elder in charge of a church has no voice in the affairs of that church, except advisory, unless he be a member. The only officers of the church are the moderator, the deacons and the clerk. These officers are elected and hold their office until their successors are elected and in case of the deacons ordained; the moderator and clerk require no special setting apart. The moderator's duty is to preside at the meetings, the clerks to record the proceedings of the business meetings, the deacons' to attend to the financial affairs of the church under instructions of the members. They have of themselves no authority to bind the church.

They are trustees of the church property which is in their names. The number of deacons is usually three or more. Baptistically speaking the place where the members meet, if it belongs to them, is the church house, if it does not it is their meeting house or meeting place. The old Baptists never called any building "a church." An elder in the Baptist church is an ordained minister or a member licensed to preach the word.

These prefatory remarks, I think, are necessary for the proper understanding of the subject I am to discuss, viz: the Baptist Church on Sweetwater (Creek) between the towns of Sweetwater and Philadelphia, called in the records of that church, the Sweetwater church and sometimes known as the Cleveland Baptist Church. I make no apology for writing of it. Not to give some account of that church in a history of the valley, which I am attempting to write, would be something like enacting the play of Hamlet with the character of Hamlet left out. It was the earliest church organized by people of this valley of which I have any knowledge; the number and prominence of its membership makes it historically speaking far the most remarkable church in the valley of any denomination whatever. I think it proper to state that no one has requested me to write this nor do I know that any one expects me to. What I say is entirely voluntary and without consultation with any of the members.

ORGANIZATION OF THIS CHURCH. BELIEF SET FORTH.

On the first Saturday in June, 1820, a number of persons met at the house of Dan'l Duggan on Fork Creek and a church was constituted with the following Declaration of Principles. (We give these in full as they are short, clear and concise and so that it can be known what that church believed.)

We believe:

1. That the scriptures of the Old and New Testaments are the infallible word of God and the only rule of Faith. and Practice.

2. There is only one true God and in the Godhead or Divine Essence there are Father, Son and Holy Ghost equal in Power and Glory.

3. That by nature we are fallen and depraved creatures and it is not in man's power to recover (of) himself from the fallen state he is in of his own free will and ability.

4. That Salvation, Regeneration, Justification and Sanctification are by the Life, Death, Resurrection, Ascension and Intercession of Jesus Christ.

5. That the saints will finally presevere through Grace to Glory.

6. That Baptism by Immersion is the only mode warranted by scripture and true believers are the only proper subjects to receive the same.
7. That the salvation and joys of the righteous will be everlasting and the punishment and torment of the wicked eternal.
8. That it is our duty to be tender and affectionate to each other and in all things to try to promote the happiness of the children of God and in all things to set forth the declarative glory of God.
9. We believe in the Resurrection of the dead and the general judgment by Jesus Christ.
10. That no minister has a right to the administration of the ordinances only such as are regularly baptized, called and come under the imposition of hands by a Presbytery.
11. That it is the duty of all church members to attend our church meeting, especially male members, and to admonish and deal with each other for the neglect of the same.
12. That a Reception or Exclusion of church members ought to be by a unanimous voice of the church or the members present.

Those who signed the foregoing articles at that meeting were:
Male members: Dan'l Duggan, Samuel Jameson, John Fine, Robert Gregory, John Dillard, William Y. Arthur, Jeremiah Selvege and Moses McSpadden; Female members: Eunice Duggan, Rebecca Jamieson, Nancy Fine, Sally Dillard, Mary Carter, Mary Selvege, Joanna McSpadden and Elizabeth Taylor; 8 male and 9 female members.

Elders present at the signing of the Constitution were: Geo. Snider and Obed Patty.

Geo. Snider was Moderator and Moses McSpadden was elected Clerk.

RULES OF DECORUM.

13 rules of decorum (parliamentary proceedings) were adopted. These were mostly such as might govern any deliberative body with the exception that it was made the duty of the Moderator to open the door of the church for the reception of new members at every business session of the church. (By session is meant the members of the church present sitting as a committee of the whole.) A person could become a member of the church in two ways: By letter from another Baptist church or by profession of faith and baptism. There were three ways of getting out of the Baptist church: By Death, Exclusion or by Letter. Even when a letter of Dismission was granted the church claimed jurisdiction over the conduct of the member "until joined to one of like faith and order."

No business relative to the finances of this church was transacted in the early days, whatever may be the custom there now, except on Saturday. Not even a collection was taken up on Sunday. The financial affairs were looked after by the Deacons.

No person can have any conception of the polity of a Baptist church until he grasps the idea that, as stated, each is an independent sovereignty. There is no appeal from its action to any Association or higher earthly power. It is complete in itself.

A Baptist church in relation to the conduct of its members toward each other might well adopt the motto: "Liberty, equality and fraternity," for as heretofore stated it is a pure democracy. By this phrase is not meant the "liberte, egalite and fraternite" of the French

Revolution, for that took no account of God or the Church. For this reason it was foredoomed to failure. It is not possible to change the customs, habits and religious thought of a people of a sudden by legislative enactment or legal process. This is the slow work of centuries. It has been said divers times (by whom first said I know not nor does it matter) "that if there were no God it would be necessary to promulgate a belief in one," a belief in the existence of the Supreme Being and a future state of rewards and punishments being essential to the well being and good order of society and that there should be a means of communication, revelation or otherwise, between the creature and the Creator. True the heavens show forth the power and glory of God, but you might gaze upon them for a thousand years and you would deduce therefrom no precept like the golden rule: "Whatsoever ye would that men should do to you, do ye even so them." This when translated and personified into action by the parliaments of the nations would become true "liberty, equality and fraternity. No war, no prisons, no poverty. The good and great in increasing numbers are bending their efforts in that direction. It has been the dream of poets through the ages, a dream perhaps not to have a perfect realization but none the less beautiful and enchanting one. It shines transcendant, the triple star of hope, on the night gloom of a tear dimmed and misery cursed world. Blot out this aspiration and the inhabitants of earth would be ruled by a multiplicity of tyrannies.

As stated in a former article some time since this church called Bethel was organized at Dan'l. Duggans on Fork Creek on the first Saturday in June, 1820. Occupation of land in the Hiwassee District was not permitted until this year and therefore the country was thinly populated. This shows the zeal which inspired the early settlers for their church and its work.

The Meetings Where First Held.

The meetings were held at D. Duggan's until and including the first Saturday in August, 1821. It was then decided for the convenience of scattered membership to hold two meetings of the church in each month, one on

Fork Creek on the second Saturday and one on Sweetwater on the fourth Saturday in each month. Accordingly on the fourth Saturday following (August, 1821), a meeting was held at Jno. Fine's. He lived in a log house which is still standing on the hill above the double spring at the southwest boundary of Sweetwater corporation line where the water works pumping station now is. At this meeting there were several accessions to the church. At the same meeting a committee was appointed to meet at Thomas Wilson's on August 31 to purchase land on which to build a meeting house and report at next meeting. James Sewell was moderator and Sam'l. Jameson, clerk. It can be seen from this that when anything needed to be done these people did not let any grass grow under their feet.

The Fork Creek branch of the church were not far behind. At a meeting at Joseph McSpadden's on the second Saturday in October Robert Gregory, Wm. Arthur and John Dillard were made trustees to purchase a site near McSpadden's for the erection of a church house and a school-house.

The Parent of Other Churches.

This church has been the parent of other churches. We know of no more satisfactory way of showing this than by giving some excerpts from the records of the church.

"Fourth Saturday in Feb., 1822. Trustees reported that they had purchased two acres of land from Mr. Hugh Boyd agreeable to orders at January meeting and had a bond for title for the same, which was received by the church. Ordered next meeting to be held at Mr. Boyd's." (Probably not a member of the church or he would have been called "Brother.")

"Stage Stand on Sweetwater 4th Saturday in June, 1822. A proposition having been made by Bro. Jameson for the part of Bethel church that lies on Sweetwater to become a separate constituted body, it is therefore agreed and ordered that Brother Sewell and Fine be appointed delegates to attend upon the brethren at the next meeting on Fork Creek to let them know our intention and select those acquiescing in such a measure to attend with us on that business the next meeting at Bro. Cleveland's."

"Church meeting at E. Cleveland's 4th Saturday in Sept., 1822. Ordered that the church formerly called Bethel be hereafter permanently established on Sweetwater and be known in future as Sweetwater church."

"Cleveland's 4th Saturday in October, 1822. Decided to build a church near his (Cleveland's) house. He promised a donation of land for building site and also land for a grave yard. Committee appointed to attend to the business.

"Fourth Saturday, April, 1834. Church requests ministerial brethren to hold a meeting at school house near Bro. Fine's on the second Saturday in each month."

"4th Saturday, April, 1835. Members joining the church at the school house near Bro. Fine's have the privilege to hold membership in the church on Pond Creek or wherever they may select."

"4th Saturday in January, 1846. The church took into consideration the building of a brick meeting house and then drew subscription paper for the purpose of obtaining subscribers to accomplish the same and made Bro. D. Ragon our Trustee for the cash subscription to collect and pay over the same. Also to Bro. R. Snead appointed to collect the trade part of our subscription. Brethren D. Ragon, R. Snead and John Pennington made Trustees to superintend and carry on the work, to make all contracts and to value all labor that may be done, and (do) all things that may attain to the building of the same."

On February 27, 1847, Eli Cleveland conveyed to the united Baptist church on Sweetwater the tract of land as follows: "Beginning at the railroad near Cleveland and son's fence and running with said fence around to the ford of the creek, thence up said creek to the foot log, thence with the lot to the corner bars, thence straight to the railroad, thence with said road to the beginning, containing five acres more or less. To be used for the following purposes: The lot at the meeting house to be extended so as to include said meeting house to be kept forever as a place for the worship of God, the balance of said piece of land to remain forever uninclosed for passways, the hitching of horse, etc. Second: Lot including the graveyard with as much more land adjoining the same as may be necessary for burying the dead. The said church or no other person or persons to have the right or privilege of selling, transferring or conveying the said pieces of land for any purpose than the ones above mentioned."

He also confirmed this deed by his will in the following words bequeathing to ——— his real estate except "The part I gave to the United Baptist Church of Christ so long as they should wish to meet for the worship of God; but if they should fail to meet for that purpose it is no longer theirs and in that case to belong to my son. I except also a piece of land for a public burying ground whereat is now to be enlarged from time to time as it may be used for this purpose, so as to be confined to the bend of the creek and to the railroad."

This is quoted for the purpose of showing the extraordinary foresight of giving and having given the amount of land so donated for church and cemetery and protecting the interests of the church and the public. It was also a new departure to have the church house and burying ground nearly a quarter of a mile distant from each other and not in close proximity, as was customary in those days. There is much ground subject to be used for a cemetery yet remaining at this date (1911).

The word "railroad" in the above deed and will is liable to be misleading. At the time (1847) the right of way had been graded in preparation for receiving the ties and iron, but they had not been laid down. Part of the grade on right of way was used as a public road. The iron on the right of way was not laid until 1852.

I have not yet found out where Mr. Boyd lived or what was done with the land for which bond for title was given. I would also like some information as to where the frame church was built on the Cleveland land. I do not know as yet where the "stage stand," referred to in the minutes of the church was. The public road, so far I am aware from Philadelphia to Reagan is the same (in 1911) almost as in the days of the old stage route before the completion of the East Tennessee & Georgia Railroad.

The location of the Fine school-house spoken of was in the bend of the creek about one-fourth mile west of Sweetwater Cemetery. The building was a one-story log house about 35 by 20 feet. It was used not only for school purposes but for preaching and sometimes for justice's trials. The cleared land around was sometimes used too for "musters" i. e., militia drill, which were in the early settling of the country obligatory.

THE BAPTIST CHURCH IN SWEETWATER—ITS LEGISLATION AND EXECUTIVE ACTIONS.

As a Baptist church has no book of rules or constitution, one must look to what it does in its business meetings to form an idea of how its members interpret certain passages of scripture; to find out what they consider mandatory or prohibitive or what is merely advisory; what one must do or refrain from doing or what is only suggested as best to do under certain circumstances. No church or sect would likely claim that St. Paul's ban on marriage was susceptible of a world-wide application or that under any and all circumstances woman should always keep silent in public. Nor should the special treatment or medical advice of St. Paul to Timothy, "Take a little wine for the stomach's sake," be used by all persons indiscriminately. What was Timothy's special disorder, how much is "a little" and what proportion of alcohol did the wine contain? None but the Friends, I believe, take literally the passage counselling no resistance to assault or oppression, but when smitten on one cheek offer the other also. Few sects but take the words "to wash one another's feet" as anything but advisory or as exhortation to practice humility rather than exalt one's self among the brethren.

In the early days this church took more account of the daily business life than is customary now. When any one made a complaint to the church on a business day meeting that he had been cheated or defrauded by a member of the church, it was usual, if the charge was not frivolous, to appoint a committee of several members, known for their fairness and impartiality, to investigate the matter and make a report. Dishonesty in trade was considered as grave an offense as lying, stealing or drunkenness or unfaithfulness to the marriage vows. They held that cheating was rarely accomplished save by lying and misrepresentation. This committee heard both sides and made their recommendation to the church. If the charge was sustained, the offender was required to make restitution, and, if he refused or failed to do so and proved obstinate, non-fellowship or exclusion was declared. (See minutes of second Saturday of May, 1822.) The difference between non-fellowship and exclusion, as I understand it, as practised by this church was that, in case of the former, repentance and restitution usually restored one to membership; in the latter case the readministration of the ordinance of baptism, just as if he had never before joined the church, was necessary to full membership. In the days of Huss or Martin Luther they would have been called Anabaptists.

CHURCH ACTION ON SEVERAL QUESTIONS COMING BEFORE THEM.

"4th Saturday of May, 1823.—A question arose as to the saints' washing of feet. After some debate on the subject it was conceived to be a duty (by some) held out by the example of the Saviour's followers to pursue (see John, Chap XIII.) to be kept up at every sacramental occasion."

"A further question arose in the church whether it would be out of order or whether or not it was outside of duty to open a door for experience at any other time or place beside the regular meeting." Both questions were laid over.

"4th Saturday in June, 1823.—Subject of Saints' Foot Washing taken up. Agreed to attend to that ordinance the following Sunday after divine service." (The writers information is that it was afterward discontinued as not being at any time an essential part of the church service.)

"4th Saturday, July, 1823.—After debate decided to be improper to open the door of the church except at regular meetings." (Supposedly for the reason that it required a unanimous vote for admission and then no complaint could be filed when done at regular meetings.)

"4th Saturday, May, 1831.—A complaint was made to the church of a sister who had been communing with the Cumberland Presbyterians. She refused to apologize to the church or acknowledge that she had committed an error. Non-fellowship was declared."

"4th Saturday in January, 1832.—Resolved, That any male member failing to attend two meetings in succession shall be required to give a reason for his absence, unless the cause be known by some brother present." Resolved—"That any member drinking ardent spirits until the effect is perceptible shall be treated with as drunk."

Eli Cleveland, Moderator.
R. Snead, Clerk.

4th Saturday in May, 1835.—Resolved—"Whereas there are difficulties and disputings about missionary societies, associations, etc., much to the hurt of Zion, we the church at Sweetwater propose to our sister churches, within the bounds of Sweetwater Association, to meet with us in associate body at Chestuā meeting house, on Tuesday before the 4th Saturday in July next, for the purpose of consulting the best means to unite and bring about a union among the churches and brethren of the association and to consult and unite upon the best plan, according to the word of God, for the spread of the Gospel; churches to send letters and delegates. Brethren Cleveland, Snead and Taliaferro were appointed delegates to the meetings. Thus this church aligned itself with the Missionary Baptists in contradistinction to those who opposing Foreign Missions and the payment of Pastors were sometimes termed "Hard Shell" Baptists. My information is that at the association held at Chestua a majority of the churches declared themselves in favor of both Home and Foreign Missions. All the delegates sent by the church on Sweetwater were in favor of Missions. However as Pastors both brethren Cleveland and Snead refused pay for their services, not because they thought it wrong to pay preachers, but, as they were well off financially without the salary, the church they thought could more profitably apply the money to other uses.

A number of the brethren at different times were "unfellowshipped" for the offenses of "non attendance," "swearing," "drunkenness," "fighting," more for non-attendance on church meetings than for any other offense; a few for gambling. One brother in February, 1855, was non-fellowshipped for "betting on a shooting match" although that was not contrary to the laws of the State of Tennessee.

The recorded cases of gambling in the Bible are not numerous. Samson (Judges, Chaps. XIV. and XV.) bet with his friends "thirty linen garments and thirty changes of raiment." He thought he was betting on a "sure thing" and, as frequently happens, lost. He did not have the wherewith to pay. The way he got the means to liquidate his "debt of honor" was anything but creditable. Samson was not a good loser. He spoke disrespectfully of his wife and left her with her parents. They soon got rid of her. The train of consequences were woeful all the way through. The Romans were great gamblers. They even cast lots for raiment of the Saviour.

Some Church Statistics.

From the inception of this church in 1820 up to and including the year 1872 there were more than 700 persons became members. The high water mark of membership was reached in 1869, when the number of members became 289. The average of number would be from 159 to 160 according to church reports sent to the different associations. It would require too much space to give all those who have been members of this church.

I would suggest however, if it is not already done, that the clerk of the church or some one compile an alphabetical list, giving the names of those who have been members, the date of admission, when died or dismissed,—a simple church history, so that such information could be obtained without having to search through the whole of the church records. We give below some of the patronymics or surnames of the membership with the number in brackets, where there are several of the same name, for the first fifty years of this church or a little more than half of its existence.

Adams, Alexander, Allen, Arthur, Allison, Barnes, Brewer, Beaty, Burns, Bodkins, Brown, Boyd, Bowman, Byrum (7), Burch, Brazeale, Berry, Bryant, Cleveland (20), Callaway (10), Carter (8), Chesnutt (4), Cooper, Cannon, Davis (3), Duggan, Dillard (3), Edwards (6), Esman, Fine (3), Fry, Fryer, Ferguson, Franklin, Grummett, Grady, Grisom, Harrison, Hathaway, Harris, Hatchett, Hudson, Hyde, Hill (3), Hood (2), Hagen, Humble, Harless (6), Hight, Houstaign, Haskins, Kelly, Kyle, Isbell, Jameson, Johnson (18), Jones (22), Kell, Lilard (5), Latham, Lord (3), Laws (12), Lewis, Mrs. M. C. Lenoir, Mary Hogg, Leonard, Jackson (7), Mc-

Spadden, McGuffey, McFalls, McMinn, McGuire, Moon, Martin (9), McNabb, Maberry, Miller (9), Moore, Montgomery, Moffett, May, Nichols, Nelson, Pharis, Purdy (5) Philpot, Pennington (10), Potter (6), Ragon (13), Ruth (14), Reed, Reynolds, Plemmons, Stephens (6), Snead (5), Selvage (5), Shelton, Stone, Scott, Snow, Stansbury, Turner, Taliaferro, Taylor, Tewell, Van, Wallens (3), Watkins (3), Walker (5), Wilson (7), Winters, Yoakum (5), Young. Of these 700 members about 15 were colored. Of these there were both put together only thirty-four non-fellowships and exclusions, in the first fifty years the church had an existence. Most of these were for the charges of drunkenness, profanity, fighting, dishonesty, gambling, non-attendance and communing with other sects or "societies." This would be, rating the average membership at 150, less than one-half of one per cent. of exclusions per year.

During the time specified 1820-1872 the moderators elected by the church have been O. Patty, James Sewell, Eli Cleveland, Robt. Snead and S. J. Martin; the pastors, E. Cleveland, R. Snead, I. B. Kimbrough, J. P. Kefauver, D. M. Breaker; the clerks, Moses McSpadden, Samuel Jameson, Wm. Johnson, John Pennington, Norris C. Hood, R. Snead, Wm. Lillard, W. E. Johnson, W. E. Jordan, F. K. Berry; the deacons, Saml. Jameson, John Fine, R. Snead, W. H. Montgomery, D. Ragon, Nelson Miller, Jesse F. Jones, F. M. Pennington, W. E. Johnson and Jos. Ragon.

POLITICAL DISCUSSIONS IN CHURCH AN INJURY TO IT.

One reason for the great prosperity and increase in membership of this church from 1865 to 1870 was that no member was permitted to discuss the war or political parties inside of the church house during the Civil War or directly thereafter. This made it possible for all who attended church to meet on terms of amity and equality. During the sixties various Baptist churches in East Tennessee were rent and torn asunder so that it took years to recover.

Members were sometimes excluded merely for the part they took in the war. The discussion of state and national questions, which divide political parties, from the pulpit or in church meetings, nearly always is an injury to the church and rarely makes the political parties any better. In this particular church during the Civil War they prayed in public neither for the success of the armies of the Union or the Southern Confederacy whatever they may have done in private. True they prayed that the war should end and brother cease to shed the blood of brother.

There were members of this church who had sons on different sides of the struggle and it was generally understood, and the rule was observed, that the right and wrong of the war, slavery or secession were not to be discussed in and around the church. Hence when the troops disbanded and came home there was little to apologize for or take back and all met on a friendly footing.

The greatest number of accessions to this church in one year was in 1866 under the pastorate of Elder I. B. Kimbrough. So far as I am aware, no one knew on which side he stood during the Civil War. When asked the question he would reply that he was a preacher of the Gospel and not a politician or fighter. Yet he was a fearless man, none more so.

One Sunday he had an appointment, not at Sweetwater Church but a considerable distance from there. Some of the tough element in the neighborhood had threatened him. On that Sunday he arose in the pulpit and coolly remarked: "I am told on good authority that I am not going to be allowed to preach here today. I have had many appointments in the years that I have been preaching and have always filled them. By the help of God and these (here he placed a couple of six shooters on the pulpit before him) I expect to fill this one, you can listen or not just as you see fit." He was not interrupted during the sermon nor afterward.

He was pastor of the church on Sweetwater during the year 1866. On the last days of October that year there was a protracted meeting and a great revival. There were sixty-seven accessions to the church, fifty-six of them by experience and baptism. Some of those joining had fought on different sides during the Civil War, and some of them were approaching middle age.

It was told in the country around that there was to be such a baptising as had never been known in this section before. A great concourse of people gathered there; they came from up and down the valley, from Pond Creek, Piney and the Flatwoods.

The day turned out to be very raw and chilly. Many doubters confidently asserted that few would have the nerve to be immersed under the circumstances. But all were there to a man and to a woman. Not one of the fifty-six held back or failed to stand the trying ordeal. The rite was performed in the creek not far from the church, when old soldiers who had fought each other valiantly in battle joined hands and marched into the water singing "Blest be the tie that binds our hearts in Christian love." To me the ceremony was exceedingly impressive. Yet some were inclined to be sorry for them or sneer, "Poor thing, she will catch her death of cold, look how she shivers." "How foolish to risk their health in such a manner, thinking God will take care of them." "I'll bet that old fellow don't like a rebel any better than he did before." "There's one they ought to hold under till he blubbers, 'taint the first time he's been dipped." These were mostly asides on the outskirts of the crowd and not really intended to interrupt the proceedings; yet I thought from how many points the same can be looked at. Take an example:

Jumbo was the largest elephant ever in capitivity. Notwithstanding his size (he was about twelve feet tall at his shoulders); he was docile and affectionate in disposition. He and the baby elephant were almost constant companions and Jumbo felt himself responsible for his welfare and safety. On one occasion a train of Barnum & Bailey's circus was wrecked. Jumbo owing to his great strength soon extricated himself from the wreckage and could have got safely away. Just then he heard the trumpeting of the baby elephant which was almost paralyzed by fright. He turned, caught and threw the baby elephant from the track but was himself somehow caught in the debris and crippled so he had to be killed. This was what an elephant did. The owners had the skin stuffed and placed on a wheeled platform. On the circus tour in the grand entry Jumbo looking quite lifelike was drawn around the ring by four elephants making stately strides while the band played the funeral march of Chopin. The baby elephant whose life he had saved toddled along behind. This made some laugh, as that is what they went there for, but most of the 15,000 people present appreciated the solemnity of the scene. As for myself I would have not have complained if that had been all I saw for the price of admission.

The Sweetwater church for many years owned a lot in Philadelphia, donated to them by Robt. Cleveland. On Saturday before the fourth Sunday in June, 1872, the Sweetwater church relinquished its title to the church in Philadelphia. Previous to this on Saturday before the fourth Sunday in May of that year letters of dismission were granted the following members in order to constitute a church at Philadelphia:

J. J. and Tabitha Swanner, H. H. Porter, Anderson and Phoebe Burns, Lavenia and Sanford Burns, C. F. and Mary Thompson, Cornelia Porter, B. F. Stansbury, Elizabeth Edwards, D. D., and Susan Kelly, Joseph Purdy, D. R. and Elizabeth Kelly, Lilah and Josephine Miller.

So the church on Sweetwater is remarkable both on account of its own membership, and as being the mother of several other prosperous churches.

The Baptist Church on Pond Creek and Its Successor, the First Baptist Church at Sweetwater.

On the 20th of November, 1824, there met at John Howell's in McMinn County, the following brethren and sisters: John and Millie Hancock, Thomas and Rufus Walden, James McClure, Barclay McClure, Wm. F. Briant, Wm. Jones, Jane Jones. They proceeded to organize a Baptist church and enunciated a declaration of faith and rules of decorum, not essentially different from the Baptist Church on Sweetwater. Wm. F. Briant was elected clerk.

Some time afterward a small church and a shed for camp meeting purposes was built near where J. N. Heiskell now lives on Pond Creek; I do not know the date of erection of either but it must have been some time in the later twenties.

The church was reasonably prosperous. In October, 1827, it had fifty-seven members.

Samuel Jamieson was clerk from 1827 to 1830. Wm. F. Briant was clerk to March, 1833. William Harralson from 1833 to 1838. James A. Small from 1838 to 1842, and then Thomas Dean until March, 1845. E. A. Taylor until 1860. Elder William Jones was pastor from 1831 to 1833. Elder R. H. Taliaferro from 1833 until March, 1841, when Elder Robert Snead was elected pastor. He was pastor until 1857.

This church was missionary in faith. It was recorded in the minutes that on the first Saturday in January, 1837, Wm. F. Briant and eight others, had left Pond Creek church, they say, "on account of the Missionary Bible Society and contributions to foreign missions"; therefore the church considered them "not of us" and their names were erased from the church book.

On the first Saturday in December, 1844, some half dozen members were excluded for joining, what they denominated, the Christian Church, often termed the Campbellites. For these causes, and the unsuitability of the church building and the inconvenience to the members to attend at that place on the first Saturday in June, 1854, it was decided to endeavor to build a house of worship at the town of Sweetwater. In July, 1854, the church appointed brethren R. Snead, John Fine, Major Wallis, J. S. Taylor and E. A. Taylor, to control the fund for the building of the meeting house there. From that time until January, 1857, there was little business transacted at the Pond Creek Church and few members received. This was the last meeting at the Pond Creek church house.

The First Baptist Church at Sweetwater.

I. T. Lenoir promised to donate a lot at the corner of the Athens road and Monroe Street for the location of a Baptist church to be the successor of the Pond Creek Baptist Church. Taking him at his word the committee appointed by Pond Creek Baptist Church proceeded to procure funds and erect a building thereon.

This building was not ready for occupation or holding meetings until August, 1860. At that time Mary Caroline Lenoir, Esther E. Yearwood, Elizabeth Cleveland, Elizabeth Bailey, James J. and Mary E. Sheldon, were received by letter, and W. B. Lenoir by experience.

On the first Saturday in December, 1860 there joined the church by experience and baptism: John A. Rowan, Thomas D. Taylor, Isaac and James Murray, Martha L. and Mary E. Taylor, Nancy Fine, Mary Rowan, John H. and Caroline Johnson, and by enrollment Mrs. Mary Rowan. W. H. Taylor was appointed clerk, and Elder Robert Snead was moderator. These continued in their offices during 1861 and 1862. The first pastor of the church elected in January, 1861, was H. W. Taylor, of Deep Spring, Grainger County, Tenn.

In August, 1861, there were received by letter, Elder W. A. Nelson and sister, M. M. Nelson.

The last church meeting held during the Civil War, was in August, 1862. From that until the summer of 1865 the church was occupied and used by the soldiers of one army or the other, Union or Confederate, for hospital and other purposes, so that church meetings could not be held. The first recorded church meeting after that was in August, 1865, when W. A. Nelson was moderator and E. A. Taylor, church clerk. Federal troops again occupied the church in latter part of 1865. There is no recorded meeting until the first Saturday in July, 1866. Then J. J. Sheldon was elected clerk and R. Snead, moderator. J. J. Sheldon continued in office and acted as clerk on the first Saturday in January, 1868. He died on January 18, 1868.

Up to the first Saturday in April, 1868, Elder R. Snead usually preached for the church although not a regular pastor; then brother J. F. Kefauver was called to the pastorate, and was pastor until May, 1870. The pastors of the church, from that time until 1889 were as follows: J. B. Lee, 1870—February, 1873; C. L. Bowling, August, 1875—July, 1876; T. A. Higdon, July, 1876—June, 1877; J. L. Lloyd, December, 1877—December, 1878; W. C. Grace, April, 1879—December, 1882; D. M. McReynolds, November, 1883—April, 1889:

The following were clerks from the death of J. J. Sheldon: E. A. Taylor, January, 1868—January, 1876;

W. B. Lenoir, February, 1876—April, 1881; John N. Janeway, November, 1881—July, 1887; Thomas M. Sample, October, 1887—September, 1888; W. Morriss, October, 1888—April, 1889.

After the death of I. T. Lenoir, in December, 1875. it was discussed by the deacons of the church and others, whether he had made a deed to the lot occupied by the Baptist church, to the deacons of the church and their successors, and if such deed had been recorded, if such deed was in existence. There was no record of such deed and if it had been made it was not to be found. It was especially important as there was some talk of building a parsonage on the lot and they wished a clear title to it for church purposes. Therefore in the year ——— W. B. Lenoir, the heir-at-law of I. T. Lenoir, conveyed to the deacons of the church and their successors the lot which the members of the Baptist church claimed they were entitled to, specifying in the deed that it should not be sold and should be used only for church purposes. As the membership of this church was small and few of them were in anything but moderate circumstances when it was decided to build the parsonage, subscriptions were solicited by E. A. Taylor and others, to help us to build the parsonage. The subscriptions were liberal and came in from various sources and places. Among other subscriptions were $39.25 from the Baptist church at Madisonville, $35.00 from the First Baptist Church at Knoxville, $30.45 from the East Tennessee Baptist Association and $5.00 from the Brownsville Church in West Tennessee. Thus a very neat and commodious parsonage was built at a cost of about $900. This building was commenced on the 23rd of August, 1880; the house was occupied the 22nd day of January, 1881, probably by the Rev. W. C. Grace, who was pastor of the church at that time.

In ——— the church decided that they would build a new church building as the old one was not convenient or commodious. They wished to sell the old property for what they could get for it but they were debarred from doing so by the provisions of the deed from W. B. Lenoir. The committee from the church solicited him to make a deed to the church without any reservation. He was loath to do so fearing that the same thing might happen as happened in the case of the Baptist Seminary; that they might lose the new church property by mortgages or mechanic's liens. But after much solicitation and promises, on the part of the church people that they would not attempt to build a church to cost more than they had valid subscriptions for and they could pay for, he consented. Therefore on —— —— he conveyed to —— trustees the old church and parsonage property by warranty deed. This helped considerably in the building of the new church which is a credit to the membership and an ornament to the town. This is the most expensive and modern in its appointments of any church building in Sweetwater.

Methodist Episcopal Church, South,

Was the second church of any denomination built in Sweetwater. On the 15th of June, 1858, I. T. Lenoir conveyed to the stewards of the Methodist Episcopal Church, South, the following described property: Beginning at the corner of Monroe and High streets, thence westwardly with Monroe Street 250 feet to —— Street, thence at a right angle to Monroe Street to Henry Mayes' line, thence eastwardly with Wright Street to High Street, thence with High Street 180 feet to the beginning, containing about one acre. The consideration expressed was $100 dollars. This was never paid but was merely named that the church might have a clear deed to the property. There was no alley there then as there is now, and the location was considered ample for the building of both church and parsonage.

The first pastor in charge was the Rev. Kelly. In 1861 the Rev. J. W. Bowman was P. C. In 1862 James Atkin was P. E., and again in 1866. J. H. Brunner, P. E. in 1867-69; R. M. Hickey 1868-69; C. Long 1869-73.

In the year ——, owing to the growing need of the church, it was decided to sell the old church building and site and erect a new building on some other location. Half of the original lot conveyed by I. T. Lenoir, to the stewards of the church had already been sold to help pay for repairs to church damaged during the Civil War and purchase a parsonage for the church.

A lot for parsonage was bought, located just across the street from the Methodist church. This was afterwards sold, along with the church lot and building as part of a building fund for a new church. As the church had acquired a title to the Victoria College, formerly the Masonic Lodge building, it was determined to build a church there. J. W. Clark was chairman of the building committee. He spent much of his time and money in the erection and construction of the same. He and J. K. Brown were the largest contributors. I have no schedule showing who were the subscribers to the building fund, but I am satisfied the above statement is true.

The new church building was completed in the year 1892 and the parsonage a little later. I have not access to the reports of the building committee, therefore do not wish to make an estimate of its cost, but it was considered the most costly church building and parsonage, up to that time, in the town. It would take up too much space to give the late history and statistics of this or any other church in Sweetwater.

The Presbyterian Church at Sweetwater.

On the 12th of January, 1861, I. T. Lenoir conveyed to J. H. Patton and F. Bogart, trustees for the Presbyterian church, a lot in the town of Sweetwater, opposite to where the Eagle Flouring Mill now stands and on a part of which is now a planing mill, near the Madisonville road: fronting on Walnut Street 190 feet and running back 110 feet to an alley, thence with that alley to the street on the Heiskell line, thence with that street to Walnut. This is not the deed description but merely for purposes of identification. It was the intention of I. T. Lenoir to donate the lot with the provision that it was to be used for church purposes. However, the elders and members of the church thought better to pay for the lot, so that if they wanted to sell it, at any time, and locate the church elsewhere, they could do so.

This church was built by the new school branch of the Presbyterian church, and the people building it were members of the Presbyterian church at Philadelphia, Tenn. The largest contributors were John Ramsey,

Charles Owen, Alex. Biggs and William Patton. The building was commenced in 1857 and it was finished in the latter part of 1858 or the early part of 1859. This church was used by the Union Sunday-school until 1872, at which time the Methodist and Baptist churches established Sunday-schools of their own. From the time the Union Sunday-school began its meetings in the Presbyterian church John Ramsey was superintendent, to the time of his death in 1872.

The first pastor after the church was organized was the Rev. Thomas Brown, of Philadelphia, Tenn. The elders were Jno. Ramsey and Charles Owen. The Rev. Thomas Brown was pastor from its organization to some time in 1860 when the Rev. Thomas Bradshaw succeeded him. During 1863 and 1864 the Rev. Wm. Brown, of Cleveland, Tenn., preached for the church. These data were gotten from Mrs. Martha Waren.

If there are any session books extant as to the early organization of the church, I have not discovered where they were. From October, 1866 to the present, 1916, the history of the church is clearly set forth in the minutes of the session.

Up to October, 1866, there were two separate congregations in Sweetwater and the surrounding country, the old and the new school. The old school had held their meetings in the old Cumberland Presbyterian Church. At that date the members of the new school, and some members of the old school church, met as a congregation, and took a vote as to whether they should join the old school or new school branch of the church. They decided to unite and join the new school. Of this meeting George A. Caldwell was moderator and the elders were James Montgomery, Jno. Ramsey, E. E. Johnston and R. A. Ramsey, who was elected clerk of the meeting.

At a congregational meeting of the church on March 17, 1867, Jno. Ramsey, formerly an elder in the new school church, and R. A. Ramsey, formerly an elder in the old school, were unanimously elected elders. James Montgomery asked to be excused on account of age and infirmity. J. H. Patton, S. Y. B. Williams, W. L. Ramsey and Frank Bogart were elected elders. From that time for twenty years J. H. Patton was clerk of the session.

The Rev. W. W. Morrison from March, 1867 until November, 1872, preached twice a month for the church. The Rev. James Wallace was pastor from November, 1872, until May, 1889. From that time to January, 1891, there was no regular supply. On the last date the Rev. E. C. Trimble began to preach for the church. He, with his family, took possession of the parsonage, next to the new church on the 12th of February, 1891. He left Sweetwater on October 3, 1892. The Rev. J. L. Bachman then supplied the pulpit for six months, and he was continued as supply until he was elected pastor. This position he has held up to the present, 1916.

THE NEW PRESBYTERIAN CHURCH.

In the latter part of 1885 the building of a new Presbyterian church began to be agitated. The principal reasons for the building of the new church were that the majority of the members in town lived on the west side of the railroad and owing to the number of trains on the railroad it was inconvenient to get to it and dangerous for children, and that the church was antiquated and uncomfortable and not suited to the growing membership. Therefore on February 22, 1886, at the session of the church, the board of deacons were directed to canvass the congregation to ascertain what sum could be obtained for that purpose. In May, 1886, the deacons reported that a sufficient amount had been subscribed for the building of the church, to cost $6,000 or more. In June, 1886, an executive committee, consisting of Jno. M. Jones, chairman, J. H. Patton, James A. Wallace, F. Bogart and A. R. Melendy were appointed. They were to select a location and superintend the building of the church. A lot was purchased from Mrs. Ada Mayes, and dirt was broken on the present site in July, 1887. Bina Young was the contractor for the building of the church. In the church minutes, page 191, we find the following: June 2, 1888. The executive committee appointed June 16, 1887, to sell the old church house and build a new one, having performed that duty, called for a congregational meeting on this day, which was held in the new church house at 8 o'clock at night, according to previous arrangements and notice, at which time the following programme was observed:

1. Long metre Doxology, "Praise God from whom all blessings flow."
2. Invocation, by the pastor, Rev. James A. Wallace.
3. Treasurer's Report. Jno. M. Jones.
4. Tender of the church to congregation, with deed and keys, by A. R. Melendy.
5. Reception of the church, for congregation, by Elder J. F. Owen.
6. Reply of congregation to committee, by Rev. J. L. Bachman.
Reading Scriptures, Rev. Dugald Munroe.
Prayer, Rev. T. H. McCallie.
Singing 100th Psalm by the congregation.
Opening and First Sermon by Rev. J. A. Wallace, from Text 1 Timothy 3:5, "The Church of God."
Prayer, Rev. Geo. F. Robertson.
Singing by choir and congregation, Hymn 567, "Dear Shepherd of thy people hear."
Benediction, by Rev. James A. Wallace, Pastor.
June 3, Sabbath, 10:30 o'clock A. M.
Anthem, by choir.
Invocation, Rev. T. H. McCallie, D. D.
Singing 137th Psalm, 2nd part, "I love thy kingdom Lord."
Reading Scripture, Rev. J. L. Bachman.
Prayer, Rev. Dugald Munroe.
Hymn, 119, "All hail the power of Jesus' name."
Dedicatory Sermon, Rev. T. H. McCallie, from Text Matthew, 6:10, "Thy Kingdom come."
Dedicatory Hymn, number 568, "Here in Thy name, eternal God."
Benediction by the Rev. T. H. McCallie.

At a session of the elders at the Bank of Sweetwater, John M. Jones, chairman of the building committee, made a final report of subscriptions collected, the summary of which is as follows: Subscriptions paid, $6,167.85. Amount paid Bina Young, contractor, for bare church building, $5,138.50. Cost of lot, purchased from Mrs. Ada Mayes, grading, pavement, furnace and some other expenses, $1,029.35.

This does not include the cost of fresco decorations and other expenses inside the church. The whole cost of the church was about $8,000.00. Of this amount the Misses Coffin and Mr. Jno. H. and Mrs. Inman, nee Margaret Coffin, contributed about $4,000.00. In addition to this amount and not included therein, the parsonage was built at a cost of $2,100. To the fund for the building of the parsonage the Misses Coffin were far the largest contributors.

THE UNION INSTITUTE BUILDING.

The public schoolhouse, one-half mile southwest of Sweetwater Depot, has been several times referred to in this history. In that only summer schools could be taught with comfort, and then the larger students had to study out of doors. Public schools were all mixed schools, namely, for both males and females, and there seemed to be a public sentiment here during the fifties a growing against them. A new building for a schoolhouse, therefore, became a necessity.

In 1857 various citizens of Sweetwater and surrounding country met and decided to build a schoolhouse at or near the town. A stock company was formed, with twenty dollars for each share, upon which shares each stockholder was entitled to vote in the election of trustees according to the number of shares he held. On the 14th of October, 1857, E. A. Taylor, I. T. Lenoir and S. J. Rowan were elected trustees. They purchased lot No. 126 in the town of Sweetwater and erected a school building thereon, costing about $1,500.00. Lot 126 was bounded by High, Walnut, Church and Wright Streets.

The lower story of the building was used as a school for males and the upper for females. Mrs. H. M. Cooke was employed by the trustees to teach the females, and Professor Gabriel Ragsdale the males. He was not a moral suasionist, but believed in a liberal application of the rod. This was in 1858-59.

GEORGE LACON LEYBURN

Was born May 21, 1839, in old Laconia, in the extreme southern part of Greece; hence the name Lacon. His father, a distinguished Presbyterian minister, was missionary to Greece at the time. He took the degree of A. B. at Washington College, afterward Washington and Lee University, Lexington, Va., in the class of 1858. Though only nineteen years of age he was first honor man in his class. He was especially proficient in Greek. He was the first college graduate to teach in the First Civil District of Monroe County. He taught at the Union Institute in the years 1859-60. He then resigned, contrary to the wishes and solicitations of the trustees, to take a theological course. Before completing his ministerial education he joined the Confederate army. He was first lieutenant of Company A, Thirty-fourth Virginia Infantry, Wise's Brigade. He served four years. After the war he was pastor of Presbyterian churches as follows: Winchester, Va., 1867-75; missionary to Greece three years; his father died there in August, 1875; pastor Lexington, Mo., 1878-88; Booneville, Mo., 1889-96; Newbern, N. C., 1896-1900; four years Superintendent of Home Missions for Synod of Missouri; pastor Lexington, N. C., 1904-08; in November, 1908, after an operation for appendicitis resigned pastorate and went to California. Father of four children, all married; one daughter and three sons.

The next teacher of males in Union Institute was Oscar W. Muller. He was born in Prussia on September 9, 1834. He came to this country in 1846. He was a graduate of Hiwassee College in the class of 1859. He taught in Union Institute, 1860-61. He then enlisted in Confederate States army as first sergeant in Company C (Captain W. L. Clark's) Second Regiment, Tennessee Cavalry. He married Miss Eliza A. Clark on July 27, 1869. Like the true Prussian he was a great believer in efficiency. He is a farmer and surveyor and resides near Hiwassee College (1916). He was the last male teacher in the Union Institute until the close of the Civil War.

The next teacher was John W. Robertson, formerly of Meigs County. He was also a student of Hiwassee College and a college mate of W. T. Lenoir. He served in the Confederate army. He taught in the Union Institute in 1866-67. He moved to Texas in 1867, obtaining his demit from Sweetwater Lodge, No. 292, F. and A. M., on August 27th in that year. He became quite a prominent lawyer in that State.

Following J. W. Robertson was Rev. W. H. Crawford. He was born near Limestone, in Greene County, on March 4, 1822. He was educated at Doak—now Tusculum—College in Greene County. He was ordained a minister in the Cumberland Presbyterian church by East Tennessee Presbytery. He affiliated with Sweetwater Masonic Lodge in December, 1870. He was teacher and was pastor of the Cumberland Presbyterian church at the same time, is my remembrance. He went from here to Kingston. He had a family. Hon. W. L. Welcker, of Knoxville, married a daughter of his.

Following Rev. W. H. Crawford, Professor R. H. Ramsay became the teacher. He came from Milledgeville, Ga., or somewhere near there to Madisonville, Tenn., in 1865. He taught there as principal in Bolivar Academy for several years. He was a very brilliant man and made quite a reputation as an educator. I never knew a man who was more conversant with the best books in English literature. In mental aberration or melancholia, due to drink, he threw himself from the county bridge over the Tennessee River at Chattanooga. He was dead when reached. He was buried at Sweetwater. This was in the fall of 1890. He was on his way to Mississippi to take charge of a school. He had taught there the year previous.

In November, 1871, the stockholders met and decided to sell the property, to be used for school purposes. As matters were, it was the understanding that the building was to be used for school purposes; legally it was owned by a stock company, and could be used for any purpose. It was agreed that the first thirteen who subscribed fifty dollars each should be directors of the institution. They were: J. W. Clark, T. G. Boyd, Isaac Benson, W. B. Lenoir, James M. Browder, Thomas Yearwood, Matt Carter, R. F. Scruggs, N. I. Mayes, J. E. Ramsey and J. H. Patton. In order that this whole amount, $650.00, should be used for the fitting up and repairing the building and not go into the pockets of stockholders of the Union Institute, the following stock was donated to the new directorate: T. Yearwood, 4 shares; T. G. Boyd, 2; F. Bogart, 3; Charles Owen, 2; D. Heiskell, 16; R. Snead, 5; H. B. Yearwood, 4; J. W. Goddard, 6; Mrs. M. A. Reagan, 15; I. T. Lenoir, 35.

From the fall of 1874 till the summer of 1884, J. L. Bachman, D. D., taught in the Union Institute. Then a charter was obtained for Sweetwater College. It was decided to build a larger schoolhouse elsewhere, to sell the Union Institute building and lot and apply the proceeds to Sweetwater College. This was located in the northwest part of the town. The sale was at auction to the highest bidder on the 2nd of October, 1885, and W. B. Lenoir became the purchaser.

Soon afterward Dr. S. B. Cook bought a half interest in the property, and he and W. B. Lenoir fitted out the lower story as a theatre, auditorium and music room. In 1886 Dr. Cook sold his interest to W. B. Lenoir, who made extensive improvements on the grounds and building.

On December 26, 1887, W. B. Lenoir conveyed this property to W. H. H. Ragon, John S. Young and nine others of Monroe County, and J. F. Christian, of Meigs Company, J. P. Parker, of James County; C. C. Samuel, of Bradley County, as trustees, the property "to be used for females of the white race under control of the Baptist denomination of the State of Tennessee.

The building on lot 126 was used from 1886 till 1898 by these trustees and their successors for the purposes expressed in the deed. In the meantime during these years, '86-98, the trustees solicited and obtained large subscriptions, amounting to $12,000 to $15,000. They built a large addition to the old building, and in this a school was run for females under charge of J. H. Richardson and wife. They also purchased the lot 127 in the plan of the town of Sweetwater, and got permission from the board of mayor and aldermen of the corporation to close up the street between.

On the 30th of September, 1898, W. C. Grace, president; D. L. Smith, secretary; R. F. Scruggs, treasurer; James May, W. H. Smith, T. R. Wagner, Joseph Janeway and E. A. Taylor, of the Board of Trustees of the Baptist Seminary, conveyed to the Trustees of Sweetwater College, consisting of F. A. Carter, D. C. Young, John L. Brown, D. L. Smith, A. B. Scruggs, Harry Heiskell, G. A. McLin and others mentioned (Reg. Bk., No. 5, pp. 57-60), conveying as Trustees, "not otherwise," lots Nos. 126 and 127: Beginning at the corner of Wright and Church Streets, thence with Church Street to Morris Street; thence with Morris to High Street; thence with High to Wright Street; thence with Wright Street to beginning. The reasons given in the deed mentioned for sale of the property are as follows:

"Whereas, we, the Trustees of Sweetwater Seminary, in an honest endeavor to build good buildings for said Sweetwater Seminary and attach good grounds to the same and to run and establish a good school in the same and the purposes of the people who have subscribed and paid same to us and for the Baptist denomination; and, whereas, the Seminary has become involved in a debt of about twenty thousand dollars and said Baptist denomination and the people of the country have failed to pay said debt, and the Trustees have had to borrow the money and pay off many of these debts; and, whereas, some eight or nine thousand dollars of said indebtedness is still due and owing, and some of us Trustees are personally involved for same and have now an offer of ten thousand dollars for the building and grounds, which comes from the Trustees of Sweetwater College for the purpose of still using the building and ground for school purposes, we have, therefore, accepted said offer of ten thousand dollars rather than force said Seminary and grounds to sale, in order to retain it to the town, community and people for educational purposes; therefore," then follows description, etc.

From 1898 until 1902 school was taught there by J. L. Bachman, D. D., and others. It was taught in the name of Sweetwater College.

From 1902 to and including part of 1909, Colonel O. C. Hulvey ran a military school in the building. It was called the Tennessee Military Institute (T. M. I.). In that year, 1909, a very large building was erected one mile north of Sweetwater Depot. Colonal O. C. Hulvey moved to this and continued his school under the name of Tennessee Military Institute.

Mr. and Mrs. E. F. Rowland ran a female school in the Union Institute. Mr. Rowland died in 1910, and it was run two more years under the charge of Mrs. E. M. Rowland.

Then from 1913-1916 school for females was taught in the building, with W. S. Woodward as principal. This school was under charge of Carson and Newman College of Jefferson City, Tenn.

A public high school is now (1916) taught in the Union Institute, which is under the charge of Professor R. M. Ivins.

SWEETWATER LODGE 292, F. AND A. M.

On November 3, 1860, a dispensation was granted by the Grand Lodge of Tennessee, to constitute a lodge at Sweetwater to the following named brethren, mostly if not entirely members of the Tellico Lodge No. 80:

William B. Sample, S. Y. B. Williams, James A. Wright, J. C. Starrett, A. A. Humphreys, J. A. Rowan, H. B. Yearwood, R. F. Scruggs, I. T. Lenoir, William H. Taylor.

The said brethren were constituted into a regular lodge, No. 292 F. & A. M. The proceedings of this lodge are not known until the date given below for the reasons hereafter stated. At a meeting of the lodge on December 25, 1863, it was recited as follows: "Upon examination it was found that the record book, ledger and papers containing lodge matter were all gone. * * * The hall having been broken open by Federal soldiers." W. H. Taylor was W. M. at this meeting. The lodge met in the second-story of the Taylor building, then occupied by S. Y. B. Williams, afterwards the J. E. Williams building. At an election of officers held the following were named: W. B. Sample, W. M.; J. M. Sample, S. W.; F. B. Carter, J. W.; S. Y. B. Williams, treasurer; S. P. Haynes, tyler; J. H. Patton, secretary.

These officers served until December 22, 1865. The succeeding officers and their years of service are as follows:

1869—W. L. Clark, W. M.; N. P. Hight, S. W.; T. G. Boyd, J. W.; R. F. Scruggs, treasurer; J. H. Patton, secretary; J. W. Goddard, tyler.

1870—W. L. Clark, W. M.; N. P. Hight, S. W.; T. G. Boyd, J. W.; R. F. Scruggs, treasurer; J. H. Patton, secretary; A. M. Dobbins, tyler.

1871—W. L. Clark, W. M.; L. Forkner, S. W.; N. I. Mayes, J. W.; R. F. Scruggs, treasurer; J. H. Patton, secretary; A. M. Dobbins, tyler.

1872—T. G. Boyd, W. M.; J. H. Pickel, S. W.; H. L. Fry, J. W.; R. F. Scruggs, treasurer; J. H. Patton, secretary; A. H. Murray, tyler.

1873—W. L. Clark, W. M.; A. A. Humphreys, S. W.; W. B. Lenoir, J. W.; R. F. Scruggs, treasurer; J. H. Patton, secretary; A. M. Dobbins, tyler.

1874—N. P. Hight, W. M.; A. A. Humphreys, S. W.; Jo. W. Robertson, J. W.; R. F. Scruggs, treasurer; J. H. Patton, secretary; A. M. Dobbins, tyler.

1876—W. L. Clark, W. M.; A. A. Humphreys, S. W.; Jo. W. Robertson, J. W.; R. F. Scruggs, treasurer; J. H. Patton, secretary; C. Cannon, tyler.

1877—J. H. Pickel, W. M.; J. W. Robertson, S. W.; J. H. Montgomery, J. W.; R. F. Scruggs, treasurer; J. H. Patton, secretary; C. Cannon, tyler.

1878—W. B. Sample, W. M.; W. L. Clark, S. W.; W. B. Lenoir, J. W.; R. F. Scruggs, treasurer; J. H. Patton, secretary; C. Cannon, tyler.

1879—J. L. McKinney, W. M.; W. L. Clark, S. W.; W. B. Lenoir, J. W.; R. F. Scruggs, treasurer; J. H. Patton, secretary; C. Cannon, tyler.

1880—J. W. Robertson, W. M.; S. B. Cook, S. W.; W. B. Lenoir, J. W.; R. F. Scruggs, treasurer; J. H. Patton, secretary; C. Cannon, tyler.

1881—J. W. Robertson, W. M.; J. L. Bachman, S. W.; W. B. Lenoir, J. W.; R. F. Scruggs, treasurer; J. H. Patton, secretary; C. Cannon, tyler.

1882—Jo. W. Robertson, W. M.; J. L. Bachman, S. W.; W. N. Lybarger, J. W.; R. F. Scruggs, treasurer; F. Bogart, secretary; C. Cannon, tyler.

1883—Jo. W. Robertson, W. M.; W. B. Lenoir, S. W.; J. L. Bachman, J. W.; R. F. Scruggs, treasurer; F. Bogart, secretary; C. Cannon, tyler.

1884—W. L. Clark, W. M.; J. L. Bachman, S. W.; J. H. Montgomery, J. W.; R. F. Scruggs, treasurer; G. F. Hicks, secretary; D. W. Butt, tyler.

1885—S. B. Cook, W. M.; J. S. Young, S. W.; J. I. Carter, J. W.; R. F. Scruggs, treasurer; G. F. Hicks, secretary; C. Cannon, tyler.

1886—S. B. Cook, W. M.; G. F. Hicks, S. W.; Jno. B. Carter, J. W.; R. F. Scruggs, treasurer; R. W. Brown, secretary; C. Cannon, tyler.

After the close of the war from 1865, until 1875, the lodge prospered exceedingly, and there were many additions to the membership. One reason for this was that it was conceded and believed that the Masonic fraternity had helped very much to mitigate the horrors of the Civil War. Favors were shown to brethren on the different sides, Federal and Confederate, and treatment given which would not have been extended to other than Masons.

In July, 1868, the lodge decided to build a new hall instead of meeting in rented property. As a building committee there were appointed: R. F. Scruggs, I. T. Lenoir, J. H. Pickel, J. H. Patton and W. L. Clark. Besides the money in the treasury the members contributed very liberally to the building of the new hall. A lot was purchased where the M. E. Church, South, and parsonage now stand, and a hall was erected at a cost of more than $5,000.

The first meeting held in the new hall was on Friday, November 19, 1869. The lower part of the building was used as a school room. It was first rented to Mrs. Helen M. Cooke in 1870.

In the year 1873 some of the brethren, especially those in the country, became dissatisfied with the location of the hall. There was no convenient hitching place for their horses nearer than the public square around the depot. A committee was appointed to report what could be done about a new and better location for a hall. In November, 1873, the committee reported that a third story on M. Carter's building, could be added at a cost of about $2,500; they therefore decided to sell the old property and accept Mr. Carter's offer.

On November 28, 1873, the lodge passed a resolution to sell to the Methodists for $5,500, and donate $2,000, for purpose of establishing a female school of high grade. This amount of $3,500 was subscribed mostly by the citizens of Sweetwater and country around, and to which fund many, not Methodists, subscribed liberally. Therefore in pursuance of this resolution of the lodge, on February 2, 1874, a deed was made to certain trustees for a female high school, to be under the charge of the Athens District Conference.

The first meeting of the Masonic Lodge in their new hall over the Carter building was on May 14, 1875. A deed to the hall in the third story of the building was made by Mat Carter to Lodge 292 F. & A. M. on September 1, 1876. The Masons still (1916) hold their meeting there.

At a meeting of the lodge April 14, 1871, by a unanimous vote the lodge subscribed to the Masonic Home

Mission School $1,000. This sum was to be paid in annual installments of $100 each, the first installment to be due in November, 1873.

From the names of those present at masonic meetings after the reorganization of the lodge we find that the following besides the charter members belonged to Lodge 292 previous to 1864, as they were mentioned afterward as being present at lodge meetings and are not afterward among the affiliates or afterward made master Masons:

S. B. Haines, J. M. Sample, F. B. Carter, D. P. Forkner, Thomas Forkner, M. T. Stanfield, John Forkner, W. A. Nelson, W. L. Clark, J. H. Patton, Thomas Upton, W. H. Cooke, Jno. W. Lotspeich, W. L. Price, J. G. Parshall, J. H. Taylor and Charles Cannon.

List of affiliates and those made master Masons up to 1886: T. C. Bellamy, 26 May '65; T. G. Boyd, 22 June '66; Frank Bogart, 6 August '65; T. J. Ballard, 12 August '65, died 12 July '69; L. F. Briant, 25 September '65; D. A. Browder, 22 September '65, died 6 April '83; W. L. Ballard, 9 March '69; T. L. Brown, 20 August '69; M. K. Benson, ———; J. L. Ballard, ———; J. E. Bilderback, 25 September '65; T. R. Bradshaw, 23 June '65; J. M. Browder, 23 November '65; J. S. Burnett, 20 October '66; J. A. Bilderback, 11 February '80; J. P. Brown, aff. (80) 8 July '70; N. C. Carter, 26 January '66; dem. 10 March '76; Mat Carter, 17 April '67, died 28 April '85; J. A. Crowder, 26 August '67; W. J. Clayton, 26 June '79; M. B. Caldwell, 3 February '71; Wm. Cannon, 24 November '65; Robt. Carter, aff. (80) 22 March '67; W. H. Cooke, dem. to No. 134 25 April '69; W. H. Crawford aff. December '70; L. L. Calloway, aff. 10 September '75; A. G. Carden, dem. 7 January '76; A. M. Dobbins, 28 July '65; A. S. Dickey, ———; H. P. Dickey, 20 October '66, buried by Masons 28 July '70; A. J. Dickey, 22 September '69; S. B. Cook, aff. 19 January '78; J. L. Bachman, 26 February '80; L. W. Brown, 21 May '80; D. W. Butt, 28 April '82; J. I. Carter, 9 May '84; G. M. Cline, aff. 21 August '85; R. W. Brown and J. B. Carter on 27 November '85; W. M. Edwards, 20 October '66; Lawrence Forkner, 27 April '65, buried 1 September '81; Wm. Foote, 28 October '65, exp. December '68; H. L. Fry, 10 November

'68; Wm. Foster, 28 October '65; Thomas A. Forkner, 25 July '85; J. G. Forkner, ———; M. B. Goddard aff. (Athens) 25 May '66; J. W. Goddard aff. (Loudon), 24 August '66; W. W. Grubb, aff. 11 October '72; W. C. Grace aff. (115), 29 August '79; Wm. Harrison, 8 December '66; N. P. Hight aff. (Mo.), 23 November '66; A. A. Humphreys, reaff. 22 March '72; E. T. Hale, aff. 30 January '74; dem. 12 October '77; Hicks G. F. aff. 20 January '80; John H. Johnston, 23 June '65; Jos. Janeway, aff. (Loudon) 23 February '66; J. Harvey Johnston, 28 September '66; E. C. Jones, 23 February '66; Eli C. Jones, 13 May '70; John M. Jones, aff. 4 December '81; J. F. Key, 25 May, '66; W. T. Lenoir, 25 September '68; J. D. Low, 25 September 65; W. T. Lenoir, 30 June '71; Noah Lybarger, 2 May '79; dem. 3 February '82; S. J. Martin, 1 November '65; Martin G. W., 7 November '65, died 6 March '70; W. G. McKenzie, ——— dem. 4 July '73; A. H. Murray, 4 September '65, ———; N. I. Mayes, 9 September '68, ———; Jas. McGuire, ———; O. W. Muller, ———; J. H. Montgomery, 3 November '66, ———; J. L. McKinney, aff. 6 September '78; A. R. Melendy, 28 February '85, ———; J. F. Owen, aff. (204), 27 April '66, ———; J. C. Pennington, 28 July '65; B. M. Porter, 22 June '66, dem. 30 June '71; Wiley Patton, 27 April '67, ———; J. H. Pickel, 5 May '68, ———; W. W. Pickel, 26 June '69, ———; W. L. Price, ——— dem. 23 February '72; J. E. Roberts, 25 September '65, ———; J. Crockett Rowan, 2 March '67, dem. 27 August '67; John W. Robertson, 30 July '67, dem. 27 August '67; J. H. Rowan, ———; F. M. Rowan, ——— Josiah K. Rowan, 27 August '67, dem. 11 June '70; Joseph W. Robertson, 23 February '72; A. C. Small, 28 July '65, ———; T. H. Small, 4 November '65, ———; G. G. Stillman, ———, died 29 July '72; J. N. Stamper, 27 October '65, ———; James Sample, 27 August '67, ——— dem. 2 December '70; J. C. Starrett, ———; A. J. Stradley, aff. (484) 12 February '86; J. H. Taylor, ———; N. G. Vineyard, 1 July '65, ———; W. A. Upton, 25 October '67, dem. 11 February '81, he died in Texas; S. E. Young (392) aff. 11 February '81, ———; Jno. S. Young, 6 June '84, ———; J. L. Willson, 12 August '65; W. P. Willson,

———; A. W. Ward, 27 July '69, ———; S. H. Willson, May '65, ———; C. I. Wright, 8 September '65, ———; S. M. Walker, 10 January '70, ———; C. B. Woodward, February '73, dem. 7 January '76.

SWEETMATER CHAPTER R. A. M., No. 57.

Of date the first day of January, 1866, John Frizzell, G. H. P. of Tennessee, granted to the following companions: John F. Slover, Richard C. Jackson, A. D. Rhea, S. B. Haines, W. A. Nelson, William G. Horton, I. N. Clark, J. B. Pickens, H. M. Rice, I. C. Grant and R. L. Scott, a dispensation empowering them to open and hold a chapter of Royal Arch Masons in the town of Sweetwater, Tenn., to be called Sweetwater Chapter No. 57.

In pursuance of said dispensation on January 22, 1866, John F. Slover, H. P., with the other proper officers, opened and held a chapter in their hall at Sweetwater. G. G. Stillman was made secretary.

Appended to the by-laws of this chapter, published by the Forerunner office at Sweetwater, Tenn., in 1868, the names of the officers and members of this chapter follow:

W. H. Cooke, H. P.; N. P. Hight, K.; F. Bogart, S.; T. G. Boyd, C. H.; W. L. Clark, P. S.; Charles Cannon, R. A. C.; R. F. Scruggs, Treas.; J. H. Patton, sec'y.; E. F. Sharp, G. M., 3rd V.; W. L. Price, 2nd V.; I. T. Lenoir, 1st V.; J. W. Goddard, Sent.; G. G. Stillman, R. A. M.; C. H. Matthewson, R. A. M.; A. D. Rhea, R. A. M.; Morgan Bryan, R. A. M.; T. J. Ballard, R. A. M.; T. N. Epperson, R. A. M.; Wm. P. McKamey, R. A. M.; Sam'l. Reese, R. A. M.; I. B. Kimbrough, R. A. M.; H. J. Foote, R. A. M.; Frank Felts, R. A. M.; W. C. Peak, R. A. M.; J. J. Harrison, R. A. M.; E. C. Jones, R. A. M.; Wm. Osborn, R. A. M.; J. C. Starrett, R. A. M.; O. C. Carter, R. A. M.; Jas. P. Galyon, R. A. M.; W. N. B. Jones, R. A. M.

This chapter prospered for some years and greatly assisted financially the Sweetwater Lodge No. 292, F. & A. M. to erect the two buildings they constructed, the hall on the hill and the third story of the Carter building. It was the understanding with the chapter and the Master Mason's Lodge that the chapter should hold its meetings in the hall and own their proportionate part of the buildings, although not so expressed in the deed.

With the formation of new chapters their territory was much reduced and it was hard to secure a quorum for the transaction of business. In 1887 the Grand Chapter of the state of Tennessee revoked their charter, since which time there has been no chapter in Sweetwater.

THE NEWSPAPERS OF SWEETWATER.

The first paper published in Sweetwater was "The Sweetwater Forerunner." Volume 1 No. 1 was dated September 1, 1867. It was a four-page paper about half the size of the usual weekly. Editor and proprietor, H. L. Fry. Subscription price was $2 per year. We find this among the editorials in the first paper.

"Last night was a terrible night.—The storm raged all night, and is not over with. Saturday, September 21, 1867, will be, in all time to come a memorable day in the history of Sweetwater. Amid the flashing of lightning and muttering and bellowing of thunder the greatest event that has ever transpired within her limits is taking place; the first newspaper ever printed in Sweetwater is being published. Long may the day be remembered and may it be pointed to with just pride as the commencement of a new epoch in the history of the village."

There were also poets in those days. Note these lines in that issue from J. A. H.:

A WARNING.

"Old bachelors arise, away,
  Shake off the fleas and dust,
If you on earth expect to stay,
  In woman put your trust.
A married man is right in town
  With a pocket full of rocks,
A wife to fix his clothes up brown
  And darn his ragged socks."

Advertisements in the issue were:

Hight & Scruggs, General Merchandise and Produce; N. I. Mayes, D. S.; Stock & Roberts, Commission Merchants, Cartersville, Ga.; Glenn, Wright & Carr, Commission Merchants, Atlanta.

The Forerunner was enlarged in May, 1868, and was published by Fry and Fisher. From December 17, 1868, to March, 1869, Charles M. Fisher was sole proprietor. He was from Richmond, Va., and was apparently finely educated and very versatile. He was the best all round newspaper man, the finest flute player and the most accomplished "boozefighter" that ever lived in the town.

He never wrote out his editorials; he just set them up and rarely looked them over. They were absolutely correct in spelling and grammar and were well expressed. He was a fluent writer although he did not write at all.

I heard that after he left Sweetwater he became a derelict and a tramp printer. He was such an entertaining companion and so fine a musician that drinks were easy for him to procure.

In March, 1869, C. B. Woodward bought out the paper and became its editor and proprietor. On September 1, 1869, he changed its name from "Forerunner" to "The Sweetwater Enterprise." He ran this paper until the early part of 1876, when Joe Ivins took charge and conducted it until after the November election. The paper was then suspended. Hight and Scruggs acquired a title to the outfit. In December, 1876, J. H. Bean of Knoxville bought the paper and press from them and published the paper on January 1, 1877, under the name of "The Monroe Democrat." He was editor and proprietor until the 1st of January, 1880, when he sold out to D. B. Grace.

He kindly furnishes the following information:

"David B. Grace went from Birmingham, Ala., in 1880, to pay a visit to his father, F. M. Grace, who was professor of English in Hiwassee College. Finding that J. H. Bean was desirous of selling the Monroe Democrat he bought him out and ran the paper for four years, returning to Birmingham in 1884. During the four years Mr. Grace ran the paper it never missed an issue. On one occasion the supply of paper ordered failed to arrive, and on Wednesday afternoon Mr. Grace went down to Athens on the train and bought five hundred sheets of paper from Mr. (Sam. P.) Ivins, of the Athens Post, and brought it with him on the train to Sweetwater. Thus the Democrat came out in time Thursday morning. While Mr. Grace published the Democrat there was no other paper in Monroe County. The Democrat printed the legal notices and these, together with the liberal patronage of the Sweetwater merchants and those of Knoxville, gave the paper a good advertising patronage. Mr. Grace was at the time a young man without experience, but he was ably assisted by his father, Dr. Brunner, Mr. W. B. Lenoir, Dr. Bachman and others." (Note: The assistance I gave him was to drop in his sanctum, read his exchanges and talk to him about the Sweetwater girls.—W. B. L.)

"In 1884 Grace sold the Democrat and returned to Birmingham. There he assisted in founding the Evening Chronicle, and afterward served as editorial writer on the News, which had been merged with the Chronicle. He also acted as assistant editor on the Age-Herald. He is now engaged in general literary work."

After Mr. Grace disposed of the Democrat J. S. Yearwood became the editor and proprietor. (See H. B. Y.) He ran the paper till W. B. Lenoir purchased from him in March, 1889. W. B. L. ran the paper till the fall of 1891 when he was bought out by F. H. Sruggs of the News. The Monroe Democrat, as its name would indicate, was always a democratic paper.

The Sweetwater News

Began to be published by F. H. Scruggs as editor and proprietor in 1886. He published it under that name until the fall of 1891. After F. H. S. purchased the Monroe Democrat from W. B. Lenoir he ran the merged papers under the name of the Democrat-News till his death which occurred on July 8, 1895. This paper was then suspended and the printing presses and the type sold to Mr. Martin of the Loudon Record.

Not long after the suspension of the Democrat-News J. M. Kirkland ran a small paper for several months which he called the "Ruby Wave." He then enlarged it and changed the name to Sweetwater Courier. This paper he conducted for about two years.

The Sweetwater Telephone.

The latter part of 1895 D. L. Smith and others formed a stock company and on January 1, 1896, commenced the publication of The Sweetwater Telephone. D. L. Smith was editor of this paper until September 1, 1907. Then at a reorganization of the stock company D. L. Smith became president and James M. Pardue, editor and manager. D. L. Smith died November 19, 1912.

J. M. Pardue has had a controlling interest in this paper for six years up to present (1916).

LEGISLATORS IN THE GENERAL ASSEMBLY OF TENNESSEE, RESIDENTS OF SWEETWATER VALLEY.

Sweetwater Valley has had its share of lawmakers in the General Assembly, and they have all been farmers except three—one of these three was a farmer when he was elected.

Those representatives living in the valley when elected were: General James H. Reagan, senator Twenty-first General Assembly, Monroe and McMinn, and also in the Thirtieth General Assembly, the first to hold its meetings in the state capitol. Reagan's history is given elsewhere in this book.

Hon. Few Hall Gregory was a representative in the Twenty-third General Assembly, elected in 1839. See Gregory elsewhere in this book.

Colonel Jno. Ramsey was elected representative from Monroe to the Twenty-seventh General Assembly. His opponent was Wm. Heiskell. An account of this race and his history is given in this book.

Hon. George W. Gaines, formerly of the fourteenth civil district of Monroe County, was living with his son-in-law, Dr. F. Bogart of Sweetwater, when elected to the Legislature in 1865. This legislature has no regular number and is known as the "Brownlow Legislature." In his race he received the Democratic vote of the county. He was a Union man during the war but opposed the disfranchising legislation and other violent measures passed by that assembly.

Hon. Jesse F. Owen was elected in 1869 to represent Monroe County in the Thirty-sixth General Assembly. For further history see Owen in this book.

General J. C. Vaughn was a senator from the seventh senatorial district to the Thirty-seventh General Assembly. He was speaker of that body. His history is given in this book.

Hon. S. J. Martin was representative from Monroe and Loudon counties in the Thirty-eighth General Assembly. For history see Presley Cleveland family.

Hon. William Cannon was elected to the Fortieth General Assembly as the representative from Monroe and Loudon counties.

Hon. W. B. Sample was a representative of Monroe and Loudon counties in the Forty-first General Assembly, although he did not reside in the first civil district of Monroe County nor in Sweetwater Valley, but close to the line between first and second districts, and his post-office was at Sweetwater. His team of oxen and his corn-cob pipe were frequently seen in our town. On election day in November, 1878, a large crowd smoking cob pipes went in a body to the polls and voted for Sample. He was called the farmer's candidate.

Hon. J. R. Love was representative from Monroe County in the Forty-fourth General Assembly, elected in November, 1884. Died during his incumbency. For sketch of him see Reagan family.

Hon. D. R. Nelson was a member of the Forty-sixth General Assembly as a senator of the sixth district. (See Nelson.)

Hon. W. L. Brown was senator from the sixth senatorial district in the Forty-seventh General Assembly. History in this book.

W. N. Hoge was a representative from McMinn County to the Forty-eighth General Assembly. At the time of his election he resided near Reagan Station. Previous to his election he occupied several important county offices.

W. G. Lenoir was a joint representative for Knox and Loudon counties in the General Assembly. He was elected in November, 1910, as a fusionist. He was a zealous prohibitionist and was a prominent factor in state-wide legislation while he was a member.

Hon. James M. Pardue was representative from Monroe to the Forty-ninth General Assembly. He is the present (1916) senator from the district comprised of Knox, Blount, Monroe and Polk counties. He is a lawyer by profession and now (1916) editor of the Sweetwater Telephone. He was born in Loudon County and came to Sweetwater twenty years ago.

Hon. J. C. Waren was a member of the Fifty-sixth General Assembly as the representative from Monroe County. For further history see Colonel Jno. Ramsey in this book.

Hon. James May was senator from the 6th district in the Fifty-fifth General Assembly. He was born in Knox County on October 10, 1863. He came to Sweetwater in November, 1896. He embarked in the hardware business in which he remained eighteen years. He was mayor of Sweetwater for eight years. He was married to Prudie C. Howard of Fork Creek on December 21, 1887. He was prison commissioner for East Tennessee, under Governor Hooper, 1912-14. He had charge of the penitentiary farm near Nashville which he ran successfully, clearing $55,000 over and above expenses during his incumbency. His children are Ethel, Beulah and Earl. Earl is a member of the firm of James May & Son at Sweetwater.

SOME TRANSACTIONS IN HORSES IN 1863.

In the last years of the Civil War East Kentucky, East Tennessee, Western North Carolina and North Georgia were infested with various bands of horse thieves, robbers and bushwhackers. Sometimes several of these bands acted in common after the John A. Murrell style. Others chose a leader and acted independently. Often they claimed to affiliate with one or the other side in the civil contest. The union bushwhackers claimed that they did not rob and kill Union men and the Rebel bushwhackers that they did not rob and murder Southern sympathizers. As notable examples we might mention Tinker Dave Beattie and Champ Ferguson in the Cumberlands and Goldman Bryson and Lyons in the Smokies. I presume if we ever have a war with a foreign country we will likely have American and hyphenated-American bushwhackers.

In the sections mentioned in 1863 and 1864 no man's life or property was safe. If a soldier deserted from either army he usually stole a horse as an additional means of safety in getting away and also to secure a valuable piece of property.

In this section horse stealing was very common in 1863. In May of that year my father, I. T. Lenoir, had a fine horse stolen from a barn near his home located about one and a half miles south of Sweetwater. It was stolen by a deserter from the 10th Confederate, Colonel Goode's Cav., Regt. of conscripts. My father got on his track and followed him to the Sand Mountains of Alabama now the richest, then the poorest section of the state. He failed to find his own horse but his expedition was not fruitless. One day in following a supposed clue he came across a rough looking sand-mountaineer who was riding a fine roane mare. He engaged him in conversation and on close inspection he was confident that he had seen the animal he was riding hitched in Sweetwater several times and was convinced that she had been stolen. He told the fellow he had come after that horse and to throw down his rifle and dismount. This he at first refused to do, but my father reasoned with him in such a way that he finally did as requested. He then ordered him to walk back the way he came and not to turn round or look back. When he had gotten some distance off, father himself lost no time in returning, fearing he might be pursued. The mare, as it turned out, belonged to Mr. Robert Wright of Fork Creek Valley. It would have been a fine joke on father if he had not succeeded in finding the owner.

After the sand mountain episode, we took precautions to prevent the horses from being stolen. Our barn had some stables which could only be reached through a passage which was closed at each end by a gate. The gate at one end was padlocked and the one at the other end, least used, was fastened by a large wood screw through the slat into the latch; thus the gate could not be opened without taking out the screw. We did not think a thief would catch on to the scheme without waking the negro or myself up. We slept in the barn loft as additional protection against thieves. But "the best laid plans of mice and men gang aft agley."

On Sunday the 5th of July, 1863, I persuaded one of the neighbor boys to go with me to Craighead Lake in the Bat Creek knobs for a swim. The lake then was considerably larger than now. We did not particularly need to go in bathing, but we had heard the Rev. Mr. Bradshaw preach for an hour and a half in the morning and we thought we were entitled to an afternoon off. For fear of embarrassing complications we thought best not to consult our parents about the trip. We remained in the water considerable time trying to outswim the mellow bugs, with which the surface of the lake abounded. This made me sleep sounder in the barn loft than usual that night. So when the thief came Sunday night, as he told me afterwards about 11 o'clock, I did not wake and neither did the darkey that was with me.

In the morning the gate was wide open and a horse was gone. The thief, in trying to get the horse out, had started to cut the latch in two. He found that would take too long. He accidentally discovered how the latch was fastened and unloosed the screw with his knife, which happened to be a strong one.

The horse stolen was one easily described and identified. He was a large rawboned bay horse, about sixteen and a half hands high and had a very large head and had a couple of large warts on his jaws. A blind bridle was missing but he got no saddle. He stole a saddle in Dancing Branch neighborhood. We heard of that on Monday. We found out on Tuesday that a man Carter had left the 6th Georgia, Hart's Regiment without a furlough and that he had volunteered from Towns County, Ga. Mr. W. H. Taylor, son of E. A. Taylor, and a former merchant in Sweetwater, had married a Miss Bradshaw of Towns County, Ga. Her mother still lived there and Mr. Taylor was acquainted in that section. He told my father he would go with me to get the horse and, if possible, the man that stole him. I was anxious to go as I was much chagrinned at my father's saying ironically what a fine guard I was. So we made our arrangements to start from Sweetwater next morning, Wednesday.

To show how thoughtful my father was I remember a little circumstance. He knew that it gave me a bad headache not to have coffee for breakfast as I had always been used to it. He suggested that I get my mother to put me up some coffee to take along. This was not to be given out where we stopped, but if I got the headache for lack of it, the grounds were to be drank from a cup mixed with cold water from some spring by the roadside. On trying the experiment when the headache came on, I found it worked like a charm. Coffee in the Confederacy owing to the blockade of the ports in 1863 was exceedingly scarce and high in price when it could be obtained at all. As a substitute parched rye and wheat were used. It tasted all right like postum but did not have any kick to it like real coffee.

But to resume my narrative: We, Taylor and myself, left Sweetwater in the morning. He rode a good horse of father's; I rode a horse rather on the pony order, which I had purchased from a Texas ranger. His name was Craig. He wanted to sell the horse to me because his ankle had been rope scorched and he was temporarily disabled. I paid for him $100.00 in Confederate money. One was about as unsafe possession as the other. I was rather proud of my trade, as that was the first horse I had ever bought.

The result proved that he was a very hardy animal but rather a tiresome saddler. We, W. H. Taylor and myself, stayed at Austin Fry's the first night. He then lived on Conasuaga Creek three miles this side of the toll gate on the road from Madisonville to Murphy, N. C. He was an old acquaintance of my father and used to reside near Reagan's Station. There at Fry's we heard nothing of the man and the stolen horse but on reaching the toll gate at the foot of Unaka Mountain we were told that our man had passed through the gate there. This was encouraging and we determined to push rapidly on. There were only two routes he could take, either up the Hiwassee River towards Murphy or the one to Ducktown going south and crossing the Hiwassee River at Taylor's Ferry near where Apalachia now is. We concluded to risk the Murphy route as we thought Carter had gone that way with the stolen horse. We did this though we had been told by Mr. Fry that that route was very dangerous. He said: "I would not undertake what you two are trying to do for my hat full of gold. The country east of the mountains towards Murphy is full of bushwhackers who do not hesitate to commit any sort of depredation." Mr. Fry some weeks before had been shot in the shoulder from ambush and narrowly escaped with his life. He was at the time we stopped with him carrying his arm in a sling in consequence of his wound. Goldman Bryson's notorious gang were then in process of formation. From the toll gate for twelve miles we saw no one, though that is no evidence that we were not ourselves seen, till we reached the Beaver Dam country on the Hiwassee River ten miles from Murphy; there we passed a man with Federal blue pants on driving two calves hitched to the front wheels of a wagon. Two or three miles further on we met a man carrying a fiddle and a bow in a sack. He was about the only man we saw that day who looked cheerful and did not eye us with suspicion. I supposed he thought that no one would be mean and heartless enough to hurt a good fiddler however steeped in crime he might be. Not far from Hanging Dog Creek we saw Jim Reddicks, so Taylor said his name was, plowing corn in a field. We questioned none of them. We did not care about advertising our business.

We stopped at Murphy where we arrived about the middle of the day, and got our dinner at S. W. Davidson's. He kept hotel in an old frame building, now torn down, which occupied the lot under the large elms and aspens opposite the site of the new Regal Hotel. At this town we made some inquiries but found out nothing of consequence. We were there about an hour and a half. We had come twenty-five miles and still had twenty-nine to go if we reached Mrs. Bradshaw's, Mr. Taylor's mother-in-law. She lived four miles east of Hiwassee, Towns County, Ga. When dark came upon us we were ten or twelve miles from our destination, but we thought it better to arrive in that neighborhood at night so that no one could have any idea who we were or what our business was. We did not want it known there were any strangers there. It must have been nearly midnight when we arrived at Mrs. Bradshaw's. Her son was away in the army and Mrs. Bradshaw being naturally excited at any one coming at that time of night and a visit from him was entirely unexpected that Taylor could hardly convince her that he was her son-in-law. When he knocked, "Who's there?" she asked. "Billy Taylor." "What Taylor?" "Della Bradshaw's husband." She finally became convinced of his identity and let us in and told us where we could get feed for our horses. We had traveled fifty-four or fifty-five miles that day and I was so thoroughly weary that it seems to me I was asleep before I hardly got my clothes off. When I had slept for about ten minutes, as I thought, Taylor awakened me out of the shortest night's sleep in my experience. He said it was near sunrise and we must be up and doing. After considerable inquiry in the neighborhood we found that Carter's wife had lived not very far from Mrs. Bradshaw's but had left sometime previous for parts unknown. They told us however that Mrs. Carter's father lived in Ducktown and that his name was Borong. So about 10 a. m. we left for that place to find out what we could there. That night we stayed at a Mr. Martin's about six miles southeast of Murphy. Next morning bright and early we were on our way. We had traveled for about an hour and were a short distance from the bridge over the Notla and we came to the forks of the road, when Taylor remarked "Lets get off our horses and have a consultation." I noticed that he had been unusually silent and serious for the last mile or two of our journey and looked as if in a deep study. When we dismounted he did not say anything for some time; then he said: "I believe Mr. Fry was right and I feel it my duty to say to you that we ought not to risk our lives for the sake of a horse that may be stolen again and may soon be impressed for the service of one army or the other. I think we had better return by way of Murphy and let the horse go." "From what Mr. Fry said," I answered, "will it not be as dangerous to return that way as to go on." "Well I'm going back," he said, "what are you going to do?" and he turned his horse's head in the direction of Murphy. "I'm going to get that horse," I replied, "that's what I came for. I'm not going back home and have Pa saying I should have prevented the horse from being stolen and when he sent me after him I did not make the proper effort to get him. I do not suppose I could take the horse and man back by myself but I'm going to get that horse or know the reason why I can't." I rather thought he was bluffing and I concluded to put up one myself. Still there was no decision. After some little time he offered as a compromise that he would go to Ducktown with me and if we found out nothing there we would return home by the most feasible route. I agreed. We had not gone far till he remarked: "The fact is I could not go back and face your mother and father if I had deserted you and anything happened to you." That was the way I had him sized up but I did not think it policy to tell him so then. We then wended our way to Ducktown, a long, long, lonesome road and one of the most hilly I've ever traveled. There is not I believe a hundred yards at one place of level road, or was not at that time, between Notla Bridge and Ducktown. (Why the name Ducktown I've often wondered, for I have never seen a duck there, wild or tame.)

When we reached Ducktown we found Mr. Borong was engaged in roasting copper ore so as to form it into mattes. This was the crude form in which the copper was hauled to Cleveland, Tenn. The copper mined at Ducktown then was mostly used by the Confederacy. Mr. Taylor asked Mr. Borong if he had seen his son-in-law or if he had passed through. He said he had two or three days previously and told when asked what kind of a horse Carter was riding. He further informed us that his daughter was up in Fannin County, Ga., near Morganton and he thought his son-in-law had gone to where she was. Mr. Taylor then informed him that Carter was riding a horse that was stolen in Sweetwater Valley but we did not know how he got it but if he came by the horse honestly he would be protected. Mr. Borong said that his son-in-law had told him that he was absent from his regiment on furlough and that he had swapped for the horse. He said that he had no desire to shield his son-in-law if he was a thief. We thought he was honest and meant what he said but still we preferred not to take any chances and lost no time in getting to Morganton, which place we reached about sundown. We put up at the hotel. Taylor left the hotel soon to hunt up the sheriff of the county. He made arrangements with him to get a deputy or two and hunt up our man and horse. He kept this secret from me and they did not start on the expedition until after I had gone to sleep. As the slang phrase goes "he put one over me."

He woke me up very early in the next morning (Sunday) and said we were ready to start home. "What, without the man and horse?" I asked. "No, we got them." I was in no good humor about his leaving me behind the night before but consoled myself that I had got a good night's rest, and that my horse was fresh.

Taylor got no more than two or three hours rest at most. He had also thought best to hire a horse for the night and let the one he had been riding get a good feed and rest so that we would be ready for any contingencies.

Taylor told me how they had captured Carter. He

would, they thought, likely be in the woods or on the watch in the day time and the best chance to get him would be at night. Taylor, the sheriff and one deputy, I think, found out that Carter was suspected to be with his wife about five miles from Morganton towards Noontootla Creek. They reached the cabin he was in about midnight. They surrounded the house and knocked at the door and the sheriff, when Carter's wife answered, told her he wanted to see her husband. She denied his being there. The sheriff said: "I know that is not so; I know he is in there. You better tell him to come out or let us in." He finally after much parley came out and surrendered. But there was no horse in the stable or near the house. When asked what he had done with him he denied having had any such horse. Taylor said that partly by threats and partly through his wife's persuasion they got Carter to take them about a half mile from the house out in the woods to where the horse was tied. However they found no saddle and Carter had to ride bareback. Taylor and his party reached Morganton about 2 in the morning. The sheriff took charge of the prisoner and let Taylor sleep awhile. Before sun up we were on our way back with the captured man and horse, and truly glad that we had come out right so far. One of the sheriff's deputies escorted us for four or five miles on our return as we did not know what Carter's friends might attempt to do. We did not intend to give them any time to "mobilize." The officer untied him and turned him over to us and we hurried on our way. We wanted to get out of Georgia into Tennessee in short order and we were not going to be bothered leading the horse he was riding and we warned him not to try to escape. We knew the bringing him out of Georgia into Tennessee was entirely illegal both from a civil and a military point of view. We had no order from Colonel Hart or any commanding officer to arrest him as a deserter and we had no warrant for his arrest from any civil authorities in either Tennessee or Georgia. We had no requisition from Governor Harris of Tennessee to the governor of Georgia. We did not know even where Governor Harris was and the governor of Georgia was at Milledgeville. There were no telephone, telegraph or railroad lines nearer than the E. T. & Ga., now the Southern Railway. How much it cost to get him out of Fannin County I do not now remember. I expect though as much as the horse was worth. We had plenty of money along and even some money besides Confederate. We knew though that Carter was in no shape to appeal either to the civil or military authorities. On more than one account however we were anxious to get out of Georgia as soon as possible.

After we traveled eight or ten miles Carter asked us by what route we intended going back. Taylor told him we thought of crossing at Taylor's Ferry and thence by the toll gate to Sweetwater the way he came. At this he was very much pleased, entirely too much so we thought. It would have been best for him to have dissembled and looked pained. After discussing the matter in a low tone, so that he could not hear, we fully determined to come back by Ducktown, down Ocoee, by Benton and Athens. When we came to the Taylor's Ferry road and we took the other route he called our attention to the fact that we were taking the wrong road. When we told him we had changed our minds and were not going that way he seemed very much disappointed and tried to get us to take the Taylor's Ferry route. This strengthened us in our determination to do the opposite. So we came down the Ocoee River for many miles. We saw nobody for nearly a half day's travel. About the only thing that attracted our attention except the scenery, and we were not thinking of that, was a gray rebel roundabout coat lying on a rock beside the road. The rapid river was on one side of us and a steep mountain on the other. We paused not to investigate but wondered whether some poor fellow had met his fate and been thrown into the river. We were then, if I mistake not, in the Frog Mountain region, where even now after fifty years have passed, accidents sometimes happen to travelers, especially deputy revenue collectors. That night (Sunday) we stayed at Captain Hanna's, six miles east of Benton in Polk County. We asked Captain Hanna if he could get any one to guard our prisoner while we slept. He said that he owned a boy that was half nigger and half Indian,—nigger enough to obey orders and Indian enough to be watchful and not afraid of anything and was trusty. When we told the half-breed that we would pay him well if he did not let the man escape, he put his hand on his gun and smiled significantly and seemed much pleased with his job. We ate dinner at Mrs. Matthews near Athens the next day, it being Monday, July 13, 1863. Mr. Taylor that afternoon turned off at Reagan's to go to his father's on Pond Creek. As we had gotten to be very good friends in our two days' acquaintance I was satisfied that my companion would come quietly, however, reluctantly, with me to my father's. This he did. My father, I. T. Lenoir, then lived one and a half miles south of Sweetwater. The horse and I were glad to get home and mother was delighted to see me but I do not think she surmised that I had been absent on anything but a rather wearisome mountain trip. Father and a rebel soldier by the name of James Wilson from Owen County, Ky., relieved me of Carter and turned him over to the Confederate authorities at Sweetwater. I heard afterward that he was sent to Richmond to be punished as a deserter.

When I told my father what risks we ran on the trip did he embrace me and say I was a young hero? Nothing of the kind; but he did say that I was very, very foolish when I learned the existing conditions not to turn back—horse or no horse. I considered this unkind, as that was the nearest I ever came to doing the Casabianca act—except his was a ship and mine was a horse. I up and told my father that we brought back our own horse and not somebody else's like he did from Alabama and remarked more forcibly than grammatically that "If another horse gets stole it can just stay stole so far as I am concerned." I was just 16 then and this was my declaration of independence on July 13 instead of the 4th.

Now in the six days we were absent I estimate that we traveled 264 miles over rough roads, up and down mountains, fording many rivers and creeks which any serious rise would have rendered impassable. But the weather was fine and the five nights we spent away from home we were fortunate in having good stopping places. My horse was small but I did not myself then weigh more than 115 pounds, and I was accustomed to riding. We were in the saddle at least thirteen hours a day. We could get no corn for our horses but had to depend for feed on sheaf oats and new hay. The latter part of our journey we were also encumbered with a prisoner.

And all this "much ado" was about a warty horse which one of Sherman's bummers not long afterward "confiscated" and probably after he had ridden him as far as he could force him to go, left him to die by the roadside.

Carter did not strike me as being a bad man but was rather the victim of circumstances. He was about 27 or 28 years of age he said when he joined the army and had been married several years. He was very ignorant and unlettered. His volunteering as well as I could understand came about in this wise. The secession ladies of Hiwassee, Ga., and the country around made a flag, baked a big dinner, advertised a rally, got a politician to make a speech: "That the Yankees wanted to take our property, free our negroes, violate state rights and force us into submission." They waved the stars and bars, the fifer played Dixie, the drummer rattled the snare drum. "Fall in line, boys, we wont be gone more than three or four months, and come back covered with glory. Whoopee! Hurrah!" Now the fellow had no property, had never seen a half dozen black folks in his life, knew nothing of state rights and secession. But he thought it would be great to ride a horse, wear a uniform, lie around the camp fire, like he used to do coon hunting, and crack jokes with the boys. And what a good thing it would be not to have to plow, in a rocky, stumpy new ground and still have his family taken care of. Just a picnic all the time! Then he soon found out what war was. He heard from home that his wife was sick and his children were hungry. He asked for a furlough. Men were too scarce and he was refused. He stole a horse between suns and went anyhow. He got caught. He was returned to his command. He was probably tried by court martial for desertion. He was sentenced. A squad was ordered to take him to Richmond and report back in half an hour. Thus ended the chapter for him. The pity of it was he did not realize what it was all about. "What the difference?" you might say. "He was nothing but a Georgia cracker;

just 'poor white trash'." True; yet he was a human being; there were wife and children; they loved him, needed him.

But most of the persons mentioned above have long since passed away. Taylor died in Paris, Texas, a year and a half ago. Were it pertinent to this history it might be interesting to note the changes commercial and physical a half century has wrought in the regions we traversed on our trip; how the rivers and creeks we forded are now spanned by steel bridges; how their waters once crystal have been discolored by wood and chemical acids; how the fish have been killed off by tan bark ooze and sawdust; how most of the mountains have been denuded of their magnificent forest trees; how the whole country has been crisscrossed by telephone and telegraph wires; how the whistle of the locomotive breaks the once quiet and stillness of the valleys and mountains; how the waterfall of the streams has been utilized to furnish light and power to distant cities; especially how the talc, marble, gold, iron, manganese and copper have added untold millions to the wealth of the nation, in so much that the production of the Ducktown region alone for the last fifty years would be equal to the assessed valuation of all the property in the city of Knoxville; how the log cabin has given place to the pretentious colonial dwelling; how summer residences and hotels dot the landscapes; but to do this would require a book.

And here's the conclusion of the matter:

> The icy rills in leafy vales,
>   That once did quench the thirst of deer,
> The tourist there stale jokes retails
>   And in their waters cools his beer;
> And where the huntsman, gun and dogs,
>   Did chase fierce bruin to his lair,
> The two-step girl in summer togs
>   Hunts down the tired millionaire.

A War Episode.

From a paper prepared by Mrs. M. T. Williams, entitled "Reminiscences of the Bushwhackers," J. C. Vaughn, Chapter U. D. C., by permission, we make the following extracts: Mrs. Williams relates that shortly after the Battle of Philadelphia, in October, 1863, she and her husband and children were spending a quiet evening at home, not expecting any unusual happening, but, she says: "On glancing up we saw a company of bushwhackers approaching us, who however passed diagonally by us going toward the Tellico River. We sat and watched them pass out of sight. My husband left immediately, as I supposed, to go to the woods to look after his stock, as the only way we could keep stock to work the land was to hide it in the woods. But instead of going there he went to Colonel C. M. McGhee's. (Here Mr. Williams takes up the story.) "From Colonel McGhee I secured one of his fleetest (race) horses. I went (post haste) to Sweetwater to notify General Vaughn, who was there reorganizing his regiment, which had not been exchanged after the Battle of Vicksburg. General Vaughn, after getting the information, at once took command of a company or small squadron of cavalry, of the 8th Tennessee, commanded by Captain McGentis containing also a few soldiers from different commands, who chanced to be on hand, and started late in the evening in pursuit of the bushwhackers. I had just got to Sweetwater off of Wheeler's raid and volunteered to go along. I took supper at Madisonville with Bob Houston who went with us. We rode to near Coco Creek that night where the command rested until near morning. Meantime I had scouted the country and found that the bushwhackers had struck the old turnpike road at Coco Creek and gone on in the direction of North Carolina. Dressed as a Yankee soldier I acted as scout and went on in advance of General Vaughan and the command to locate the crowd. We overtook them at Evans' Mill on Beaver Dam Creek, in Cherokee County, N. C. When I rode into them I turned back and notified General Vaughn, when he notified Captain McGentis to charge them at once. We killed two and captured seventeen, including Lieutenant Conley, a Yankee officer with Bryson. We lost one man killed. I chased Bryson some distance but he, being better mounted than I, got away from me in the mountains. Captain Jim Taylor, with a squad of Indians, trailed him across the mountains a few days afterwards, perhaps the next day, and killed him on Coco Creek, near where he lived. However that did not break up the bushwhackers in Monroe County.

THE TOWN OF PHILADELPHIA.

I have access to a map owned by W. C. Cannon, of Philadelphia, which purports to be a certified copy of the original map of Philadelphia, which William Knox had laid off in 1822 or prior thereto. This map was copied from one drawn by Robert Wear. The numbers of the lots ran from 1 to 70, commencing at the northwest corner of the town in the bend of the creek number one and ending in number seventy on the west side of what is known as the Bacome Branch. The map shows the purchasers of lots up to April, 1822, at which time about twenty-five lots had been sold. James Price was the purchaser of lot number one, and Joseph Price, the brother of James Price, purchased lot number two. Most of the names mentioned as purchasers of lots are unfamiliar to the present generation. Few of their descendants are now living in this section. Jacob Pearson purchased lots numbers ten and eleven, opposite to where the mill now stands. Jacob Pearson built the brick house which stands west of the spring, where Mrs. W. G. Lenoir now (1916) lives. Lot No. 39, now owned by Robert Mims, formerly the home of Robert Cleveland, was bought by John Grigsby. Lot No. 58 was the one on which Matthew Nelson, former treasurer of the State, built the log house in which he lived and which is still standing. Lot No. 18, where the Presbyterian church now stands, was purchased by Amos Chesnut. Lots Nos. 19, 20 and 21 were purchased by Richard Hill, John Haskins and Hiram Lambert, respectively. Lot No. 28, where Dr. Ben Franklin once lived and now owned by John Thompson, was purchased by Jonas Israel. Lots Nos. 45, 46 and 47 constitute the public square of the town.

THE PRESBYTERIAN CHURCH OF U. S. A. AT PHILADELPHIA

Was organized in 1820 by the Rev. William Eagleton and first had a temporary place of worship in the town. The first building was a brick which was erected about 1829 in the cemetery north of the creek and town. This building was destroyed by fire during the Civil War. The present building was erected during 1872 and was dedicated on September 22, of that year. The church at Philadelphia was called the Mt. Zion Church. During its early days Revs. William Eagleton, Abel Pearson and Hilary Patrick were its ministerial supplies. In 1828 the Rev. Thomas Brown became its pastor and remained in charge until 1872. The Rev. Thomas Roberts served the church in the years of 1872 and 1873. The Rev. C. E. Tedford was pastor from June, 1874, until June, 1877; the Rev. Donald McDonald 1877 to 1883, inclusive; the Rev. Joseph Clements 1884 to 1886 and the Revs. J. H. McConnell, James McDonald and P. M. Bartlett were temporary supplies until 1892 when the Rev. J. B. Creswell took charge in May of that year and remains the pastor until this time (1916).

The following persons have served as elders:
In 1827, Moses Renshaw, James Patton, Stephen Low, Robert Shaw, James Martin, Thomas Craighead, Jacob Pearson, John Ramsey, Cummings McCoy.
In 1833, James Taylor and Stephen Dillard.
In 1843, James Harrison, M. D., William Rodgers, M. D.; in 1850, Thomas McCauley; in 1851, David F. Jamieson; in 1854, A. W. Cozart; in 1857, Solomon Bogart; in 1877, W. L. Brown; in 1885, George C. Ruggles; in 1891, Samuel J. Sparks.
Clerks of the Session: In 1827, Cummings McCoy; in 1829, John Ramsey; in 1843, William Rodgers; in 1846, Dr. James F. Harrison; in 1857, Solomon Bogart; in 1877, W. L. Brown.

THE BATTLE OF PHILADELPHIA.

As this was the only important engagement fought within the bounds of Sweetwater Valley during the Civil War, it would be pertinent and interesting to relate some of the occurrences which led up to it, before giving the reports of the commanders on each side, which I hereto append.
The latter part of August, 1863, General Burnside with a large force of cavalry and mounted infantry, having crossed the Cumberland Mountains, struck the railroad at Lenoir's Station, now Lenoir City. The Confederate forces did not attempt to resist their approach. They had previously prepared the Loudon Railroad bridge for destruction by distributing inflammable material on it, and on ———— they set fire to it and burned it to prevent pursuit. The object of the Confederates was to concentrate somewhere about Chattanooga and to defeat Rosecrans in his flank movement on that place. So, after the battle of Chickamauga, on the 19th and 20th of September, 1863, cavalry was sent towards Knoxville by the Confederates to drive the Federals out of the country and prepare the way for Longstreet's forces to come afterwards. In the Confederate official reports there seems to be some confusion as to who was the senior officer in the Second Cavalry Brigade, Colonel G. G. Dibrell and J. J. Morrison both signing themselves as commanding officers. It seems that the Second Cavalry Brigade was divided into two parts and approached Philadelphia, where Wolford's Brigade of Cavalry was encamped, by different routes. Colonel Morrison came through Bradley County, passing in the neighborhood of Georgetown, where they encamped for a couple of weeks. They crossed the Hiwassee River, partly by fording and partly by ferrying, between Charleston and the Tennessee River, and, as Colonel Morrison in his reports relates, traveled very rapidly through Meigs and Roane Counties to get between Loudon and Philadelphia to cut off Wolford's forces from their base at Loudon. The forces under his command, though not so stated by him in his official report, were the Sixteenth Battalion and the Sixth and First Georgia Cavalry, commanded by Colonel Morrison. Scouts were sent ahead by him to ascertain, if possible, the location of the Federal pickets, the whereabouts and number of the Federal troops and their contemplated movements. For this duty Private J. A. Reagan and five others from Neil's Battalion

were sent with instructions not to spare their horses and to report as soon as possible. They returned and made a clear and satisfactory report. Colonel Morrison's command succeeded in concealing their movement and struck the railroad at the old Cannon residence, one and one-half miles northeast of Philadelphia.

Colonel G. G. Dibrell, with the Fourth Tennessee Cavalry, with some parts of the Third, Thirty-first and Fifty-ninth Tennessee Regiments acting as mounted infantry, approached by way of Charleston, Athens and Sweetwater. The engagement was fought on the morning of October 20th. There were some pickets stationed near the Cleveland church. A small party of Confederates, in order to make a complete surprise, attempted to get behind them by the road which crosses the railroad near the old Lillard place, between the Cleveland church and Philadelphia, but these pickets happened to see them and made their escape to Philadelphia. They reported to General Wolford that the Confederates were coming from Sweetwater. When the Confederates found out that the pickets had not been captured they came on as rapidly as possible. About this time the Federals became aware that a force of the enemy were approaching from the direction of Loudon. They made a charge on Morrison's command with the intention of breaking through and escaping to Loudon, where the infantry was encamped. For the space of fifteen or twenty minutes there was a very hotly contested engagement, and although Colonel Morrison's command was forced back for a short distance, they succeeded in blocking the exit of the Federals towards Loudon. About that time they were attacked by the forces under Colonel Dibrell from the Sweetwater side. Those of Wolford's command that were not taken prisoners crossed Sweetwater Creek at and below the town of Philadelphia, making a disorderly retreat, each man for himself, going around to the north of Morrison's command, most of them finally reaching Loudon.

The forces reported as being under command of Colonel Wolford were the First, Eleventh and Twelfth Kentucky Cavalry and the Forty-fifth Ohio (mounted) Infantry. A rather amusing circumstance of how tables can be turned is well illustrated by the following incident: Private Henry Sawtell, of Neil's Battalion, while on a scout near the Thomas Osborne place, ran upon a foraging party of Federal soldiers. He was captured and taken to Philadelphia and placed under guard. When the Confederate forces reached Philadelphia they found that he had taken several of his guards prisoners and was on guard over them.

The results of the battle may be seen by the official reports of the battle, by each side, appended. The Federal forces undoubtedly lost all of their baggage, wagons and cannon—as to the number of prisoners taken there is some discrepancy.

DATA ON THE BATTLE AT PHILADELPHIA, TENN., FROM OFFICIAL RECORDS OF THE WAR OF THE REBELLION.

Official Records of the Union and Confederate Armies, Series 1, Vol. 21, Part. 1.

Report of Major-General A. E. Burnside to Major-General Grant:

General:
On the 20th instant, Colonel Wolford's Cavalry Brigade, at Philadelphia, was surprised by the enemy's cavalry and driven back to Loudon, with the loss of six mountain howitzers and a considerable

number of men. Colonel Wolford reports his loss at 100. The enemy has been driven back again beyond Philadelphia, and are said to be concentrating at Sweetwater a heavy force of infantry, cavalry and artillery. The reports of the number of the enemy are indefinite, except as to the presence there of Stevenson's Division of Infantry and of some 3,000 or 4,000 cavalry. I have re-enforced the garrison of Loudon and shall leave for there at once; from there I will endeavor to telegraph you more definitely. We have had a good deal of rain. Trains late, and I fear much of our supplies will be very badly delayed by high water and bad roads. It is reported from several sources that a considerable force under Joe Johnston has left Bragg's army.

A. E. BURNSIDE, Major-General.

Report of Colonel Frank Wolford, First Kentucky Cavalry, commanding cavalry brigade:

Loudon, Oct. 20th, 1863.

About ten o'clock this morning I got information that about 1,500 Rebels had attacked my wagon train, six miles from camp. I sent Colonel Adams with the First and Eleventh Kentucky Cavalry, who got in the rear of the enemy and were cut off by some 3,000 Rebels. I soon after got information that a large body of Rebels were coming up from Sweetwater. I then mustered up the rest of my men, amounting to about 700, and attacked them and drove them back several times. After driving, they re-enforced, attacking us from every side. Our artillery fired their last round. I rallied my men and charged through, saving most of men and several prisoners. We had several killed and several taken prisoners. I am confident we killed more of them, and took more prisoners than they did of us. We have lost some of our wagons and baggage and some of our artillery—perhaps all of it. The enemy are in large force, both infantry and artillery, with several heavy pieces of the latter.

WOLFORD, Colonel.

To Gen. Burnside.

Return of casualties in the Union forces engaged at Philadelphia, Tenn., October 20th, 1863:
Killed: 1 officer and 6 enlisted men.
Wounded: 1 officer and 24 enlisted men.
Captured or Missing: 7 officers and 440 enlisted men. Total, 479.

Report of Colonel George G. Dibrell, Eighth Tennessee (Confederate), commanding cavalry brigade:

Headquarters Second Cavalry Brigade,

Philadelphia, October 20, 1863, 5 P. M.

Dear Sir:
The colonel commanding instructs me to say that he engaged the enemy in front of this place at 8 o'clock to-day. After a sharp artillery duel of an hour or more the guns of Colonel Morrison's Brigade were heard in the enemy's rear. Colonel Dibrell immediately charged into the town. The enemy was completely routed. We captured all his wagons, ambulances, tents, cooking utensils, all his artillery, about 400 prisoners and at least that many small arms. The colonel cannot speak too highly of his officers and men. The rout

is not yet over; prisoners, horses and mules are hourly coming in. Our loss is nothing.

By order of Colonel G. G. Dibrell, commanding Second Cavalry Brigade.

DIXON A. ALLISON,
Acting Assistant Adjutant-General.
To Major-General Stevenson.

Report of J. J. Morrison, First Georgia Cavalry, commanding cavalry brigade:

Headquarters Second Cavalry Brigade,

Lenoir's House, Philadelphia, Tenn., October 20th, 1863.

General:
I have the honor to state that, agreeable to your instructions, I succeeded in getting between Philadelphia and Loudon, after making a march of fifty miles in fifteen hours. Found the enemy (Colonel Wolford's Brigade) in line of battle. Sent one regiment to Loudon to make demonstration to prevent Colonel Wolford's force being augmented by forces from Loudon. I attacked him at once with the remainder of my forces, numbering 1,200. After a very severe fight, with twice my number pitted against me, supported by six pieces of artillery, I succeeded in completely routing him, capturing all of his artillery (six pieces), entire wagon train, with many fire-arms and ammunition. Captured 400 prisoners. My loss will foot up 10 killed, 68 wounded and 70 missing. The whole command acted very gallantly. I will report at full at earliest opportunity.

I am, general, your obedient servant,

J. J. MORRISON,
Colonel, Commanding Second Cavalry Brigade.

P. S.: Colonel Wolford fell back in great confusion upon four regiments of infantry at Loudon. Night prevents me from pursuing him.

A REMINISCENCE OF COLONEL FRANK WOLFORD.

Some time in September, 1863, Wolford's Brigade of Cavalry camped at Sweetwater. The space between the hotel and the big springs was then woodland, and was a favorite camping place for soldiers of both armies. A day or two after Colonel Wolford's command came I went to the town of Sweetwater to look around. I asked some of the soldiers questions and displayed, as the soldiers thought, quite too much curiosity. So they proceeded to arrest me and took me before the Provost Marshal. He asked me what I was doing and why I came inside the lines. I told him I came on business and wished to see Colonel Wolford. He questioned me as to my sympathies in regard to the war. When I told him I was a Southern sympathizer he told me I would have to take the oath to support the United States government. I answered him I preferred not to do so. He said if I did not he would give me a nice little trip up to Camp Chase. I respectfully informed him that I did not see what good that would do as I was a non-combatant, and asked if I could see the commanding officer. I was detained some little time after that, when for some reason, Colonel Wolford came into the Provost's office. He may have heard that a spy had been arrested in camp. I explained to Colonel Wolford that some of the command were encamped on my father's land, that the soldiers being near the corn fields were taking corn. If this was according to his orders I would like to get something for it. He then told me he would have the commissary issue me a voucher for everything his soldiers took. I then told him my father was away from home and that my mother would like to have a few soldiers to guard our premises, and would prefer to have some Kentuckians. He replied that he would do so and "such as would give protection." I told him also that I would like to have a pass so that I could go in and out of the lines at any time so I could attend to whatever was needing looking after. He gave me the pass and at the same time he said to the Provost Marshal: "Captain, we are not making war on boys." This produced quite a change in his manner toward me.

According to promise, he sent four guards, I think of the First Kentucky Cavalry, who were quite polite and attentive. While they stayed at our place they feasted on turkey, pies, cake and wine. They were relieved from other duties while on guard at our home, and when the command was ordered away, as I remember, in about ten days' time, they expressed very many regrets.

I thought Colonel Wolford was a grand old man if he was surprised and did get whipped at Philadelphia. When the soldiers got corn and other supplies for the brigade, he gave me, in my father's name, vouchers, omitting the words "on proof of loyalty." This, too, when my father at that time was a refugee in Georgia. These were the only vouchers that were ever paid my father, I. T. Lenoir, or myself by the United States government. What a contrast was Wolford's conduct to that of Return J. Meigs, Claim Commissioner! One would expect of him, as his mother lived for a while in this Valley, and he was personally known to my father, that he would treat him with some measure of justice, but the claims for wood and ties, got for the use of the railroad taken over by the United States government, and for hay, corn and wheat, attested by vouchers and sworn to by reliable witnesses, filing with the same the oath of amnesty which I. T. Lenoir took at Loudon in 1864, after he returned home from Georgia, were disallowed by him and were refused reconsideration.

LOUDON.

When I contemplated writing the history of the early settlers of Sweetwater Valley it was my intention to take in that part of it which was formerly a part of Roane County, but time and space and the difficulty of access to the records at Kingston prevented me from so doing. The task set for myself was greater than I thought. But as I have almost two years issue of the Loudon Free Press, which commenced publication on November 20, 1852, I feel that I ought to publish some excerpts from the same, the facts contained in which might otherwise not be preserved. Even previous to the publication of the Loudon Free Press there appeared in the Athens Post of November 7, 1851, an advertisement of James H. Johnston, stating that on Thursday, the 27th day of November, 1851, there would be a sale of 200 town lots at Blairsport or Blairs Ferry (afterwards Loudon) at public auction. I presume the sale took place. It was not stated what particular lands were to be sold. This sale was very widely advertised in papers from Richmond, Va., to Augusta, Ga. How many lots were sold or what prices they brought I have not found out. This was the first example of systematic "booming" that I know of occurring in this part of East Tennessee. So the laying out of towns on paper, and the selling at auction, as in the late eighties and early nineties, was really nothing new to Loudon people.

The editors and proprietors of the Loudon Free Press were Jno. W. and Samuel B. O'Brien. It was excellently printed on good linen paper and well edited. It contained many well written articles and various important advertisements of railroad and large business enterprises. Not only those in Loudon but many from cities of Tennessee and large cities in the east. Among other things there was a half column advertisement of the Saturday Evening Post. There were also the following advertisements:

Orme, Wilson & Co., Merchants. This Wilson was R. T. Wilson, afterwards so well known as a banker in New York. Lenoir & Goddard, merchants in Philadelphia, Tenn. Notice May 13, 1853, of Wm. and W. A. Lenoir, executors of Wm. B. Lenoir, deceased. Advertisement of the firm of William, W. A., B. B., and I. P. Lenoir, cotton factors, millers, farmers and merchants at Lenoir's. On November 20, 1854, were also the law cards of Hopkins & Stephens, Welcker & Key, of Chattanooga, Tenn., Gahagan & Wright of Madisonville, William G. McAdoo, Thos. C. Lyon, Maynard & Vaughn of Knoxville, and N. A. Patterson of Kingston.

Track laying of the E. T. & Ga. R. R. reached Blair's Ferry, afterwards Loudon, in May or June, 1852. This made Loudon the terminus of the railroad until 1856, on account of the difficulty at that time, of bridging the Tennessee River. This caused Loudon to be very much "boomed." The optimistic claimed that it would become a rival of Knoxville as it was exceedingly uncertain when the railroad would be completed, and as Loudon had railroad transportation to the south which Knoxville did not.

In the issue of the Free Press of August 26, 1853, noting the town improvements it mentioned those who were about to complete buildings and residences, as follows: R. T. Wilson, E. P. Clark, James W. Clark, W. R. Hurley, H. Ingalls, W. B. McInturf, Joseph Rowan and L. A. Markum. The New School Presbyterian Church, the Episcopal Church, the parsonage were completed and the work on the Cumberland Presbyterian had been commenced.

Some time in the year 1853, date not at hand, Loudon was incorporated, for the issue of the Free Press for January 11, 1854, stated that an election had been held, and that the following were elected: W. T. Low, mayor; H. Bogart, recorder; B. F. Davis, treasurer; R. T. Wilson, H. Ingalls, J. H. Leuty, and J. W. O'Brien, aldermen. Thomas Russell was unanimously elected city constable.

Under the heading: Facts about the Hiwassee and East Tennessee and Georgia Railroad, there is given, in this book, a schedule of trains between Loudon and Dalton, Ga., published in the Athens Post of August 10, 1852, which recites that the "down train" leaves at 4 a. m. and the "up train" arrives at 6:35 p. m., making a round trip daily. In the Loudon Free Press of March 14, 1854, the time of departure from Loudon for Dalton was 5:45 a. m. and the time of arrival from Dalton was 3:09 p. m.

The elevation of Loudon as given to the Free Press by Mr. Pritchard, chief engineer of the E. T. & G. R. R., is 814 feet above the sea level.

Comparative population of Loudon and Sweetwater on the dates given below, taken from the United States census:

Loudon.		Sweetwater.
1860.	1,292	not given
1870.	1,357	1,609
1880.	832	1,335
1890.	942	879
1900.	875	1,716
1910.	995	1,850

In the Free Press of July 25, 1854 is an editorial, "Come Back," pleading with those, who had fled from the cholera to return, as the panic had subsided, that the disease which was afflicting the people was not Asiatic cholera but was malignant cholera morbus. It says that there are a thousand and one silly reports circulating through the country. "To set these rumors aside we will state that with the exception of Mr. Strange there has not been a case since last Wednesday. Mr. Strange was attacked Tuesday night, he was relieved of cholera, and died on Friday of typhoid fever." The editorial goes on:

"The weather continues warm but the atmosphere is quite lively and a gentle breeze is constantly playing through our office. So come back, ye fugitive inhabitants of Loudon! And, oh, ye Iron Horse! why standest thou quaking in the distance? We little thought that your iron nerve would quail at the sight of five or six cases of cholera. Oh, ye hotelkeepers, return! The danger is now past and you can all come back swearing that you were not scared. Since the 9th inst. we have had the following deaths in town, with cholera symptoms: N. D. Sutton, taken on Saturday about one o'clock, died Sunday about three o'clock; Mr. Taylor, a blacksmith, died on Saturday after a short illness; Harvey Erskine, colored, taken on Sunday night, died after an illness of twelve hours; W. P. Truitt, taken on Sunday morning, died on Tuesday at three o'clock."

Editorial a week later says:

"Since our last we have had but one death by cholera in Loudon, Mrs. Dialtha Donohoe. One at Philadelphia, Mrs. J. W. Clark; one near Philadelphia, Mr. Gilbreath. * * * We verily believe there is less apprehension relative to cholera felt in Loudon than there is in any point in fifty or a hundred miles of this place."

In the Athens Post of September 29, 1854, there is a comparative table of the rainfall in July, August and September, 1853 and 1854; for Nashville and vicinity:

	1853.	1854.
July	7 inches	1 1-2 inches
Aug.	6 inches	1-2 "
Sept.	6 1-3 "	1-4 "
Total	19 1-3 "	2 1-4 "

A difference of more than 17 inches in Nashville. It is probable the difference might have been equally as great in this section. This drouth may account for the terrible devastation of the cholera in the year of 1854.

AFTERTHOUGHTS.

I hope this book will be criticised; for a work of this kind which is not will attract little attention; but I trust that the criticisms will be made with some degree of fairness, just as I have tried to treat with fairness those I have written about.

I will, no doubt, be blamed for mistakes I did not make and for many that I did make. I have endeavored to give the old settlers and their descendants, wherever they are found, with as great accuracy as I was able. Some, though not a large proportion, have failed to answer the letters addressed to them. Quite a few letters have been returned unclaimed, as those not living where written to at last address, or passed beyond the reach of the U. S. mail.

I will be criticised for writing about some people I did give sketches of and because I failed to write of others I should have written about. Possibly I did not have sufficient accurate information to justify. I have not tried to give a history of families who came to this section later than 1865. That is more than a half century ago. Even of those who came previous to that time, and did not stay long enough to leave their impress upon the country and were merely transients, it would hardly be expected I should treat.

I will, doubtless, be blamed for not dwelling more at length on the material resources and manufactures of our section. But it must be remembered that previous to 1865 there were no mills of any kind, except a few small custom mills, and not a bank within the bounds of Sweetwater Valley until a much later date. The check and deposit habit had not been acquired.

The old settlers of the valley were thrifty people but I have laid much greater stress on character than accumulated land and dollars.

What constitutes a community as well as a state has been fitly answered as follows:

"What constitutes a State?
  Not high raised battlements or labored mound,
Thick wall or moated gate;
  Not cities proud with spires and turrets crowned,
Not bays and broad-armed ports,
  Where, laughing at the storm, rich navies ride;
Not starred and spangled courts,
  Where low-browed Baseness wafts perfume to Pride;
No, men, high-minded men—
  Men who their duties know,
But know their rights and knowing dare maintain;
  Prevent the long-armed blow, .
And crush the tyrant while they rend the chain;
  These constitute a State."

If I have not missed my estimation gravely, of such were those of our valley and with more excellent characteristics added thereto.

I close this work with quite a feeling of relief. It has been much more troublesome, far more expensive and taken much longer time than I anticipated, even after the families whom I was investigating rendered me all the assistance in their power. Some had kept no records and many had had their records destroyed by war, flood and fire. It is also with a feeling of some sadness that I finish the compilation of the work. It has brought me in personal touch, and also into correspondence with many friends of my youth who I had almost forgotten or only faintly remembered; and in correspondence with them they brought to mind many circumstances which but for that I would never have thought of again.

The publication of this book about the old families may cause some who are dear friends or relatives to get into correspondence with each other and bring to their knowledge those who are far separated.

I can not write finis to this book without making some acknowledgment to some who especially assisted me; most of these have been laides, who, as is usual, take more interest in personal history than men. I thank especially for assistance, Mrs. J. N. Heiskell, Miss Ran Yearwood, Mrs. Sarah Willson, of Niota, Tenn., Mr. W. P. Jones of Pond Creek, Mrs. Robert Stickley of Memphis, and Mrs. Julia R. Love, and the record clerks of Monroe County at Madisonville, Tenn., and Hon. W. L. Brown of Philadelphia.

With this I make my bow to the public as an author.

INDEX

Axley, Rev. James	51-58
Axley, Samuel	68
" James	68
" Brunner	68
" Fred & M.	68
Allison, John(Johnson)	59-61, 64-66
Adkins, Nettie	75-81
" Annie M.	62, 111
" Henry	264
Aiken, S. J.	181
Anderson, Capt. John	319
Avery, Waightstill	193, *29
Bachman, Samuel*	260
" Rev. J. L.	140-354-375
" Bessie	141
Bayless, Milton	271
" William	133-261
Bartlett, Rev. William	140
Bacome, Arch	180
Bellamy, T.W.	84
Bean, JoeIII	
Bellamy, Andrew	84
Berry, F.K. Sr. Family	82 & 101
Blair, Smauel	67
" (Ferry)	152 & 219
Bland, Mary	117
" Elizabeth	117
Boyd, Dr. H.T.	325
Bogart, Solomon Family	05-155-339
Bogart, Dr. F.	86
" Dr. Will	86
" W.J.N.	87
" Margaret	155
" Susan	110'
Bowman, John D. Family	110
Boykin, D.C	174
Boyd, Mrs. H. T.	206
Brakebill, J. H.	69
" Austin	70
Bradley, John	349
" Henry Family	348
Bradshaw, Rev. T.R.	166
Brandon, Jane	151
Brewster, Mrs. Elizabeth	248
Bryant, Louis	275
Browder, William Family	72
Browder, John J.	75
" Amanda J.	75
" J. M.	77
" J. P.	79
" Mrs. C. O.	313
" Nancy J.	74 & 143
Bryan, William	71
Brown, John	76
" Hon. Jon, K.	76 & 373
Brown, Rev. William	474
" Rev. Thomas Family	85, 89, 166
	252, 374
Brown, W. L. Family	90, 390
" William	159
Brunner, Rev. J. H.	30
Bushong, Josie	175
Burns, Riley	231, 273
Buchanan, Elizabeth	312
Bushwhackers	403
Byrd, Emma	78
Browder, W. D.	80
Browder, D. A.	80
Browder, Horace	79 & 104
" C. D.	80
" David D.	81
" Charles O.	81
Byrd, Ernest	145
Brownlow, Hon. John B.	37
Calloway, Maj. John Fam	90
" Thomas H.	92
" Marshall	93
" Jophew	94
" H. L. W.	94
" Mary	95
" James	133
Campmeetings	55
Caldwell, G.L. Family	83
" Martha	115
Cannon, Family	109
" Louisa	146
Carter, R. L.	105
" Matt	144 & 349
" Fred A.	351
"Mrs." "	207
Cecil. H. L.	77
Cherokees	26,28,34,37,43,44
" Dream of Big Chief	41
Childress, David Burton	112 & 155
" John	114
CHURCHES_	147
CUMBERLAND PRESS	163, 166, 168

PRESBYTERIAN CHURCH	139,89,140 268,285, 273	Fine, John	147
		Finley, John B.	157
		Foland, G. H.	71
BAPTIST	147, 213,244,355	Forshee, M. J.	71
METHODIST	129, 132, 133, 372	Fouche, Jesse	70
City Beautiful League	204	Fry, William	269
Cleveland, Caroline	82	" Austin	151
" Eli, Sr.	90,91,103	Fryer, Rev. J. H.	166
" Eli, Jr.	158	FEDERAL ROAD	44
" (Family)	97		
" Sir Guy	97	Gaines, John R.	131
" Robert M.	104, 368	Gallaher, Rev. James	56
" Robert R.	104, 368	Gilman, Mrs. W. D.	206
" Presley (Family)	106, 33	Glaze, Henry (Fam)	152
" Harvey H.	109,275	Goddard, Sarah J.	154
Cline, George	108	" Thornton	154
College, Victoria	129, 373	Green, Douthardd	69
Cline, Polly	338	Gregory, Dr. Few Hall	158
Clark, Mrs. Bland	124	Griffin, Sarah	84
" James W.	127	Griffitts, William	280
" Capt. W. L.	129		
" Mrs. Ida	124	Haun, William	70
Colquit, Edd	71	Haun, N. W.	169, 225
Cooke, Robert	94	Hardin, J. A.	77, 78
" Helen Library	11, 126, 272,377,387	Harrison, Dr. William	177
		Hartsell, Susan B.	260
Cooper, James	114	Heiskell, Ed	104,174
Copenhaven, Robert C.	131	" Dan	159,168
COURT-COUNTY	227	" William McBride	170
Cozart, Abe W. Family	115	" S. G.	161
Crockett, David	314	" William	161,278
Cunningham, (Family)	132	" Luther M.	171
" Patton	135	" Hugh B.	172
" Pickle	142	" James M.	174
Cuson, George M.	115	Heabler, Amanda J.	349
Coffin, (Misses)	352,376	" Belle	317
Craighead Lake	392	HIWASSEE PURCHASE	147, 197
		HIWASSEE COLLEGE	158
DeArmond, Alan B.	105	Hill, Dr. Ira L.	145
Dickey, A.J.	75	Hotchkiss, Claiborne	149
" D.W.	76, 131	Hogg- (Family)	208
" Joseph H.	155	" Thomas	209
" Hugh	76	" Dr. Sam	210-212
Dobbins, Arch, M.	157	Holt, Frank A.	348
Dow, Lorenzo	56	HORSE STEALING	391
Earnest, Cynthia	66	Hunt, Oscar-	
" Mary Ann	66	Ella Axley-	68
Edmondson, Cap. J.P.	240	Hull, S.	69
Eggers, Herman R.	275	Hudson, B. F.	104
Embree, J.G.	76	Hulvey, Col. O. C.	125
Engleman, J.G.	76	" Col. Charles N	157
		Heiskell, Harry	174

Harrison, Maggie J.	232	McGuire, Josiah	70
IVINS, R. M.	275,379	" Frank	83
Jackson, Andrew	211,-341	MASONS	59, 61, 380,385
" Rev. Frank	351	Matlock, Henry M.	94
"JERKS" The	56	Martin, S. J.	108
Janeway, Rev. Joe	175	Martin, (Family)	250
Johnston, Josiah K.	178	Magill, R. E.	351
Johnson, J. A.	104	" Nathaniel	351
Johnson, Gideon B.	349	" J. A.	140
Jones, John M. SR.	321, 351	Mayes, Henry	234
" Joe D.	176,337,339	" Mrs. Ada Reagan	243, 375
" Paul	177	Manis, (Family)	249
" Matt	177	McReynolds, David	96
" Jesse F.	178	McGhee, Rev. J.	115
" Nancy	178, 806	McLin, Charles E.	127
" Reps	335	McBride, Elizabeth	162,169
Kerr, Rev. D. M.	154	McCroskey, Rev. Solon	169
" Rev. W. M.	177	McKnight, George M.	252
Keller, H.	69	McElwee, Frank B.	334
Kimbrough, Lois	68	Milligan, W. C.	181
Kimbrough, Jacob	323	Mims, Robert L.	229
" I. B.	336	Melendy, Dr. A. R.	249
Kinser, Adeline	154	MOUSE CREEK	15
		MOUNDS, INDIAN	70
Legislators	389	Moser, Kittie	70
Land Title	45	Montogomery, John B.	103
Lackey, Dr. J. B.	181	" Mary I. Magill 351	
Lenoir, W. F.	185,182	Morrison, Rev. W. W.	375
" Myra Ann	294	Muller, Oscar W.	377
" W. B.	195	Moore, Thos, (Family)	251
" I. T.	198,200,317, 225	McGhee, Charles M.	41
" Mary C. H.	212	Moon, John	280
" W. B.	214	NEWSPAPER, FIRST, Sweetwater	
" W. F.	226,230	Forerunner C611	152, 384
" W. T.	226	Nelson, Hon, Matthew	255
" W. G.	228	" William C.	256
" Henry L.	231	" Sydney	101, 256
Lenoir City	196	Neil, Sterling	257
Leyburn, George L.	231		
Lillard, (Family)	231	Orr, Irby (Family)	269
Library, Helen M. Cooke	123,772	Orr, Mary C.	152
Loudon, Fort	27,28	Orr, A. Q.	156
Loudon, Town of	409	Osborne, Lafayette	158
LOUDON FREE PRESS 223	226, 409	" Harriete	230
Lotspeivh, E. J.	75	Owens, Charles	258, 265
" John	66,232	" (Family)	260
Lowery, Reece	270	" Jesse F.	264
Lowry, J. W.	310	" Ross	264, 317
" Harrison	337		
:" Mrs. M. C.	337	Patton, W. M.	136
Love, Julia R. Family	310	" Amanda	108, 324
" Col. James R.	310	" Mary J.	262
		" Mary	263
		" Francis A.	270,324

Patton, Anne E.	324	Sneed, Rev. Robert Family	221,370
Parsley, Stephen	271	Sheldon, James J.	317
Pardue, Robert	274	Scruggs, Dr. R. F. Family	313,168
" Rev. H. Clay	274	Scruggs, Margaret O.H.	174
" John	274	Scruggs, Dr. A.	174
" William	274	Sizer, J.B.	252
Patterson, Sarah H.	173	Scruggs, Rev. John	313, 343, 347
Parker, Dr. M. C.	237,347	Sneed, Robert	95, 99
Pennington, Wm. Family	273	Sneed, Wm. F.	179
" H. B.	143, 273	" T. E.	339
" John	101	Steele, Sarah	150
" Mary Ann	109, 275	Starrett, J. C.	150
Penland, R. N.	125	Stillman, Mrs. Julia	139, 320
Pickel, Johnathan	142	" George C.	318, 319
" William	145	Stakely, William	164,225
PHILADELPHIA, TOWN OF	254,260	St. John, F. B.	311
	404	SLAVERY	215
Battle of	227, 296,403	SWEETWATER-PLAN OF	224
	405	SWEETWATER VALEY	32, 65
Plemings, William	70	Smith, Andrew	116
Pope, James	275	Taylor, Jabin S.	150
Price, W. L.	271	Taylor (Family)	222
Reagan, James K.	307	Tedford, R. A.	140
" Joseph	231	Thatcher, L. P.	113
Reagan, Gen. J. H.	218, 286, 304	Thomas, William	248
	253	Tipton, Harris	257
Reagan, W.B.L.	300		
" Genealogical Table	308	TRADES, Horses	391
" Mrs. J. A.	206	Trimble, Rev. E. C.	375
" Maj. J. A.	311		
" Station	15,286	Vaughn J. C.	225, 326
Ramsey J.M.G.	39	Walker, Hon, Joseph	336
" Col. John	276	" S. M.	336
" R. J.	282, 283	Warren, Capt. J. C.	102
Rausin, V. T.	83	" Mrs. J. C.	281
RAILROADS - 200,218,255,292,290		Wallace, Rev. James	375
	270	Webb, John	209
Rowan, Frank	280	" George	95
" S. J.	285	Wheeler, General	223
" John A.	336	Wilson, W. Y.	274
Rowland, J. T.	286	" W.P.	94
Rutherford, William	283	" James	95
" John F.	285	Williams, S.V.B.	338
		" J.W.P.	339,156
SCHOOLS Unnion Institute	377	Wright, James, A.	179
George L. Leyburn	377	Upton, Thomas L.	335
O. W. Muller	377	Upton Inn	335
Sweetwater College	377	Yearwood, (Family)	340
Tenn. Military Institute	377	" R. J.	103
Sweetwater High School	377	" James F.	263
		" Miss Ran	344
Shell, Christian	319	" Thomas	346
Sheldon, Mary E.	130	Young, D. C.	112
		" C. E.	125,227

Young,	Col. S. E.	325
"	Ross	327
"	John-Scott	348
"	Bina	375

www.ingramcontent.com/pod-product-compliance
Lightning Source LLC
Chambersburg PA
CBHW071140300426
44113CB00009B/1029